THE COMPLETE HOUSEPLANT SURVIVAL MANUAL

THE COMPLETE HOUSEPLANT
SURVIVAL MANUAL

ESSENTIAL KNOW-HOW FOR KEEPING (NOT KILLING!)
MORE THAN 160 INDOOR PLANTS

BARBARA PLEASANT

PHOTOGRAPHY BY ROSEMARY KAUTZKY

The mission of Storey Publishing is to serve our customers by publishing practical information that encourages personal independence in harmony with the environment.

EDITED BY Gwen Steege

TECHNICAL EDIT AND PLANT KEY BY Elizabeth P. Stell

ART DIRECTION AND COVER DESIGN BY Kent Lew

TEXT DESIGN AND PRODUCTION BY Vertigo Design and Cynthia McFarland

PRODUCTION ASSISTANCE BY Jessica Armstrong and Jennifer Jepson Smith

COVER AND INTERIOR PHOTOGRAPHS © Rosemary Kautzky, except for those on pages 110, 111, and 192 ©MACORE, Inc.

ILLUSTRATIONS © Christine Erikson

INDEXED BY Stepping Stones Indexing Services

For additional information please contact Storey Publishing, 210 MASS MoCA Way, North Adams, MA 01247.

Storey books are available for special premium and promotional uses and for customized editions. For further information, please call 1-800-793-9396.

Printed in China by R.R. Donnelley

10 9 8 7 6 5 4 3 2 1

LIBRARY OF CONGRESS CATALOGING-IN-PUBLICATION DATA

Pleasant, Barbara.
The complete houseplant survival manual / by Barbara Pleasant ; photography by Rosemary Kautzky.
p. cm.
Includes index.
ISBN-13: 978-1-58017-569-2; ISBN-10: 1-58017-569-4 (pbk. : alk. paper)
1. House plants. I. Title.

SB419.P573 2005
635.9'65—dc22

2005014205

CONTENTS

HOW HOUSEPLANTS EARN THEIR KEEP

For the past two centuries, mankind has been playing with houseplants as if they were pretty toys. We have appreciated their beauty and suspected their power to enrich our lives, yet we are only now learning how they also can foster something everyone wants: to feel happy. The science of happiness is still in its infancy, but houseplants, it seems, have been doling out doses of happiness for a long time. And, with the increasing availability of bright blooming houseplants (which get the highest smile ratings), more and more people are discovering the joys to be found in indoor gardening.

We hope you are one of these people. This book is designed to meet the needs of houseplant growers of all skill levels, from newbies, who often feel a bit anxious about doing the wrong thing and causing their plant to suffer, to experienced plant keepers, who sometimes want to know more about a plant's background and superior forms that might be available. The plant profiles in Parts 1 and 2 describe how to care for 150 beautiful blooming and foliage houseplants, including many selections that have entered retail markets only in the last ten years. General information on houseplant care is covered, encyclopedia style, in Part 3.

Before we jump into that green world, a short review of how houseplants came to be is in order, as well as an inventory of the benefits they bring to the people who grow them. When it comes to houseplants, history, healing arts, environmental sciences, and interior design intertwine in unique and life-enhancing ways. Expanding your awareness of what houseplants can do will give you a new appreciation for indoor plants wherever you are lucky enough to encounter them — from the waiting room at your dentist's office to your own kitchen windowsill.

A Brief History of Houseplants

When did people begin keeping indoor plants? It wasn't so long ago, because people had neither plants nor hospitable indoor environments until modern times. The forerunners to houseplants were medicinal herbs, which monasteries and apothecaries struggled to keep alive in dim, drafty indoor spaces when protected courtyards would not do. The advent of glass windows (which began appearing in Europe in the late 1600s but were not commonplace for another 200 years) were quickly followed by the culture of citrus fruits — the first plants to be widely grown "under glass" in early conservatories. But it was not until plant exploration boomed in the nineteenth century, coupled with the increased availability of window glass, that people had real choices in houseplants and suitable environments in which to grow them. Blown-glass tableware, and even stained glass, predate clear window glass by several hundred years, because forming molten glass into a flat surface is much trickier than creating small pieces or variously shaped bubbles. It's interesting to imagine the excitement people felt when window glass made it possible to enjoy indoor light year-round — a huge change from pulling closed dark shutters every time a cold wind blew. The next step was to see if plants could also make use of light that came through wavy glass windows.

Social changes supported the move to grow plants indoors. During the Victorian era (1837 to the early 1900s), a nicely kept formal parlor became a symbol of middle-class respectability, and a proper parlor included plants. Many of these plants remain popular today because of their ability to adapt to low light — aspidistra, sanseveria, ferns, and palms. Geraniums also became a fashion craze, and small terrariums planted with tiny tropicals provided the middle class with miniature versions of the glassed-in conservatories kept by the rich. In 1936, George Orwell used the aspidistra as a symbol for the

Miniature greenhouses, or terrariums, were one of the first methods employed for keeping plants indoors.

English middle class's preoccupation with propriety in his comic novel *Keep the Aspidistra Flying.*

Meanwhile, in North America, the first half of the twentieth century was a quiet era for houseplants, but they came back into style with a vengeance in the 1960s and 1970s. As part of the back-to-nature movement, people got into green things again, and a new generation of plants was ready to fill the need. Dorm rooms were decked out with dracaenas and philodendrons, and sparsely furnished apartments became jungles of jade plants, crotons, and cacti. Then, as the flower power generation became more involved in careers, raising families, and keeping up yards, their houseplant collections thinned.

But changes are afoot. The generation that embraced houseplants in the 1970s is rediscovering old green friends and making many new ones. The roles houseplants play in peoples' lives have changed, too. Instead of symbolizing social status or the need for a cleaner, greener world, houseplants are valued for all the things they do, from providing companionship to purifying the air to helping fragile bodies heal. We no longer grow houseplants to impress other people. We grow them to please and nurture ourselves.

How Houseplants Heal

We assign our plants personalities and genders, and even guess at their taste in music. Like animal pets, plants welcome us home when we've been away, respond to our care by growing healthy and strong, and draw us into very real relationships. This process can be healing in itself. When people have been badly hurt by others, or face the task of rebuilding a shattered life, therapists and recovery programs often suggest that they begin healing by nurturing a houseplant. Even a simple relationship such as that between a pothos and its keeper is rife with lessons about understanding, responsibility, and patience.

Clockwise from top: *Dendrobium* (spray orchid), clivia, *Faucaria* (tiger's jaws)

Just What the Doctor Ordered

BASED ON THE CONCEPT THAT PLANTS AID HEALING, horticultural therapy is practiced in nursing homes, rehabilitation centers, and schools worldwide. In situations where outdoor gardening activities are not practical — for example, in nursing homes or Alzheimer's units — houseplants provide a green connection that enhances healing, decreases frustration, and stimulates memory. And, because of its connection with nurturing and light, working with houseplants is increasingly recommended as a primary therapy for people who suffer depression due to Seasonal Affective Disorder.

Popular gift plants include *(clockwise from left)* tulips, cineraria, begonias, hyacinths, and primroses.

Our subtle belief in the healing power of indoor plants is reflected in the gifts we send to those who are sick and grieving. As well as the message to "Feel better," remember that you can use living plants to send other positive messages: "Good luck in your new business venture," "Congratulations on your new home," and "Thanks for a job well done" are commonly written on notecards accompanying houseplants to their new homes. At work and at home, houseplants enter our lives as legacies that remind us of milestone events.

Indeed, more houseplants are given as gifts than are intentionally selected by the people who want to grow them — and sometimes this creates a problem. We are often faced with the challenge of accommodating a plant chosen by others because of its beauty, and this story does not always have a happy ending. If you've struggled in the past to please gift plants that never seemed satisfied, don't be discouraged. Instead, get to know the best sites you have for growing

houseplants, and choose species that are likely to prosper. The returns for sharing your home or office with vigorous plants are enormous.

Hardworking Houseplants

The workplace has become home to many pet plants, which is good for workers, employers, and their customers. When you set aside a little space in a work cubicle for a leafy friend, its constant companionship is soothing to the body, mind, and soul, which improves your morale.

The presence of plants at work has other payoffs. Plants actually make for better work, as has been validated in several studies. For example, in a five-story office building in England, four stories were stocked with houseplants. A year later, a clear correlation was found between the plantless floor and increased absenteeism and reduced productivity. In a controlled experiment at Washington State University, students working in a computer lab were more productive and made fewer mistakes when houseplants were within easy view.

Several other studies have found that houseplants improve students' performance in schools. Because so many bodies are present in classrooms, all breathing in oxygen and exhaling carbon dioxide, carbon dioxide levels are often four to five times as high as they should be. Plants take in carbon dioxide and give off oxygen, so they are a natural choice for helping to set things right. Numerous school systems now recommend keeping classrooms, corridors, and cafeterias well stocked with houseplants. Reducing high carbon dioxide levels helps students stay alert while creating a much more wholesome environment for learning.

The explanation for improved work and school performance in the presence of houseplants goes beyond plants' abilities to restore healthful oxygen levels. After all, if we could feel smart and positive and well by breathing more oxygen, we would all be walking around wearing oxygen tanks. It is also likely that, in addition to the oxygen plants are putting out, their benefits encompass what they are taking away. As part of their normal transpiration processes, houseplants also clean the air of gaseous chemicals.

NASA scientists have validated the ability of many plants to remove from the air pollutants ranging from ammonia to xylene. Paints, carpeting, furniture, and even our clothing give off pollutants, which can build up to toxic levels in tightly insulated spaces. Houseplants ease this situation (though a large number of houseplants are needed to purify badly tainted air). In new homes or buildings, where indoor chemical pollution is likely to be most acute, a strong case can be made for bringing in as many green plants as the space can hold. Among houseplants, the most efficient air purifiers are heavy transpirers, or species that cycle a lot of water from roots to leaves, such as palms, rubber plants, and corn plants (*Dracaena*). However, any green plant deserves some credit for making indoor air better for people to breathe.

It is a fact that being near plants improves the quality of every breath you take, but excellent air does not fully explain how a houseplant sitting on the corner of a desk can improve test scores, or how plants in a room increase a hospital patient's tolerance for pain. Even a simple green scene, such as a sanseveria stationed in a classroom window, can soothe and inspire while quietly ridding the air of excessive carbon dioxide. Clearly, living with plants is good for us, so it makes perfect sense to share our indoor space with generous green friends.

Low-maintenance sanseveria provides the calming effect of plants at the same time that it purifies the air.

There may be more to this story, because certain aspects of our relationships with plants are beyond the scope of science. Yet there is one basic principle that may be at work here. The green world of trees and grasses is our natural home. It's where we got our start, and though climate-controlled indoor spaces are comfortable, something important is missing. That something affects our attitudes, work performance, ability to tolerate physical and emotional discomfort, and other variables that add up to happiness.

Cultivating Creativity

In making the case for houseplants, one unsung variable is creativity — another fascinating characteristic unique to humans that, when worked regularly like a muscle, makes us feel vibrantly alive. Enter the practice of interiorscaping, in which plants are used as living art. The large windows present in modern homes and offices, particularly those employed in passive solar design, create ideal canvases for tapestries of foliage. Where windows are not available, green plants grown beneath bright supplemental light dramatically transform the mood and vibrancy of any indoor space.

Indoors as well as outdoors, artfully arranged plants evoke a feeling of completion that goes far beyond fads or styles. The business world has learned that good interiorscaping creates the impression of prosperity, which is tightly linked to customer confidence — a well-trodden path to success. Perhaps this is why houseplants are so popular as gifts to new businesses. They also create a welcoming environment in airports, malls, and other public places, where a high priority is given to making the place feel comfortable and inviting.

Wherever houseplants live, they must be given appropriate care in order to flourish, which is the main goal of this book. Whether you enter the houseplant world on purpose or by accident, good care gives plants a fair chance to proclaim themselves as the sovereign life forms that they are, eager to demonstrate their ability to enliven a tabletop, windowsill, or vacant corner. As a plant's keeper, you become part of its performance. This book will be your tutor in that role, so that as you include plants in your interior spaces, you, too, will come a little closer to having a happy life.

An eye-catching assortment of easily grown succulents.

HOW TO USE THIS BOOK

The world of houseplants is huge and varied, so this book is organized to help you quickly and easily find the information you need. It is divided into three main parts — two plant directories and an in-depth encyclopedia of houseplant care. The first A–Z plant directory contains information on blooming houseplants, which are grown as much for their flowers as for their foliage, and the second A–Z directory covers foliage plants, which typically do not produce flowers. Each directory is alphabetized by botanic name: For a translation of botanic to common, and common to botanic names, see pages 356–366. (For an explanation of botanic nomenclature, see page 267.)

Within each A–Z directory, groups of closely related plants (for example, several kinds of cacti in the blooming section and several kinds of ferns in the foliage section), are discussed together, since they share common needs. The whys and hows of caring for these plants are covered in detail in short introductions to each group. The introductory coverage often includes a reference chart to help you compare the characteristics and cultural requirements of individual species and a group roundup of frequently seen problems. Each species then gets its turn in the spotlight.

Many houseplants stand alone, with no close relatives with whom they might be confused. The plant profiles describe each plant's size and appearance, its preferred growing conditions, the best methods for propagating the plant, and tips for selecting varieties and displaying them to maximum advantage. The individual profiles conclude with a troubleshooting section to help you identify and correct common plant problems. If you find the remedies given in the troubleshooting sections too brief, look at the more detailed information in Part 3: Houseplant Care, which begins on page 247. If you have any questions about the terminology used in this book, you can consult the Glossary, beginning on page 332.

Key to Success

If growing houseplants is a new venture for you, or if you think you may not be able to provide the right spot for many of them, look for this icon at the top right of some entries. These are the plants that thrive in a wide range of light and temperature conditions or aren't very fussy about their water needs.

Plants that don't get this signal aren't necessarily difficult to grow, but check out the ⬥ in the specifications. This indicates that if you pay attention to that particular need, you're more likely to succeed with that plant.

WHAT PLANT DO YOU HAVE?

The first step is to identify the houseplant you want to study. This may or may not be provided on a plant tag stuck into the pot. If you know either the plant's botanical or common name, you can look at the botanic-to-common or common-to-botanic cross reference lists (page 340) or the index to locate detailed information about the plant. But often foliage plants, in particular, are simply labeled "foliage plant" or "tropical plant." Use the following Plant Identification Guide, which is designed to help you name your plant, and then refer to the entry in Part 1 or 2 for all you need to know to help it not only survive, but thrive.

TO LEARN MORE

If you find yourself feverishly interested in a certain type of plant, look into the plant societies and specialty mail-order nurseries listed in Resources for Houseplant Lovers (page 337). These organizations and companies share your passion and can greatly add to the satisfaction of growing beautiful houseplants.

IT'S NOT UNUSUAL TO ENJOY YOUR HOUSEPLANTS without knowing their names. Cuttings from friends, supermarket finds, or even plants from nurseries may not be identified, or may be identified incorrectly. But with a proper identification, you're more able to meet your plant's needs. This key helps you observe and classify your plant's characteristics, starting with 5 main, color-coded categories:

- Plants with small "oranges" present
- Plants with no ordinary leaves
- Plants with spines or hairs on leaves or stems
- Plants with no spines but with flowers
- Plants with no spines and no flowers

For instance, your plant has smooth stems (no spines) but it does have flowers, so you go to the heading "No spines, flowers present," where you have 4 more choices. Because your plant has very showy flowers and plain green, straplike leaves, you're led to 6 plants that fit that description. Make your match by comparing the photo and description to your plant. *Note:* Plants listed as "no flowers present" may in fact bloom, but the key was developed to help you identify them either way. Also, the term "flowers" in this chart may refer to colorful bracts.

Small "oranges" present

- *Citrus × citrofortunella mitis* (pp. 88–89)
- *Solanum pseudocapsicum* (pp. 148–149)

No ordinary leaves

Small rounded shapes close to soil

- *Lithops* (p. 84)

Many rounded "beads" on long drooping stems

- *Senecio rowleyanus* (p. 87)

Many spines or hairs on leaves or stems (flowers may or may not be present)

Velvety purple hairs

- *Gynura* (pp. 204–5)

Velvety hairs barely visible

- *Kalanchoe tomentosa* (p. 83)
- *Saintpaulia* (pp. 140–41)

Stems covered with sharp thorns (small leaves usually present, red flowers may also be present)

- *Euphorbia milii* (pp. 96–97)

Plants columnar or tubelike and spiny

- *Aporocactus flagelliformis* (p. 67)
- *Cereus peruviana* (p. 68)

Plants rounded (may be clustered) and spiny

- *Echinopsis* (p. 69)
- *Gymnocalycium mihanovichii* (p. 70)
- *Mammillaria* (p. 72)
- *Parodia* (p. 73)
- *Rebutia* (p. 74)

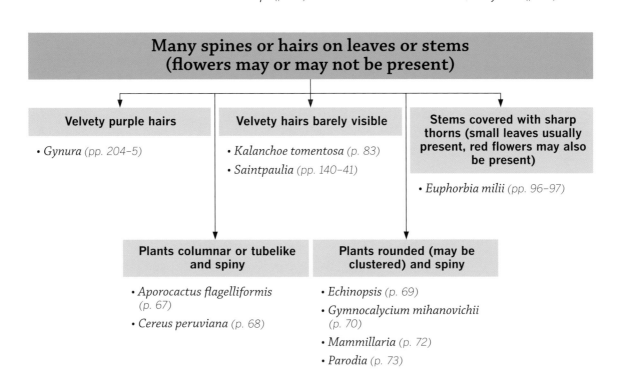

No spines, flowers present

Leaves showy; flowers sometimes present

- *Begonia rex* (p. 13)
- *Begonia × corallina* (p. 12)
- *Oxalis regnellii* (p. 50)
- *Saxifraga stolonifera* (pp. 142–43)
- *Tradescantia albiflora* (pp. 244–45)
- *Zebrina pendula* (pp. 244–45)

Flowers showy and leaves showy or patterned

- *Abutilon* (variegated forms) (pp. 2–3)
- *Aechmea fasciata* (p. 23)
- *Ananas comosus* 'Variegatus' (p. 24)
- *Aphelandra squarrosa* (pp. 6–7)
- *Cyclamen* (pp. 92–93)
- *Paphiopedilum* (some forms) (p. 128)
- *Vriesea splendens* (p. 30)

Flowers strongly fragrant

- *Citrus × citrofortunella mitis* (pp. 88–89)
- *Freesia corymbosa* (p. 44)
- *Gardenia jasminoides* (pp. 102–3)
- *Hyacinthus orientalis* (p. 46)
- *Jasminum polyanthum* (pp. 112–13)
- *Lilium longiflorum* (p. 47)
- *Narcissus* (p. 49)

Flowers showy and leaves plain green (or with only slight markings)

LEAVES STRAPLIKE

- *Billbergia nutans* (p. 25)
- *Clivia miniata* (p. 43)
- *Guzmania lingulata* (p. 27)
- *Muscari armeniacum* (p. 48)
- *Narcissus* (p. 49)
- *Tillandsia* (p. 29)

LEAVES NOT STRAPLIKE

Flowers large:

- *Anthurium* (pp. 4–5)
- *Cattleya* (p. 125)
- *Euphorbia pulcherrima* (pp. 98–99)
- *Hibiscus rosa-sinensis* (pp. 110–11)
- *Hippeastrum hortorum* (p. 45)
- *Paphiopedilum* (p. 128)
- *Phalaenopsis* (p. 129)
- *Spathiphyllum* (p. 125)
- *Zantedeschia* (p. 52)

Individual flowers small (often clustered):

- *Begonia* (pp. 12–14)
- *Exacum affine* (pp. 100–101)
- *Kalanchoe blossfeldiana* (p. 83)
- *Oncidium* (p. 127)
- *Primula* (pp. 132–33)
- *Saintpaulia* (pp. 140–41)

Flowers medium size:

- *Abutilon* (pp. 2–3)
- *Achimenes* (p. 41)
- *Columnea gloriosa* (pp. 90–91)
- *Dendranthema morifolium* (pp. 94–95)
- *Dendrobium* (p. 126)
- *Hatiora* (p. 71)
- *Rhododendron* (pp. 134–35)
- *Rosa* (pp. 136–37)
- *Schlumbergera* (p. 75)
- *Senecio × hybridus* (pp. 144–45)
- *Sinningia speciosa* (pp. 146–47)
- *Streptocarpus × hybridus* (pp. 146–47)
- *Tulipa* (p. 51)

No spines, no flowers present

Leaves solid green, bluish, olive or gray-green

LEAVES SMALL, OVAL, OR ELONGATED WITH POINTED TIP

- *Cissus antarctica* (pp. 168–69)
- *Ficus benjamina* (p. 198)
- *Ficus pumila* (p. 201)

LEAVES LARGE, OVAL, OR ELONGATED WITH POINTED TIP

- *Aspidistra eliator* (pp. 160–61)
- *Cordyline terminalis* (pp. 172–73)
- *Dracaena* (pp. 178–79)
- *Ficus elastica* (p. 199)
- *Philodendron* hybrids (p. 234)
- *Spathiphyllum* (pp. 150–51)

LEAVES NEEDLELIKE

- *Araucaria heterophylla* (pp. 158–59)
- *Asparagus densiflorus* (p. 185)
- *Rosmarinus officinalis* (pp. 138–39)
- *Tillandsia* species (p. 29)

LEAVES FLESHY

Rounded:
- *Crassula ovata* (p. 79)
- *Lithops* (p. 84)
- *Plectranthus australis* (pp. 130–31)

Pointed and forming rosettes:
- *Agave* (p. 77)
- *Echeveria* (p. 80)
- *Faucaria* (p. 81)
- *Haworthia* (p. 82)

Flattened segments:
- *Hatiora gaertneri* (p. 71)
- *Schlumbergera* (p. 75)

Long and narrow:
- *Aloe* (p. 62)
- *Sanseveria trifasciata* (p. 85)

Small, overlapping in drooping "tails":
- *Sedum morganianum* (p. 86)

LEAVES NARROW, STRAPLIKE

- *Asplenium nidus* (p. 190)
- *Beaucarnea recurvata* (pp. 162–63)
- *Billbergia nutans* (p. 25)
- *Chlorophytum comosum* (pp. 166–67)
- *Clivia miniata* (p. 43)
- *Guzmania lingulata* (p. 27)
- *Hippeastrum hortorum* (p. 45)
- *Pandanus veitchii* (pp. 226–27)
- *Tillandsia* (p. 29)

LEAVES COMPOUND (FEW TO MANY SMALLER LEAFLETS MAKING UP EACH LEAF)

Plant size small to medium:
- *Cissus rhombifolia* (pp. 168–69)
- *Cyrtomium falcatum* (p. 191)
- *Davallia* (p. 192)
- *Nephrolepis exaltata* (p. 193)
- *Oxalis regnellii* (p. 50)
- *Polypodium aureum* (p. 194)
- *Pteris* (p. 195)

Plant size medium to large:
- *Chamaedorea* (p. 220)
- *Chamaerops humilis* (p. 221)
- *Chrysalidocarpus lutescens* (p. 222)
- *Dizygotheca elegantissima* (pp. 176–77)
- *Howea* (p. 223)
- *Phoenix* (p. 224)
- *Rhaphis excelsa* (p. 225)
- *Schefflera* (pp. 238–39)

LEAVES HEART-SHAPED

- *Anthurium* (pp. 4–5)
- *Epipremnum aureum* (pp. 180–81)
- *Philodendron erubescens* (p. 233)
- *Philodendron scandens oxycardium* (p. 235)
- *Tolmiea menziesii* (pp. 242–43)
- *Zantedeschia* (p. 52)

Leaves strongly fragrant when rubbed

- *Rosmarinus officinalis* (pp. 138–39)
- *Pelargonium* (pp. 104, 06, 08)

Leaves colorful or strongly patterned

LEAVES NARROW, STRAPLIKE

- *Aechmea fasciata* (p. 23)
- *Ananas comosus* 'Variegatus' (p. 24)
- *Chlorophytum comosum* (pp. 166–67)
- *Cryptanthus acaulis* (p. 26)
- *Dracaena marginata* 'Tricolor' (pp. 178–79)
- *Neoregelia carolinae* 'Tricolor' (p. 28)
- *Vriesea splendens* (p. 30)

LEAVES SMALL TO MEDIUM

- *Cissus discolor* (pp. 168–69)
- *Ficus benjamina* (variegated form) (p. 198)
- *Fittonia verschaffeltii* (pp. 202–03)
- *Hedera helix* (some forms) (pp. 206–07)
- *Hypoestes phyllostachya* (pp. 208–09)
- *Peperomia* (pp. 228–29)
- *Pilea cadierei* (pp. 236–37)
- *Saxifraga stolonifera* (pp. 142–43)
- *Tradescantia albiflora* (pp. 244–45)
- *Zebrina pendula* (pp. 244–45)

LEAVES LARGE

- *Aglaonema commutatum* (pp. 156–57)
- *Begonia rex* (p. 13)
- *Caladium* (p. 42)
- *Calathea* (pp. 164–65)
- *Codiaeum variegatum pictum* (pp. 170–71)
- *Cordyline terminalis* (pp. 172–73)
- *Dieffenbachia* (pp. 174–75)
- *Dracaena* (pp. 178–79)
- *Epipremnum aureum* (pp. 180–81)
- *Maranta leuconeura* (pp. 210–11)
- *Philodendron* (pp. 232–35)
- *Sanseveria trifasciata* (p. 85)
- *Schefflera*, variegated form (pp. 238–39)
- *Syngonium podophyllum* (pp. 240–41)

LEAVES FANCY SHAPE (DEEPLY CUT OR LOBED)

- *Abutilon* (pp. 2–3)
- *Cissus rhombifolia* (pp. 168–69)
- *Fatshedera lizei* (pp. 182–83)
- *Ficus lyrata* (p. 200)
- *Hedera helix* (pp. 206–07)
- *Monstera deliciosa* (pp. 212–13)
- *Philodendron bipinatifidum* (p. 232)

PART 1

BLOOMING HOUSEPLANTS

Abutilon hybridum ah-BU-te-lon hi-BRI-dum

ABUTILON, FLOWERING MAPLE

Flowering maple *(Abutilon)*

ABUTILON IS CALLED FLOWERING MAPLE because of the shape of its broad, five-lobed leaves, but it is in no way a maple. It is more closely related to the hollyhock and to the weed known as velvet leaf. When given good light and proper care, abutilon rewards its keeper by producing papery blossoms on drooping stems nearly year-round. Flowers may be red, yellow, pink, orange, or peach, depending on variety. Some varieties feature leaves mottled with yellow, but the strongest growers have solid green leaves. Abutilon plants tend toward legginess, so it is important to prune them back by one-third their size in the spring, just before the most vigorous flush of new growth begins. Also pinch back stems occasionally through the summer to promote a full, bushy shape. Regular pruning makes it easy to keep an abutilon less than 18 in/45 cm high and wide. If you want an upright plant to 36 in/1 m tall, tie long branches to sturdy stakes.

SPECIFICATIONS

Light: Bright indirect light from a south or west window.

Temperature: Average room temperatures (65–75°F/18–24°C) year-round.

Fertilizer: *From spring through fall*, feed every 2 weeks with a balanced houseplant fertilizer. *In winter*, feed monthly, as plants grow more slowly.

Water: Water thoroughly and then allow plants to dry until the top inch of soil feels dry to the touch before watering again. Mist every few days in winter to prevent problems with spider mites when the air is very dry.

Soil: Any peaty potting soil; never add lime, as abutilon likes acidic soil conditions.

◆ Repotting: Repot young plants every 6 months or so to accommodate growing roots. After plants fill an 8 in/20 cm pot, usually when they are 3 years old, propagate new plants from stem tip cuttings and discard the parent plant.

Longevity: Plants become woody and unattractive by the time they are 3 or 4 years old, but can be kept indefinitely by propagating stem tip cuttings.

Propagation: Take 4 in/10 cm-long stem tip cuttings in spring or summer and set them to root in damp seed-starting mix as described on page 299. Use rooting powder. Transplant to potting soil after 4 to 6 weeks, setting three rooted cuttings in a 6 in/15 cm container.

Selections: Abutilon has been extensively hybridized, so there are dozens of named cultivars. Those with mottled or variegated foliage are best grown as foliage plants, because they tend to be weak bloomers.

Display tips: In addition to being grown in pots or hanging baskets, abutilon can be trained to assume a treelike shape by tying the main stem to a sturdy stake and pinching off all branches that emerge from the lowest 15 in/38 cm of stem.

TROUBLESHOOTING

Plant does not bloom.
CAUSE: Not enough light, or needs additional fertilizer.
REMEDY: Move plant to a place where it will get bright natural light half the day. Switch to a high-phosphorous fertilizer. Some plants bloom very little in winter, but vigorous hybrids should bloom year-round with good light and regular feeding.

Flowers and low leaves drop.
CAUSE: Uneven watering, resulting in some roots remaining dry; too much direct sun.
REMEDY: Rehydrate pot as described on page 328. In summer, move plant to a place where it will be protected from hot midday and afternoon sun.

Sticky leaves; small insects present on leaves.
CAUSE: Aphids.
REMEDY: Prune plant to remove badly infested leaves. Clean thoroughly with plenty of water every 3 days for 2 weeks. See page 269 for more information on controlling this pest.

Leaves are pale and stippled with yellow dots; faint webbing on leaf undersides.
CAUSE: Spider mites.
REMEDY: Isolate plant, and prune off and dispose of badly infested leaves. Clean undersides of remaining leaves with warm, soapy water. Mist daily for a week and see if plant shows signs of recovery. If plant has a stem that is not infested, attempt to propagate its tip, because seriously damaged plants may not be worth saving.

FAMILY: ARACEAE   ORIGIN: CENTRAL AND SOUTH AMERICA

Anthurium hybrids an-THUR-i-um
ANTHURIUM, FLAMINGO FLOWER

Flamingo flower (*Anthurium hybrid*)

THE COLORFUL, WAXY, HEART-SHAPED SPATHES of anthurium, which are often seen in cut-flower arrangements, are the reward for growing this tropical plant. Older anthuriums were temperamental, but advances in breeding in the last few decades have resulted in plants that are much more lush, compact, and willing to flower. Blooms, which are really bracts, last for up to 8 weeks, and many vigorous hybrids bloom nearly year-round, taking a brief break in winter. Very compact plants grow to only 12 in/30 cm tall, but larger ones may grow to 18 in/45 cm tall and wide. Flower colors include white, orange, and pink.

Do provide ample humidity by keeping your anthurium on a tray filled with damp pebbles or in a room with a humidifier. To keep leaves glossy and free of pests, wipe leaves clean from time to time with a damp cloth or clean plant with a fine spray of warm water. Do not allow pets to chew on anthurium foliage, as it contains calcium oxalate crystals and several toxic proteins that can cause severe mouth burning or skin irritation in all mammals, including humans.

SPECIFICATIONS

Light: Bright to moderate, with no direct sun.

Temperature: Average to warm (65–80°F/18–27°C). Plant grows best when there is little difference between daytime and nighttime temperatures.

Fertilizer: *From spring through late summer,* feed plants monthly with a high-phosphorus plant food. *In fall and winter,* feed every 6 weeks with a balanced fertilizer. Newly purchased plants often have time-release fertilizer in the pot and need no feeding until plant is repotted.

Water: *In spring and summer,* water frequently to keep soil lightly moist. Leach pots once or twice in summer as described on page 263. *In fall and winter,* water less, but do not allow soil to dry out. Maintain moderate to high humidity.

Soil: A peaty potting soil, such as African violet mix.

Repotting: Repot annually in spring, shifting plant to a slightly larger pot. Set plant high, so the crown sits just above the soil line. If roots show at the surface between repottings, cover them with moss or a light sprinkling of potting soil.

Longevity: 5 years or more; indefinitely when propagated by division.

Propagation: When plant produces a new crown more than an inch away from the main one, gently pull it away when repotting plant and set it in a small container. With good care, it should begin blooming after about a year.

Selections: Look for named varieties, many of which will have trademarks on the plant tags. These are hybrids bred for compact growth and heavy flowering.

Display tips: Keep plant in a handsome ceramic pot that coordinates well with the color of the blooms. Snip out central flower to prolong the life of the colorful spathes and to avoid pollen on tabletops.

TROUBLESHOOTING

Plant does not bloom.
CAUSE: Young age; too little light; too much nitrogen fertilizer.
REMEDY: Plants do not bloom until they are about 1 year old. To promote bud formation, move plant to a bright place, such as filtered light from a south or west window. After buds open, move plant to lower light. Check the fertilizer analysis to make sure the second number (phosphorous) is higher than the first one (nitrogen).

Leaves turn yellow.
CAUSE: Overwatering.
REMEDY: Check drainage holes to make sure they are not plugged by debris. Water less, and consider repotting plant using a peaty soil mix that includes perlite. Anthuriums need a little air around their roots.

Lower leaves are yellow with brown tips.
CAUSE: Overfertilization.
REMEDY: Leach pot as described on page 263. Resume feeding after a month, mixing fertilizer at half the normal strength. Brown leaf tips without yellowing may be a sign of extremely dry air. In this case, increase humidity.

Small insects flit about at soil's surface.
CAUSE: Fungus gnats.
REMEDY: Allow surface to dry between waterings. See page 270 for other control measures for this pest.

FAMILY: ACANTHACEAE   ORIGIN: BRAZIL

Aphelandra squarrosa

ah-fee-LAN-druh squar-OH-sa

ZEBRA PLANT, SAFFRON SPIKE

Zebra plant
(*Aphelandra squarrosa*)

APHELANDRA'S GLOSSY GREEN LEAVES marked with bold white leaf veins are reason enough to grow this plant, which matures into a 4-foot-tall, evergreen shrub in its tropical homeland of Brazil. Potted plants usually grow to no more than 15 in/38 cm tall and are best kept in pots no larger than 6 in/15 cm in diameter. Most people obtain a blooming aphelandra, which shows a lovely cluster of yellow bracts from which emerge delicate, yellow, tubular flowers. The flowers last only a few days, but the bracts often persist for 4 to 8 weeks. After the bracts deteriorate, clip them off and allow the plant to rest in a cool room for about 2 months. As light becomes more abundant in late spring, move plant to a bright place near a south or west window, but not in direct sunlight. Or, shift it to a shady porch or patio. When exposed to bright light for 3 months, aphelandra will usually rebloom in the fall, its natural bloom season. Light intensity rather than day length triggers flowering. A zebra plant may not bloom when kept in low light, but it will earn its place with its exotic foliage.

SPECIFICATIONS

⚠ Light: *In spring and summer,* bright. *In fall and winter,* moderate.

Temperature: Warm (65–80°F / 18–27°C).

Fertilizer: *From spring through fall,* feed every 2 weeks. Leach pots twice during the summer (see page 263). *In winter,* feed only every 6 weeks.

Water: Keep soil constantly moist. Do not let this plant dry out. Maintain moderate to high humidity.

Soil: Potting soil amended with peat moss or African violet mix.

Repotting: Annually in spring to refresh soil. Keep plants slightly rootbound.

Longevity: 1 to several years; indefinitely if propagated from rooted cuttings.

Propagation: Take stem tip cuttings in spring and root as described on page 299. Use rooting powder to speed rooting.

Selections: The most common cultivar, 'Dania', has emerald green leaves with white veins. The white venation is more dramatic in 'Apollo'. 'Red Apollo' features stems and leaf undersides blushed with red.

Display tips: Wipe leaves often with a damp cloth to keep them glossy. Display in a prominent place in fall, when the plant is in bloom.

TROUBLESHOOTING

Leaves become crinkled or curled.
CAUSE: Too much light.
REMEDY: Move plant to a shadier location.

Growing tips wilt.
CAUSE: Soil too dry.
REMEDY: Aphelandra requires constant moisture, which can be a challenge in summer when the plant is kept in bright light. Rehydrate pots that may have dried out in the center (see page 328). This often happens with rootbound plants grown in a peaty potting mix.

Lowest leaves wilt and drop off.
CAUSE: Too dry; too wet; excessive fertilizer.
REMEDY: Maintain constant moisture and reduce strength of fertilizer solution. Leach pots to remove possible accumulated salts (see page 263).

Small yellow spots on leaves; tiny flying insects are present.
CAUSE: Whitefly.
REMEDY: Isolate plant and install sticky traps as described on page 278.

Plant is weak; grows slowly; small flying insects present.
CAUSE: Fungus gnats.
REMEDY: The moist, peaty soil aphelandra prefers is attractive to this irritating pest. Keep soil slightly dry for several days, then trap larvae with potato pieces as described on page 271.

White cottony masses on stems.
CAUSE: Mealybug.
REMEDY: Remove mealybugs with a cotton swab dipped in alcohol or vegetable oil. Follow other control measures described on page 273.

Small sucking insects on leaf undersides and new leaves.
CAUSE: Aphids.
REMEDY: Clean plant thoroughly with water, then spray with insecticidal soap. See other control measures on page 269.

Begonias

Angel-wing begonia
(*Begonia* × *corallina*)

NAMED AFTER SEVENTEENTH-CENTURY, French-born plantsman Michel Begon, the begonia family includes more than 900 species, and there are ten times that many named hybrids. Most begonias grown as houseplants come from tropical regions, so they are warm-natured plants. All begonias have fleshy stems and lopsided leaves, with half of the leaf larger than the other half. Leaves vary in shape from elongated hearts to pointed, ivylike forms, and some begonias have rounded leaves with scalloped edges. Begonia flowers are either male or female. The male flowers tend to be short lived, while the female flowers persist for weeks as enclosures for winged seedpods.

Numerous "outdoor" begonias can be grown indoors for short periods, including the wax begonias used as indestructible bedding plants in the summer garden, and tuberous begonias, often grown in hanging baskets kept outdoors in shady areas. Yet three types of begonia make superior houseplants: angel-wing begonias, fancy-leafed begonias, and winter-blooming begonias. Each type is discussed in detail on pages 12–14, since each has unique characteristics.

Caring for Begonias

Begonias vary in size, longevity, and their most remarkable features. Angel-wing begonias make wonderful houseplants, since they produce showy leaves and pretty flowers. They are also reasonably long lived and easy to propagate by rooting stem cuttings. Fancy-leafed begonias are more challenging to grow, but their stained-glass leaves are among the most painterly plants in existence. Most people use winter-blooming begonias as short-lived color plants for winter windowsills. When the last flowers fade, you can discard the plants or keep them long enough to propagate new plants from rooted stem cuttings.

Light: Begonias need moderate light in summer, so they fare well when grown near an east window or under fluorescent lights. Those that bloom benefit from increased light in winter, when they perform best near a south or west window.

Temperature: Protect plants from chilling, as they are easily damaged by temperatures below 55°F/13°C. A temperature range of 65–75°F/18–24°C is ideal for most begonias.

Fertilizer: A steady diet of liquid fertilizer diluted to half the normal strength will keep begonias happy. Feed plants every 2 weeks while they are actively growing. Flowering begonias benefit from a high-phosphorous plant food. With fancy-leafed begonias, a balanced plant food is fine.

Water: Begonias are easily damaged by overwatering, yet they also suffer when their soil becomes extremely dry. Watering practices vary slightly with begonia type, but as a general practice it is prudent to allow the top inch of soil to become nearly dry between waterings. Begonias need moderate to high humidity. Make use of trays filled with dampened pebbles or use a humidifier in areas where you grow begonias. Avoid frequent misting, which can lead to problems with powdery mildew. Because of their need for humidity, begonias are good plants to grow in the same room with orchids, bromeliads, or ferns.

Winter-blooming begonia
(*Begonia × hiemalis*)

Soil: Provide begonias with a peaty yet well-drained soilless mix, such as African violet soil. Many good-quality potting soils that include perlite, which lightens the mix texture, are satisfactory for these plants. Heavy soil that dries slowly is not a good choice for begonias.

Repotting: Begonias often are sorted according to their root types, which can be fibrous or tuberous or include a thick rhizome that spreads over the surface of the soil. Root type influences container size and shape. Angel-wing begonias have fibrous roots and grow best when slightly rootbound in smallish pots. Most fancy-leafed selections develop rhizomes that grow near the soil's surface, so the best containers for them are broad and shallow. Winter-blooming begonias usually need no repotting unless you want to shift them to a more decorative container.

Be careful not to plant any begonia in a large pot, as this can lead to problems with overwatering and root rot. After repotting, tap on the sides of the pot to tamp soil into place, but do not press it down hard with your fingers. A bit of air left in the potting mix is good for begonias.

Pruned stems from angel-wing begonias make good cut flowers.

Propagating: All begonias can be propagated by setting stem tip cutting to root in a warm, humid environment. Fancy-leafed types can be propagated from petiole leaf cuttings, as is done with African violets (see page 302). They have the further distinction of being the only commonly grown houseplants that will develop plantlets when a leaf is pinned to the surface of dampened seed-starting mix. Although interesting, this method is slow compared to rooting petiole leaf cuttings, and not nearly as dependable. Some begonias can also be grown from seed, though hybrids are best propagated vegetatively, by rooting stem cuttings or leaves.

Small details: Begonias often react badly to changes in their environment, so it is wise to provide special care when bringing a new one into your home or office. Buy from a local source if possible, or purchase a small plant if it must be shipped. Reputable suppliers will ship plants only in warm weather. When you get the plant home, protect it from exposure to drafts and dryness by enclosing it in a loose plastic bag for a few days. Babying the plant along during its first few weeks in its new location can make a dramatic difference in a begonia's short- and long-term welfare.

TROUBLESHOOTING

Leaves turn yellow or brown and fall off.
CAUSE: Overwatering.
REMEDY: Keep plants in small pots and water only after the surface becomes dry. Cool conditions and oversized pots contribute to this problem.

Tan spots on leaves; plants rot at the base.
CAUSE: Botrytis, a fungal disease.
REMEDY: If possible, remove affected leaves and propagate new plants from clean stem tip cuttings. This disease is common with rooted cuttings, and is best prevented by using a clean, pathogen-free rooting medium.

Spots with yellow halos on leaves.
CAUSE: Bacterial leaf spot.
REMEDY: On angel-wing and fancy-leafed begonias, remove affected leaves and increase air circulation. Dispose of infected winter-blooming begonias, as they carry this disease throughout their systems.

Flowers twisted and distorted, especially on winter-blooming begonias.
CAUSE: Thrips or mites.
REMEDY: See page 276 and check for presence of thrips. If present, pinch off affected leaves and buds and dispose of them. With good care, plants should rebloom in a few weeks. Mites are a more persistent pest. If flowers and new leaves are distorted, but no thrips are present, assume mites are the problem and dispose of the infested plant.

White powdery patches on leaves.
CAUSE: Powdery mildew, a fungal disease.
REMEDY: Remove affected leaves at the first sign of this disease. Increase air circulation around the plants. Older leaves are more susceptible than young ones, so propagating new plants annually is a good preventive strategy.

White cottony creatures on stems and leaves.
CAUSE: Mealybugs.
REMEDY: Isolate plant, and remove mealybugs by hand using a cotton swab dipped in alcohol. Repeat every 5 days until problem is controlled. Do not use oil sprays on begonias to control mealybugs or other pests.

Leaves of fancy-leafed begonias become pale and brittle.
CAUSE: Excessive light; dry air.
REMEDY: Move plant to a spot with reduced light and increase humidity. When new leaves appear with good color, propagate a few to grow a new plant.

Getting to Know Begonias

In addition to the three types of begonias described below, there are many more available from specialty greenhouses and collectors.

Botanical name	Common name	Features	Ease of culture
Begonia × corallina, other species and hybrids	Angel-wing begonia	Clusters of pendant flowers, winter through spring, on evergreen plants with beautiful leaves on canelike stems.	Vigorous hybrids are moderately easy to grow.
Begonia rex, B. masoniana, other species and hybrids	Fancy-leafed begonia	Small flower clusters are usually pinched off; plants are grown for their technicolor leaves.	Somewhat temperamental, these plants are easy for some people and challenging for others.
Begonia × hiemalis	Winter-blooming begonias	Lovely double camellia-type blossoms in bright primary colors.	Purchased in bud, these plants provide dependable color for several months, but they are challenging to regrow in subsequent seasons.

Fancy-leafed begonias show mesmerizing variegation patterns.

Begonia × corallina, other species and hybrids be-GO-nee-uh ko-ra-LEE-nuh

ANGEL-WING BEGONIA, CANE BEGONIA

Angel-wing begonia
(*Begonia × corallina*)

WITH MARVELOUSLY MARKED LEAVES and elegant pendant flower clusters, angel-wing begonias are the best types to grow as houseplants. There are dozens of species and named hybrids, which vary in size, leaf variegation, and flower color. Dwarf selections grow to only 12 in/30 cm and can be kept as table plants, while large ones become nearly shrublike within a few years' time, often growing more than 36 in/90 cm tall and wide. Bloom time varies with cultivar, but most angel-wings bloom best in late winter and spring. The varieties named below are among the strongest rebloomers, often producing several flushes of flowers at different times of year.

SPECIFICATIONS

Light: *In spring and summer,* bright filtered light with no direct sun. *In fall and winter,* bright light, including up to 4 hours of direct sun.

Temperature: Average room temperatures (65–75°F/18–24°C) year-round.

◆**Fertilizer:** Feed every 2 weeks with a high-phosphorous plant food mixed at half the normal strength.

Water: Allow soil to become dry to within 1 in/2.5 cm of the surface between thorough waterings.

Soil: A light, peaty soilless mix such as African violet potting soil.

Repotting: Repot annually in spring, shifting plant to a slightly larger container. Add pebbles or broken crockery to the bottom of the pot to increase weight and improve drainage. Very large specimens may need staking.

Longevity: 4 to 5 years, or indefinitely when propagated from stem tip cuttings.

Propagation: In spring or summer, root nonflowering stem tip cuttings in perlite, seed-starting mix, or a half-and-half mixture of peat moss and sand, as described on page 300.

Selections: 'Bubbles' is naturally dwarf, and produces orange-red flowers almost continuously. Pink-flowered 'Looking Glass' grows 12–36 in/30–90 cm tall, and features metallic silver leaves with olive green veins and red undersides. The dark reddish leaves of 'Cracklin Rosie' are speckled with pink, while long-limbed 'Sophie Cecile' has green leaves speckled with white. For hanging baskets, white-flowered 'Orococo' is a real beauty, with ivy-shaped, green-gold leaves edged with dark red.

Display tips: Angel-wing begonias are beautiful year-round, and deserve a prominent position where they can be admired constantly.

Begonia rex, B. masoniana, other species and hybrids bee-GO-nee-uh REKS, b. may-so-nee-AN-uh

FANCY-LEAFED BEGONIA, PAINTED-LEAF BEGONIA, REX BEGONIA, IRON CROSS

Rex begonia (*Begonia rex*) and iron cross begonia (*B. masoniana*)

BREATHTAKING TO BEHOLD, fancy-leafed begonias produce large leaves, to 6 in/15 cm long, dramatically marked with silver, green, pink, and burgundy. They need slightly less light than blooming begonias, and do well when grown under fluorescent lights. Pinching off buds and blossoms helps to maintain large, healthy leaves. To provide the high humidity these begonias crave, cover plants with a plastic tent at night, which works like a humidity chamber.

Fancy-leafed begonias sometimes shed their leaves and become dormant in winter. When this happens, clip off the withered leaves, allow the soil to become almost dry, and enclose the pot in a plastic bag. Keep it at 60°F/16°C until new growth appears, 6 to 10 weeks later.

SPECIFICATIONS

Light: Bright indirect light or fluorescent light year round.

Temperature: Average room temperatures (65–75°F/18–24 cm) year-round.

Fertilizer: *From spring through fall,* feed every 2 weeks with a balanced houseplant fertilizer. *In winter,* feed plants monthly unless they are dormant.

Water: Water lightly yet frequently to keep soil constantly moist, but avoid overwatering. Plants need moderate to high humidity, but heavy misting can cause spots to form on leaves. Use trays filled with moist pebbles, a humidifier, or a plastic tent instead.

Soil: Use a light-textured, fast-draining medium such as African violet mix.

Repotting: Using shallow pots, repot plants in early spring so the rhizome is barely visible at the soil's surface. Repot dormant plants as soon as new growth appears.

Longevity: Individual plants grow for 2 to 3 years, but can be kept indefinitely when propagated from stem or leaf cuttings.

Propagation: You can divide rhizomes when repotting, but it's safest to root medium-sized leaves in early summer; handle these like petiole leaf cuttings see page 302.

Selections: 'Iron Cross' begonia (*B. masoniana*) features apple green leaves marked with dark brown crosses; leaves have a distinctively puckered texture. Leaves of various *B. rex* and *B. boweri* hybrids may be spotted, as in varieties with 'Tiger' in their name. Other hybrids show flaming variegation patterns in pink, silver, and various shades of green.

Display tips: Young plants are ideal for tank-sized terrariums. Larger plants demand exacting care and high humidity.

FAMILY: **BEGONIACEAE**   ORIGIN: **HYBRID OF TUBEROUS AND WAX BEGONIA SPECIES**

Begonia × hiemalis bee-GO-nee-uh hy-MA-lis
WINTER-BLOOMING BEGONIA, REIGER HYBRID BEGONIA

Winter-blooming begonia
(*Begonia × hiemalis*)

CREATED IN 1955, WINTER-BLOOMING BEGONIAS are usually called Reiger hybrids. Ongoing breeding work continues to improve these plants, which are increasingly available on the brink of bloom in early winter. Mature plants in full flower stand 12–18 in/30–45 cm tall. They feature numerous camellia-like blossoms, to 2 in/5 cm wide, that may be red, pink, salmon, orange, or yellow. To prolong flowering time, gingerly pinch off individual flowers as they fade.

These plants are bred for a single season of enjoyment, but it is possible to keep them from year to year. When flowering subsides, taper off water and allow plants to become nearly dry. Cut foliage back to 3 in/7.5 cm, allow plants to rest for 6 weeks, then commence watering. When new stems are 3 in/7.5 cm long, cut them off and root them; discard the parent plant. In the fall, keep plants in natural light, since short days (less than 12 hours long) and cool nights trigger the formation of buds.

SPECIFICATIONS

Light: Near a cool, bright window.

Temperature: *At night,* 60°F/16°C. *During the day,* 70–75°F/21–24°C year-round.

Fertilizer: Feed every 3 weeks with a high-phosphorous fertilizer mixed at half the normal strength.

Water: Allow soil to dry to 1 in/2.5 cm below surface between thorough soakings. Keep plants on trays filled with damp pebbles to increase humidity.

Soil: Fast-draining mix that includes peat and perlite, such as African violet potting soil.

Repotting: Should plants become rootbound, shift them to slightly larger pots.

Longevity: 6 months, or indefinitely when propagated from stem tip cuttings.

❶ Propagation: After plants have been cut back, rested, and begin to regrow, take 3 in/7.5 cm–long stem cuttings and root them in damp perlite, seed-starting mix, or a half-and-half mixture of peat moss and sand, as described on page 300.

Selections: Labeled as 'Eliator' or 'Reiger' hybrids, it is best to buy plants that show good bud color but have not yet begun to bloom.

Display tips: These are ideal plants for a sunny winter windowsill, where they can be teamed with amaryllis, cyclamen, and other winter-blooming plants.

Bromeliads

COMMONLY KNOWN AS THE PINEAPPLE FAMILY, bromeliads grow wild in the rain forests of South America. The first bromeliad brought to Europe was indeed the pineapple, which Columbus found growing in the West Indies in 1493. After that, nearly 300 years passed before other bromeliads were introduced to the civilized world. These plants were grown in the conservatories of wealthy Europeans, and only gradually made their way into the houseplant world. Compared to other houseplants, bromeliads are definitely newcomers.

All bromeliads are members of the Bromeliaceae family, which includes many plants that grow in the crotches of tree limbs, others that anchor themselves to rocks, and some that sink their roots into the forest floor. Bromeliads are unique in their ability to absorb moisture and nutrients from the air through tiny leaf scales, called trichomes. In addition, many species form rosettes of stiff leaves that overlap at the base to form a reservoir that holds water. Often called a cup or tank, this reservoir provides the plant with water and

Blushing bromeliad
(Neoregelia carolinae 'Tricolor')

nutrients, which are released as insects and forest debris caught in the cup slowly decay.

In homes and offices, most bromeliads need a moderately moist environment where they can receive direct light for half the day. Some species tolerate dry air better than others, but all bromeliads grow best when humidity levels hover around 50 percent. They are therefore good plants to partner with ferns and other plants that need moist air. Bromeliad roots are quite skimpy, so they can be kept in smallish pots. For a dramatic display, you can grow young plants tethered to pieces of wood or large stones, with their roots wrapped in sphagnum moss.

The bracts of many bromeliads, such as this scarlet star *(Guzmania lingulata),* color up as the plants prepare to bloom.

All bromeliads bloom, usually when the plants are 3 to 5 years old. The blooms are actually clusters of colorful bracts, from which small, often vividly colored flowers emerge. The bracts persist for several weeks. After a bromeliad blooms, it slowly dies. But before it expires, the parent plant produces several offsets, or pups, which grow from the leaf crevices of the outermost leaves. When the pups are a third the size of the failing parent plant, they can be cut away, repotted, and grown into the next generation (see page 20).

Caring for Bromeliads

Read below about the best potting soil and watering and fertilization practices for bromeliads. Never use any type of oil to clean bromeliad leaves or control pests, since oil can interfere with the work of the leaf scales. Also be careful where you place bromeliads, since the plants easily fall over when they become top-heavy, and some species have sharp spines along the edges of the leaves.

Light: Bromeliads vary in their preferences for light. Those with stiff leaves, such as urn plant and variegated pineapple, need more light than species that have more pliable foliage, such as queen's tears. The plant profiles that follow give specific light recommendations, but you also can memorize the phrase "soft leaf/soft light, hard leaf/hard light," as a good rule of thumb. In simple terms, bromeliads with soft leaves do well when grown near an east window, while those with hard leaves prefer the stronger light found by a west window. Soft-leafed bromeliads are often kept indoors year-round, while those with stiff leaves enjoy spending part of the summer outdoors in a place that receives a few hours of morning or afternoon sun.

Temperature: Average room temperatures are fine for most bromeliads, which should never be chilled by temperatures below 60°F/16°C. Some species, such as scarlet star (*Guzmania*) and flaming sword (*Vriesea*) resent temperatures above 80°F/27°C, so they are best kept indoors in climates with very warm summers. Others, particularly air plant (*Tillandsia*) and variegated pineapple (*Ananas*), are much more likely to bloom if treated to a warm summer outdoors. When moving plants outdoors in summer, gradually accustom them to increasing light levels, and never place them where they must endure intense midday sun. When shifted to bright light too quickly, bromeliad leaves can sunburn.

Fertilizer: Bromeliads are not heavy feeders, but they grow better when fed regularly in summer. Most grow best with an all-purpose liquid plant food diluted to half the normal strength. With most bromeliads, it is best to spray the fertilizer solution on the leaves and into the tank, while also dribbling a small amount into the soil. See the plant profiles for specific feeding recommendations for each species.

As bromeliads reach maturity, which usually takes 3 years or more, you can encourage the formation of flowers by feeding them a small pinch of Epsom salts (magnesium sulfate). Mix it into the water or fertilizer. The magnesium helps to initiate flowers. Another method for encouraging flower formation is to enclose a mature plant in a clear plastic bag along with a ripe apple or several apple cores for 1 to 2 weeks. The ethylene gas given off by the apple helps initiate bud formation. To avoid overheating, be sure to keep the plant out of direct sun when it is enclosed in a plastic bag.

Water: Most bromeliads gather water in their tanks, or reservoirs, and only a little moisture from natural rainfall penetrates the leaves to reach the roots. Keep this in mind when watering bromeliads. Many bromeliads are sensitive to minerals and chemicals in tap water, so they prefer rainwater or distilled water. Slow growth or browning of leaf tips can be due to hard water.

When watering bromeliads, spray a little water on the leaves, replenish the water in the reservoir, and dampen the soil only when it becomes very dry. A few species need more moisture in their soil, but as with other houseplants, overwatering greatly increases the risk of root rot, especially in winter when temperatures may be cooler. It is also good maintenance to dump out any water left in the reservoir after 10 days or so before refilling it with a fresh supply. If lifting the plant to empty the reservoir is too cumbersome, you can remove the old water with a bulb-type turkey baster. Place slightly less water in the reservoir when the plants produce a flowering spike. Excessive water left sitting in the cup can cause the base of a flower spike to rot.

Soil: Most bromeliads take up nutrients and moisture through their leaves and cups, so they do not depend on their roots for sustenance the way most other plants do. And, because many bromeliads are tree-dwellers, their roots are accustomed to sudden flushes of moisture followed by periods of dryness. Fast drainage is therefore important, along with some air in the root zone. To meet these needs, use a special bromeliad mix comprised of 1 part peat moss,

1 part sand or perlite, and 1 part chopped, decomposed tree bark or pine needles. This is an acidic mix, which is good. Never add lime to potting mixes used for bromeliads. If you prefer, potting soil developed for use with orchids is suitable for bromeliads.

Repotting: Bromeliads have scant root systems, and most grow best when kept in small pots. Restricted roots also control the plants' size and may help them to flower, too. Young plants that are actively growing usually benefit from yearly repotting, which is best done in spring. After 2 to 3 years, plants often can be held in a 5–6 in/12.5–15 cm pot until they bloom and produce offspring. Whether you are repotting a large plant or small offsets, watch the planting depth and be careful not to set plants too deeply. Deep planting can cause a bromeliad to rot. If the plant has such skimpy roots that it will not stay upright in its new container, surround it with a "fence" of wood skewers pushed into the soil. Remove them in a month or two, after the plant has established a sound anchor of new roots.

Graceful queen's tears (*Billbergia nutans*) gets its common name because of the drops of nectar that frequently "weep" from its pendulous blossoms.

Wait until bromeliad pups are at least one-third the size of their parent plant to cut them away and repot them in small containers.

Giving pink quill (*Tillandsia cyanea*) a cool winter's rest increases the chance that mature plants will bloom.

Propagating: Bromeliads are grown from offsets, often called *pups*. Some species develop offsets before they flower, but it is more typical to see pups emerging after the parent plant has bloomed and begun to decline. If desired, you can trim back the failing leaves of the parent plant to give the pups more light, but do not remove it too soon. The offsets feed off of the deteriorating tissues of the parent plant.

Remove and repot the pups when they are one-third to one-half the size of the parent. It is usually best to do this by repotting the entire family. Use a sharp knife to separate the pups, and pot them in a lightly moist potting mix. Planting the offsets in a very wet medium can cause them to rot. Offsets that grow quickly may need repotting in only six months, but most grow slowly, and can wait until spring to be moved into a slightly larger container.

Small details: Patience is important with bromeliads, which must be mature before they will bloom. Under ideal conditions, the bromeliad life cycle is completed in 3 years, but plants often need a year or two longer when grown indoors. When buying plants, choose those that have not yet bloomed or have just begun to show a flower spike. Bromeliads in full bloom will expire within a few weeks, and you will have to wait years for another good show of flowers.

TROUBLESHOOTING

Tips of leaves turn brown.
CAUSE: Conditions are too hot or too dry. In winter, increase humidity by placing plant near a humidifier or misting it every other day. In summer, move plant to a shady place outdoors. Use a spray bottle to water the leaves, reservoir, and roots of the plant. Bromeliad pots should never be allowed to become completely dry.

Brown spots on leaves.
CAUSE: Sunburn.
REMEDY: Expose plants to direct sun gradually, especially in summer when sunlight is very intense.

Plant rots at the base without blooming.
CAUSE: Soil is too wet; insufficient air circulation.
REMEDY: Plants that develop root rot often cannot be saved.

Plant does not bloom.
CAUSE: Immature; receives insufficient light.
REMEDY: Move to a slightly brighter location. Keeping plants in small containers helps encourage flower formation. Most bromeliads do not bloom until they are at least 3 years old. See "Fertilizer" on page 18 for more tips on promoting bromeliad flowers.

Flower spike rots at the base.
CAUSE: Too much water in reservoir.
REMEDY: Reduce the amount of water placed in the reservoir after the flower spike emerges. Instead, water plants by spraying the leaves until thoroughly wet, then dribbling water into the pots.

Offsets die without rooting.
CAUSE: Offsets taken when too small; humidity too low.
REMEDY: Wait until the parent plant is nearly dead to remove pups. For the first 3 to 4 weeks after repotting offsets, enclose them in a plastic bag to maintain very humid conditions.

Brown disks on leaves.
CAUSE: Scale insects.
REMEDY: These sucking insects occasionally infest bromeliads. Gently remove by hand by scraping them off with your fingernail. Repeat every few days, then spray plants with insecticidal soap after testing plant for tolerance. See page 273 for more on this pest.

White woolly patches on leaves, especially in crevices between leaves.
CAUSE: Mealybugs.
REMEDY: Mealybugs are an occasional problem on bromeliads. Remove with a cotton swab dipped in alcohol; repeat every 3 days until the plants are clean.

Bromeliads with soft, arching leaves, such as queens' tears (*Billbergia nutans*), require less light than those with stiffer leaves.

Getting to Know Eight Beautiful Bromeliads

In the following pages, eight of the most popular, easy-to-grow bromeliads are described in detail. They are listed in alphabetical order by botanical name, but you may not know a bromeliad's botanical name if you bought it without benefit of an identification tag. This chart will help you identify which bromeliad you have, so that you can then turn to the appropriate plant profile to get to know your bromeliad better.

Botanical Name	Common Name(s)	Description
Aechmea fasciata	Urn plant, silver vase plant	Stiff gray-green leaves form an upright vase shape. Mature plants produce pinkish orange bracts.
Ananas comosus 'Variegatus'	Ivory pineapple, variegated pineapple	Long green leaves with ivory edges studded with sharp spikes. Mature plants produce small, brown pineapples at their tops.
Billbergia nutans	Queen's tears, friendship plant	Long, leathery green leaves arch outward. Mature plants produce bright red bracts on arching stems.
Cryptanthus acaulis	Earth star, starfish plant	Small plants comprised of wavy, sharp-tipped leaves, often with red, pink, and green longitudinal stripes. Flowers are hidden by foliage as plants grow into clumps.
Guzmania lingulata	Scarlet star	Glossy, dark green leaves arch outward. Mature plants produce showy bracts that may be wine or bright red, orange, yellow, mauve, or lavender, depending on variety.
Neoregelia carolinae 'Tricolor'	Blushing bromeliad, cartwheel plant	Leaves with cream stripes down the centers spiral outward to give plant a flattened shape. As plant develops low flowers, the leaf bases turn red.
Tillandsia species	Pink quill, air plant, sky plant	Thin, scaly leaves have a grasslike texture. Plants have very few roots, and are usually grown on a piece of wood or mounted in a seashell.
Vriesea splendens	Flaming sword, painted feather, zebra bromeliad	Stiff, light green leaves feature bands of brown or mahogany. Mature plants produce a long flower spike topped with bold orange-red bracts.

FAMILY: **BROMELIACEAE**   ORIGIN: **BRAZIL**

Aechmea fasciata ak-MEE-uh fa-see-AH-tuh

URN PLANT, SILVER VASE PLANT

Urn plant (*Aechmea fasciata*)

THE STIFF, UPRIGHT SHAPE OF URN PLANT serves it well in its natural habitat — the floor of South American rain forests. The tough, arching leaves have a waxy finish, which helps the plant gather water in its reservoir. Individual leaves can grow to 15 in/37.5 cm long, and well-grown plants may reach 20 in/50 cm in height. Mature plants produce a quilled, pinkish orange bract that persists for 4 to 6 weeks. If a 4-year-old plant shows no signs of blooming, try pushing it along with Epsom salts and ethylene gas released by fresh fruit (see page 18). Spring is the best season to induce bloom; bright light also promotes flowering. After flowering, urn plant usually produces two to three pups.

SPECIFICATIONS

Light: Bright light from an east or west window.

Temperature: *In summer*, plants enjoy moving outdoors, provided temperatures range between 70–85°F/21–30°C. *In fall, winter and early spring*, average room temperatures (65–75°F/18–24°C).

Fertilizer: *In summer*, feed monthly with a liquid plant food mixed at half the normal strength. Spray it on the leaves, fill the reservoir at least 1 in/2.5 cm deep, and also fertilize the roots. *In winter*, feed plants every other month.

Water: Replenish water in the reservoir when it dries out, at least every 10 days. Lightly water the roots weekly in summer, less often in winter. Do not allow the roots to dry out completely in any season.

Soil: Orchid potting soil or a bromeliad mix (see page 18).

Repotting: Repot young plants annually in spring until they fill an 8-inch pot.

Longevity: Plants mature in 3 to 4 years.

Propagation: Divide and repot offsets when they are 4 to 6 months old and at least 6 in/15 cm tall.

Selections: In addition to the green-leafed form, 'Purpurea' features leaves blushed with maroon, and 'Variegata' has creamy longitudinal stripes on the leaves.

Display tips: Grow urn plant in its own pot near plants with lush green foliage, such as ferns or flowering houseplants that need abundant light. Young pups can be mounted on a piece of wood for one season.

FAMILY: **BROMELIACEAE**   ORIGIN: **BRAZIL AND PARAGUAY**

Ananas comosus 'Variegatus' ah-NAH-nus ko-MOH-sus
IVORY PINEAPPLE, VARIEGATED PINEAPPLE

Ivory pineapple
(*Ananas comosus* 'Variegatus')

THE SAME SPECIES AS THE EDIBLE PINEAPPLE, ivory pineapple is grown primarily for its long leaves with creamy margins studded with sharp spines. Plants can get quite large, to 36 in/90 cm tall and 6 ft/1.8 m across, but keeping them in 8 in/20 cm pots helps to control their size. Plants that are 5 to 6 years old produce a pinkish fruiting spike that slowly grows into a small brown pineapple over a period of 3 months. Although it lacks the sweet flavor of cultivated pineapples, which grow in hot sun, it is fun to watch as it matures.

Potted pineapples benefit from strong light and warm temperatures, so it is best to move them outdoors in summer. Gradually accustom the plants to increased light. Move the plants back indoors when nights begin to cool in the fall, and then place them in a very warm, brightly lit location.

SPECIFICATIONS

Light: *In summer,* move plant outdoors to partial sun. *In fall, winter and early spring,* a half day of direct light from an east or west window.

⬥ **Temperature:** *In winter,* warm (above 65°F/18°C). *In summer,* very warm (to 85°F/29°C).

Fertilizer: *From late spring through summer,* feed plant every 2 weeks with liquid plant food mixed at half the normal strength. *In winter,* feed monthly.

Water: *In summer,* provide moisture by thoroughly spraying the leaves with water twice weekly. Also water the roots when the top half of the soil becomes dry. *In winter,* plants kept indoors need less water due to lower temperatures and less sun. Use similar practices about once a week.

Soil: Orchid potting mix or African violet soil. This bromeliad needs a heavier soil than most other species.

Repotting: Every 2 years in spring. When repotting, do not press the soil down, as this plant likes a little air around its roots. Wear gloves and long sleeves when handling this spiny plant.

Longevity: Individual plants live 5 to 6 years.

Propagation: If the plant produces a fruit, cut off its top when the leaves in the rosette are 4 in/ 10 cm long, allow it to dry for a day, and then pot it in a lightly dampened mixture of peat moss and sand. You also can pot up offsets that emerge after the parent plant begins to die.

Selections: You can grow a regular pineapple by cutting off the top and rooting it, but the variegated form makes a much more attractive houseplant.

Display tips: This plant needs plenty of room and abundant sun. It makes a good floor plant in rooms with large windows, particularly when grown in close company with tropical-looking palms.

Billbergia nutans bil-BER-gee-uh NOO-tans

QUEEN'S TEARS, FRIENDSHIP PLANT

Queen's tears (*Billbergia nutans*)

POPULAR AND EASY TO GROW, queen's tears gets its name from the tendency of the flowers to weep droplets of nectar. It is also a willing producer of offsets, which can be shared among friends, hence its other common name, friendship plant. Young plants grow into upright rosettes. As the leaves age, they arch outward. Mature plants are typically 16 in/40 cm tall and up to 30 in/75 cm wide. Plants bloom when they are 2 to 3 years old, usually in spring, bearing pendant red or pink bracts with green, purple, or yellow flowers inside. Too much light can make the leaves take on a reddish cast, but increased light levels available outdoors in summer encourage mature plants to bloom the following spring. This bromeliad tolerates dry indoor air better than others, but still benefits from being kept in a spot where it can be misted often to increase humidity.

SPECIFICATIONS

Light: *In summer,* partial shade outdoors. *In fall, winter and early spring,* bright light from an east or west window.

Temperature: *In summer,* enjoys warm temperatures outdoors (65–80°F/18–27°C). *In fall, winter and early spring,* cool to average room temperatures (60–75°F/ 16–24°C); can tolerate brief winter chilling to 40°F/4°C.

Fertilizer: *In spring and summer,* feed leaves and roots with houseplant fertilizer mixed at half the normal strength every two weeks. *In fall and winter,* feed monthly.

Water: *In spring and summer,* water the leaves, reservoir, and roots as needed to keep the cups filled and roots lightly moist. *In fall and winter,* keep slightly dry to reduce problems with root rot.

Soil: Bromeliad mix or orchid potting soil.

Repotting: Annually in spring until plant fills a 5 in/12.5 cm pot. Then wait until after flowering to repot offsets.

Longevity: Individual plants usually live for 3 years.

Propagation: When parent plant fails after flowering, use a sharp-tipped knife to cut it off at the soil line. Repot pups when they are about 6 in/15 cm tall.

Selections: This plant is usually sold by species or common name. Buy plants that have not yet produced flowers.

Display tips: Grow in a hanging basket or suspended pot at eye level, where the arching leaves and pendant flowers can be seen up close.

Cryptanthus acaulis and hybrids

krip-TAN-thus uh-CAL-is

EARTH STAR, STARFISH PLANT

Earth star (*Cryptanthus acaulis*)

A SMALL BROMELIAD, earth star is an excellent choice for humid rooms where space is limited. Mature plants are only 5 in/12.5 cm high and 6 in/15 cm across. Unlike other bromeliads, earth star's flowers are small and hidden, so it is grown primarily for its starry, sharp-tipped wavy leaves. The coarse leaf scales are easily seen on most cultivars, and they do a good job of absorbing moisture and nutrients. Strong light intensifies the leaf colors of pink or variegated earth stars. Older plants often flatten out a bit before they bloom, and then slowly fail. Use scissors to trim back the leaves by half their length, which speeds the growth of the emerging offsets.

Because of its small size, earth star is the preferred bromeliad for growing in homes. Its unique texture brings surprising drama when earth star is grouped with ferns and other foliage plants that like high humidity.

SPECIFICATIONS

Light: Bright light from an east or west window.

Temperature: Warm (60–80°F / 16–27°C) year-round.

Fertilizer: *In spring and summer,* spray leaves monthly with a houseplant fertilizer mixed at half the normal strength. *In fall and winter,* feed every other month.

Water: *In spring and summer,* water as often as needed to keep the roots lightly moist. *In fall and winter,* water less often, but do not allow the roots to dry out completely.

Soil: Regular potting soil amended with one-third part peat moss, or use orchid potting soil.

Repotting: Repot every 2 to 3 years in spring, handling the plant gently to avoid injuring its sparse, shallow roots. This plant does well in a broad container.

Longevity: Up to 10 years, or indefinitely when propagated from offsets.

Propagation: Cut away pups and repot them when they are half the size of the parent plant. Keep newly potted pups in a warm place, enclosed in a loose plastic bag for a month to increase humidity.

Selections: Some earth stars feature all-green leaves, while others have red, pink, and green longitudinal stripes. 'Areltey' is quite pink, with gray-green stripes down the center of each leaf. 'Black Mystic', also known as 'Black Magic', has leaves mottled with irregular zebralike dark bands. A unique earth star, *C. sinuosus* 'Cascade', produces pups on long stolons, reminiscent of a spider plant.

Display tips: Young plants make good additions to terrariums. Older plants grown in pots are ideal for low windowsills, where they can easily be viewed from above.

FAMILY: **BROMELIACEAE**   ORIGIN: **CENTRAL AND SOUTH AMERICA**

Guzmania lingulata and hybrids

goos-MAN-ee-uh lin-goo-LAH-tah

SCARLET STAR

Scarlet star *(Guzmania lingulata)*

MANY OLDER STRAINS OF SCARLET STAR grew quite tall, but most modern named varieties are smaller, reaching a mature size of 10 in/ 25 cm tall and 12 in/30 cm wide. This bromeliad has a rather upright posture, and its glossy green leaves add to its appeal. A flamboyant bloomer, in its third or fourth year scarlet star produces a brightly colored quilled spike, which emerges just above the foliage in the plant's center. As the flower spike fades, usually 6 or more weeks after it appears, pups emerge from near the base of the plant. Although scarlet star appreciates high humidity, it is less demanding of light than other bromeliads, and often grows beautifully in the bright artificial light of offices.

SPECIFICATIONS

Light: Moderate to bright year-round, with no direct sun; grows well with bright fluorescent light.

Temperature: Average to warm (65–80°F/18–27°C) year-round.

Fertilizer: Feed monthly year-round with a houseplant fertilizer mixed at half the normal strength. Feed leaves, roots, and reservoir.

Water: Keep cup filled with at least 1 in/2.5 cm of water, and dribble enough water to the roots to keep them lightly moist. Empty old water from cup every 2 to 3 weeks and promptly replace it. Leach pots once during the summer to remove accumulated salts (see page 263).

Soil: Bromeliad or orchid potting soil.

Repotting: Repot annually in spring until plant fills a 6 in/15 cm pot. Small pots help induce blooming in mature plants.

Longevity: Individual plants live 3 to 4 years.

Propagation: Remove offsets and pot them up when they are at least 3 in/7.5 cm tall. Maintain high humidity for a month after potting up the pups.

Selections: There are numerous named varieties. The most popular is 'Luna', which produces a mauve spike. Others bloom yellow, red, or pinkish lavender. Varieties with reddish leaf markings often are not as vigorous as green-leafed selections.

Display tips: The handsome glossy leaves are spineless, so this bromeliad poses no danger when placed near activity areas. Moving a blooming plant to slightly lower light helps to intensify the color of the bracts.

Neoregelia carolinae 'Tricolor'

nee-oh-ree-GEE-lee-uh ka-roh-LIN-uh

BLUSHING BROMELIAD, CARTWHEEL PLANT

Blushing bromeliad
(*Neoregelia carolinae* 'Tricolor')

BLUSHING BROMELIAD GETS ITS NAME from the way the leaves in the center of the plant turn bright red as the plant begins to flower (see photo on page 15). The blossom itself is not showy and stays nestled deep in the crown. However, the colored vase persists for a few months, until the parent plant dies back and makes way for three or more new offsets. Full-sized blushing bromeliads, sometimes called "neos," become broad, flat-topped plants, 25 in/62.5 cm wide and 12 in/30 cm tall, and plants of any size need abundant warmth and humidity. To grow well, they must feel convinced that they are in a jungle, yet they also need abundant sun. This bromeliad is therefore not for everyone, but is a good choice if you have a bright sunroom that is kept humid at all times.

SPECIFICATIONS

Light: Bright light with a half day of direct sun year-round. Responds well to being grown in a sunny yet humid place outdoors in summer.

Temperature: Average to warm room temperatures (65–80°F/ 18–27°C), with no chilling below 50°F/10°C.

Fertilizer: Feed monthly with a high-phosphorous (low-nitrogen) fertilizer mixed at half the normal strength. Feed the leaves, roots, and reservoir.

Water: Keep roots lightly moist, and replenish water in reservoir every 10 days, or more often in summer. This bromeliad grows best in high humidity, above 50 percent.

Soil: Potting soil amended with one-third part peat moss, or African violet soil.

Repotting: Repot annually in spring until plant fills a 5 in/ 12.5 cm pot.

Longevity: Individual plants live 3 to 4 years.

Propagation: Wait until the parent plant dies back to pot up offsets, which often have very skimpy roots. Keeping newly potted offsets in a warm, humid enclosure, such as a roomy plastic bag, speeds the rooting process.

Selections: There are numerous named varieties, most of which have cream stripes in their leaves. 'Martin' is quite vigorous, as is the slightly smaller 'Compacta'.

Display tips: Because of its large, spreading shape, this bromeliad needs plenty of space. It is at its best when viewed from above.

Tillandsia species and hybrids til-AND-see-uh

AIR PLANT, SKY PLANT

TILLANDSIA BROMELIADS are the rootless wonders of the plant world. Some species do have roots, but these are used primarily to anchor the plants in place. Tillandsias take up moisture and nutrients through the leaves, and only one species, *T. cyanea* (pink quill), can be grown in a pot. Others can be pinned, tied, or even glued onto a mount, such as a gnarled piece of wood or a seashell. All are small plants with thin, gray-green leaves that seldom spread more than 6 in/15 cm high and wide. Like other bromeliads, tillandsias bloom and then produce offsets. Giving them a cool winter rest increases the probability that mature plants will bloom. Most tillandsias reach maturity in 3 to 5 years.

Pink quill *(Tillandsia cyanea)*

SPECIFICATIONS

Light: Bright light from an east or west window, with some direct sun in winter but not in summer.

Temperature: *In spring, summer and early fall,* warm (to 80°F / 27°C). *In winter,* a cool rest in the 60°F/16°C range.

Fertilizer: *In spring and summer,* feed plants every 2 weeks by spraying them with a high-phosphorous fertilizer, mixed at half the normal strength. Plants take up the nutrients with their leaf scales. *In fall and winter,* no feeding is needed.

Water: Spray plants with water twice weekly, until they are thoroughly wet. The applied water should dry within 4 hours. Do not soak the base of the plants.

Soil: None needed for most selections. A bit of sphagnum moss can be used to create a nest for air plants. Grow pink quill in orchid soil.

Repotting: Reposition as needed to accommodate new growth, usually only every 2 to 3 years.

Longevity: Individual plants live 5 years or more.

Propagation: Detach offsets when they are one-third the size of the parent plant. Small holes drilled in an old piece of untreated wood make a good temporary home for these babies.

Selections: Pink quill can be grown as an individual specimen in a pot. Most other air plants are sold by common name, or may be labeled as *T. ionantha.* Spanish moss is *T. usneoides.*

Display tips: Use a rasp to create crevices or depressions in a nicely figured knot of wood and install three air plants to create a tree garden.

FAMILY: **BROMELIACEAE**   ORIGIN: **TROPICAL AMERICA**

Vriesea splendens and hybrids

VREE-see-uh SPLEN-dens

FLAMING SWORD, PAINTED FEATHER, ZEBRA BROMELIAD

Flaming sword (*Vriesea splendens*)

ONE OF THE SHOWIEST BROMELIADS, flaming sword features stiff, arching leaves banded with maroon, which form a tight vase in the center. Mature plants grow 20 in/50 cm tall and 24 in/60 cm wide. Flaming sword is not as easy to grow as some other bromeliads, but it will succeed when provided with bright light, warm temperatures, and moderate to high humidity. If all goes well, a 3- to 4-year-old plant will reward you with a tall, flattened flower spike, which is usually bright red, with small yellow flowers emerging from the bracts. The spike persists for several weeks, after which the plant slowly declines while producing one or more offsets. Wait until the parent plant is quite far gone to propagate a new plant from the pup.

SPECIFICATIONS

Light: Bright indirect light year-round, with some direct sun in winter.

Temperature: Warm (70–80°F/ 21–27°C) year-round.

Fertilizer: Feed monthly with an all-purpose houseplant fertilizer mixed at half the normal strength. Feed the leaves, roots, and reservoir.

Water: Keep soil lightly moist at all times, and refill reservoir every 2 weeks with fresh water. Mist weekly, and keep in a humid room.

Soil: Bromeliad mix or orchid potting soil.

Repotting: Repot young plants after 2 years, and limit pot size for mature plants to 6 in/15 cm.

Longevity: Individual plants live for 3 to 4 years.

Propagation: After flowering, this bromeliad usually produces one robust pup. Allow it to grow until it is at least 8 in/20 cm tall before detaching it, potting it up, and discarding the parent plant.

Selections: There are many named varieties, which vary in leaf variegation and the shade of the flowering spike. Purchase plants that have not yet bloomed, or have just begun to produce a flowering spike.

Display tips: The dramatic leaf colors make this plant a strong focal point even when it is not in bloom. Because of its width, it is a good plant to display on a raised platform, with smaller ferns or other low-light plants beneath it.

Bulbs, Corms, and Tubers

Bright tulips, forced into bloom in pots, are an easy way to bring springtime indoors.

GROWING BEAUTIFUL INDOOR FLOWERING PLANTS from onion-shaped bulbs, nubby corms, or fleshy tubers planted in pots carries with it the same excitement as growing flowers from seeds, only better. Bulbs, corms, and other types of storage roots are packed with the nutrients plants need to grow and bloom, and some actually contain the cells of the flowers to come. Provide these plants with light and temperature regimens that suit them, and you will be delighted with the bursts of color at different times of the year.

This chapter includes twelve blooming plants that are grown by planting dormant roots of one kind or another. Those included here are commonly sold as indoor plants, and can be expected to bloom for more than 3 weeks when given adequate care. Some, such as oxalis, bloom almost year-round.

Bulbs, corms, and tubers vary in their need for and tolerance of cold, so they are broadly divided into two groups: spring-flowering bulbs and warm-natured bulbs. Most spring-flowering bulbs

Λ summer-blooming bulb in the garden, clivia can be forced for early bloom indoors in February or March.

Bulbs as Houseplants

The plants in this section are organized into the two broad groups listed below. I refer to all as "bulbs" in the interest of simplicity, though some grow from corms and tubers, which are quite different from true bulbs in terms of botanical structure. See the chart on page 39 for further guidance on plant characteristics and seasonal growth cycles. The plant profiles, which are listed by botanical name, provide detailed information on how to grow each plant for maximum satisfaction.

Spring-Flowering Bulbs

Botanic Name	Common Name
Hyacinthus	Hyacinth
Muscari	Grape hyacinth
Narcissus	Daffodil, paperwhite
Tulipa	Tulip

Warm-Natured Bulbs

Botanic Name	Common Name
Achimenes	Cupid's bow, orchid pansy
Caladium	Angel wings
Clivia	Kafir lily
Freesia	Freesia
Hippeastrum	Amaryllis
Lilium	Easter lily
Oxalis	Shamrock
Zantedeschia	Calla lily

are planted in fall, after which they must have several weeks of chilling before they will bloom in spring. Warm-natured bulbs, corms, and tubers that do not require chilling are regarded as "summer" bulbs, though some of them bloom in winter and spring. Most warm-natured bulbs need a dry rest period between cycles of active growth.

Forcing Spring-Flowering Bulbs

When spring-flowering bulbs are grown for indoor bloom, the process is called "forcing" because it tricks the bulbs into behaving as if they have been grown outdoors through a long, cold winter. With the exception of paperwhite narcissus (see page 49), spring-flowering bulbs require a minimum chilling period of 8 to 15 weeks before they will bloom. Part of the chilling period can take place in your refrigerator, but most spring-flowering bulbs also need time to grow roots in cold soil before they start expending their energy putting out leaves and flowers.

Stores and mail-order companies begin selling spring-flowering bulbs in late summer and early autumn. As soon as you buy them, put the bulbs in your refrigerator (keep them in perforated plastic

Very fragrant signs of spring, grape hyacinth (*Muscari* species) are ideal bulbs for forcing.

Spring-flowering tulips and hyacinths frame this bright arrangement of other seasonal favorites (*from top to bottom,* cineraria, winter-blooming begonia, primrose).

bags). Store them away from apples and other fruits, which give off ethylene gas that can cause bulbs to rot. On a calendar, write down the date when you put your bulbs in the refrigerator — the official beginning of their chilling period.

How you approach the next step, planting the bulbs, depends on two things: your climate, and whether or not you have a place where the planted bulbs can be held at temperatures between 35–45°F/ 2–7°C for another couple of months.

Where winters are cold. Rig up a "chilling chamber" by placing the planted, lightly dampened pots in a cooler, plastic storage bin, or stout cardboard box kept on your porch or patio, or perhaps in an unheated garage. Then fill the box with chopped bark or other loose mulch material. If you want to keep the pots clean, enclose them in plastic bags before filling in around them with mulch. Stored in such a box, the bulbs should not actually freeze, and will be out of the reach of mice and squirrels, who like to eat bulbs for breakfast.

Where winter are warm. If your winter temperatures stay above 50°F/10°C or you simply have no space outdoors to use as a chilling chamber, you can plant bulbs in pots, water them lightly, enclose them in plastic bags, and return them to your refrigerator. This takes up refrigerator space, but most people can find room for a few small pots on the back of a middle shelf. Another option is to find a garden center (or mail-order company) that sells pre-chilled bulbs. These can be planted as soon as you buy them, though you'll still need to keep them in a cool place for a few weeks while the bulbs grow roots.

Fragrant paperwhite narcissus need no chilling period, and they can even be grown in a container filled with pebbles and water.

Hyacinths fill the room with their heavy fragrance.

Potting Up Spring-Flowering Bulbs

You can force bulbs in any containers that have drainage holes in the bottom and are at least three times as deep as the height of the bulbs. These can be the same containers in which you plan to display the bulbs when they bloom, or you can use small individual pots. Later on, when the chilling period is over and the bulbs produce their first green growth, you can gently transplant them to prettier containers if you like.

All-purpose potting soil is fine for forced bulbs, and you can mix in some small pebbles or gravel if desired to give the pots extra weight. Plant bulbs pointed side up, only so deep that the tops of the bulbs are barely covered with soil. Water the pots until the soil around the bulbs is thoroughly dampened, and move them to their chilling chamber. Then forget about them until the chilling time is up.

When your calendar says that the bulbs have chilled long enough (counting any time they spent in the refrigerator), examine the containers and look for the two signs that the bulbs are ready to come inside: roots showing in the pots' drainage holes, and a green shoot emerging from the tops of the bulbs. Move the containers to a cool room where temperatures are 50–60°F/10–16°C, such as your basement or a spare bedroom where the heat can be turned off. If the coolest spot you can manage has little light, don't leave the bulbs there for more than a week or so. If the place has light, the bulbs can stay there for 2 to 3 weeks. During this time they will slowly grow leaves and the flower buds will begin to appear. If you can, step up light but not temperature during this period.

Three weeks after being brought indoors, your bulbs will be well on their way to blooming. At this point they need abundant light and constant gentle moisture, but they may grow too fast if kept in a very warm spot. To make flowers last as long as possible, keep the bulbs in your coolest room at night. This is also the best way to handle purchased plants that are already coming into bloom (be sure to choose pots in which the buds have not yet opened).

Forced spring-flowering bulbs grow in such cramped conditions that it is difficult for them to store up the nutrients needed to bloom again if forced a second time the following year. However, small bulbs such as grape hyacinth and other "little" bulbs, discussed on page 36 in "Spring Surprises from Small Packages," can sometimes regain the strength they need to prosper if they are fed and watered regularly until they can be transplanted to the garden in mid- to late spring. In general, it is best to discard forced

SPRING SURPRISES FROM SMALL PACKAGES

Muscari (see page 48) are the most dependable and long-flowering of the so-called "little" spring-flowering bulbs, but several other species, described below, can be forced into bloom in the same way. Garden centers sell these bulbs alongside tulips and daffodils in the fall. Plant little bulbs close together in small pots, and allow them 12 to 15 weeks of chilling time. Expect the flowers to last about 2 weeks indoors. Like grape hyacinth, these little bulbs often do well when transplanted to the garden after their indoor blooms have faded. Here are some others to try:

- *Chinodoxa luciliae,* often called glory-of-the-snow, produces 8 in/20 cm–tall stems studded with up to a dozen small, starry, blue or pink flowers.
- Crocus hybrids bloom only for a week or so, but they are a beautiful way to celebrate the coming of spring on a cool windowsill. Plants grow to only 6 in/15 cm tall.
- *Iris reticulata,* or dwarf iris, features showy but short-lived blossoms in shades of blue, often with white or yellow markings, that grow only 4–8 in/10–20 cm tall.
- *Puschkinia scilloides,* or striped squill, looks like a tiny, 6 in/15 cm–tall hyacinth, with blue blossoms marked with darker blue stripes.
- *Scilla* species, including *S. bifolia, S. mischtschenkoana, S. peruviana,* and *S. siberica,* feature dainty little blue or white blossoms on stems that grow 4–8 in/10–20 cm tall.

Framed by their dark green foliage, the white trumpets of Easter lilies appear especially pristine.

Pots of caladiums can be sunk in the garden in summer, and brought back indoors when temperatures drop in the fall.

hyacinths, daffodils, and tulips after they have bloomed. If you want to grow bulbs that can be brought back into bloom year after year, the best candidates are achimenes, amaryllis, and some of the other warm-natured bulbs discussed on the following pages. But do not bypass spring-flowering bulbs just because they are one-shot wonders. A plant-lover's life is incomplete without the occasional fragrance of hyacinths or the cheery company of miniature daffodils.

Growing Warm-Natured Bulbs, Corms, and Tubers

The bulbs in this group come from different parts of the world, from the tropics to the arid temperate climate of South Africa, so they are not all grown the same way. Oxalis is nearly perpetual, hardly ever needing a rest period, while amaryllis, clivia, and most others do best when allowed a period of dormancy. Indeed, the seasonal light and temperature cycles of warm-natured bulbs vary so much that few generalizations can be made.

Most warm-natured bulbs that grow well indoors need a period of bright light or cool temperatures to coax them into bloom; many respond well to winter sun. In summer, they are best grown in shadier spots and can be moved outdoors onto a porch or patio provided they are not exposed to temperatures below about 55°F/13°C. If you have a garden, you can even bury the pots halfway in loose soil, which insulates the roots from daily temperature fluctuations and helps keep them moist at the same time.

Most warm-natured bulbs have in common a need for regular fertilization before and after they bloom. You might expect this with plants that, while somewhat seasonal, still grow for a long time. A high-phosphorous plant food is ideal for these plants.

Perhaps the best thing about warm-natured bulbs is that they provide bursts of color at different times of the year. You can have achimenes and caladiums through the summer, amaryllis in winter, clivia in late winter, and calla lilies in spring. While one species is at rest, there is always another ready and waiting to take its place. Whether you start with purchased plants or dormant roots, most warm-natured bulbs can be counted upon to reward their keepers with several seasons of delight. The plant profiles provide detailed information on the life cycles and cultural requirements for these beautiful plants.

Potted amaryllis bulbs fill a bright window in winter.

TROUBLESHOOTING BULBS

No leaves or flowers.
CAUSE: Bulbs have died, usually because fungi entered them. Infected bulbs rot and feel light or mushy when you remove them from the pots. Spring-flowering bulbs that freeze hard for a long time frequently rot when they thaw.
REMEDY: Discard bulbs and potting soil, and thoroughly clean pots. Start over in the proper season with bulbs from a reputable supplier. Use clean, uncontaminated potting soil.

Leaves appear, but no flowers.
CAUSE: Improper storage, especially at high temperatures, can cause the flowering parts of the bulb to die, though the leaf-producing tissues survive. Small, low-quality bulbs may lack sufficient specialized cells to develop flowers. High-nitrogen fertilizer also can cause plants to produce lush leaves and few flowers.

REMEDY: Buy bulbs soon after they become available, bypassing those that have been on store shelves a long time. Obtain the biggest and best bulbs or tubers you can find, and buy from a reputable dealer.

Leaves emerge from near the side of the pot.
CAUSE: Bulb or corm was planted upside down.
REMEDY: The tops of bulbs and corms are usually pointed, but if you can't tell the top from the bottom, plant the root on its side.

Leaves grow slowly and buds drop off before flowers open.
CAUSE: Dry conditions; trauma from environmental change.
REMEDY: Increase water and humidity. Avoid moving plants at the early bud stage of development.

Leaves look fine but buds drop off before flowers open.
CAUSE: Sudden change from cold to warm conditions.

REMEDY: When spring-flowering bulbs are moved from their chilling chamber, keep them in a cool room for at least a week. The change from cold to warm should be as gradual as possible.

Plants grow tall and have trouble staying upright.
CAUSE: Too warm during early growth phase, or not enough light.
REMEDY: Crowding bulbs helps dwarf their topgrowth, as does growing them in a cool room. Do not move to a warm place until buds are ready to open. Light-starved plants stretch toward the brightest light.

Leaves look unhealthy and show tiny yellow dots.
CAUSE: Spider mites.
REMEDY: See page 274 for the best ways to control this pest. Discard infested plants that are short lived, because spider mites can easily spread to other plants. When purchasing plants, check them thoroughly for this and other pests.

Twelve Top Bulbs, Corms, and Tubers to Grow Indoors

Botanical Name	Common Name	Type of Root	Chilling Required	Seasonal Characteristics
Achimenes species	Cupid's bow, orchid pansy	Small, pinecone-shaped tuber	None	Plant in early spring for bloom in summer through fall. Dormant in winter.
Caladium hybrids	Caladium, angel wings	Knotlike, fleshy corm	None	Plant in spring for colorful leaves for 6 months or more. Dormant in winter.
Clivia miniata hybrids	Clivia, Kafir lily	Ropelike rhizomes	5 weeks in fall	Evergreen; blooms in late winter, rests in fall
Freesia corymbosa	Freesia	Shriveled corm	Two months of heat treatment; no chilling	Start corms in fall for winter bloom, or early winter for late-winter bloom. Dormant in summer.
Hippeastrum hortorum	Amaryllis	Bulb	None	Plant in fall or winter for bloom 6 to 8 weeks later. Dormant in late summer and fall.
Hyacinthus orientalis	Hyacinth	Bulb	12 to 15 weeks	Plant in fall for bloom in late winter and spring. Bulbs may be forced only one time.
Lilium longiflorum	Easter Lily	Bulb	None	Plants purchased in spring bloom for 3 to 4 weeks. They can then be planted outdoors or discarded.
Muscari armeniacum	Muscari, grape hyacinth	Bulb	10 to 14 weeks	Plant in fall for bloom in spring. Bulbs may be forced only one time.
Narcissus species and hybrids	Daffodil, narcissus	Bulb	12 to 15 weeks for daffodils, none for paperwhites	Plant in fall for bloom in late winter and spring. Bulbs may be forced only one time.
Oxalis regnelli	Oxalis, shamrock plant	Small bulblike tubers, called pips	None	Blooms almost year-round with occasional rest breaks
Tulipa species and hybrids	Tulip	Bulb	At least 14 weeks	Plant in fall for bloom in spring. Discard bulbs after forcing.
Zantedeschia hybrids	Calla lily	Tuber	None	Plant in fall for bloom in late spring or early summer. Dormant in late summer.

Container-grown bulbs and tubers each have distinctive bloom seasons, making it easy to share the company with blooming bulbs during every season of the year. *Clockwise, from top left:* Oxalis, achimenes, paperwhite narcissus, and freesia

Indoors in winter or outdoors in summer, the varied colors and textures of succulents make them ideal plants for displaying in groups.

Achimenes species and hybrids ah-kih-MIN-ees

ACHIMENES, CUPID'S BOW, HOT WATER PLANT, MAGIC FLOWER, ORCHID PANSY

Cupid's bow (*Achimenes* hybrid)

THERE IS AN UNDENIABLE ALLURE to a beautiful blooming plant that grows from tiny rhizomes planted indoors in spring, blooms prolifically from summer to fall on a bright windowsill or shady patio, and then becomes dormant in winter, when space is needed by other plants. This is the life cycle of achimenes, a relative of African violet that can be grown in hanging baskets or pots, and blooms in colors ranging from rich blues and purples to yellow, salmon, red, and pink.

Plant the dormant rhizomes, which resemble tiny pinecones, in a 3–6 in/7.5–15 cm container in spring. Set them 1 in/2.5 cm deep in African violet potting soil, and keep the container lightly moist at around 70°F/21°C. Pinch the stem tips when they are 3 in/7.5 cm long to promote branching. Through the summer, grow the plants indoors or out, in a bright location where temperatures range in the 70°sF/20°sC. Fertilize weekly with a high-phosphorous plant food. In October, allow the plants to dry until the foliage withers to brown. Gather the rhizomes and store them in bags, padded with a handful of dry peat moss or vermiculite and kept at 60°F/16°C. In spring, discard any rhizomes that are small or shriveled, and replant the rest.

SPECIFICATIONS

Light: Bright filtered light.

Temperature: Nearly constant at about 70–75°F/21–24°C.

Fertilizer: Feed weekly with a high-phosphorous fertilizer while plants are actively growing. Stop feeding in late summer.

Water: Provide as much luke-warm water as needed to maintain constant, even moisture.

Soil: African violet mix.

◆ Repotting: Replant the best rhizomes in spring in fresh soil.

Longevity: Many years.

Propagation: Replanting of rhizomes; rooted stem tip cuttings.

Selections: Grown in hanging baskets, the cascading types are easy and rewarding. Fine varieties include pink 'Charm' and blue 'Blue Monarch'. The best reds are hybrids such as 'Inferno' and 'Scorpio'.

Display tips: Achimenes are spectacular when grown in a hanging basket at eye level.

FAMILY: **ARACEAE**   ORIGIN: **SOUTH AMERICA**

Caladium hybrids ka-LAY-dee-um

CALADIUM, ANGEL WINGS

Angel wings (*Caladium* hybrid)

CALADIUMS DON'T REALLY BELONG among the flowering plants, since they only occasionally produce finger-shaped flowers. Yet each colorful heart-shaped leaf easily does the work of ten flowers. Caladiums are among the showiest houseplants you can grow, with large nodding leaves in pink, green, red, and white, often with contrasting veins and edges.

Grow caladiums in summer, when warm temperatures and abundant light prevail. Purchase tubers in spring and plant them in pots, no more than 3–6 in/7.5–15 cm pot; cover tubers with 1 in/2.5 cm of potting mix. Water well, and set in a warm place, such as atop your refrigerator. Leaves will begin to unfurl in a few weeks, and will get bigger and better as they are exposed to more light and warmth. Move them outdoors only if temperatures there will not dip below 60°F/16°C at night. If you want to keep plants from year to year, allow the pots to dry until the leaves wither in the fall. Clip off the old leaves, and then store the pots in a closet or other dark place where temperatures will remain above 55°F/13°C. Repot the tubers in fresh soil the following spring.

SPECIFICATIONS

Light: Bright to moderate light.

Temperature: Warm to very warm (70–85°F/21–29°C) during active growth.

◆ Fertilizer: Feed plants weekly with a high-nitrogen foliage plant food. Caladiums are all leaf, so they benefit from abundant nitrogen.

Water: Keep soil constantly moist, and maintain high humidity.

Soil: Any good potting soil.

Repotting: Move to larger pots if the plants become rootbound during the growing season.

Longevity: Showy season lasts 6 months or more. Tubers can usually be grown in pots for 2 years before they lose quality, evidenced by sparse, undersized leaves.

Propagation: In spring, cut off any sections of root that appear shriveled and dead, and replant the healthy section.

Selections: Dwarf 'Miss Muffet' has creamy white leaves liberally sprinkled with red spots. All varieties with 'Florida' in their name tolerate cool conditions better than most larger caladiums.

Display tips: Place caladiums where you want to evoke a tropical feel. They are a wonderful way to color up collections of tropical foliage plants.

Clivia miniata hybrids KLY-vee-uh min-ee-AH-ta

CLIVIA, KAFIR LILY

Clivia (*Clivia miniata*)

FIRST COLLECTED IN 1815, clivia is easy and exciting to grow as an indoor-outdoor houseplant. Plants more than 3 years old can be counted upon to bear clusters of 10 to 20 tubular orange, salmon, red, yellow, or white flowers in late winter. Atop thick, ropelike roots, deep green strappy leaves 2 in/5 cm wide and 24 in/60 cm long persist year round, and the plants get bigger and better with time. A special temperature regimen is needed to make a clivia bloom, but this is easily accomplished by keeping the plant outdoors in fall during the last month before the first frosts arrive, and then moving it to your coolest indoor room and keeping it rather dry until midwinter. After this cool, dry rest, a gradual increase in water, coupled with normal room temperatures, leads to a beautiful show of blossoms in February or March.

SPECIFICATIONS

Light: *Indoors in winter,* moderate light from an east window. *Outdoors from late spring to fall,* mostly shade with no midday sun.

Temperature: *From midwinter to spring,* average room temperatures (60–75°F/16–24°C) indoors. *In summer,* warm temperatures (70–80°F/21–27°C) outdoors. *In fall,* cool temperatures (35–55°F/2–13°C) outdoors.

Fertilizer: *Spring to fall,* feed every 2 weeks with a balanced or high-phosphorous plant food. *In winter,* do not feed.

Water: *Spring to fall,* keep soil lightly moist. Leach pots in summer to remove accumulated salts (see page 263). *In fall and early winter,* allow a dry period, watering only enough to keep leaves from wilting. *During the second half of winter,* gradually increase water.

Soil: Orchid potting mix.

Repotting: Plants like to be root-bound, and need repotting only every 3 years. Use a broad, heavy pot to prevent toppling.

Longevity: 10 to 20 years, or indefinitely when divided every 5 to 7 years.

Propagation: Purchased plants are grown from seed. At home, it is best to cut off the flower stalk at the base when the blossoms shrivel, and propagate clivia by carefully dividing old plants. Young, growing crowns survive repotting better than older ones.

Selections: Orange, red, and salmon strains are much more affordable than comparatively rare yellow or white clivias.

Display tips: Celebrate clivia's bloom season by moving the plant to your most often-used room when the flowers appear.

Freesia corymbosa FREE-see-uh ko-rim-BOH-suh

FREESIA

Freesia (*Freesia corymbosa*)

THE SAME SWEET FREESIA FRAGRANCE found in bath and body products can be experienced straight from the blossom when you grow these delightful flowers indoors. Doing so requires that you mimic the climate in their native home of South Africa — this is not difficult, but it is quite different from the way other blooming bulbs are handled. The temperature regimen freesias need is easily accommodated by planting them in early fall.

Begin in summer by keeping little freesia corms in a very warm (80°F/27°C) spot for two months, such as atop your refrigerator or hot-water heater. Plant the conditioned corms in well-drained pots, six to eight to a 6-inch pot. After watering, keep the pots at average room temperatures for a month. Move them to a cooler (60°F/16°C), brightly lit room for 2 weeks while the buds form. Get them situated in a cool window as the blooms open. Freesia stems often grow 18 in/45 cm long and need to be taped or staked to hold them upright. After the flowers fade, continue to feed and water the plants until they die back. Allow the pots to dry completely, gather up the corms, and repeat the cycle.

SPECIFICATIONS

Light: Bright light from an east or west window.

Temperature: Cool (55–65°F/13–18°C) during their active growth period.

Fertilizer: Feed every 10 days with a balanced or high-phosphorous plant food.

Water: Keep soil lightly moist during the growth period, but avoid overwatering the plants.

Soil: Any well-drained potting soil.

Repotting: Replant yearly, after the annual warm-temperature conditioning period.

Longevity: Several years.

Propagation: When repotting, sort the corms and discard very small ones or those that are old and woody, then replant the healthiest specimens.

Selections: Freesias are available in single- and double-flowered types, in individual colors or mixtures. Those with single flowers are not as prone to falling over as are heavier double-flowered strains.

Display tips: Freesias in full flower will fill a window and perfume a room. If they become too rangy, cut the stems and use them as cut flowers.

Hippeastrum species and hybrids

hip-ee-AS-trum hor-TOR-um

AMARYLLIS

Amaryllis
(Hippeastrum hortorum)

A FAVORITE BULB TO BRING INTO BLOOM in winter, amaryllis often are sold in kits that are marketed especially for the Christmas holiday season. These big, dependable bulbs bloom in red, white, or pink, and there are many bicolors.

All amaryllis bloom 6 to 8 weeks after planting. Set bulbs in a container that leaves only 2 in/5 cm to spare between the bulb and the pot's edge. Good drainage is essential, as is setting the bulb high in the pot, so the top third of the bulb is exposed. Water well and place the planted bulb in a cool (60°F/16°C) place for a month, until a 6 in/15 cm shoot appears. Then move it to good light and feed it with a balanced fertilizer every 10 days. Most big bulbs produce two flower stalks. After the flowers fade, cut off the stalks and continue to feed and water the plants. In late summer, allow the plants to dry very gradually. Cut off the old leaves, and let the bulbs rest in a cool (50°F/10°C) place for at least 10 weeks. Repot firm, healthy bulbs 6 to 8 weeks before you want a repeat show of flowers

SPECIFICATIONS

Light: Bright light during active growth period

Temperature: Cool (55–70°F/ 13–21°C) during early growth and flowering, followed by warmer temperatures (70–85°F/21–29°C) after the flowers fade.

Fertilizer: Feed with a balanced all-purpose plant food every 10 days.

❖ Water: Keep soil lightly moist during the active growth period. Induce dormancy by allowing the pots to gradually dry out in mid- to late summer.

Soil: Any good potting soil, or a three-way mixture of peat moss, sand, and potting soil.

Repotting: Replant each year in winter, after bulbs have rested for 10 to 15 weeks.

Longevity: Several years.

Propagation: Very vigorous varieties may produce offset bulbs around the mother bulb. Allow these to remain attached for two seasons before breaking them off and planting them in their own pots.

Selections: Pale pink and white 'Appleblossom' is an old favorite. 'Scarlet Baby' and 'Baby Star' are more compact and often produce numerous blooms followed by offset bulblets.

Display tips: Tall amaryllis look best when grouped with low-growing foliage plants, so that the dramatic flowers rise from a sea of green.

FAMILY: **LILIACEAE**   ORIGIN: **TURKEY**

Hyacinthus orientalis hybrids

hi-uh-SIN-thus or-ee-en-TAL-is

HYACINTH, DUTCH HYACINTH

Hyacinth (*Hyacinthus orientalis*)

BEAUTY, FRAGRANCE, AND EASE OF CULTURE have made hyacinths the most popular bulb to grow indoors. Each bulb produces a robust spike packed with sweetly scented florets, which come in various shades of blue and pink, as well as white, red, yellow, and coral. Tremendously reliable, an old Persian saying summarizes their allure: "If you have two coins, use one to buy bread, the other to buy hyacinths, for the joy of your spirit."

To coax hyacinths into bloom indoors, follow the instructions in the section "Forcing Spring-Flowering Bulbs," on page 32, allowing at least 12 weeks of chilling time. Hyacinths can be left out in the cold for much longer, and bringing forced bulbs indoors one at a time helps stretch the bloom season. You can grow hyacinths in soil, decorative pebbles, or in plain water. Garden gift shops sell hourglass-shaped hyacinth vases that hold the bulb in place while allowing sufficient room for the roots. Hyacinth flowers last about 2 weeks when the plants are kept in a cool room. Sadly, hyacinths that are forced to bloom indoors never regain their strength and are best discarded after the flowers fade.

SPECIFICATIONS

Light: Bright.

⬥ Temperature: Cool (45–65°F / 7–18°C) during indoor growth period.

Fertilizer: None required, but a little liquid fertilizer added to water helps to support long-lasting flowers.

Water: After the bulbs begin to grow, water them lightly yet frequently to keep the soil lightly moist. When grown in water, only the roots should be suspended in water.

Soil: Any fast-draining potting soil; hyacinths can also be grown in water, pebbles, or glass marbles.

Repotting: If desired, shift growing bulbs to decorative containers when you bring them indoors in late winter.

Longevity: 6 months.

Propagation: Discard bulbs after they bloom. Buy new ones each fall.

Selections: Choose varieties based on color, such as pink 'Anna Marie', blue 'Delft Blue', or soft coral 'Gipsy Queen'. Although less uniform, 'Festival' French-Roman hyacinths produce multiple flower spikes from each bulb.

Display tips: Enjoy the fragrance of hyacinths by keeping them in frequently used rooms during the day. To prolong flower life, move them to your coolest room at night.

Lilium longiflorum LIL-ee-um lon-je-FLOR-um

EASTER LILY

Easter lily (*Lilium longiflorum*)

THE PURE WHITE BLOSSOMS of Easter lilies signify the sacred side of spring, and they are among the most popular of all blooming houseplants. Yet they do not naturally bloom in spring, but rather in summer. Greenhouse growers coax them into bloom at exactly the right time by using elaborate temperature, light, and water regimens.

To make sure that a purchased plant keeps its good looks for a long time indoors, choose one that shows only one or two partially opened buds. When you get the plant home, remove any plastic or foil wrapping that blocks the drainage holes (see "Fixing Floral Wrappings," page 260), water as needed to keep the pot moist, and keep the plant in a cool room where temperatures are 60–65°F/ 16–18°C, especially at night. When the blossoms open all the way, use a small pair of scissors to snip out the anthers, which prolongs flower life and prevents the scattering of pollen on furniture. After the blooms fade, Easter lilies can be planted outdoors, where they are hardy to Zone 5. Following a year of adjustment, they normally bloom in early summer when grown outdoors.

SPECIFICATIONS

Light: Bright.

Temperature: Cool to average room temperatures (60–75°F/ 16–24°C) during active growth period.

Fertilizer: Feed with an all-purpose plant food every 2 weeks if you plan to keep the plant as a garden lily. No fertilizer is needed for plants that will be discarded when their blooms fade.

Water: Water lightly yet frequently to keep the soil lightly moist.

Soil: Most plants are grown in a peaty mix. (Outdoors, plants need excellent drainage and rich, moist soil.)

Repotting: Not needed. (When planting outdoors, set bulbs 6 in/ 15 cm deep.)

Longevity: 3 to 4 weeks indoors (outdoors, several years).

Propagation: Easter lilies grown in containers become too weak to propagate.

Selections: Seldom sold by variety name. Choose plants based on size and vigor.

Display tips: If you force a few grape hyacinths or other little bulbs, you will stand a good chance of having blooming companions for an Easter lily purchased in spring.

Muscari armeniacum, other *Muscari* species mus-KAR-ee ar-mee-nee-AK-um

MUSCARI, GRAPE HYACINTH

Grape hyacinth
(*Muscari armeniacum*)

THERE ARE MANY FORMS OF MUSCARI, all of which produce unusual rounded flower clusters on upright stems that resemble elongated bunches of grapes. Most bloom in shades of purple, and there are white forms, too. The flowers are very slightly fragrant; they often last a month when grown indoors under cool conditions.

Unlike other spring-flowering bulbs, grape hyacinths have a dual life cycle. A few grasslike leaves emerge soon after the bulbs are planted in fall, and more leaves appear with the flowers in spring. If planted outdoors after they have been forced for one season in a pot, the bulbs become dormant in summer. They then grow a thick tuft of leaves in the late summer which persists well into winter.

Follow the instructions in "Forcing Spring-Flowering Bulbs" on page 32, allowing a 10-week chilling period. White selections need 14 weeks of chilling. Flowers appear about 3 weeks after the pots are brought into warmer quarters. If you have no garden yourself, don't hesitate to give your tired muscari to a friend who has a place to put them into the ground.

SPECIFICATIONS

Light: Bright.

◆ **Temperature:** Cool (40–65°F/ 4–18°C) during active growth period.

Fertilizer: Feed actively growing plants every 10 days with an all-purpose plant food.

Water: Water lightly yet often to keep soil a bit moist at all times.

Soil: Any potting soil that drains well, or a half-and-half mixture of potting soil and sand.

Repotting: Plant out in the garden after blossoms fade, setting bulbs 3 in/7.5 cm deep.

Longevity: 6 months to many years; these are excellent bulbs for naturalizing in the garden.

Propagation: Seldom needed. (Outdoors, very crowded clumps can be dug and divided in summer after the foliage fades.)

Selections: 'Christmas Pearl' requires less chilling than other varieties. 'Valerie Finnis' has refined pale lavender blooms.

Display tips: Tuck pots into a pretty basket and hide the containers from view with moss or pine needles. Purple muscari look great with dwarf yellow daffodils or white Easter lilies.

Narcissus species and hybrids nar-SIS-us

DAFFODIL, PAPERWHITE NARCISSUS

Paperwhite narcissus
(*Narcissus jonquilla*)

THE LARGE DAFFODILS that are commonly grown outdoors can be forced into bloom in pots, but smaller selections, such as those found within the *N. cyclamenius* species, often do a better job of holding their lovely heads high. They also feature backswept petals that suggest the presence of wind. Mature height is usually less than 12 in/30 cm, though height varies with variety. To grow them, follow the instructions in "Forcing Spring-Flowering Bulbs" on page 32, allowing 12 weeks of chilling. Expect the plants to bloom about 4 weeks after the containers are brought indoors. The flowering period lasts 2 to 3 weeks, so if you buy the plants in pots, choose specimens that have not yet begun to bloom.

Paperwhite narcissus (*Narcissus jonquilla*, Tazetta type) are from warmer regions of Asia, and they need no chilling to promote bloom. Bulbs begin growing as soon as they are planted, with fragrant blossoms appearing after 3 weeks. Flowers last 2 to 3 weeks, so it's important to purchase plants that are just beginning to bloom. Growing paperwhites sold in kits is a good introduction to the art of growing indoor bulbs.

SPECIFICATIONS

Light: Bright.

⬥ Temperature: Cool (45–65°F/ 7–18°C) during the active growth period.

Fertilizer: Feed weekly with an all-purpose plant food when plants are growing.

Water: Keep soil moderately moist at all times.

Soil: Any potting soil, with pebbles added to improve drainage and add weight.

Repotting: Not necessary.

Longevity: 3 months for paperwhites, which are best discarded after they bloom. Miniature daffodils can be shifted to the garden, where they are likely to prosper for many years.

Propagation: Not needed.

Selections: Among little daffodils, yellow 'February Gold' is dependable in pots and often persists in the outdoor garden. 'Jenny' opens yellow and ripens to pure white. If you find the fragrance of paperwhites too musky for your taste, seek out 'Grand Soleil d'Or', which has a sweeter scent. Paperwhites often need staking to remain upright.

Display tips: Slip containers of yellow daffodils into small wicker baskets. With close attention to watering, paperwhites can be grown in damp pebbles in containers that lack drainage holes.

Oxalis regnellii oks-AL-is reg-NEL-ee-i

OXALIS, SHAMROCK PLANT

Shamrock plant (*Oxalis* hybrid)

THIS IS ONE OF THE EASIEST flowering houseplants to grow, often producing white or soft pink flowers continuously, except for a brief break in winter. The dainty flowers are held above the triangular, clover-like leaves. Oxalis plants do not require a period of dormancy, but if they are forced into one by dryness or an infestation of spider mites, you can cut off all the leaves, repot the bulblike pips, and have a healthy flowering plant in a matter of weeks.

Oxalis is happy to grow in filtered sun indoors year-round, or you can move it outside to a shady patio or balcony in the summer. Good light intensifies the leaf colors with strains of burgundy or variegated leaves. Very hot, humid conditions may slow down the production of flowers, and low light levels in winter often lead to a short period of no flowers. Oxalis is sensitive to salt buildup in containers, but you can prevent damage to roots by flushing the pots thoroughly with plenty of clean, room-temperature water every 2 months.

SPECIFICATIONS

Light: Bright to moderate year-round.

Temperature: Average room temperatures (60–75°F/16–24°C) year-round.

Fertilizer: Feed plants every 2 weeks with a balanced or high-phosphorous plant food.

Water: Light, frequent waterings are needed to keep large plants constantly moist. Leach pots occasionally to dissolve accumulated salts.

Soil: Any good-quality potting soil.

Repotting: Move plants to larger pots should they become crowded, or when salt deposits accumulate in containers.

Longevity: Many years.

Propagation: This plant can be divided with ease, whether it is in active growth or dormant. Pull apart the roots, dividing a large, 8 in/20 cm-wide mass into three smaller clumps. After repotting, snip off any damaged leaves.

Selections: Many strains have leaves that are green on top and burgundy beneath, but leaves of 'Triangularis' are burgundy on both sides. 'Fanny' features green leaves with silver margins.

Display tips: The delicate simplicity of oxalis works well with light-colored ceramic containers.

Tulipa species and hybrids too-LIP-uh
TULIP

Tulips (*Tulipa* hybrid)

OF ALL THE BLOOMING PLANTS you can grow indoors, tulips offer the widest range of color, and even carefully selected mail-order bulbs are quite inexpensive. You can force any type of tulip, but varieties that grow very tall or produce extremely large flowers often fall over when grown indoors. Triumph tulips seldom have these problems, so they are the favorite type for forcing.

Follow the instructions in "Forcing Spring-Flowering Bulbs" on page 32, allowing 14 weeks of chilling time. Deep containers help accommodate tulip bulbs' extensive roots. When buying potted tulips in December and January, look for plants with buds that have not yet opened, and keep them in a cool, well-lighted room. Warmth makes potted tulips bloom very quickly, and also limits how long the flowers last. Even in a cool room, forced tulips usually hold their blossoms only 2 weeks. Large-flowered tulips that are forced to bloom indoors are best discarded after the flowers fade, but you may have luck transplanting smaller "species" tulips to your garden when the weather begins to warm in the spring.

SPECIFICATIONS

Light: Bright.

🌡 Temperature: Cool (45–65°F/ 7–18°C) during active growth.

Fertilizer: None required, but a little liquid fertilizer added to water helps to support long-lasting flowers.

Water: Keep soil lightly moist while the plants are actively growing.

Soil: Any clean potting soil, with pebbles added to increase weight.

Repotting: If desired, shift growing bulbs to decorative containers when you bring them indoors. When tulip roots are too restricted, they may fail to flower well.

Longevity: 6 months for large-flowered tulips, which are best discarded after they bloom. (Small species tulips that are transplanted to the garden may persist for many years.)

Propagation: Not needed.

Selections: Triumph tulips are uniform and dependable, growing about 14 in/35 cm tall. Smaller, more long-lived species tulips, such as fragrant *T. batalinii* and *T. humilis*, grow to only 6 in/15 cm tall and make fine companions for other spring-flowering bulbs.

Display tips: Make the most of tulips' formal demeanor by slipping the plants into ceramic or brass containers. To prolong flower life, move blooming tulips to your coolest room at night.

Zantedeschia hybrids zan-tuh-DES-kee-uh

CALLA LILY, ARUM LILY

Calla lily *(Zantedeschia)*

IN STORES AND FLORAL SHOPS, Easter lilies often share company with lovely potted calla lilies, which bear colorful, cupped, spade-shaped blossoms in pink, yellow, white, rust, and many bicolors. The flowers usually last 4 to 6 weeks, and many varieties also feature pretty speckled foliage. Callas grown outdoors often reach 36 in/90 cm in height, but those bred for container culture are usually 12 in/30 cm high and wide. Plants may be brought back into bloom in future seasons provided you give them a dry rest period in late summer. Allow the plants to dry until the leaves wither, clip off the old foliage, and keep the pots very lightly moist in a cool, shady spot. In winter, a fresh pot of soil, along with warmth, moisture, and bright light, will quickly bring them back to life.

SPECIFICATIONS

Light: Bright.

Temperature: Cool (60–75°F / 16–24°C) in winter and spring, warming to moderate (70–85°F / 21–29°C) from summer to fall.

Fertilizer: Feed plants every 3 weeks with a high-phosphorous plant food while the plants are actively growing.

Water: Keep soil lightly moist when rhizomes are just beginning to grow. Increase water as plants attain full growth so that roots stay constantly moist. Reduce water in late summer, allowing plants to dry almost completely while they are dormant.

Soil: Any good potting soil that drains well.

Repotting: In early summer, shift newly purchased plants to one-size-larger pots, disturbing roots as little as possible. In subsequent seasons, repot tubers in late fall, smooth side down, before coaxing them out of dormancy.

Longevity: 3 to 5 years.

Propagation: Unless you live in Zones 8 to 10, where callas can be grown outdoors as perennials, discard rhizomes that fail to produce a good show of flowers, and replace them with newly purchased plants or rhizomes. Pot-grown callas usually become weaker rather than stronger after several seasons.

Selections: Choose plants based on flower color and health. Most callas grown in containers are compact hybrids of *Z. rehmanii*.

Display tips: Clip off stems as flowers fade, and enjoy your calla as a foliage plant for 2 to 3 more months.

Cacti and Succulents

Tho ghostly gray leaves of an *Echeveria* keep their calm cool year round, and the plants require very little care.

SEMI-SUCCULENT HOUSEPLANTS

Here are several wonderful houseplants that are technically considered succulents, although their leaves are flat rather than plump. (Page numbers refer to profiles on these semi-succulent plants.)

Ponytail palm
(Beaucarnea recurvata),
(page 162)

Crown of thorns
(Euphorbia milii), (page 96)

Poinsettia
(Euphorbia pulcherrima),
(page 98)

Peperomia
(Peperomia caperata),
(page 228)

A GEOLOGIC DRAMA occurring slowly over a period of about 20 million years is credited for the emergence of cacti. Sixty million years ago, in the "before cactus" era, regions such as the American Southwest, central Mexico, and southern Brazil, now rich in cacti, enjoyed moist, tropical climates. As mountains pushed up, stopping the inflow of moisture, plants adapted to increasingly dry conditions by storing up water in their leaves and stems. Gradually leaves became spines, useful for protection from predators and as built-in sunscreens, and stems fattened into globes, columns, and other shapes designed to retain moisture. In the "after cactus" era (which began 40 million years ago), cacti became well established in numerous niches: on sandy ground, between rocks, and even growing on trees. Because most cacti produce flowers loaded with pollen that is spread from plant to plant by bees and other insects, cacti constantly cross-bred, resulting in thousands of diverse species.

And so, though it is tempting to think of cacti as very primitive plants, the opposite is true. They are actually highly refined flowering perennials. Classification of cacti is incredibly complex and confusing, and even the most knowledgeable cactus experts sometimes have trouble identifying obscure species. The one characteristic that wins a plant a place in the Cactaceae family is the presence of areoles — the specialized buds from which spines and new bodies (stems) grow. In some genera, for example Echinopsis, the areoles are easily visible. In others they may be impossible to see unless you are a sharp-eyed botanist, but they are there.

All cacti are native to the Western Hemisphere. Succulents, which owe their existence to climate changes not quite as extreme as those that created cacti, are found on all continents, but most come from Africa, Asia, Europe, and Australia. Some succulents, such as living rocks (lithops), use their entire bodies to store moisture, but most have stems studded with juicy, water-retentive leaves. Sorting through the two groups is difficult enough without mixing them up, so they are listed separately in this chapter. The descriptive chart of nine easy-to-grow cacti on page 65 is followed by individual plant profiles. In similar fashion, eleven succulents are summarized in the chart on page 76, followed by detailed profiles of each species. However, because cacti and succulents have similar cultural needs and share pest problems, general aspects of their care will be discussed together, and the Troubleshooting instructions on page 64 covers both.

A columnar cereus cactus will grow slowly for decades with minimal care.

A PRICKLY PROBLEM

Cactus spines hurt, and some cacti have a special type of barbed spine, called a *glochid*, that sticks in skin like a tiny fishhook. To be safe, display cacti away from activity areas, and always keep them out of the reach of children. Suggestions for handling cacti when repotting them are given below, but even with the most careful handling, accidents happen. The best way to remove a cactus spine tip from human skin is to press a piece of very sticky tape against it and lift it right out. If you keep cacti, never be without a roll of sticky tape! If the tape trick doesn't work, coat the affected area with white glue, allow it to dry, and then peel it off.

Caring for Cacti and Succulents

If you have a bright south window or other spot that gets strong sun for at least 4 hours a day, you have a good place to grow cacti and succulents. All cacti and succulents tolerate dry indoor air well, though they vary in how dry they like conditions to be. Species that come from jungle environments, such as the well-known Christmas cactus or the tiny succulents known as haworthias, demand regular watering, while desert cacti and agave are able to go weeks or months without any watering at all. Learn the preferences of each plant you adopt, not only in terms of water but in terms of rest period. Cacti are never fully dormant, but all of them need a rest period if they are to produce flowers. The same goes for many succulents — for example, kalanchoe. The timing and temperature of the rest period for various species are included in the plant profiles that follow. To fulfill the rest requirements of any cactus or succulent, appropriate changes in location are usually needed.

Cacti and succulents grown together in dish gardens are lovely, and some people grow their collection in a large tray that fills an entire windowsill. Arid dish gardens work well as long as the plants have similar seasonal needs. However, if cactus flowers are a high priority, it is often simpler to meet a plant's needs for water, light, fertilizer, and temperature if it is kept in an individual pot. Cactus flowers last only 1 to 3 days, but the flowers are often gigantic compared to the size of the plants that bear them.

Cacti and succulents often show best if the surface of the soil is covered with small stones, gravel, or sand, so that it mimics a desert landscape. You can arrange a pebble mulch in a pattern by using two or three different colors to form an attractive design. The pots themselves can be plain terra cotta, or you can use more colorful ceramic or painted pots. Any container that provides excellent drainage will do for cacti and succulents.

Light: Most cacti and succulents are pleased to spend part of their time in baking sun, so they love spending the summer outdoors. Place them where they will get some direct sun but are sheltered from heavy rain. Cacti and succulents are indeed sun-loving plants, but they can get sunburn; to keep this from happening, gradually expose plants to increasing amounts of light. For example, if you plan to move a plant outdoors in summer, first shift it to a sunny west window for a few weeks in spring. After nights warm into the 60°F/16°C range, move the plant to a shady spot outdoors. After 2 weeks, it should be ready for partial sun. When kept outdoors in

Summering outdoors, two agaves share quarters with a selection of other succulents. Many succulents propagate themselves so freely that they are often traded among friends.

CACTI OR CACTUSES?

What's the proper word for more than one cactus — cacti or cactuses? Both are correct! Feel free to use whichever word sounds best to you.

summer, most cacti and succulents are happiest with no more than 5 hours of direct sun; some grow best with only 2 or 3 hours. And, although some species may be fine in a very sunny spot, if you acclimate them to full sun it becomes more challenging to get them ready to come back indoors in the fall. This, too, should be a gradual process, in which the plants are moved as needed to slowly accustom them to reduced amounts of light. You also can keep your cacti and succulents indoors year-round. Bright light from a south or west window is needed in summer.

Indoors in winter or outdoors in summer, the varied colors and textures of succulents make them ideal plants for displaying in groups.

Most cactus collectors enjoy the challenge of coaxing plants into bloom, which is not difficult if the plants are fully mature and a few basic needs are met. In the wild, many cacti develop seed-filled berries, or even edible fruits, after the flowers fade. This seldom happens with cacti grown as houseplants.

Many *Mammillaria* cacti sport a thick growth of fine hair, which protects them from hot sun.

Temperature: In winter, when most cacti and succulents prefer a cooler place to rest, a minimally heated room in which temperatures drop below 60°F/16°C at night is ideal. See the plant profiles for the temperature preferences of individual species. Some cacti must have a very cool resting place in winter if they are to set flowering buds.

Fertilizer: Cacti and succulents grow slowly, so they have less need for nitrogen than many other houseplants. The typical analysis of special cactus fertilizers is 2-7-7, which means they have a low concentration of all nutrients, particularly nitrogen. If you do not want to invest in a special fertilizer for one or two cacti but want to meet their special needs, use a high phosphorous (low-nitrogen) fertilizer mixed at half the normal strength. Fertilize cacti and succulents only during their periods of active growth.

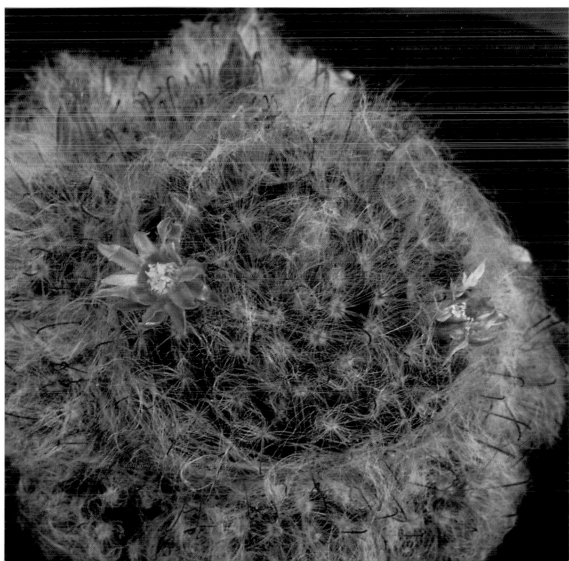

Water: Overwatering in winter, when most cacti and succulents are at rest, is the most common reason for plant failure. Instead of soaking the roots, you might try spritzing water with a pump spray bottle, or dribbling small amounts from the tip of a thoroughly cleaned squirt bottle, like those used for dishwashing detergent. With clump-forming cacti and succulents, water only around the outside edge of the clump. Most cacti and succulents will begin to shrivel if they are underwatered, but they recover quickly when adequately hydrated. Rehydrate dried-out pots by watering the plant lightly two or three times. Cacti and succulents are prone to rot if their roots become soaking wet.

Most agaves have prickly spines, which limits their display to low-traffic areas.

A variety of cacti thrive in a broad, shallow container in potting soil amended with sharp sand or a specialty mix designed for cacti.

Easter cacti (*Hatiora* hybrids) look similar to Christmas cacti, but they bloom and rest on a different schedule.

Cacti and succulents need more water in warm, sunny weather, their season of new growth. Again, it is better to water cacti lightly yet frequently than to give them too much water at once. In general, succulents need about twice as much water as cacti. However, leaves of succulents that form round rosettes often serve as funnels that collect water. This is okay once in a while, but try not to fill the rosettes with water more than once every few weeks, especially in winter.

Most cacti and succulents like low humidity, but extremely dry conditions can contribute to problems with spider mites. Mist resting plants from time to time, even if you do not water their roots. To a cactus or succulent, this is similar to being exposed to dew or fog, which for some species is a natural source of moisture. Jungle plants are especially appreciative of occasional misting when they are kept in places with very dry air.

Soil: Cacti and succulents need a very fast-draining soil, since many of them evolved in areas that receive only 2 in/5 cm of rain each year. Regular potting soil with sharp sand or grit (rock crushed into .25 in/.6 cm-diameter pieces) added is fine, or you can buy potting soil specially made for cacti. Another option is to amend potting soil with perlite instead of sand. However, perlite is very light compared to sand or grit. In addition to improving drainage, sand or grit add weight to containers, which helps prevent toppling. When blending your own potting soil for cacti and succulents, mix 1 part sand, grit, or perlite to 2 parts potting soil. Adding a .5 in/ 1.25 cm layer of pebbles to the bottom of containers adds bottom weight and enhances drainage.

Repotting: Cacti and succulents should be repotted when they grow to within 5 in/1.25 cm of the edge of their container, or when they are so rootbound that they make little new growth. Some species, especially rat's tail cactus and donkey tail, are very difficult to repot when the plant becomes large. If you can't repot a large plant without damaging it, propagate it instead.

Most cacti and succulents grow well in broad, shallow containers. However, those that grow upright, or species with more extensive roots, may need deeper pots. You are less likely to overwater cacti grown in tight quarters, so it's best to repot them into containers only slightly larger than the ones they have outgrown.

There are safe ways to handle cacti when repotting so that neither you nor the plant suffer injuries. Before you begin, run a knife around the inside of the pot to make the cactus easier to remove. If the cactus is growing in a dish garden, use a knife to cut a circle around the plant about 1 in/2.5 cm beyond its outer edges. Next, wrap the cactus with a band made of strips of folded newspaper, held snugly with a gloved hand. Thick leather or rubber-coated gloves are best.

Place a layer of pebbles in the bottom of the new pot to improve drainage, and add 1–2 in/2.5–5 cm of potting soil (see page 314). Make sure the soil mixture in the new container is lightly moist before replanting the cactus. Use a spray bottle to mist the roots as you set the cactus in place, and then mist the soil as you fill in around the edges with a long-handled spoon. Use a small brush to clean off any potting mix that became caught in the spines. Blow through a drinking straw to dislodge debris that will not brush away. Add a decorative mulch of pebbles or sand, and set the repotted plant in a bright yet sunless place for a few days. Wait about a week before you begin watering freshly repotted cacti.

Although they last but a few days, cactus flowers feature rich colors and simple, refined forms.

Most succulents do not have spines, so they are easier to repot than cacti. With succulents, the biggest challenge is to handle the plants very gently, because succulent leaves often break off at the slightest touch. When repotting very delicate succulents, it can help to wrap them with a cloth throughout the operation.

Propagating: The easiest way to prolong the life of a beloved cactus or succulent is to propagate it from cuttings. Rooting is generally fastest at about 70°F/21°C, and cacti and succulents root best when they are entering their most active period of new growth. Late spring or early summer is usually the best time to propagate plants from rooted cuttings. When rooting either cacti or succulents, use a half-and-half mixture of peat moss and sand, a soilless mix used for seed starting, or cactus potting soil from a newly opened bag.

Most cacti develop pieces that are joined to the parent plant. Use a sharp, clean knife to sever a healthy young offset or pad from the parent plant, allow the cut end to dry and callus for a couple of days, and then plant it in a clean container filled with a half-and-half mixture of potting soil and sand. Keep it in a shady place, and water lightly every few days to keep the soil lightly moist. Expect roots to form in about a month, but wait another few weeks before repotting the plant into a permanent pot.

Cacti that do not show obvious places where they are joined to the parent plant also can be propagated from cuttings, though this involves cutting off the top of the plant. However, if a columnar cactus has developed black rot at its roots and is failing fast, severing its crown and setting it to root is usually the best alternative.

Many cactus collectors learn to graft plants, which is not difficult. It is also rather straightforward to start many cacti from seeds. However, both of these projects are best undertaken with the help of a good cactus book.

Succulents are among the easiest houseplants to propagate, since they typically develop offsets, or babies, which cluster around the parent plant. Others are very easy to root from stem cuttings. Again, the best season to propagate succulents is late spring or early summer, when plants are entering their period of most active growth. When propagating succulents, allow the severed offsets or cuttings to dry for at least a day before repotting them. The callus that forms over the cut section of the stem or root helps protect the plant from rotting when it is planted in an appropriate rooting medium.

Many cacti are easily propagated by cutting away offsets that grow at the base of a parent plant. Allow the cut surface to dry into a callus for two days or more before transplanting it to a small container.

A Fresh Start with Aloe

The healing properties of fresh aloe gel seem almost magical, but a small mountain of scientific research explains how it helps minor burns disappear overnight. Aspirin-like salicylates soothe the pain, other enzymes reduce inflammation, and meanwhile additional chemical components increase blood flow to the injured area and kill a range of bacteria that might attempt to enter the wound.

After breaking off an aloe leaf to treat injured skin, can you propagate the tip to grow a new plant? Many have tried and all have failed, though it is sometimes possible to propagate aloe using the basal section of an outer leaf. The leaf can be a partial one, from which the tip has been harvested and the wound has dried into a callus, but it is essential that it include the curved "heel" that attaches to the main stem near the soil line. Set the leaf atop a small container filled with cactus potting soil, and use a small piece of wire to pin the base to the soil. Mist lightly from time to time to keep the leaf from drying out too quickly, but do not keep the leaf or the potting soil constantly wet. The cluster of new plantlets that forms along the lowest edge of the leaf will draw the moisture they need from the parent leaf. Until they develop roots, they have little use for water. When the plantlets are more than 1 in (2.5 cm) tall and the parent leaf has shriveled, cut it away and pot up the babies.

Small details: With cacti and many succulents, plant identification can be difficult. If you don't know what species you have, use the chart on page xiv to narrow the possibilities. Then check the plant profiles for more specific information. If you're still stumped as to what plant you have, there are several sites on the Internet where you can look at pictures of various species, and others where you can post a picture of your cactus and get help identifying it from other cactus lovers. Try using "cactus identification" as a search phrase with your favorite search engine when seeking to identify a cactus. With succulents, you will get the best results by using the genus name, for example "Echeveria," as the search word.

In the plant profiles that follow the charts, you will meet nine cactus species and eleven succulents that are popular houseplants. All are easy to grow, and many will produce exotic flowers when given the right regimen of care. But even without flowers, the symmetry of spines, well-defined shapes, and ease of care of cacti and succulents are reason enough to enjoy them as houseplants.

Echeverias are perhaps the most painterly succulents you can grow, and the symmetry of their leaves is often spellbinding.

TROUBLESHOOTING

Base of plant near the soil turns black.
CAUSE: Root rot, which spreads to the body of the plant.
REMEDY: Overwatering contributes to this problem, but it sometimes happens even when plants are properly watered. Poor air circulation can add to the problem. If possible, scrape away the black portions of the plant with a small serrated knife. Allow the callus to heal before watering the plant. In severe cases, propagate the plant from a healthy tip, offset, or stem cutting.

Plant appears shrunken and wrinkled.
CAUSE: Too little water.
REMEDY: Give the plant a light watering and mist it with a spray of water. Water again the following day, being careful not to drench the soil. Wait 3 days and water again; by then the plant should be plumped up nicely.

Brownish to gray patches on leaves; body of cactus appears yellowish.
CAUSE: Sunburn.
REMEDY: Move plant to a shadier spot. Make sure that plant is very gradually exposed to increasing amounts of sunshine.

Round to angular brown spots form on cactus and increase in numbers.
CAUSE: Corking, which can be caused by fungi, usually following a bruise or other physical injury.
REMEDY: Reduce water and fertilizer and increase air circulation around the plant. Overfeeding that leads to soft, succulent growth contributes to this problem.

Plant appears pale and pocked with tiny yellow specks.
CAUSE: Spider mites.
REMEDY: Isolate plant. *Cacti:* Clean by laying plant on its side and dousing the body with warm water.

Succulents: Spray with warm water. When dry, spray plant with insecticidal soap. Dispose of badly infested plants.

White, woolly deposits on plant body or leaves.
CAUSE: Mealybugs.
REMEDY: Isolate plant, and remove as many mealybugs as possible with a toothpick. Lay plant on its side and spray with a neem-based insecticide or insecticidal soap. See page 272 for more information on this common houseplant pest.

Plant appears stunted; shows little if any new growth.
CAUSE: Root mealybugs.
REMEDY: Remove plant from pot and inspect roots for signs of light-colored, slow-moving insects that look like bits of mold. Rinse roots; spray with a neem-based insecticide. Repot plant in clean pot with fresh soil.

Brown disk-shaped insects attached to plants.
CAUSE: Scale, an occasional problem on cacti and succulents.
REMEDY: Isolate plant and remove scale with a toothpick. (On cacti, scale tend to cluster near the areoles, where spines emerge.) Repeat every few days until plant is clean.

Plant does not bloom.
CAUSE: Immature age; too little summer light in summer; insufficient winter rest.
REMEDY: Many species do not bloom until the plants are more than 3 years old. Acclimate plant to strong sunlight for several weeks in summer and keep it in your coolest well-lit room in winter. Use a high-phosphorous fertilizer. See plant profiles for species-specific details on improving bloom.

New growth is crooked or uneven.
CAUSE: Too little light, often combined with too much fertilizer.
REMEDY: Gradually move plant to brighter light. Remove misshapen parts if possible.

Flowers fade within 1 day.
CAUSE: Many cactus flowers are naturally short lived.
REMEDY: You can extend the life of blossoms on Christmas cactus and some other species by keeping them in a cool location, away from bright sunlight, when they are in bloom. Avoid moving cacti when they are in bloom.

Small, wedge-shaped insects are present on stem tips of succulents.
CAUSE: Aphids.
REMEDY: Clip off badly damaged stems. Use a fine spray of warm water to remove as many aphids as possible. Spray survivors with insecticidal soap. See page 269 for more information on managing this pest.

Getting to Know Your Cacti

To help make plant identification simple, cacti and succulents are sorted into groups, with cacti summarized here and succulents appearing on page 76. Remember: Cacti have spines, while succulents seldom do. Succulents also have leaves, which are absent in cacti. Listed in alphabetical order by botanical name, the following nine species of cacti are popular and easy to grow.

Botanical name	Common name	Description
Aporocactus flagelliformis and hybrids	Rat's tail cactus	Long, trailing stems grow over container edges and become vertical. Mature plants produce showy flowers in spring or early summer.
Cereus peruviana	Peruvian apple cactus, column cactus, Peruvian torch	Two forms include tall, columnar types with 8 prominent lobes, and smaller, twisted types with wildly convoluted ridges.
Echinopsis hybrids	Sea urchin cactus	Ribbed round cacti grow into clusters and bear showy funnel-shaped or daisylike flowers on tubular stems in summer.
Gymnocalycium mihanovichii 'Red Cap'	Red top cactus, ruby ball	Green rootstock, round or columnar, topped with ball-shaped red top; top also may be yellow, pink, or orange.
Hatiora gaertneri	Easter cactus	Dark green pads with notched edges joined in a chainlike pattern form stems. Large showy flowers in spring.
Mammillaria species	Powder puff, snowball, golden star, lady fingers, many others	Numerous species, all small, in variable shapes, bloom at a young age. None have ribs. Spines grow from raised knobs, called tubercules.
Parodia species, formerly called *Notocactus*	Ball cactus	Rounded ball shaped cactus, usually less than 4 inches across, with ribs and symmetrical spines. Blooms in summer.
Rebutia species	Crown cactus, cluster cactus, red crown	Small rounded cactus develops numerous offsets that cluster around the parent plant. Blooms in spring following winter rest, numerous colors.
Schlumbergera hybrids	Christmas cactus	Dark green pads with notched edges joined in a chainlike pattern form stems. Large showy flowers in winter.

Living stones (*Lithops*) fascinate their keepers with their curious life cycles.

Clockwise from top left: Aloe *(Aloe barbadensis)*, crown cactus *(Rebutia* species), hen and chicks *(Echeveria* species) (both bottom photos)

Aporocactus flagelliformis and hybrids

ap OR-oh-cak-tus fla-jel-ih-FOR-mis

RAT'S TAIL CACTUS

Rat's tail cactus
(*Aporocactus flagelliformis*)

A FAST GROWER, the stems of rat's tail cactus can lengthen by 3 in/ 7.5 cm or more each year, eventually growing to 4 ft/1.2 m long. Showy flowers appear in spring and early summer. Though the flowers last only a few days, new ones continue to open for several weeks. They are most numerous on the previous year's growth. A natural creeper adapted to growing in rocky ledges and trees, rat's tail cactus develops little roots along the stems, making it easy to propagate. Stems of the original species have very shallow ridges, but numerous hybrids have dark green, deeply ridged stems. These large-flowered hybrids are less demanding of bright light and produce very large flowers in unusual colors including purple, pink, and bright orange. The ancestral species blooms violet red.

SPECIFICATIONS

Light: *In spring and summer,* bright, or move to a half-shaded place outdoors. *In fall and winter,* bright light increases flowering in spring.

◆ **Temperature:** *In spring and summer,* average room temperatures (65–75°F/18–24°C). *In fall and winter,* quite cool (50–55°F/ 10–13°C).

Fertilizer: Begin feeding in late winter with a cactus fertilizer or high-phosphorous fertilizer mixed at half the normal strength. Continue regular light feeding until late summer. Do not feed in fall and early winter.

Water: *In spring to midsummer,* water thoroughly, allowing soil to almost dry between waterings. *In fall and winter,* water less frequently, but do not allow soil to dry out completely. Dry stem tips are a symptom of insufficient water.

Soil: Cactus potting soil, or regular potting soil amended with sand.

Repotting: Repot young plants each year in midsummer. Older plants can be repotted less often.

Longevity: Many years if propagated from stem cuttings.

Propagation: Take 6 in/15 cm-long stem cuttings in early summer, allow the cut ends to dry for 2 days, and then set them to root in damp potting soil.

Selections: Buy plants in bloom if you want a certain color.

Display tips: This plant is most spectacular when grown in a hanging basket. The short spines are sharp and treacherous, so keep the plant well away from activity areas.

FAMILY: **CACTACEAE**   ORIGIN: **BRAZIL, URUGUAY, ARGENTINA**

Cereus peruviana SER-ee-us pe-ROO-vee-an-uh

PERUVIAN APPLE CACTUS, COLUMN CACTUS, PERUVIAN TORCH

Peruvian apple cactus
(*Cereus peruviana*)

CEREUS CACTI OF THIS SPECIES include two very different forms often grown as houseplants. Most common are tall, columnar specimens, which are the mysterious night-blooming cereus. Only very old specimens bloom, but when they do the show is spectacular. Large white flowers to 6 in/15 cm long open at night and close the next morning. In the wild, the flowers give rise to edible red fruits that resemble apples. When kept as houseplants, these cacti are best appreciated for their upright form. They like to be moved outdoors in summer, an operation that must be undertaken carefully since the plants are quite heavy and well armored with tiny spines.

A subspecies with a remarkably globular, convoluted form, *Cereus peruvianus monstrosus* stays smaller, growing to less than 24 in/60 cm tall. This is an excellent cactus for beginners. It seldom blooms, though very old plants may occasionally produce short-lived white flowers in summer. This clublike cactus resembles a green sculpture, and it is very long lived and dependable. Some forms are much more attractive than others.

SPECIFICATIONS

Light: *From late spring to early fall,* bright; consider moving plant outdoors into dappled sun. *In winter,* bright light from a south or west window.

Temperature: *From late spring to early fall,* warm (70–80°F/ 21– 27°C). *In winter,* cool (50–65°F/10–18°C).

Fertilizer: *From spring through fall,* feed monthly with a balanced houseplant fertilizer. *In winter,* do not feed.

Water: Allow soil to become almost dry between waterings. The plant should become slightly spongy, then plump up noticeably after watering.

Soil: 3 parts cactus potting soil to 1 part sterilized garden soil (the garden soil gives the medium a slightly heavy texture).

Repotting: Repot young plants every 2 years in spring. Older plants may be repotted only every few years.

Longevity: 20 years or more.

Propagation: Cuttings root easily.

Selections: With the columnar form, look for pots in which three plants have been established as a group. Among *C. p. monstrosus* selections, the 'Ming Thing Blue' cultivar features exotic swirled lobes in a blue-green jade color. Its sculptural quality is awesome.

Display tips: Columnar types are prone to toppling and have sharp spines, so give them a wide berth in high-traffic areas. Use 'Ming Thing' or other attractive selections as focal-point plants in groupings of cactus or other succulents.

Echinopsis species and hybrids   eh-kin-OP-sis
SEA URCHIN CACTUS, PEANUT CACTUS

Sea urchin cactus
(*Echinopsis* species)

THE SEA URCHIN CACTUS lives up to its name by developing huge flowers on tubular stems, which emerge in clusters from the round cactus bodies in summer. Many species are similar, and some bloom only at night. Named hybrids that have been developed for strong flower production often bloom two or three times in the summer provided they enjoy a cool, dry rest period in the winter.

There are hundreds of other species within the *Echinopsis* genus, which now includes cacti that were long known under other names, including *Lobivia* and *Trichocerus*. All share a need for cool, dry winters and a tendency to bloom at night. Some common "peanut" cacti are included in this group, and they are very easy to grow. To promote strong blooming, feed them regularly through summer and keep them cool through winter so they can set flower buds.

SPECIFICATIONS

Light: *From late spring to early fall,* a half-shaded spot outdoors. *In winter,* bright light near a south or west window.

◆ **Temperature:** *From late spring to early fall,* warm (70–80°F/21–27°C). *In winter,* cool (55–65°F/13–18°C).

Fertilizer: *In spring and summer,* feed plants monthly with a balanced fertilizer. *In late fall and winter,* do not feed.

Water: *In spring and summer,* water more often than other cacti, allowing soil to almost dry between waterings. *In late fall and winter,* keep plants very dry. Mist occasionally during winter rest period.

Soil: Cactus soil, or potting soil amended with sand.

Repotting: Repot when plants need more space, preferably in summer after flowers have faded. Pot up offsets after they grow to more than 1 in/2.5 cm in diameter.

Longevity: Many years if offsets are rooted every 3 to 4 years.

Propagation: Offsets; seeds.

Selections: The many named varieties vary in flower size and color. Orange-flowered 'Paramount' is a common parent, yet there are at least a dozen more available, some with contrasting midribs. All are beautiful.

Display tips: One of these cacti in full bloom forms a bouquet of exotic blossoms, which makes an awesome table centerpiece.

FAMILY: **CACTACEAE**   ORIGIN: **SOUTH AMERICA**

Gymnocalycium mihanovichii 'Red Cap'

jim-no-kal-EE-see-um mi-han-oh-VIK-ee-i

RED TOP CACTUS, RUBY BALL CACTUS

Red top cactus
(Gymnocalycium mihanovichii)

THIS ATTENTION-GETTING CACTUS is really two cacti in one. The red top, a mutant form of *Gymnocalycium* that lacks chlorophyll but features bright red, orange, yellow, or pink color, is grafted onto a more vigorous green cactus. The green cactus feeds itself and the grafted top, and both gradually grow larger. After several years, red top may produce pink flowers in summer, provided the plant gets a cool rest in winter. Old, well-pleased plants also develop round offsets just above the graft union. The trickiest part of growing this cactus is getting the light right. The colorful cap can burn in bright sun, but the green part needs bright light in order to photosynthesize light energy for the whole plant.

SPECIFICATIONS

Light: Bright light but not direct sun year round.

Temperature: *From spring through fall,* warm (70–80°F / 21–27°C). *In winter,* move to a cooler spot (50–60°F/10–16°C).

Fertilizer: *In spring and summer,* fertilize monthly with a balanced liquid plant food mixed at half the recommended rate. *In fall and winter,* do not feed.

Water: Allow soil to become nearly dry between waterings, but not so dry that the cactus becomes spongy. Reduce water in winter, but do not let the soil dry out completely.

Soil: Cactus potting soil, or regular potting soil amended with a little sand.

Repotting: Repot every 1 to 2 years to accommodate growing roots and refresh the soil.

Longevity: 5 to 10 years, or sometimes longer.

Propagation: Offsets that form on older plants can be grafted onto various green cacti, but they will not root and grow on their own.

Selections: These cacti are often sold unlabeled, so simply choose a plant that appeals to you. The green rootstock may be a round ball cactus or a more upright column. Both parts will grow larger with time.

Display tips: One little red top makes a good focal point in a dish garden planted in a southwestern-style bowl. As the cactus grows, plant it in its own pot and rear it as a specimen plant for your kitchen windowsill.

Hatiora gaertneri and hybrids (formerly known as *Rhipsalidopsis gaertneri*)

hay-tee-OR-uh gart-NAR-ee

EASTER CACTUS

Easter cactus *(Hatiora gaertneri)*

EASTER CACTUS LOOKS VERY MUCH like the more popular Christmas cactus, but it blooms in spring rather than winter. A rain forest native, it adapts to less light than other cacti, and needs more water. Unlike Christmas cactus, this species is easily stressed by cool temperatures and should be brought indoors in early fall and kept in a bright room through winter. Allow it a cool, dry rest period after flowering stops in late spring, but otherwise treat Easter cactus like most of your foliage houseplants. Easter cactus is notorious for shedding its buds if it is moved during its flowering period. Locate the plant in a spot where it can stay put from late winter to late spring.

SPECIFICATIONS

Light: *In summer,* bright. *In spring, fall, and winter,* filtered indoor light.

Temperature: *In summer,* warm (70–80°F/21–27°C). *In spring, fall, and winter,* average room temperature (65–75°F/18–24°C).

Fertilizer: *From early summer through fall,* feed every 2 weeks with a cactus fertilizer, or a high-phosphorous fertilizer mixed at half the normal strength. *In winter and spring,* feed monthly.

Water: *In spring,* allow plants to dry out for a month after flowers fade. *Through summer and early fall,* keep soil lightly moist. *In winter,* allow soil to almost dry out between modest waterings. Shriveled stems indicate too little water.

Soil: Any good potting soil.

Repotting: Repot young plants annually in early summer. Older plants may be repotted every 2 to 3 years.

Longevity: To 6 years, or indefinitely when propagated from stem cuttings.

Propagation: Take stem cuttings consisting of two to three pads in summer, allow the cut ends to dry for a day, and then plant in moist potting soil. Keep in a shady place until new growth appears.

Selections: Buy plants in bloom to be sure of getting the color you want. Various shades of orange and pink are available.

Display tips: Grow in a hanging basket that can be suspended at eye level. Or, plant in a ceramic pot in a spring pastel color that coordinates nicely with the color of the blooms.

Mammillaria species   mam-il-AIR-ee-uh

POWDER PUFF, SNOWBALL, GOLDEN STAR, LADY FINGERS, MANY OTHERS

Powder puff
(*Mammillaria* species)

THIS HUGE GENUS INCLUDES more than 250 species, which are often called "mamms" by devoted collectors. They are easy cacti for beginners, and so small that they work well in dish gardens. With mammillarias, the biggest problem may be identifying what you have, since species vary in shape and appearance. All are small, rarely growing more than 8 in/20 cm tall or wide, and they lack ribs. Instead, tufts of spines emerge from raised knobs, called tubercules, which are arranged in symmetrical patterns and are densely crowded near the crown. Mammillarias flower at a young age, and the flowers, which are borne from creases between the tubercules, usually appear in a circular, wreathlike pattern.

To encourage blooms, which appear in late spring or summer, keep plants cooler in winter than in summer. Most species are hardy to 32°F/0°C, but it's best to keep them above 50°F/10°C. Dry winter conditions help flower buds to form. These cacti enjoy warm temperatures in summer, though they should be kept in a spot where strong summer sun is limited to 4 hours each day.

SPECIFICATIONS

Light: Direct sun 4 hours daily, or bright light all day, year-round.

⚠ Temperature: *From late spring to early fall,* warm (70–85°F/ 21–29°C). *In winter,* cool (50–65°F/ 10–18°C).

Fertilizer: *In spring and summer,* feed monthly with a cactus fertilizer, or a high-phosphorous plant food mixed at half the normal strength. *In fall and winter,* do not feed.

Water: Allow soil to become almost dry between waterings. In hot summer weather, plants may need water twice weekly. Water very sparingly in winter.

Soil: Cactus soil, or potting soil amended with one-third sand.

Repotting: When grown in broad, shallow containers or dish gardens, plants need repotting only every 2 to 3 years.

Longevity: Many years.

Propagation: Offsets; seeds.

Selections: Puffy white hairs cover the ball-shaped powder puff or snowball cactus (*M. bocasana*). Golden star or lady fingers (*M. elongata*) is fast and easy to grow. Many other species are available.

Display tips: Grow in shallow containers weighted with gravel in the bottom. Mammillarias are wonderful subjects for indoor windowboxes that include a variety of small cacti.

Parodia species (formerly known as *Notocactus*) pair-OH-dee-uh

BALL CACTUS, SILVER BALL, YELLOW TOWER, TOM THUMB CACTUS

Ball cactus (*Parodia nivosa*)

FOR 60 YEARS, THESE SHOWY LITTLE GLOBES were called *Notocactus*, and many catalogs (and plant tags) still use that genus name. Now renamed *Parodias*, there are 100 species, several of which make excellent houseplants. Old favorites like silver ball cactus (*P. scopa*) are easy to grow, bloom willingly, and adapt well to life in homes and offices. Most parodias are round and ribbed, grow to less than 10 in/25 cm tall, and often feature showy spines arranged in a symmetrical matrix pattern. After several years, some ball cacti produce small offsets near the base. Flowers appear near the crown, and may be yellow, orange, pink, or red, depending on the species.

In their native habitat, parodias receive warm rain often in summer and experience dry, temperate winters. If you mimic this pattern, your parodias should do well. Ball cacti thrive when allowed to spend the summer outdoors in a half-shaded spot.

SPECIFICATIONS

Light: *From late spring to early fall,* partial shade outdoors. *In winter,* bright light from a south or west window.

Temperature: *From late spring to early fall,* warm (65–85°F/18–29°C). *In winter,* cool (55–65°F/13–18°C).

Fertilizer: *From late spring to late summer,* feed monthly with a balanced liquid fertilizer. *In fall and winter,* do not feed.

Water: *From late spring to early fall,* water as often as needed to keep soil lightly moist. *In winter,* allow soil to become almost dry between waterings.

Soil: A very sandy yet humus-rich mix, such as cactus soil amended with a small amount of sand.

Repotting: Repot only when the plants reach the edge of the pots, usually only every 2 to 3 years.

Longevity: Many years.

Propagation: Seeds; offsets.

Selections: Silver ball cactus (*P. scopa*) is widely available and easy to grow. It features showy white hairs in tufts at the spines, and yellow to yellow-orange flowers. Yellow tower cactus (*P. leninghausii*) elongates as it grows, and is well armed with long yellow spines. Fast-growing Tom Thumb cactus (*P. mammulosa*) has a barrel shape, and often blooms repeatedly in summer.

Display tips: Place ball cactus on a low table where the patterns formed by ribs and spines can be easily seen. Combine young plants with other cacti and succulents in small dish gardens.

FAMILY: **CACTACEAE**   ORIGIN: **ARGENTINA**

Rebutia species   ree-BOOT-ee-uh
CROWN CACTUS, CLUSTER CACTUS, RED CROWN

Crown cactus
(*Rebutia* species)

NATIVE TO HIGH ELEVATIONS of the South American Andes, these small cacti bloom willingly in spring and summer provided they are given a cool, 3-month-long winter rest. Flower buds develop near the base of the plant or in crevices between the mother plant and its offsets. Plants with many offsets may produce a dozen tubular blossoms, which may be white, pink, yellow, orange, or red, depending on the species.

Rebutias may be sold as individual plants or included in dish gardens. Once a plant grows into a flattened head about 2.5 in/6.25 cm across and 1.5 in/3.75 cm tall, it begins propagating itself into a cluster. With good care, a clump up to 6 in/15 cm across will develop within 3 to 4 years. In summer, carefully remove offsets with a gentle twist and transplant them to individual containers or a new dish garden.

SPECIFICATIONS

Light: *From spring through fall,* bright light. *In winter,* rest in moderate light.

⬥ Temperature: *From spring through fall,* average room temperature (65–75°F/18–24°C). *In winter,* rest in a cool room (50–65°F/10–18°C).

Fertilizer: Feed once in spring, and a second time in late summer, with a balanced liquid plant food.

Water: *From spring through fall,* allow soil to become nearly dry between waterings, but do water regularly. *In winter,* water lightly only every 7 to 10 days.

Soil: Cactus potting soil, or regular potting soil amended with grit or sand.

Repotting: Every other summer, or as needed to provide room for new offsets.

Longevity: Many years due to ease of propagation. Discard old plants when they lose color and lack vigor, which is often due to root rot.

Propagation: Offsets; seeds.

Selections: These cacti may be labeled by species name, or you may get a mystery rebutia in a dish garden. Of more than 40 species grown by collectors, the red-blooming *R. minuscula* is famous for producing large red flowers at a young age.

Display tips: Individual plants look great in a dish garden, but a large cluster, set in a shallow pot, becomes spellbinding when it is in bloom. In good years, blooms of some species are so numerous that they nearly cover the plants.

Schlumbergera hybrids   shlum-bur-JER-uh

CHRISTMAS CACTUS, THANKSGIVING CACTUS, HOLIDAY CACTUS

Christmas cactus
(*Schlumbergera* hybrid)

THESE HEAVY-BLOOMING RAIN FOREST NATIVES are easy to grow, and they are available in a huge range of colors. The intensity of bloom depends on climactic factors: bright light in summer and fall, combined with days that gradually become shorter and cooler. It is therefore ideal to move plants outdoors in summer, and keep them there until night temperatures dip down to 40–50°F/4–10°C. When you bring them in, keep them in a cool room that stays completely dark after sunset. Buds will develop in early winter, at which time plants should be moved to where you want them to bloom. Once plants begin blooming, they may drop their blossoms if exposed to any type of stress. This is why plants that are bought in bloom often shed their buds and blossoms. With less shifting about after buds form, plants that shed their buds one winter will bloom beautifully the following year.

SPECIFICATIONS

Light: *From late spring to fall,* bright. *From late winter to early spring,* rest in moderate light.

Temperature: *From late spring to late summer,* warm (65–80°F/ 18–27°C). *In fall and winter,* cool (50–65°F/10–18°C).

Fertilizer: *From spring through summer,* feed every 2 weeks with a balanced fertilizer, mixed at a slightly reduced rate, or use a high-phosphorous plant food. *In fall and winter,* feed monthly.

Water: *From spring through fall,* keep soil lightly moist. *In winter,* allow soil to almost dry out between modest waterings. Shriveled stems indicate too little water.

Soil: Any good potting soil.

Repotting: Repot young plants annually in early summer. Older plants may be repotted every 2 to 3 years.

Longevity: 5 to 6 years, or indefinitely when propagated from stem cuttings.

Propagation: Take stem cuttings consisting of two to three pads in early summer, allow the cut ends to dry for a day, and then plant in moist potting soil. Keep in a shady place until new growth appears.

Selections: Buy plants in bloom to be sure of getting the color you want. Light pink and lilac shades are especially beautiful.

Display tips: Grow this cactus in a broad pot that can be placed on a tabletop when it blooms. Christmas cacti also are easy to grow in hanging baskets.

Eleven Super Succulents

Listed in alphabetical order by botanical name, these eleven species of succulents are popular and easy to grow.

Botanical Name	Common Name	Description
Agave species	Agave, American aloe, century plant	Vase-shaped or rounded plants comprised of stiff-spined leaves; most are quite large.
Aloe barbadensis, A. vera	Aloe, burn plant	Plump green or variegated leaves fan out from a central base; sap has medicinal value.
Crassula ovata	Jade plant	Shiny, plump green leaves on plants that assume a treelike shape as they mature
Echeveria species and hybrids	Hen and chicks	Round rosettes of succulent leaves in a range of colors eagerly produce offsets that can be grown into new plants.
Faucaria tigrina, F. felina	Tiger's jaws	Unusual incurved spines on leaf edges resemble sharp teeth; the "jaws" open as the leaves mature.
Haworthia species and hybrids	Haworthia	Very small succulents of variable shape and color; the miniatures of the succulent world
Kalanchoe blossfeldiana hybrids	Kalanchoe, flaming Cathy, flaming Katy	Robust winter-blooming plants with glossy green leaves
Lithops species	Living stones, split rocks	Unusual small succulents resemble stones with a cleft in the center.
Sanseveria trifasciata	Mother-in-law's tongue, snake plant	Stiffly upright variegated leaves slowly form clumps; very easy to grow.
Sedum morganianum	Donkey tail, burro's tail	Closely spaced succulent leaves clothe long stems that often cascade over the sides of the container.
Senecio rowelyanus	String of pearls, bead plant	Leaves are small round beads, usually green, attached to thin stems.

Agave species   ah-GAH-vee

AGAVE, AMERICAN ALOE, CENTURY PLANT

MORE THAN 450 SPECIES OF AGAVE have been identified, and several make excellent houseplants provided you can give them abundant natural light. This is easy in summer, when agaves love to be moved outdoors, but they need bright light in winter, too. The easiest agaves to keep indoors are small ones, such as little princess agave (*A. purviflora*) and *A. victoriae-reginae*, both of which grow into 10 in/25 cm, ball-shaped plants packed with spiny leaves. Many people love the widely spread, wavy leaves of variegated American agave, which grows so slowly that it can be kept as a houseplant for about 10 years. After that, it must be set free in a garden, where it is hardy to about 15°F/-9°C. Only garden-grown or wild agaves produce flowers, so don't look for blooms on indoor plants. The sap of all agaves can cause skin irritation, so be careful when handling.

Agave (*Agave parryi*)

SPECIFICATIONS

⬥ Light: *From late spring to early fall,* direct sun at least 5 hours a day. *In winter,* keep in a bright south window, where temperatures cool off at night.

Temperature: *From late spring to fall,* very warm (70–90°F/21–32°C). *In winter,* cool (50–60°F/10–16°C).

Fertilizer: *In spring and summer,* feed monthly with a balanced houseplant fertilizer. *In fall and winter,* do not feed.

Water: *In spring and summer,* use warm water, and water plants before the soil becomes completely dry. *In fall and winter,* provide only scant moisture.

Soil: Regular potting soil amended with pebbles or sand to improve drainage.

Repotting: Repot only every few years, to refresh the soil. These plants are slow growers, and are best handled as little as possible.

Longevity: 10 to 40 years, depending on species. When grown in open soil in warm, arid climates, plants often live for 50 years or much longer.

Propagation: Seeds, offsets. Agaves grown as houseplants seldom need to be propagated, which is best done in a greenhouse.

Selections: Named varieties of *A. victoriae-reginae* require a little less light than other agaves, so they are often the best choice if you live in a cool or cloudy climate.

Display tips: Grow agaves in a stout, heavy pot with a wide bottom, because plants are prone to toppling if planted in small, lightweight containers.

FAMILY: ALOACEAE   ORIGIN: NORTHERN AFRICA

Aloe barbadensis, syn. *A. vera* AY-low bar-buh-DEN-sis
ALOE, BURN PLANT

Burn Plant *(Aloe barbadensis)*

IT IS NO WIVES' TALE that the sap of the aloe plant cures minor burns and other skin problems. It really works. The most medicinally potent species is pretty, too, with plump, elongated leaves that fan out from a central base. Aloe is easy to grow, and can be kept indoors year-round or moved outside in the summer. Just be sure to make moves gradual ones. Aloe sunburns easily when moved from low indoor light to bright sun too quickly, and the plants sulk when moved from a warm, sunny porch to a dim room. When grown outdoors in mild winter climates, aloe often blooms in late winter or spring. Aloe rarely blooms when grown indoors.

SPECIFICATIONS

Light: Bright light from an east or south window.

Temperature: Average room temperatures year-round (65–75°F/18–24°C). Aloe can adapt to higher summer temperatures outdoors, and does not mind a cool winter rest.

Fertilizer: *From spring through fall,* feed plants monthly with a balanced houseplant fertilizer. *In winter,* do not feed.

Water: *From spring through fall,* keep soil lightly moist. Plants may dry out quickly on hot summer days. *In winter,* water less, but do not allow the soil to become completely dry.

Soil: Any good potting soil.

Repotting: Repot every other year in spring, or as needed to refresh the soil and give plants more room.

Longevity: Many years if propagated from offsets.

Propagation: Cut off pups (offsets) in spring or early summer. Allow the cut roots to dry for a day before potting them in clean containers.

Selections: In addition to medicinal aloe, two species are valued for their good looks. Partridge-breasted aloe, also called tiger aloe (*A. variegata*), forms a tight rosette of beautifully patterned leaves that grows only 6 in/15 cm tall. Lace aloe (*A. aristata*) is smaller, with thready leaf tips. It offsets freely, and has been hybridized with tiger aloe.

Display tips: Find a place in or near your kitchen for a small aloe plant. The more quickly a leaf is split open and placed on a minor burn, the better the burn heals.

Crassula ovata (formerly known as *C. argentea*) kras-OO-luh oh-VAH-tuh

JADE PLANT

Jade plant (*Crassula ovata*)

THE TREELIKE FORM AND SHINY LEAVES set the jade plant apart from other succulents, and it is easy to grow in homes and offices. When grown outdoors in frost-free areas, jade plants grow into 4 ft/ 1.2m-tall shrubs. Indoors, they seldom grow more than 24 in/ 60 cm tall over a period of many years. Plants more than 10 years old may flower in winter, though blooming is uncommon in indoor grown plants. Purchased plants often consist of up to five cuttings that have been rooted and grown in a single pot, which allows little room for growth. Divide crowded pots in spring, transplanting each plant to an individual container, or keep them in groups of no more than three plants in a 6 in/15 cm pot. Plenty of light and fertilizer improves the leaf color of jade plant.

SPECIFICATIONS

Light: Four hours of filtered sun daily year-round. Plants can be moved outdoors to a shady spot in summer.

Temperature: Average room temperatures (65–75°F/18–24°C) year-round. A 6-week cool (55–60°F/13–16°C) rest in winter improves the chances that older plants will bloom.

Fertilizer: *From spring through fall,* feed every 2 weeks with a balanced fertilizer mixed at half the normal strength. *In winter,* do not feed.

Water: Allow soil to become almost dry between waterings, but watch for shedding leaves or brown spots on leaves — signs that the plant needs more water. Water less in winter, but do not allow plants to dry out completely.

Soil: Regular potting soil or African violet soil.

Repotting: Repot young plants annually in spring. With plants more than 10 years old, repot every 2 to 3 years to refresh the soil.

Longevity: 10 years or more, or indefinitely if propagated from tip cuttings every 5 to 10 years.

Propagation: Take 3 in/7.5 cm long stem tip cuttings in spring. Allow the cuttings to callus for at least 5 days before planting them in a mixture of damp sand and peat moss.

Selections: Some varieties have leaves variegated with white or tinged with red. A closely related plant, money plant or silver dollar plant (*C. arborescens* or *C. cotyledon*), has flattened gray-green leaves covered with fine felt.

Display tips: Make the most of jade plant's treelike form by shifting plants to individual containers when they are about 5 years old.

Echeveria species and hybrids   ek-uh-VAR-ee-uh

ECHEVERIA, HEN AND CHICKS

Hen and chicks
(*Echeveria* species)

SEVERAL PLANTS GO BY THE COMMON NAME of hen and chicks, and it can be difficult to tell them apart. Echeverias differ from semperivums (which are hardier plants, often called houseleeks), in that echeverias have thicker, more succulent leaves and much less tolerance of cold weather. Echeverias grow into symmetrical rosettes held on short stems that may be 2–6 in/5–15 cm across, depending on cultivar. They often bloom in spring, but many growers pinch off the blooms to preserve the appearance of the rosettes. Echeverias are easy to grow and willingly produce offsets, known as *chicks,* that can be transplanted to new pots with no complications. Many varieties are blushed with red, which becomes more intense when the plants receive good light. Plants may be moved outdoors in summer or kept in a home or office year-round. As long as they get plenty of light, echeverias are very happy houseplants.

SPECIFICATIONS

Light: Bright light year-round, with some direct sun in summer.

Temperature: *From spring to late summer,* average to warm (65–80°F/18–27°C). *In fall and winter,* cool to average (55–75°F/13–24°C).

Fertilizer: *From spring through fall,* feed plants every 2 weeks with a high-phosphorous plant food mixed at half the normal strength. *In winter,* feed monthly.

Water: Provide water as often as needed to keep the soil lightly moist. Plants that dry very quickly in summer may need repotting. Water less in winter.

Soil: Cactus potting soil, or regular potting soil amended with one-fourth part sand.

Repotting: Repot every 2 years, or more often if plants outgrow their pots.

Longevity: Indefinitely, due to this plant's ease of propagation.

◊ Propagation: Remove offsets with a short stub of stem attached, and transplant them to new containers. Small offsets transplant more easily than large ones.

Selections: Choose plants based on their appearance, which varies between the red-blushed green leaves of 'Painted Lady' to the woolly felted rosettes of 'Doris Taylor' to some with frilled red edges, such as 'Wavy Curls'. Most named varieties are interspecies hybrids.

Display tips: Grow several different echeverias together in a broad bowl kept on a sunny windowsill. They also mix quite well with other succulents.

Faucaria tigrina, F. felina faw-KER-ee-uh tee-GREE-nuh
TIGER'S JAWS

THIS INTERESTING SMALL SUCCULENT grows to only 6 in/15 cm tall, but the short green or orange-blushed leaves, often speckled with white dots, provide ongoing drama. The edges of each short, triangular leaf bear incurved, soft spines that resemble teeth. The teeth interlock on young leaves, but as the leaves grow, they open until they look like dangerous jaws. Tiger's jaws gradually grows into a clump of ground-hugging stemless rosettes. Sometimes yellow flowers appear in fall, but only on mature plants that get at least 4 hours of strong sun each day all summer. This plant likes warm to hot conditions during its active growth period, so consider moving it outdoors in summer. In winter, do not allow the plant to be chilled by temperatures below 60°F/16°C.

Tiger's jaws *(Faucaria tigrina)*

SPECIFICATIONS

Light: *From late spring to fall,* partial sun. *In winter,* strong light from a south window.

Temperature: *From late spring to early fall,* warm temperatures (70–90°F/21–32°C). *In winter,* average room temperatures (65–75°F/18–24°C).

Fertilizer: *From mid-spring to early fall,* feed plants once a month with a high-phosphorous plant food. *In winter,* do not feed.

Water: *From mid-spring to early fall,* keep plants lightly moist.

In winter, allow plants to dry out between waterings. In its natural habitat, tiger's jaws collects water from dew, so misting the plant occasionally is a good practice when it is grown in a very dry room.

Soil: Cactus potting soil, or regular potting soil amended with one-third part sand.

Repotting: Repot only every 2 to 3 years, when the plant grows to within .25 in/.6 cm of the edge of the pot. Tiger's jaws has very shallow roots, so it can be grown in small, broad containers.

Longevity: Indefinitely if propagated from offsets.

Propagation: Cut offsets from a parent plant in late spring. Allow the little rosettes to dry for a day before potting them up.

Selections: This plant is usually sold by its common name. A few faucaria species lack the characteristic teeth and have small bumps along the edges of the leaves instead.

Display tips: Tiger's jaws makes an excellent centerpiece for a shallow dish garden featuring an assortment of small succulents such as echeverias and haworthias.

FAMILY: **ASPHODELACEAE**   ORIGIN: **SOUTH AFRICA**

Haworthia species and hybrids   hay-WOR-thee-uh
HAWORTHIA

Haworthia (*Haworthia* species)

COLLECTING HAWORTHIAS QUICKLY BECOMES ADDICTIVE to plant lovers who delight in small things, because haworthias are the smallest succulents of them all. Many grow less than 3 in/7.5 cm tall or wide, while some columnar types may grow to 5 in/12.5 cm tall. This genus includes more than 80 species that offer endless variation in form. Many resemble miniature aloes, a few look like tiny echeverias, and some are sedum look-alikes. They have in common a tremendous tolerance for neglect, needing only sun and occasional water to prosper for many years. A collection of several haworthias can be grown in an 8 in/20 cm-wide shallow dish kept in a sunny window. It is important to repot them every year or two. Haworthias shed some of their old roots each spring, so refreshing the soil is necessary maintenance for healthy plants.

SPECIFICATIONS

Light: Bright indirect light year-round. If you move plants outdoors in summer, gradually accustom them to increased light, as indoor-grown plants sunburn easily.

Temperature: *From late spring to fall,* warm (70–80°F/21–27°C). *In winter,* allow plants a winter rest at around 60°F/16°C, if possible.

Fertilizer: *In spring and summer,* feed monthly with a balanced houseplant food mixed at half the normal strength. *In fall and winter,* do not feed.

Water: Allow soil to become almost dry between waterings. Because of their small size, haworthias require a little less water than other succulents.

Soil: Cactus potting soil, or regular potting soil amended with one-third part sand.

Repotting: Repot in spring at least every other year.

Longevity: Indefinitely if propagated from offsets.

Propagation: Propagate offsets when repotting in spring or early summer.

Selections: Choose haworthias based on forms and colors you like. The classification of haworthias is a matter that gives plant taxonomists serious headaches.

Display tips: Haworthias are so small that they can be grown in novel containers, such as little teacups or decorative tins. When using a container that lacks drainage holes, fill the bottom with 1 in/2.5 cm of coarse gravel. Haworthias also make fine little accent plants for dish gardens planted with larger succulents.

Kalanchoe blossfeldiana hybrids

kal-AN-cho blas-fel-dee-AN-uh

KALANCHOE, FLAMING CATHY, FLAMING KATY

Kalanchoe
(*Kalanchoe blossfeldiana* hybrid)

IN THE MIDDLE OF WINTER, it's hard to resist a kalanchoe covered with clusters of red, pink, or orange flowers. The flowers last several weeks, and the plants are quite easy to grow. However, before a kalanchoe will make buds, it must be exposed to a series of long, sunny days followed by at least 2 weeks of short days, less than 12 hours long. This is easy enough to accomplish by placing plants outdoors in summer and then bringing them indoors in late fall, just before nighttime temperatures drop below about 40°F/4°C. After you bring the plant in, keep it in a room where no lights are used at night. When brought into bloom naturally, kalanchoes flower in January and February. To speed up the schedule, cover the plants with a box for 14 hours each night for 14 consecutive days in early fall, and let them have moderate light during the day. Blooms will appear about 6 weeks later. Snip off bloom-bearing branches after the flowers fade to preserve the handsome good looks of this plant.

SPECIFICATIONS

◆ Light: Bright direct sunlight indoors; filtered shade outdoors.

Temperature: *From late spring to early fall,* warm to very warm (70–90°F/21–32°C). *In fall and winter,* cool to average (50–70°F/10–21°C).

Fertilizer: *From late spring to midwinter,* feed with an all-purpose houseplant food monthly. *From late winter to early spring,* do not feed.

Water: *From spring to fall,* keep the soil lightly moist. *In winter,* allow the soil to dry out between light waterings.

Soil: Any good potting soil.

Repotting: Repot annually in early summer.

Longevity: 2 to 3 years, or indefinitely when propagated from stem cuttings.

Propagation: When plants are more than 2 years old, take stem cuttings and set them to root in small pots in late spring (see page 299).

Selections: In addition to flowering kalanchoe, other interesting species include devil's backbone (*K. diagremontiana*), which is also known as "mother of thousands" because of the way it produces tiny, rooted plantlets along its leaf margins. Panda plant or pussy ears (*K. tomentosa*) features thick gray-green felted leaves with reddish markings.

Display tips: To celebrate the blooming of flowering kalanchoe, wrap the pot with colorful cloth or paper, tied with ribbon or raffia.

FAMILY: **AIZOACEAE (FORMERLY MESAMBRYANTHEMACEAE)**   ORIGIN: **SOUTHERN AFRICA**

Lithops species LY-thops
LIVING STONES, SPLIT ROCKS

Living stones (*Lithops* species)

THERE IS LITTLE ARGUMENT that living rocks are the most unusual succulents in the world. They were not discovered until 1811, when a plant collector noticed that some of the stones underfoot were not stones at all, but living succulent plants.

Lithops are not difficult to grow provided you follow their natural growth cycle. In late winter and spring, new leaves push up through the cleft between the bodies. The new leaves take up the moisture and nutrients in the old leaves, so the plants need no water during this time. Do water them a few times in late spring, after the old leaves have shriveled away. Then allow the plants to become quite dry through summer. In fall, flower buds may emerge from the cleft provided the plants are fully mature. This is a good time to water the plants lightly for several weeks. Then let them rest again through winter, until the life cycle begins anew.

SPECIFICATIONS

◆ Light: *In summer,* 4 hours of direct sun. *From fall through spring,* less light, by an east or south window.

Temperature: *In summer,* warm to very warm temperatures (70–90°F/21–32°C). *From fall through spring,* cool to average room temperatures (55–70°F/ 13–21°C).

Fertilizer: Twice yearly, once in spring and once in fall, feed plants with a balanced, all-purpose houseplant food.

Water: Lithops have two seasons when they need light watering: in spring after new leaves have absorbed old ones, and in fall when flowers appear. At other times, keep plants very dry, watering lightly only if plants become badly wrinkled.

Soil: Cactus soil amended with sand.

Repotting: Repot only when plants outgrow containers, usually only every 5 years or so. Use 5 in/ 12.5 cm-deep pots to accommodate taproots. Set plants so that one-third of the leaves are buried.

Longevity: Many years.

Propagation: Seeds; division of old plants that have grown into large clusters.

Selections: Plants vary in color, and are sold by species name. *L. aucampiae* has sandy brown bodies with reddish markings, and blooms yellow. *L. marmorata* has gray to beige bodies with white, fragrant flowers. There are many others.

Display tips: Grow two or three different species in a broad pot, with an attractive arrangement of smooth stones to keep them company.

Sanseveria trifasciata san-suh-VER-ee-uh try-fah-see-AH-ta

MOTHER-IN-LAW'S TONGUE, SNAKE PLANT

Mother-in-law's tongue
(*Sanseveria trifasciata* 'Laurentii')

ONE OF THE MOST CAREFREE HOUSEPLANTS you can grow, sanseveria adapts quickly to life in homes, workplaces, and shopping malls. Often described as indestructible, sanseveria tolerates neglect but responds to good care by growing sturdy, sword-shaped leaves, which often are edged with yellow or white. Clean them periodically with a damp cloth to maintain a glossy sheen. Very old plants sometimes produce clusters of white flowers in winter, but most indoor-grown plants go many years between bloom cycles. This is a top houseplant for beginners, but seasoned houseplant growers also love sanseveria for its stalwart constitution and dramatic upright form.

SPECIFICATIONS

Light: *From spring through fall,* bright indirect light. *In winter,* moderate light.

Temperature: Average indoor temperatures (65–75°F/18–24°C) year-round, with no chilling below 60°F/16°C.

Fertilizer: *From late spring through fall,* feed monthly with a balanced houseplant fertilizer mixed at half the normal strength. *In winter,* do not feed.

Water: *In spring through summer,* water often enough to keep soil lightly moist. *In winter,* allow soil to become nearly dry between waterings.

Soil: Regular potting soil, possibly amended with a handful of sterilized garden soil to give it a slightly heavier texture.

Repotting: Repot as needed in spring every 2 to 3 years. As plants become taller, add pebbles or small stones to the bottom of the container to add weight, which prevents toppling.

Longevity: 20 years or more; indefinitely if propagated by division every 5 to 10 years.

Propagation: Division in early spring. Use a sharp, serrated knife to cut through the thick roots.

Selections: Standard selections such as 'Laurentii', with creamy yellow leaf margins, grow to 24 in/60 cm tall. Dwarf forms such as 'Golden Hahnii' and 'Silver Hahnii' grow to half that size, with sharply variegated leaves.

Display tips: Sanseveria's tall, linear look makes it an ideal background plant to group with other foliage plants. It moves willingly to new locations provided steady warmth is maintained.

FAMILY: **CRASSULACEAE**   ORIGIN: **MEXICO**

Sedum morganianum SEE-dum mor-ga-nee-AH-num
DONKEY TAIL, BURRO'S TAIL

Donkey tail
(Sedum morganianum 'Burrito')

NUMEROUS HARDY SEDUMS GROW in outdoor rock gardens, and several of these make good houseplants, too. The sedum known as donkey tail is too delicate for outdoors, but it makes an attractive and interesting indoor companion. Stems that emerge from the plant's crown are thickly clad with juicy, gray-green leaves, which overlap like the coarse hair on a donkey's tail. Plants that enjoy bright light in summer and a cool winter rest sometimes produce small pink flowers at the stem tips in summer. This plant's biggest weakness is its fragile leaves; a slight bump can send them falling to the floor. However, new stems constantly emerge to replace such casualties.

SPECIFICATIONS

Light: Bright light most of the year. Extra light in summer is beneficial, but be careful, because indoor-grown plants sunburn easily.

◆ Temperature: Average room temperatures (65–75°F/18–24°C). A cool winter rest, with 55–60°F/13–16°C temperatures, increases the likelihood of blooming.

Fertilizer: *From spring to late summer,* feed monthly with an all-purpose balanced houseplant food. *In fall and winter,* do not feed.

Water: *From spring through summer,* water as often as needed to keep soil lightly moist. *In fall and winter,* allow soil to become dry between waterings.

Soil: Cactus potting soil.

Repotting: Repot as needed in spring every 2 years if plant is actively growing. After plants fill an 8 in/20 cm pot, they become so fragile that repotting is difficult. Begin propagating tip cuttings when repotting becomes impractical.

Longevity: 5 to 10 years, or indefinitely if propagated from stem tip cuttings.

Propagation: Take a 3 in/7.5 cm-long tip and remove leaves from the lowest 2 in/5 cm section. Insert the stem in a half-and-half mixture of damp peat moss and sand, and keep it moist for 2 months.

Selections: This plant is usually sold by species name. One unusual cultivar, 'Burrito', features short, stocky stems thickly covered with blunt leaves. It is a little less fragile than other donkey tails.

Display tips: Grow in a hanging basket or suspended pot, so that the long stems can trail down over the edges. The gray-green leaves show especially well when this plant is grown in a dark-colored container.

Senecio rowleyanus sen-EE-see-oh roh-lee-AY-nus
STRING OF PEARLS, BEAD PLANT

String of pearls
(*Senecio rowleyanus*)

NO OTHER PLANT looks like string of pearls, with succulent leaves that grow into small, round marbles, .5 in/1.25 cm in diameter. Although dainty in appearance, string of pearls is a robust grower, quickly covering the surface of its container and then developing stems that hang over the sides of the pot. Plants grow only a few inches tall, but the trailing stems can extend 24 in/60 cm or more if they are not accidentally broken off. Mature plants that enjoy a cool rest in winter sometimes produce small white flowers, which are not showy but carry a faint cinnamon scent. If long stems become straggly, snip them off and propagate new plants from healthy stem sections.

SPECIFICATIONS

Light: 2 to 4 hours of direct sunlight year-round.

Temperature: *From spring to fall,* warm (70–80°F/21–27°C). *In winter,* cool (55–60°F/13–16°C).

Fertilizer: *From spring through fall,* feed every 2 weeks with a balanced liquid fertilizer mixed at half the normal strength. *In winter,* feed every 6 weeks.

Water: *From spring through fall,* keep soil lightly moist. *In winter,* allow soil to dry out between waterings. Beads flatten if the plant is underwatered, but this plant requires slightly less water than other succulents.

Soil: Cactus potting soil, or regular potting soil amended with one-third part sand.

Repotting: Repot annually in spring, or every 2 years if the growth of mature plants is so thick that it would be ruined by repotting. Propagate cuttings every few years, because older plants tend to decline.

Longevity: Up to 5 years, or indefinitely if propagated from stem cuttings.

Propagation: In early summer, take 4 in/10 cm-long stem cuttings, and press them into damp potting soil until the beads are almost covered. Keep lightly moist. New roots form quickly from the places where the beads join the stem.

Selections: A variegated form, in which the beads are sprinkled with yellow spots, is sometimes seen, but this plant is usually sold by its common name.

Display tips: Grow in a hanging basket, or in a broad dish so that the stems form a thick green groundcover over the surface.

FAMILY: **RUTACEAE**   ORIGIN: **CHINA**

Citrus × citrofortunella mitis

SIT-rus sit-ro-for-tu-NEL-a MY-tis

✕ CALAMONDIN ORANGE, MINIATURE ORANGE

Calamondin orange
(*Citrus × citrofortunella mitis*)

IF YOU HAVE SUFFICIENT ROOM inside a sunny, south-facing window for a 36 in/90 cm-tall plant, that plant should be calamondin orange or another small citrus fruit, such as 'Meyer' lemon. Both are easy to grow and can be counted upon to bear tart fruit almost year-round, beginning in their second year. The leaves give off a refreshing citrus scent when crushed, and the flowers are lightly fragrant as well.

The calamondin orange is a superior houseplant. A strong producer of 1 in/2.5 cm-wide, bright orange fruits, calamondin orange is actually a cross between a kumquat and an orange. The tart fruits can be used like lemons in cooking or can be made into marmalade. Taste them for bitterness first. If the rinds are very bitter, supplement the recipe with rinds from milder-flavored oranges. There is no rush to pick calamondins, as they remain in prime condition on the plants for several weeks. Young plants are available by mail, or you can grow one from a cutting taken from a friend's plant. As a precaution against citrus canker and various plant viruses, live citrus plants cannot be shipped to Arizona, California, Florida, or Texas. Shop for plants locally if you live in one of these states.

SPECIFICATIONS

◆ **Light:** Direct sun at least 4 hours a day year-round.

Temperature: Average room temperatures (65–75°F/18–24°C) year-round are ideal, though plants can accept cool (60°F/16°C) conditions in winter, and warmer (80°F/27°C) temperatures in summer.

Fertilizer: *In spring and summer,* feed plant every 2 weeks with a balanced plant food that includes micronutrients. *In fall and winter,* fertilize monthly.

Water: *In spring and summer,* keep soil lightly moist at all times. *In fall and winter,* allow the top inch of soil to dry between waterings. Mist plant twice weekly to increase humidity.

Soil: Any good potting soil.

Repotting: Repot young plants every 2 years. When 3- to 4-year-old plants fill an 8 in/20 cm pot, repot only every 2 to 3 years.

Longevity: 10 years or more.

Propagation: Root 4 in/10 cm-long stem tip cuttings in early summer (see page 299). Use rooting powder, and keep cuttings enclosed in a plastic bag to maintain high humidity. Cuttings root in 6 to 8 weeks.

Selections: When shopping for calamondin orange, buy from a reputable supplier to be sure you get cutting-grown plants. Many citrus fruits grow easily from seed, but they seldom fruit well. Very inexpensive plants are probably random seedlings that mature into substandard houseplants.

Display tips: To ensure good fruit set, dab flowers with a dry paintbrush to distribute pollen among the flowers.

TROUBLESHOOTING

Plant does not bloom.
CAUSE: Pot is too large; plant is overfertilized.
REMEDY: Keep young plants in pots no larger than 6 in/15 cm across. Reduce fertilizer, or switch to a cactus fertilizer or high phosphorous plant food.

Flowers drop without setting fruit.
CAUSE: Very dry air.
REMEDY: Keep a humidifier running in the room when flowers appear, or mist plant daily first thing in the morning. Do not mist when the sun is shining brightly, as leaf damage can occur.

Plant grows leggy, fruit causes branches to droop.
CAUSE: Needs pruning.
REMEDY: Keep older plants compact by pruning back long branches in spring. New branches will emerge from just below where older ones are tipped back.

Brown disc-shaped insects on leaves and stems.
CAUSE: Scale.
REMEDY: Several types of scale infest citrus fruits. On houseplant citrus, manage this pest by hand by removing them with your fingernail or a toothpick. Painting the scales with a cotton swab dipped in vegetable oil makes them easier to remove.

FAMILY: **GESNERIACEAE**   ORIGIN: **CENTRAL AND SOUTH AMERICA**

Columnea gloriosa hybrids

kol-UM-nee-a glo-ree-OH-sa

GOLDFISH PLANT

Goldfish plant
(*Columnea gloriosa*)

A VINING COUSIN TO AFRICAN VIOLETS, columnea is often called "goldfish plant" because of its curved tubular blossoms, which resemble leaping fish. Well-grown mature plants flower heavily in spring and summer, often producing dozens of blossoms at a time. Expect little or no blooming in winter when light levels are low. Maintaining somewhat dry soil in winter also promotes heavy spring flowering, but take care that the soil never dries out completely. In the wild, columnea grows in trees in shady tropical rain forests.

Columnea stems may grow to 36 in/90 cm long, but it is best to pinch them back to 18 in/45 cm or less, which encourages bushy growth. The arching stems typically rise 12 in/30 cm above the pot before cascading downward, so this is an ideal plant for a hanging basket. Some varieties have hairy leaves, while others feature glossy foliage. In winter, avoid wetting the leaves of either type when watering, as this can lead to problems with stem rot. Keep plant indoors in summer, as high temperatures or too much light can cause leaves to turn brown.

SPECIFICATIONS

Light: Moderate light from an east window, or fluorescent light.

Soil: Average room temperatures (65–75°F/18–24°C) year-round.

Fertilizer: *From spring through summer,* feed every 2 weeks with a high-phosphorous plant food mixed at half the recommended rate. *In winter,* feed monthly.

⬧ Water: *From spring through summer,* provide tepid water as often as needed to keep soil lightly moist. *In winter,* allow soil to become almost dry between waterings. Maintain moderate to high humidity year-round by misting plant daily or using a humidifier.

Soil: A light, porous mix such as African violet soil.

Repotting: Every 2 to 3 years, preferably in spring. Lightly prune roots of mature plants when repotting them rather than moving them into very large containers.

Longevity: 4 to 5 years, or indefinitely when propagated from stem tip cuttings.

Propagation: In spring or summer, root 3 in/7.5 cm-long, nonflowering stem tip cuttings as described on page 299. Newly rooted cuttings need to grow for at least a year before they begin blooming.

Selections: There are many named hybrids, which vary in leaf and flower color. Red-flowered 'Firebird' and 'Aladdin's Lamp' have dark green foliage, while 'California Gold', with yellow flowers edged with red, has bronzy green leaves. The red flowers of 'Light Prince' look dazzling among its white variegated foliage.

Display tips: Goldfish plant is always at its best when grown in a hanging basket.

TROUBLESHOOTING

Leaf tips turn brown.
CAUSE: Buildup of calcium in the soil.
REMEDY: Leach pots as described on page 263 monthly in summer. Use rainwater or distilled water whenever possible; avoid using a fertilizer that contains high amounts of calcium.

Leaves drop.
CAUSE: Cold conditions or very dry air.
REMEDY: Keep plant away from cold windows, as it is sensitive to chilling injury. Mist plant daily, especially in winter, or keep it in a room with a humidifier.

Stems wither and die.
CAUSE: Stem or root rot, caused by fungi in the soil.
REMEDY: Prune away damaged stem at soil line. Allow soil to dry out between waterings. Propagate stem tip cuttings from healthy stems, and pot them in fresh potting soil in clean pots. When cuttings show new growth, discard parent plant.

Leaves appear parched, with faint webbing on leaf undersides.
CAUSE: Spider mites.
REMEDY: Isolate plant, and prune off badly infested branches. Wipe leaf undersides with a soft cloth dipped in soapy water, and mist plant daily for a week. See page 274 for more information about this pest. Badly infested plants that do not quickly recover should be discarded.

White cottony deposits on stems.
CAUSE: Mealybugs.
REMEDY: Isolate plant, and pick off mealybugs with tweezers or a cotton swab dipped in alcohol. Repeat every few days until mealybugs are gone. See page 272 for more information about this pest.

FAMILY: **PRIMULACEAE**   ORIGIN: **SOUTHERN EUROPE AND TURKEY**

Cyclamen persicum hybrids

SY-kla-men PER-see-kum

CYCLAMEN, FLORISTS CYCLAMEN, PERSIAN VIOLET

Cyclamen *(Cyclamen persicum)*

THE CRISP, SHOOTING-STAR FLOWERS of cyclamens make lovely accents indoors in midwinter, their strongest season of bloom. From the centers of the plants, upright stems bear richly colored blooms with backswept petals in soft shades of pink and lilac, as well as bright red or snow white. New blooms replace the old for 2 months or more, all the while framed by lovely green heart-shaped leaves.

Many people discard cyclamens when they begin to deteriorate in spring, but they often can be brought back into bloom. Allow the foliage to dry until it withers in late spring, and then clip off the old foliage. Place the dormant plant in a cool, dark place for up to 3 months, providing just enough water to keep the roots from drying out completely. In late summer, return the container to a bright location, and repot the plant in fresh soil as soon as new growth appears. Resume watering and feeding, and blooms should emerge 2 to 3 months later.

SPECIFICATIONS

Light: Bright, including 1 to 2 hours of direct sun in winter.

Temperature: Cool (60–70°F/ 16–21°C) year-round. Plants can tolerate cold to around 40°F/4°C.

Fertilizer: Feed every 2 weeks with a high-phosphorous plant food, mixed at half strength. (Do not feed dormant plants.)

⚠ Water: Keep lightly moist at all times. Provide water by placing pot in a shallow container of tepid water for 15 to 30 minutes. When watering from the top, avoid getting water in the plant's crown.

Soil: Any good potting soil is fine. If you plan to keep a purchased plant for another year, promptly shift it to a slightly larger pot to provide room for growing roots.

Repotting: Repot soon after purchase and again following the plant's rest period, just before new growth commences in late summer.

Longevity: 6 months to several years. Regardless of age, discard plants that show weak growth or are plagued by pest problems.

Propagation: By seeds. Seeds are small and slow, so it's best to purchase new plants, which are usually seedlings less than a year old.

Selections: Varieties vary mostly in terms of size, which ranges from 6 in/15 cm tall for very dwarf selections to about 12 in/30 cm for larger varieties.

Display tips: Cyclamens are ideal plants for a sunny winter windowsill.

TROUBLESHOOTING

Leaves and flower stems collapse.
CAUSE: Dry soil.
REMEDY: Cyclamens are prone to sudden fainting spells when their roots dry out. Prompt watering will usually bring them back quickly. Stems or flowers that fail to respond to watering can be pinched off. If plants must be left unattended for a few days, move them out of the sun to help them retain water until you return.

Oldest leaves turn yellow and shrivel.
CAUSE: Accelerated aging caused by warm temperatures.
REMEDY: If possible, move plant to a place where it will remain cool at night. Pinch off old leaves as they fail and continue to feed and water plant regularly.

Mold appears near the soil's surface, some stems become limp and wither.
CAUSE: Gray mold or other stem rot.
REMEDY: The cool, moist conditions cyclamens need put them at high risk for fungal diseases that affect the crown of the plant. Try to keep the crown dry by watering plant from the bottom, or by dripping water just inside the edges of the pot. Improve air circulation by pinching out old flower stems and leaves. Discard badly affected plants.

Leaves are limp and pale; webby material on leaf undersides.
CAUSE: Spider mites or cyclamen mites.
REMEDY: Isolate plant and consider discarding it, because the ability of cyclamens to recover from a mite infestation is quite weak. If you want to try to save an infested plant, snip off badly affected leaves and treat plant with a neem-based insecticide.

FAMILY: **ASTERACEAE**   ORIGIN: **CHINA**

Dendranthema morifolium
hybrids (formerly known as *Chrysanthemum morifolium*)

den-DRAN-the-ma mor-i-FO-lee-um

CHRYSANTHEMUM

Chrysanthemum
(Dendranthemum morifolium)

COLORFUL AND AFFORDABLE, potted chrysanthemums also help remove chemical pollutants from indoor air. Their natural bloom season is autumn, but greenhouse growers bring them into bloom year-round by controlling how many hours of light the plants receive. Careful feeding regimens and growth regulators are also used to produce stocky plants crowned with large, uniform blossoms. If purchased when the blooms are just beginning to open, chrysanthemums often stay in bloom for 6 weeks or more.

Enjoy your potted mum while the blossoms last, because the plant will never look so good again. You can transplant it to a garden and possibly get another season of bloom, but many florist mums are not hardy in cold climates. Most people dispose of the plants after the last flowers fade. While you share company with them, do not allow pets to chew the foliage, which can be poisonous.

SPECIFICATIONS

Light: Bright to moderate.

Temperature: Cool temperatures (55–65°F/13–18°C). Flowers may be short lived if the plant is kept in a very warm room.

Fertilizer: No feeding is required.

Water: Keep soil constantly moist. Large plants often are quite rootbound and therefore need a little water every day.

Soil: If plants are loose in their pots, fill crevices with potting soil or sand.

Repotting: Not necessary. If you want to try growing your plant outdoors, cut back the branches to 3 in/7.5 cm long and keep the pruned plant in a cool, frost-free place until spring, after danger of hard freezes have passed. Plant it in a sunny section of your garden.

Longevity: A few weeks to a few years. Some florist mums are moderately winter hardy, and may grow as perennial plants in mild winter climates.

Propagation: If you want to grow outdoor mums, it is better to begin with a locally adapted garden mum than to use a florist mum. All chrysanthemums are easy to propagate by rooting stem cuttings.

Selections: Choose plants according to size and color. Light colors usually show best indoors. Most florist mums have dahlia-type flowers, but other forms such as spider, anemone, and rounded button-shaped blossoms sometimes are available.

Display tips: Combine small chrysanthemums with English ivy, Swedish ivy, or other trailing plants for temporary display. When plants have only a few good blossoms left, cut the stems and use them in small bouquets.

TROUBLESHOOTING

Buds fail to open.
CAUSE: Plant was severely stressed in transit or deprived of sufficient light.
REMEDY: Place plant where it will receive a few hours of direct sunlight and hope for the best. Buy plants that show one or two blossoms beginning to open.

Foliage wilts.
CAUSE: Too little water.
REMEDY: Sometimes pots are so packed with roots that the water you give them runs over the roots and down the insides of the pot rather than soaking in. Rehydrate badly dried-out roots by placing the pot in a pan of water for 30 minutes while also watering it from the top.

Small, wedge-shaped, green insects on plant stems or leaf undersides.
CAUSE: Aphids.
REMEDY: Rinse plant thoroughly with a fine spray of water. Apply a soap spray to kill any survivors. Dispose of badly infested plants.

Lower leaves turn yellow or brown while plant is still blooming.
CAUSE: This is a natural growth pattern for mums.
REMEDY: If you don't like looking at the failing foliage, cut the best bud-bearing stems, remove the lowest leaves, and display them in a vase. Cut chrysanthemum blossoms often last longer than flowers on living plants.

Euphorbia milii hybrids

you-FOR-bee-a MIL-ee-i

CROWN OF THORNS, SIAMESE LUCKY PLANT, SILVERTHORN, CHRIST'S THORN

Crown of thorns *(Euphorbia milii)*

BIBLICAL SCHOLARS CHALLENGE THE BELIEF that *Euphorbia milii* was the plant used to make Christ's crucifixion crown, yet it is still an apt name for this semi-succulent plant. In Thailand, it is often said that the plantkeeper's luck in life is foretold by the number of flowers his or her euphorbia produces. Today's hybrid versions should make you lucky indeed, because breeding improvements in the last two decades have resulted in euphorbias with bigger, more numerous blooms than ever before. The blooms are actually bracts, which persist for several weeks, and the plant's thorny, grooved stems add to its allure. Plant height, which can exceed 24 in/60 cm, is easily controlled with pruning of the growing tips.

Accepting of a wide range of temperatures, this euphorbia thrives in the dry air of modern homes and offices, and survives occasional neglect. When given abundant light and good care, it is capable of blooming almost year-round. Be careful, because this plant is poisonous if eaten, and the sap can cause skin irritation in sensitive individuals.

SPECIFICATIONS

Light: Bright, including direct sun for 3 to 4 hours each day.

Temperature: Plant grows best in average room temperatures (65–75°F/18–24°C), but can tolerate 50°F/10°C in winter and 90°F/32°C in summer.

Fertilizer: *From spring through fall,* feed every 2 weeks with a balanced, all-purpose plant food. *In winter,* feed monthly, diluting fertilizer to half the normal strength.

Water: *From spring through fall,* allow soil to dry to within 1 in/ 2.5 cm of the surface between waterings. *In winter,* when plants often rest, water less.

Soil: A light, fast-draining medium such as cactus potting soil.

Repotting: Every 2 years in late winter or early spring.

Longevity: 5 to 7 years, or indefinitely when propagated from stem tip cuttings.

Propagation: Take 3 in/7.5 cm stem tip cuttings, dip them in very warm water to stop the latex sap from bleeding, and allow them to dry for 24 hours. Keep the soil somewhat dry when rooting cut-tings as described on page 299. Cuttings root in about 6 weeks.

Selections: Red continues to be a very strong color, though Thai hybrids include plants that bloom yellow, pink, and peach. A compact patented variety, 'Short & Sweet', is often offered for sale.

Display tips: Keep plant in a very sunny window, where its thorny stems can be silhouetted by bright light.

TROUBLESHOOTING

Leaves turn yellow and drop.
CAUSE: Too much water.
REMEDY: This plant stores water in its thick stems, so it needs less water than other houseplants. Water less heavily and less often, especially in winter. Plants sometimes shed leaves in winter in response to low light, and regrow new foliage in spring.

Plant does not bloom.
CAUSE: Too young; not enough light.
REMEDY: Very young plants often do not bloom until their second spring. Strong light also promotes blooming, so consider moving your plant outdoors in summer. Then allow it to rest in a cool, well-lit room in winter. Spring is usually the strongest season for abundant blooms.

Leaves are present only at stem tips.
CAUSE: Natural growth habit, which can be improved with pruning.
REMEDY: When plants become tall and leggy, prune them back by half their size in late spring, and set the pruned growing tips to root in a separate container. New branches should emerge from lateral nodes below the pruning cut.

Small, wedge-shaped insects are present at new growing tips.
CAUSE: Aphids.
REMEDY: Various aphids that plague wild milkweeds can infest plants that are taken outdoors in summer. Clean plants with a fine spray of water, and treat with insecticidal soap if problem persists.

Euphorbia pulcherrima hybrids yu-FOR-bee-a pul-ker-EE-ma

POINSETTIA

Poinsettia
(Euphorbia pulcherrima)

THE MOST POPULAR OF ALL BLOOMING HOUSEPLANTS, yearly poinsettia sales now top 75 million plants. Almost all are sold during the winter holiday season, and plants that receive good care may keep their looks well into winter's second half. However, keeping the plants and regrowing them for a second season is quite difficult unless you live in a tropical climate where the plants can be kept outdoors. Indoors, the regrowing process involves pruning the plants hard in spring and then rooting the stem tips that emerge. Beginning in October, the plants must have 14 hours of continuous darkness nightly, for 8 to 10 weeks, before they will set buds.

Poinsettias come in various sizes, from 6 in/15 cm miniatures to big, bushy plants that stand 18 in/45 cm tall. Red and white are the most popular colors, but many others are available, including decorator-friendly shades of peach and burgundy. When buying plants, look for nicely colored bracts and deep green leaves. As soon as you bring your plant home, alter the decorative wrapping as needed to promote good drainage (see "Fixing Floral Wrappings," page 260). Poinsettias grow best when they receive bright light, but they don't mind being shifted about as needed to accommodate changing needs for space during the holiday season.

SPECIFICATIONS

Light: Bright filtered light.

Temperature: Average room temperatures (60–70°F/16–21°C). Cool conditions prolong bloom time.

Fertilizer: Not absolutely necessary, but plants purchased early in the season benefit from feeding with a high-phosphorous plant food every 2 weeks.

Water: Keep soil lightly moist at all times. Large plants often need water every other day.

Soil: Should repotting be needed, any good potting soil will do.

Repotting: Not generally needed unless stem cuttings are rooted in early summer and grown in small, 4 in/10 cm pots.

Longevity: Less than 1 year.

Propagation: Root stem tip cuttings in July and grow them outdoors in filtered shade.

Selections: There are hundreds of cultivars, and the names change often as improved varieties replace old ones. Choose plants based on colors you like, and be picky about the condition of the plants.

Display tips: Should a plant lose its leaves and become lanky while still holding bracts, cut them off and use them as cut flowers.

TROUBLESHOOTING

Bracts begin to show color but remain small and pale.
CAUSE: Plant needs more light.
REMEDY: Buying a young poinsettia in which the bracts have yet to mature is a good idea, but these plants need plenty of light and occasional feeding to help them attain perfection. After the pea-sized yellow flowers swell and open, the poinsettia is fully mature and can be placed in less light and given routine care.

Leaves drop within days after plant is purchased.
CAUSE: Chilling injury.
REMEDY: Poinsettias that are exposed to temperatures below 50°F/10°C often develop this problem. Purchase plant from a store where the plants are displayed far from cold entryways, and place plant in a roomy paper bag when carrying it to your car, which should be warm and ready to transport the plant home.

Leaves and bracts droop despite attentive watering.
CAUSE: Plant was kept wrapped in a restrictive sleeve too long; root rot due to overwatering.
REMEDY: Plastic or paper sleeves protect poinsettias in shipping, but these should be removed as soon as they arrive at the store. Do not buy plants that have not been set free from their sleeves unless they arrived at the store earlier in the day. Sleeving a plant for a quick ride home will do it no harm. Be careful not to overwater poinsettias, which often happens if the drainage holes in the bottom of the pot are blocked by decorative wrapping.

Bract color fades.
CAUSE: Too much sun.
REMEDY: Direct sun can bleach the bracts of deeply colored varieties, and the condition is irreversible.

FAMILY: **GENTIANACEAE**   ORIGIN: **SOCOTRA ISLANDS, OFF THE COAST OF EAST AFRICA**

Exacum affine eggs-AK-um a-FEEN
PERSIAN VIOLET, GERMAN VIOLET, ARABIAN VIOLET, TIDDLY-WINKS

Persian violet (*Exacum affine*)

A BEAUTIFUL BLOOMER that will bring color and fragrance to any room, exacum is often called Persian violet, but it is more closely related to garden impatiens than to true violets. Exacum can be grown outdoors in shady gardens, but it is most popular as an indoor blooming plant. The shiny green leaves studded with .5 in/ 1.25 cm-wide, bell-shaped, violet-blue flowers give this plant a refined look, and its neat, 12 in/30 cm-high, mounding form makes it a perfect fit for sunny windowsills.

As for disadvantages, exacum is a short-lived annual best regarded as a temporary color plant. If blossoms are pinched off as soon as they fade, and the plants get good light, water, and fertilizer, they may bloom for several months. More often, this plant blooms very heavily and then promptly begins to fail. For the longest possible show, choose a plant with buds that are just beginning to open, and deftly shift it to a slightly larger container. This eases watering challenges, as exacum often dries out quickly when kept in the bright light it finds most pleasing.

SPECIFICATIONS

Light: Bright light from a south, east, or west window.

Temperature: Average room temperatures (65–75°F/18–24°C).

Fertilizer: Feed every 2 weeks with a complete houseplant fertilizer that includes micronutrients.

Water: Keep soil constantly moist; mist plant regularly to boost humidity.

Soil: Potting soil amended with peat to increase acidity.

Repotting: Beneficial if plant is so rootbound that it is difficult to water. Do not disturb the roots during repotting.

Longevity: A few weeks to several months.

Propagation: Plants are usually grown from tiny seeds, which germinate in 2 to 3 weeks. Propagating plants from stem cuttings is possible, but not easy.

Selections: Most exacums feature violet-blue flowers, but varieties are occasionally offered in white or deep violet-purple. Indoors, lighter shades tend to show better than darker ones.

Display tips: Use exacum as a feature plant in your favorite room when the plant is in full bloom. Blossoms have a fleeting fragrance that is sweet yet light. When purchased in the summer, exacum can be kept outdoors on a shady patio and brought indoors when it attains full bloom.

TROUBLESHOOTING

Buds drop off before they open.
CAUSE: Shock from change of environment.
REMEDY: Find a hospitable spot for your exacum and give the plant regular water and a balanced plant food. New buds and blossoms should appear within 3 weeks.

Leaves specked with yellow; webby material on leaf undersides.
CAUSE. Spider mites.
REMEDY: See page 274 for details on identifying and treating this pest. Pinch off and dispose of all affected branches. Clean plant with a spray of water, isolate it, and mist three times daily. If problem persists, dispose of the plant.

Leaves are pale and crinkled.
CAUSE: Aphids.
REMEDY: Isolate plant and treat with insecticidal soap as described on page 278. Repeat after 5 days.

Plant wilts despite watering and gradually collapses.
CAUSE: Root rot.
REMEDY: This is not unusual with this plant. Discard the plant and thoroughly clean the container before using it to grow another houseplant.

FAMILY: **RUBIACEAE**   ORIGIN: **CHINA**

Gardenia jasminoides

gar-DEEN-ee-a jas-min-OY-dees

GARDENIA

Gardenia *(Gardenia jasminoides)*

FRAGRANT, SNOWY WHITE BLOSSOMS framed by glossy, dark green foliage make gardenia a popular gift plant. Perhaps you crave gardenia's intoxicating scent so much that you buy one for yourself, determined to grow this romantic little shrub near a sunny south window. Several varieties grow only 24 in/60 cm, and these dwarfs are often seen in stores around Easter, loaded with blossoms. Unable to resist, you snap one up.

In subsequent seasons, you will find that gardenia is not the easiest plant to bring into bloom, though plants that are happy with their situation will often bloom in late spring and again in the fall. In between, they enjoy spending the summer outdoors in a shady spot. Thoroughly clean plants before bringing them back indoors to prevent possible pest problems. In winter, keep the leaves lustrous by polishing them every 6 weeks with a soft cloth that has been lightly sprinkled with vegetable oil.

SPECIFICATIONS

Light: Bright light at least 4 hours daily, but not strong midday sun.

◈ Temperature: Cool (60°F/ 16°C) nights and warmer (75°F/ 24°C) days promote strong flowering.

Fertilizer: Feed plant every 2 weeks with a balanced houseplant fertilizer that contains micronutrients, especially iron, or use a slow-release azalea fertilizer sprinkled into the pot.

Water: Keep soil lightly moist, but do not overwater. Gardenias love high humidity, which is best provided with a humidifier or tray of damp pebbles.

Soil: An acidic mix of 2 parts potting soil and 1 part peat moss.

Repotting: Repot young plants annually in late winter until the roots fill 8 in/20 cm pots. After the root mass reaches this size, repot every 2 years to refresh the soil.

Longevity: Indoors, 10 years, more or less. Outdoors, plants live for decades.

Propagation: Root stem cuttings taken in spring or early summer. Rooting powder and high humidity are essential to success.

Selections: 'White Gem' is the most popular upright gardenia to grow in containers. Even when fully grown, it stands only 24 in/60 cm tall. Another dwarf variety, 'Radicans', has a semi-prostrate posture, which makes it a good plant for training as bonsai. A taller variety, 'Veitchii', often called everblooming gardenia, is a good choice for airy sunrooms or other large spaces.

Display tips: When your gardenia blooms, place it on a tabletop so the flowers will give off their perfume at nose level.

TROUBLESHOOTING

Leaves turn yellow though leaf veins remain green.
CAUSE: Nutritional disorder associated with high soil pH and low temperatures.
REMEDY: Move plant to a place where temperatures are above 70°F/21°C, and fertilize it with an azalea fertilizer that includes iron, magnesium, and sulfur.

Entire leaves turn yellow.
CAUSE: Overwatering.
REMEDY: Check drainage holes to make sure they are free of debris. Allow soil to dry slightly between waterings, so that the top inch of soil feels dry to the touch.

Flower buds fall off before they open.
CAUSE: Too little light, too much or too little water, high temperatures, or very dry air.
REMEDY: As soon as you see buds on your gardenia, spoil the plant by giving it perfect growing conditions. Situate it in a spot where it will get bright natural light for half the day, followed by cool nighttime temperatures. Wait until the blooms open to gently move the plant to a spot where you can easily enjoy its fragrance.

Leaves are pale with webby material on leaf undersides.
CAUSE: Spider mites.
REMEDY: Isolate plant, and spray it with water followed by insecticidal

soap. Repeat weekly until the infestation is controlled. It is best to take preventive measures by cleaning plant with plenty of warm water once a month. When bringing a gardenia indoors after a summer outside, spray it with insecticidal soap as a safety precaution.

White cottony masses on leaves and stems.
CAUSE: Mealybug.
REMEDY: Isolate plant and remove mealybugs with a cotton swab dipped in alcohol. Repeat weekly until mealybugs are controlled. See page 272 for additional information about this pest.

Geraniums

Bold and bright, geraniums are excellent candidates for summering outdoors, then bringing in to enjoy throughout winter indoors.

IN ADDITION TO THE GERANIUMS OFTEN GROWN OUTDOORS in the summer garden, there are several types that make outstanding houseplants. Historically, geraniums have been grown indoors longer than they have been enjoyed in the garden, and they are such interesting and rewarding houseplants that they definitely deserve wider use. The three types that make the best houseplants include fancy-leafed zonal geraniums, scented geraniums, and regal or Martha Washington geraniums, each of which is profiled individually in the following pages.

The geranium common name will probably persist forever, but more than 200 years ago these plants were reclassified as *Pelargonium,* a genus within the Geraniaceae family. The pelargonium name caught on in Europe, but North America has stuck by its use of the word geranium. In the interest of accuracy, they will be called pelargoniums here. However, from a practical point of view, you should be prepared to use the names geranium and pelargonium interchangeably when shopping for plants.

You will probably need to seek out houseplant-worthy geraniums. Many strains that were popular parlor plants in Victorian times have been preserved and propagated by specialty growers; they are available by mail if you can't find them locally. There also are modern varieties with much to offer, for example hybrids that combine the exotic leaf color of zonals with deliciously scented foliage borrowed from scented types, and regals that produce huge flowers in late winter.

Indeed, because pelargoniums have been so extensively hybridized, the dividing lines between the three types have become blurred. Once upon a time, zonals were grown for color, scenteds for fragrance, and regals for off-season bloom. These days, you may be able to have it all in one plant. Still, you do need to know whether your plant should be handled as a zonal, scented, or regal type. This is important, because the three types vary in their seasonality, water requirements, and a few other cultural details. Use the chart on page 106 to help identify which type of pelargonium you have, or wish to have. Then turn to the appropriate profile page for detailed information on how to bring out its best talents as a houseplant. The Troubleshooting section on page 105 explores possible problems, which all types of pelargonium have in common.

TROUBLESHOOTING

Old florets shrivel before all the buds in the cluster open.
CAUSE: This is normal for many geraniums.
REMEDY: Use a small pair of scissors to clip out the withered florets. When most of the flowers in the cluster have peaked, clip off the blossom-bearing stem where it rises from the main branch.

New leaves are small; older leaves turn yellow.
CAUSE: Insufficient fertilizer.
REMEDY: Increase feeding by adding a half ration of soluble plant food to the water at each watering, or by feeding at the rate recommended on the fertilizer package once a week.

Plants develop lush leaves but no flowers.
CAUSE: Too much fertilizer.

REMEDY: Reduce the amount or frequency of plant food. If you are using a balanced or high-nitrogen plant food, switch to high-phosphorous fertilizer.

Old leaves turn yellow, then brown.
CAUSE: This is a normal growth pattern, or plant may be reacting to reduced light.
REMEDY: When grooming plants, routinely remove old leaves that have begun to yellow. Many older leaves may turn yellow and drop if you do not prune back plants before bringing them indoors after allowing them to spend the summer on a porch or patio.

Buds have small holes in them and fail to open.
CAUSE: Small caterpillars called budworms, common outdoors but rare indoors.
REMEDY: Clip off affected buds and dispose of them. Clean plants

with a fine spray of water. New buds that emerge 2 to 3 weeks later should be free of this pest.

Rusty brown spots on leaves; affected leaves turn brown and drop off.
CAUSE: Bacterial leaf spot.
REMEDY: Trim off affected leaves if there are only a few of them. Prune off affected branches. Repot plant in fresh soil, using a clean container. If problem persists, dispose of plant and start over with a disease-free specimen.

Leaves dry and parched; faint webbing on leaf undersides.
CAUSE: Spider mites.
REMEDY: Isolate plant and attempt to control the mites as described on page 274. Discard badly affected plants, or prune them back severely and hope for the best.

Regal geraniums are often sold as winter-flowering houseplants.

Getting to Know Pelargoniums

In the following pages, the three best types of pelargonium to grow indoors are described in detail. They are listed by botanical name, which are often somewhat generic hybrids. In fact, the parentage of some varieties is so complex that species names have been dropped altogether! Name or no name, use this chart to identify what type of geranium you have, and then turn to the appropriate plant profile to get to know your pelargonium better.

Pelargonium species and hybrids	Scented geranium	Numerous species vary in size and growth habit. Leaves tend to be finely cut and slightly hairy, and release various fruity or spicy scents when crushed. Citrus-scented varieties often have small leaves and compact growth habits. Pink to white flowers appear in early summer.
Pelargonium × *domesticum*	Regal geranium, Martha Washington geranium	Potentially large plants thrive in cool weather and bloom heavily in winter when given proper care. Large, showy flowers appear in clusters, making these popular gift plants. Plants rest in summer.
Pelargonium × *hortorum*	Zonal geranium, fancy-leafed geranium	Foliage shows circular variegation patterns of green, red, and white that vary with variety and are most vivid in strong light and cool temperatures; good indoor varieties stay compact and bloom intermittently almost year-round. A few zonals have scented leaves.

Regal geraniums remain old favorites for the garden and as houseplants.

Pelargonium species and hybrids

pel-ar-GO-nee-um

SCENTED GERANIUM

Scented geranium hybrid
(*Pelargonium* 'Atomic
Snowflake')

EACH LEAF OF A SCENTED GERANIUM is laden with special cells that explode with fragrance at the slightest touch. Scents range from citrus to chocolate to rose. The apple-scented species (*P. odoratissimum*) and old-fashioned rose (*P. graveolens*) are large, vigorous plants, but many selections are much daintier in size. Nutmeg (*P. × fragrans*) is often recommended for beginners, and most citrus-scented pelargoniums are small plants that fit easily on a sunny windowsill. The leaves of most scented strains are crinkled and more finely cut than those of the zonal types. A few are valued as much for their flowers as for their fragrance, but scented geraniums are usually light bloomers.

Most scented-leaf pelargoniums never become dormant, though they are willing to rest in winter in a cool basement. If you try this method of off-season care, keep the roots quite dry, watering only enough to keep the plants from shriveling. Otherwise, keep your plant in good light year-round, but push it to produce new growth only in spring and summer.

SPECIFICATIONS

Light: Bright light from a south or west window. Many people shift plants outdoors in summer, and allow them to become semi-dormant in winter.

Temperature: Cool to average room temperatures (60–75°F / 16–24°C).

Fertilizer: *From spring through fall*, feed plants every 2 weeks with a balanced, all-purpose houseplant food that includes micronutrients. *In winter*, do not feed.

Water: Allow soil to dry to within .5 in/1.25 cm of the surface between waterings in spring and summer. Water much less in winter, but do not allow roots to dry out completely.

Soil: Any good potting soil that drains well.

Repotting: Annually in spring.

Longevity: 3 to 4 years for individual plants, which can be kept indefinitely when propagated from rooted stem cuttings.

◆ Propagation: Soon after new growth appears in spring, take 3 in/ 7.5 cm-long stem tip cuttings and set them to root as described on page 299.

Selections: Revered old varieties include 'Mrs. Taylor', with red flowers and pungent lemony leaves. 'Old Spice' smells like its namesake fragrance.

Display tips: Don't be reluctant to pinch and sniff leaves of scented geraniums. When pruning, save leaves to dry and use in potpourri.

FAMILY: **GERANIACEAE**   ORIGIN: **SOUTH AFRICA**

Pelargonium × domesticum

pel-ar-GO-nee-um do-MES-ti-kum

REGAL GERANIUM, MARTHA WASHINGTON GERANIUM

Regal geranium
(*Pelargonium × domesticum*)

REGAL GERANIUMS ARE OFTEN CALLED Martha Washingtons, the name of a once-famous cultivar. Regals are often sold as winter-flowering houseplants, and they are commonly grown outdoors in climates where nights stay cool through summer, such as the West Coast. The plants are not at all difficult to keep alive, but it can be challenging to get them to rebloom well. The key is to follow a special seasonal rhythm of care. In early summer after flowering stops, cut plants back to about 4 in/10 cm, repot them, and allow them to rest inside for a month. Give them enough water to keep them alive, but wait until midsummer to begin feeding them. When nights cool to below 55°F/13°C in fall, place plants outdoors for at least 6 weeks. Plants use this cool conditioning period to develop buds, which may not show until midwinter. Look for large, dramatic flower clusters in February or March.

SPECIFICATIONS

Light: *In winter and early spring,* bright light from a south or west window. *In fall,* filtered sun outdoors.

Temperature: *In winter and early spring,* average room temperatures (60–75°F/16–24°C). *In summer,* plants rest. *In fall,* provide 6 to 8 weeks of cool temperatures (45–60°F/7–16°C).

Fertilizer: *From late summer through winter and spring,* feed plants every 2 weeks with a high-phosphorous plant food. Do not feed in early summer when plants rest.

Water: Keep soil lightly moist at all times, allowing soil to dry to within .5 in/1.25 cm of the surface between waterings.

Soil: Any good potting soil that drains well.

Repotting: Annually in late summer, to provide clean containers and fresh potting mix.

Longevity: 3 years, or indefinitely when propagated from rooted stem cuttings.

Propagation: Root stem tip cuttings in spring or fall, as described on page 299.

Selections: The famous 'Martha Washington' variety has been replaced by more vigorous, disease-resistant hybrids such as the 'Elegance' series, which grow into large plants to 36 in/90 cm and wide, or the more restrained 'Maiden' varieties, which are easier to grow in 6 in/15 cm pots.

Display tips: Use broad pots or hanging baskets to showcase these beautiful off-season bloomers.

Pelargonium × hortorum pel-ar-GO-nee-um hor-TOR-um
ZONAL GERANIUM, FANCY-LEAFED GERANIUM

Zonal geranium
(*Pelargonium × hortorum*)

COMMON GARDEN GERANIUMS are zonal types, but there are much showier varieties that make beautiful and rewarding houseplants. These special pelargoniums have graced sunny windows for many decades. Leaf variegation often appears in halo patterns, with a red or bronze halo ringing the leaf's center, and white bands or splashes near the margin. Varieties with mostly green leaves are valued for their flowers, which often are produced year-round when plants are pruned periodically to force out new growth.

Do look into these wonderful, collectible, fancy-leafed pelargoniums, but in the meantime you can also coax bedding geraniums, which also are zonal types, into bloom. In late summer, gradually move outdoor-grown plants to shadier quarters to acclimate them to reduced light. Even when acclimated, zonal geraniums often shed half their leaves when they are moved indoors, so don't be alarmed. Clean up after them, and prune off up to half of the long, brittle branches. Blooming should resume after 3 to 5 weeks.

SPECIFICATIONS

Light: Bright light from a south or west window.

⚠ Temperature: Cool to average room temperatures (60–75°F / 16–24°C)

Fertilizer: Feed plants every 2 weeks with a balanced houseplant food that includes micronutrients.

Water: Allow soil to dry to within 1 in/2.5 cm of the surface between waterings, but do not allow the roots to become so dry that the plants wilt.

Soil: Any good potting soil that drains well; some people add a handful of sand to standard potting soil to improve drainage when potting geraniums.

Repotting: Annually in spring to provide a clean pot and fresh potting soil.

Longevity: 3 years, or indefinitely when propagated from rooted stem cuttings.

Propagation: When new growth emerges in spring, take 3–4 in/ 7.5–10 cm-long stem tip cuttings and root them as described on page 299. Some varieties are much easier to propagate than others.

Selections: Once-popular dwarf varieties with variegated leaves, such as 'Skies of Italy', are well worth seeking out. In addition, some zonals have scented leaves, including pink-flowered 'Roger's Delight', 'Prince Rupert Variegated', and many others.

Display tips: Grow geraniums in good-quality terra-cotta pots that feature simple relief patterns. Geraniums are among the cheeriest plants you can grow in an office that includes a spot of bright sunlight.

LVACEAE   ORIGIN: **CHINA**

Hibiscus rosa-sinensis hybrids   hi-BIS-kus RO-sa-si-NEN-sis

HIBISCUS, HAWAIIAN ROSE

Hibiscus (*Hibiscus rosa-sinensis*)

THE STATE FLOWER OF HAWAII, hibiscus bears the largest blossoms that can be produced by an indoor plant. Some measure more than 8 in/20 cm across, and all feature crepe-paper-textured petals that flare around a prominent yellow stamen. Individual blossoms last only 2 to 3 days, but well-adjusted plants often bloom intermittently from late spring to late fall.

Hibiscus plants need warmth, so they are best grown near a south or west window. If possible, move them outdoors in summer to a place where they will receive partial sun. Be sure to bring them back indoors before night temperatures fall to 50–55°F/10–13°C. You can control the size of your hibiscus by pruning the plant lightly in early summer and more aggressively in fall. Hibiscus blooms form on the tips of new branches, which emerge from just below where older branches are tipped back.

SPECIFICATIONS

Light: Bright, including some direct sun.

Temperature: Warm (65–85°F/ 18–29°C).

Fertilizer: *From spring through summer,* feed every 2 weeks with a balanced liquid fertilizer. *In winter,* feed monthly. Alternatively, fertilize twice yearly with a high-nitrogen, controlled-release fertilizer. Special hibiscus fertilizer has an analysis of 18-5-23.

Water: *In warm weather,* water as often as needed to keep soil lightly moist at all times. *In winter,* allow soil to dry to within 1 in/2.5 cm of surface between waterings.

Soil: A light-textured potting soil that contains perlite and peat.

Repotting: Annually in fall, prune back stems by one-third, and also trim off about one-fourth of roots before repotting.

Longevity: 5 to 10 years for most hybrids.

Propagation: Many hibiscus can be propagated by rooting 6 in/ 15 cm-long stem tip cuttings as described on page 299. Many hibiscus are grafted onto special rootstocks, so rooted cuttings may not show the vigor of their parent.

Selections: There are dozens of named varieties in shades of pink, blue, red, and yellow, with many bicolors. 'Dragon's Breath' features bold red, 8 in/20 cm blossoms with white swirls in the centers. 'The Path' is bold yellow with magenta centers.

Display tips: Grow plants in pots that can be slipped inside larger planters equipped with wheels so they are easy to move outdoors in summer.

TROUBLESHOOTING

Buds drop off soon after they form.
CAUSE: Environmental stress or weak cultivar.
REMEDY: Any type of stress that strikes when buds are swelling can cause plants to give up their will to bloom. Water attentively after buds appear, and avoid moving bud-bearing plants unnecessarily. Varieties that produce large, double flowers are more likely to drop buds than those that bear single blossoms.

Leaves turn yellow and drop off.
CAUSE: Normal in fall, but excessive leaf drop can be caused by sudden reduction in light.
REMEDY: Plants that are grown outdoors in summer — and even those kept indoors year-round — often shed some of their leaves when returned to comparatively dim indoor rooms. To keep shedding to a minimum, gradually accustom plants to less light.

Leaves appear parched, with pale yellow specks.
CAUSE: Spider mites.
REMEDY: Prevent this problem by washing off leaf undersides with plenty of water once a month. See page 276 for details on identifying this pest. If spider mites are present, isolate plant, prune off badly infested branches, and spray plant daily with water. Use insecticidal soap if problem persists.

Leaves small and misshapen.
CAUSE: Too much phosphorous in fertilizer.
REMEDY: Some hibiscus are sensitive to high amounts of phosphorous (the middle number in a fertilizer's analysis). Leach pots as described on page 263 and switch to a low-phosphorous fertilizer.

FAMILY: **OLEACEAE**   ORIGIN: **CHINA**

Jasminum polyanthum

jas-MIN-um po-lee-AN-thum

JASMINE, CHINESE JASMINE, WINTER-BLOOMING JASMINE

Jasmine (*Jasminum polyanthum*)

A VINING MEMBER OF THE OLIVE FAMILY, jasmine is grown for its twining stems, glossy green leaves, and fragrant flowers that appear in winter. This vine can be grown outdoors through Zone 8, but it is not difficult to keep as a houseplant provided you follow its natural growth rhythms. In summer, give it a very sunny spot where warmth and light will encourage vigorous growth. Move it outdoors in fall to expose it to 6 weeks of cool temperatures (40–60°F/ 4–16°C). Jasmine uses this cool period to set buds, which will remain very small until late winter. Plants typically bloom in February, when the clusters of pink buds open into starry white flowers. Fragrance is often strongest at night.

After the flowers fade, prune back the plants and allow them to rest for a month or more. Pruning is needed to control this plant's size, which can easily exceed 5 ft/1.5 m. With hard pruning in spring and occasional trimming during the summer, jasmine will grow into a graceful vine that needs little help twining around whatever support you provide.

SPECIFICATIONS

Light: *From late spring through fall,* bright light, including 4 hours of direct sun. *In winter,* moderate to bright light.

⚠ **Temperature:** *In fall,* cool outdoor temperatures (40–60°F/ 4–16°C). *In winter,* average room temperatures (65–75°F/18–24°C). *From late spring through summer,* warm outdoor temperatures (70–85°F/21–29°C).

Fertilizer: *From spring through fall,* feed every 2 weeks with a high-phosphorous plant food. *In winter,* feed monthly.

Water: *From early summer through fall,* keep lightly moist, allowing soil to dry to within .5 in/ 1.25 cm of the surface between waterings. *In fall,* water less. *In late winter and spring,* keep plant slightly dry during this resting period.

Soil: Any good potting soil.

Repotting: Annually in spring after aggressive pruning. Install some type of support when repotting plant.

Longevity: Many years, or indefinitely when propagated from stem tip cuttings.

Propagation: Take 4 in/10 cm stem tip cuttings in early summer and root them as described on page 299.

Selections: In addition to Chinese jasmine, Arabian jasmine (*J. sambac*) features stronger fragrance, but is more difficult to grow since it requires very warm, humid conditions.

Display tips: Train plant to twine around a hoop or up a slender post. Keep it in a bright window when it comes into bloom in late winter.

TROUBLESHOOTING

Plant does not bloom.
CAUSE: Lack of cool conditioning in the fall.
REMEDY: Jasmine sets its buds in the fall, and cool conditions are needed to ensure good budset. Keep plant outdoors for 6 weeks when the weather cools in the fall. If you have no place to condition plant outdoors, keep it in your coolest room in October and November.

White cottony masses on leaves and stems.
CAUSE: Mealybugs.
REMEDY: Mealybugs love this plant. If they appear in late winter, after the plant has bloomed, severely prune it before removing survivors by hand using tweezers or a cotton swab dipped in alcohol. If the problem persists, spray plant with insecticidal soap. When plant is moved outdoors in summer, natural predators may bring mealybugs under control.

Leaves turn yellow and drop.
CAUSE: Too much water, insufficient light, or needs pruning.
REMEDY: Water only enough to keep soil lightly moist. Jasmine needs strong light, and will languish in low light conditions. Plants that are not pruned hard in spring often become bare at the base as they shed old leaves.

New growth slow; few new leaves.
CAUSE: Insufficient light.
REMEDY: Place plant in a very sunny spot in spring and summer, or move it outdoors to partial shade.

Orchids

By selecting the right varieties, anyone can grow at least a few orchids successfully.

IF YOU LOVE BEAUTIFUL FLOWERING HOUSEPLANTS, sooner or later you will want to grow an orchid. Or several! It takes but a little success with these interesting plants to want more, and despite their finicky reputation, many orchids are easy to grow. In the next few pages, you will be introduced to the five types of orchids that are widely recommended for beginners: cattleyas or corsage orchids (*Cattleya*); "dens," sometimes called spray orchids (*Dendrobium*); dancing ladies (*Oncidium*); lady's slippers (*Paphiolpedilum*); and moth orchids (*Phalaenopsis*). Orchids can be costly, so it pays to learn a little about them before buying your first plants.

The Orchidaceae family is extremely large and diverse, with 28,000 species occurring in a wide range of environments, from tropical rain forests to dry alpine rock outcroppings. Orchids that adapt easily to homes and offices are mostly forest-dwellers that live in the wild on tree limbs and rocks.

Over the last 200 years — and especially in the late 1800s — orchid hunters took millions of orchids from their native habitats and shipped them to wealthy patrons. But orchids are no longer greenhouse flowers only for the rich. New methods of propagation, including tissue culture, in which thousands of plantlets can be grown in test tubes from a small piece of parent plant, and seeds sprouted in flasks under laboratory conditions, have made orchids much more affordable, while helping to prevent further pilfering of dwindling natural populations. However, because even tissue-cultured orchids do not begin blooming until they are 5 to 6 years old, orchids remain somewhat costly. And it is still true that some orchids, for example those that produce the huge blossoms used in corsages, are best grown in a greenhouse where light, temperature, and humidity can be tailored to meet the preferences of plants rather than people.

Caring for Orchids

Botanically, orchids are among the most highly evolved flowers on Earth. In orchids, the male and female flower parts are fused into one anatomical organ, called the *column*. For pollination to take place, the right insect must be drawn into the flower and then crawl about a bit, so orchid flowers have evolved with this specific purpose in mind. When you admire the intricate structures and markings in an orchid blossom, you are seeing the stage upon which a tricky pollination play will be performed.

Orchids do produce seeds, but they are extremely tiny and require the presence of helpful fungi before they can germinate and grow. In modern times, it has been learned that orchid seeds can be germinated successfully in agar jelly, and this has led to a boom in orchid hybridization. In the world of orchids, it is not only possible to cross-breed different species, but genera as well.

Light: Most orchids grow best in bright, indirect light from a south window, but lady's slippers and moth orchids need less. They often thrive in an east or west window, or when grown under fluorescent lights. To help you choose the best plants for your situation, the chart on page 124 compares the light and temperature preferences of the easiest orchids. Outdoors, place orchids in filtered shade where they will receive little, if any, direct sun, and also be shielded from prevailing wind.

Lady's slipper orchids (*Paphiopedilum* species and hybrids) need less light than other species, and each bloom includes a prominent pouch, or slipper.

The growth habits of orchids are as variable as the flowers. *Left to right:* hybrid forms of *Cattleya*, *Dendrobium*, *Phalaenopsis*, *Oncidium*, *Paphiopedilum*.

Temperature: The orchids presented here are appropriate for a range of possible growing conditions. The one thing all orchids have in common is a need for a 15–20°F/8–10°C difference between day and night temperatures. The plant profiles suggest the best range for each type of orchid, which can be cool (60°F/16°C nights and 75°F/24°C days), intermediate (65°F/18°C nights and 80°F/27°C days), and warm (70°F/21°C nights and 85°F/29°C days). There is some leeway here, but choosing an appropriate orchid for the place you have to grow it is crucial if you want a healthy, heavy-flowering plant.

Orchids benefit from being moved outdoors in summer, particularly those that like warm temperatures. Check the preferred temperature range for your plants, and wait until weather conditions are perfect to gradually accustom them to increased light. You may want to keep plants indoors that show signs of imminent bloom. Slugs, snails, and random insects find the buds irresistible. If you live in a hot climate, keep cool-natured orchids indoors through the summer. (See page 291 for more details on moving plants outdoors in summer and bringing them back inside in the fall.)

Soil: Potting soil for orchids is not potting soil at all, but rather a mixture of coarsely chopped fir bark or redwood bark, with small amounts of peat moss, perlite, or vermiculite mixed in. This mixture (or something similar; there are many variations) drains quickly and there is room between the particles for air to reach the orchid's roots. Orchid mix decomposes slowly over a period of 2 years, which is the usual repotting interval for orchids. Large garden centers stock orchid mix, or it can be purchased from orchid growers or specialty supply companies (see Resources on page 337). Orchid mix is also good for potting most bromeliads.

Fertilizer: Orchids are slow growers by nature, but they need regular feeding, since their potting medium offers meager nutrients. Many growers use the phrase "weekly-weakly" to describe their feeding practices, which consists of mixing a high-nitrogen houseplant fertilizer, such as those recommended for foliage plants, at one-fourth the normal strength, and giving it to plants

The intricate markings in orchid flowers are intended to lure pollinating insects. In the wild, many orchids require the work of obscure native bees that are as rare as the orchids they pollinate.

Orchid breeders have developed complex hybrids that often involve parents from different genera, which is an unusual accomplishment in the world of plants.

about once a week. When you see signs that your plant is developing flowers, you might switch to a dilute high-phosphorous fertilizer for a few weeks. If plants are moved outdoors in summer, you may want to increase the rate of fertilizer to one-half the normal strength to compensate for the nutrients that are washed away by frequent watering. Some spray orchids shed their leaves and rest in winter. Do not feed resting plants. The plant profiles make specific suggestions for fertilizing different types of orchids.

Water: The watering needs of orchids vary with their origins. Those that naturally grow in tree crotches or on rocks need to dry out between waterings, while ground-dwelling species, such as most lady's slippers, need a steady supply of moisture. Many orchids have swollen stems, called pseudobulbs, which function as water-holding organs. Like succulent plants, orchids with pseudobulbs can gather and store moisture until it is needed. The plant profiles give specific watering instructions, but when in doubt, err on the dry side. Orchids are easily damaged by too much water.

Many orchids bloom on arching stems, which makes them even more graceful and beautiful.

Dancing ladies orchids (*Oncidium*) are beloved for the number of small blossoms they carry at any one time.

Orchids are also sensitive to salts that accumulate in the growing medium, so they should be flushed monthly in summer. Thoroughly water plants, allow excess water to drain away, and then repeat.

The orchids described here need moderate humidity, in the 50 percent range. Mist plants often with clean rainwater or distilled water, which do not leave salt deposits on the leaves like tap water sometimes does. Mist lightly yet often, and never so heavily that water accumulates in the crown of the plant. Setting plants on a tray filled with damp pebbles increases humidity as well, as does placing open bowls of water near the plants. If you have a number of plants to satisfy that need moderate humidity, running a humidifier is an easy answer. See page 266 for more ways to increase humidity for houseplants.

Repotting: Most orchids need repotting every 2 years, but flowering is best when the plants are slightly rootbound. The main reason to repot a plant is to provide it with fresh potting medium, since orchid potting mix decomposes over time. The best time to repot an orchid is summer, or whenever the plant appears to be in a very active period of growth.

How you repot (and propagate) orchids depends on their growth habit. But don't assume that you should divide a plant that simply needs repotting. Orchids usually grow and bloom best when they are divided infrequently, and large plants are easier to care for than smaller ones. Still, understanding the growth habit of your plant is basic to proper repotting. Two terms often are used to describe the growing habits of orchids.

- *Monopodial,* or upright orchids, develop stems that emerge from a crown, or "foot." When the plant is mature, flower spikes emerge from the stem, usually in the midsection between the leaves. Lady's slippers and moth orchids are usually monopodial.
- *Sympodial,* or creeping orchids, develop a shallow creeping rhizome. The tip of the rhizome sends out a green shoot that eventually flowers. Cattleyas, dendrobiums, and oncidiums are sympodial.

By the time you need to repot your orchid, you will probably know it well enough to recognize its growth habit.

Thoroughly soak roots before repotting, which makes the roots less brittle and prone to breakage. You may need a screwdriver or table knife to pry an orchid out of a tight pot; sometimes it is necessary to shatter a clay pot to free a rootbound orchid. Examine the roots, use scissors or pruning shears that have been sterilized in boiling water to clip off any that are black or mushy, and tease out

Many fancy corsage orchids (*Cattelya*) are not difficult to grow if you can provide them with plenty of warmth.

the old potting mix. Then rinse the roots with lukewarm water to remove trapped bits of old potting mix. With creeping species that form pseudobulbs, cut off the oldest pseudobulb, with roots attached, and dispose of it.

Place broken crockery or coarse gravel in the bottom of a new or thoroughly clean pot, and fill it two thirds full with damp orchid potting mix. With sympodial orchids, set the groomed plant in the pot a little off center, so that the oldest pseudobulb is close to the edge but there is at least 1 in/2.5 cm of space between the newest growing tip and the edge of the pot. Add more potting mixture, tamping it in with a stick. When you're finished, the rhizome should still be visible at the surface, about .5 in/1.25 cm below the edge of the pot. If necessary, tie the plant to a slender stake to hold it upright. Orchid-supply companies sell special wires, called rhizome clips, that hold plants in position by anchoring them to the edge of the pot.

After grooming a monopodial orchid, place it in the center of a prepared pot, and repot it at the same depth it grew in its previous container. With all orchids, it is important to tamp the pot well to help settle the planting medium firmly around the roots. Tap the pot on a hard surface several times, and gently press it down from the top. The medium should be sufficiently firm that the plant does not fall out when you hold the container sideways.

Be careful not to overwater a newly repotted orchid. Allowing it a dry rest for a few days helps it seal off damaged roots. Wait a month after repotting to resume feeding your orchid.

Propagating: Orchids will let you know when they need to be propagated, and a close look at the plant will suggest how it should be done. Dendrobiums produce aerial roots, so you can cut off the top of the plant, with roots attached, and simply pot it up. Cattleyas, dancing ladies, and other orchids that produce pseudobulbs can be cut into clusters of three during routine repotting. Lady's slippers form clumps, which can be divided every 4 to 6 years. Moth orchids and dendrobiums often develop small plantlets, called *keikis*, on the flower stem close to the parent plant. When the keikis have three leaves and a 3 in/7.5 cm-long root, clip them off and plant them in small pot. Then baby the keiki as if it were a newly set rooted stem cutting (see page 299).

More details on propagating different types of orchids are given in the plant profiles, but these general guidelines apply:

- When propagating orchids, set the small plants in 4 in/10 cm pots so they will grow a tight, compact root system.
- Mist newly propagated plants daily for several weeks to maintain high humidity, which reduces demands on scant roots.

After propagating, orchids may not bloom for a year, or sometimes two. It is therefore wise not to propagate orchids until it is necessary, which is usually every 5 years.

Some orchids, especially dendrobiums, develop aerial roots on their stems. Cut the stem below the roots, and transplant the cutting to a small pot, kept in a warm, humid environment.

Paphiopedilum with mottled leaves, like this one, generally needs more warmth than does one with green leaves.

Small details: Take your time when shopping for orchids. It is always best to buy from a local grower so the plants will not be traumatized in shipping. Local growers also may make excellent suggestions on good beginner varieties for your area.

Instead of buying plants in full bloom, look for mature plants or those that are just beginning to produce a flower spike. Orchids that are on the verge of blooming cost a few dollars more than those that are not yet in a flowering mood. When you can "interview" prospective "or-kids" in person, look for big, plump roots and lots of them, and no bruises or soft spots on the crowns.

If you cannot buy orchids from a local grower, there are many excellent mail-order sources. The American Orchid Society (see Resources on page 339) keeps an up-to-date list at their website. Rare orchids cost much more than varieties that have been around a long time. As a beginner, it's best to stick with proven varieties.

Growing one orchid is a satisfying experience, but orchids have a way of turning people into collectors rather quickly. Keeping a collection usually requires a greenhouse, or at least a window outfitted with a greenhouse extension. If you fall in love with growing orchids, be forewarned that other life modifications will probably follow.

TROUBLESHOOTING

Plant does not bloom.
CAUSE: Improper temperature range, too much fertilizer; not enough light.
REMEDY: Orchids must have a 10–20°F/6–9°C difference between night and day temperatures, and only enough nutrients to keep them from going hungry. Plants also may not bloom if they are younger than 5 years old or are deprived of sufficient light. Most importantly, you should choose orchids that suit the growing conditions you have to offer.

Leaf tips turn brown.
CAUSE: Overfertilization; improper watering.
REMEDY: This is a common sign of fertilizer burn in orchids. Dilute the plant food to one-fourth the rate recommended on the label. Water according to the preference of the orchid you have chosen.

White cottony masses on leaves.
CAUSE: Mealybugs.
REMEDY: This is the most serious insect pest of orchids. Practice preventive care by wiping leaves periodically with a soft, damp cloth. If a plant becomes infested, isolate it and attempt to remove mealybugs by hand, using a cotton swab dipped in alcohol. See page 273 for other methods of controlling this pest.

Flowers have small, brown, circular spots.
CAUSE: Petal blight, a fungal disease.
REMEDY: Remove affected blossoms. In the future, increase air circulation around the plants to prevent the occurrence of this problem.

Leaves turn an unusually light green color.
CAUSE: Excessive sun.
REMEDY: Move plant to a shadier spot.

Leaves show unusual crinkles and blotches; new growth is slow.
CAUSE: Virus infection; several viruses infect orchids, and they can be spread by insects or by humans when plants are handled or repotted.
REMEDY: Destroy affected plants. Sterilize scissors, knives, and other cutting instruments used in repotting by dipping them in boiling water just before using them.

Leaves show ragged holes along edges.
CAUSE: Slugs or snails.
REMEDY: When plants are placed outdoors, they become easy targets for these leaf-eating pests. Place saucers of beer beside plants. The slugs will drink it, fall in, and drown. Where these pests are truly terrible, you can buy copper tape and fasten it to the tray or table upon which orchids are kept. Slugs and snails are deterred when they come upon a copper barrier.

Orchids

Getting to Know Orchids

The five species groups described below, listed in alphabetical order by botanical name, are good orchids for beginners. Start with an orchid that accepts the light and temperature range you have to offer. Master these before moving on to orchids that are more difficult to grow.

Botanical Name	Common Name	Flowers	Temperature	Light
Cattleya species and hybrids	Corsage orchid	Usually in clusters, often with frilled petals, in a range of colors including white, pink, purple, and chocolate red, most with contrasting throats. Most bloom in spring.	Intermediate to warm (60–70°F/16–21°C nights and 75–85°F/24–29°C days)	Bright year-round
Dendrobium species and hybrids	Dens, spray orchids	Arching sprays of flowers in yellow, white, red, and pink, many with contrasting throats. Some are fragrant. Most bloom in spring.	*In winter,* cool (60°F/16°C nights and days in the 75°F/24°C range); *in summer,* intermediate (60°F/16°C nights and 75–80°/24-27°C days)	Bright light year-round
Oncidium species and hybrids	Dancing ladies	Branching flower spike bears dozens of exotic flowers, usually yellow, red, mahogany, or white, some with delicious scents. Bloom time varies with variety, climate, and care.	*In winter,* cool (60°F/16°C nights and 75°F/24°C days); *in summer,* intermediate (60°F/16°C nights and 75–80°F/24–27°C days)	Bright year-round
Paphiopedilum species and hybrids	Lady's slippers, "paphs"	Flowers may be solitary or in small clusters in many colors; all have a slipper-shaped pouch. Most bloom in fall and winter.	Intermediate (60–65°F/16–18°C nights and 75–80°F/24–27°C days) year-round	Moderate year-round
Phalaenopsis species and hybrids	Moth orchids	Sprays of small flowers resemble dainty butterflies in some; others have large, 4 in/10 cm flowers; numerous colors and bicolors. Most bloom in spring, some repeat bloom.	Intermediate (65–70°F/18–21°C nights and 80–85°F/27–29°C days) year-round	Moderate year-round

Cattleya species and hybrids, and closely related orchids KAT-lee-a

CORSAGE ORCHID

Corsage orchid (*Cattleya* hybrid)

THE **TYPES OF ORCHIDS THAT PRODUCE** large, frilly blossoms used in corsages are seldom recommended as the best types for beginners, but some people are willing to go to great lengths to grow these beautiful flowers. They are least troublesome if you live in a warm climate, because they are mostly jungle plants and crave warm temperatures and high humidity. Cattleyas also need abundant light, and you can tell if your plant is getting enough by monitoring the color of its leaves. Dark, jade green color indicates too little light, in which case the plants may refuse to bloom. Plants that are stressed by too much light show very light, yellow-green leaves. Medium green leaves with a slight yellowish cast suggests you have hit the right balance.

SPECIFICATIONS

Light: Bright year-round, including some direct morning or late-afternoon sun.

Temperature: Warm (60–85°F / 16–29°C) year-round.

Fertilizer: *From late spring to early fall,* feed every 2 weeks, but leach pots monthly to remove excess salts. *In winter,* feed monthly.

Water: Allow medium to become slightly dry between thorough drenchings. Plants need more water in summer than in winter.

Soil: Orchid potting mix.

Repotting: Every 2 to 3 years, to replace potting medium that has decomposed. Add 1 in/2.5 cm or more of pebbles or other drainage material to the bottom of pot.

Longevity: Many years, or indefinitely if propagated by division.

Propagation: Divide only after plants have more than seven pseudobulbs. Separate into clumps of three or more.

Selections: If at all possible, work with a local orchid grower, because this species group is huge and varied, and plants can be quite expensive. Start with whatever orchid your expert suggests, which may be a species selection. There is tremendous variation in flower form, fragrance, and plant size. Large "standard" varieties often are easier to grow than compact miniatures, sometimes called "mini-catts."

Display tips: Showcase your cattleya when it is in bloom by keeping it in a warm windowsill in your most-often-used room.

FAMILY: **ORCHIDACEAE**   ORIGIN: **INDIA TO AUSTRALIA**

Dendrobium species and hybrids   den-DRO-bee-um

DENDROBIUM, DEN, SPRAY ORCHID, LEI ORCHID

Spray orchid (*Dendrobium hybrid*)

DENDROBIUMS ARE A LARGE GROUP of orchids, with more than 1,600 species known. They vary in their care, so plan to form a close personal relationship with a dendrobium. The best ones produce flowers that persist for many weeks, and some of the finest hybrids bloom in spring and again in late summer. Flower colors include yellow, red, pink, and violet, many with contrasting throats; blossoms have a light, fruity fragrance. Tall dendrobiums may grow to 18 in/45 cm or more, and often need staking to keep them upright.

Most dendrobiums like a strong seasonal life cycle consisting of warm, brightly lit summers with plenty of fertilizer and regular water, and a cooler winter when their soil is allowed to become almost dry between waterings. A brief but very dry winter rest, lasting only a month, encourages heavy flowering. When new roots appear near the base of the plant, begin feeding and watering the plant again. Many dendrobiums become deciduous plants as they reach maturity, shedding most of their leaves in winter.

SPECIFICATIONS

Light: Bright light year-round.

Temperature: *In winter,* cool (60°F/16°C) nights and days in the 75°F/24°C range. *In summer,* dendrobiums can adapt to very warm outdoor temperatures as long as there is a 15°F/8°C difference between day and night temperatures.

Fertilizer: *From spring through fall,* feed weekly with a balanced houseplant fertilizer diluted to one-fourth the normal strength. *In winter,* allow plants to rest, unfed, for a month or two.

⚠ Water: Allow soil to become almost dry between waterings. Dendrobiums can store water in their canelike stems; some species have pseudobulbs. Grow at 50 percent humidity.

Soil: Orchid potting mix.

Repotting: Every 2 to 3 years; likes to be potbound.

Longevity: Many years.

Propagation: Propagate from aerial cuttings taken from mature plants. Cut off tip just below where you see several aerial roots emerging, and pot the cutting. The parent plant will continue to grow. Plants sometimes produce keikis (see page 122).

Selections: There are hundreds, but two easy suggestions are *D. loddigessi*, which produces fragrant peach-colored blossoms, and 'Wonder Nishii', a long-blooming hybrid with sugar-scented yellow flowers marked with deep maroon.

Display tips: Tall types work well when staked and placed on the sill of a sunny window. Dwarf varieties can be grown in hanging baskets.

Oncidium species and hybrids on-SID-ee-um
DANCING LADIES ORCHID

Dancing ladies orchid
(Oncidium hybrid)

SOME ONCIDIUM ORCHIDS bear single flowers, but most produce swarms of flowers on branched, arching stems. Most modern oncidiums are complex hybrids involving several species, and these hybrids have several advantages. They grow faster than species selections, often bloom more than once a year, and sometimes produce more than 100 small blossoms at a time.

One of the most popular oncidiums, 'Sharry Baby Sweet Fragrance', is an excellent orchid for beginners. Comprised of one or two pairs of pseudobulbs, this modest plant sends up a branched flowering spike 18–30 in/45–75 cm long, clad with red-and-white, chocolate-scented flowers. Grow it in a heavy clay pot, and install a sturdy stake when blooming appears imminent. This orchid blooms when she's ready, which may be summer, fall, or spring. She sometimes blooms twice a year.

SPECIFICATIONS

Light: *Year round,* bright. If moved outdoors in summer, protect the plant from direct sun.

Temperature: *From late fall through late winter,* cool (60°F/ 16°C nights and days in the 75°F/ 24°C range). *In spring and summer,* intermediate (65°F/18°C nights and 75–80°F/24–27°C days).

Fertilizer: *In spring and summer,* feed every third time you water, mixing the fertilizer at half the normal strength. *In fall and winter,* feed monthly. This orchid is sensitive to fertilizer burn, so never use full-strength plant food.

Water: *In summer,* water as often as needed to keep media lightly moist. *From fall to spring,* let the plant become almost dry between thorough waterings.

Soil: Orchid potting mix.

Repotting: Every 2 to 3 years, to refresh the potting mix.

Longevity: Indefinitely, due to ease of propagation.

Propagation: When plants have developed more than six pseudobulbs, divide them into clusters of three or more when repotting. Plants should not need to be divided more often than every 7 to 8 years.

Selections: Beyond 'Sharry Baby' variations, any oncidium with "cat" in its name is a good bet. 'Bobcat' bears numerous dark burgundy blossoms on branching spikes. The blossoms of 'Wildcat' orchids are an exotic blend of red, mahogany, yellow, and white.

Display tips: Keep in a sunny east or west window when not in bloom. As the flower spike develops, put your oncidium to work as a tall, columnar floor plant.

FAMILY: **ORCHIDACEAE**   ORIGIN: **ASIA**

Paphiopedilum species and hybrids

paf-ee-oh-PED-a-lum

PAPH, LADY'S SLIPPERS

MOST OF THE 60 SPECIES OF "PAPHS" are forest ground-dwellers, so they need less light than other orchids. All produce blossoms comprised of top and side petals that frame a pouch, or slipper (*pedilium* is Latin for shoe). Blooms last for 8 weeks or longer, and colors range from dainty pinks to exotic combinations of brownish slippers flanked by wildly mottled wing petals. Bloom time varies with selection and growing conditions, and some bloom intermittently all year. These orchids are slow growers, equipped with fleshy leaves that range from 6–12 in/15–30 cm long. As a general rule, paphs with green leaves prefer cool growing conditions, while those with mottled leaves need more warmth. All need high humidity in the 60 to 70 percent range.

Lady's slippers
(*Paphiopedilum* hybrid)

SPECIFICATIONS

Light: Moderate, from an east or west window or bright fluorescent light. Keep plant in shade if you move it outdoors in summer.

Temperature: Cool to moderate (60–80°F/16–27°C), with a 15°F/8°C difference between night and day, year-round.

Fertilizer: Add a balanced houseplant fertilizer mixed at half the normal strength to the water every third watering in summer. Feed every 3 weeks in winter, diluting fertilizer to one-fourth the normal strength.

Water: Keep potting medium lightly moist at all times. Drench pots occasionally to leach out excess salts.

Soil: Orchid potting mix, with a pinch or two of lime added to reduce acidity.

Repotting: Gently repot annually, because orchid potting medium breaks down fast when it is kept constantly moist.

Longevity: Many years.

Propagation: Mature plants develop small offsets at the base, which can be cut away and repotted. Or you can allow plants to form large clumps and divide them. Division is seldom necessary more often than every 4 to 5 years.

Selections: Hybrids grow a little faster than many species selections, and tend to be heavy flowering, too. 'Darling Christiane' bears single pink-and-cream blossoms with comely freckles. 'Laser' blossoms are deep wine red.

Display tips: This is an excellent orchid to grow in a simple clay pot, which can be displayed in a prominent place when it is in bloom.

FAMILY: **ORCHIDACEAE**   ORIGIN: **TROPICAL ASIA**

Phalaenopsis species and hybrids

fay-len-OP-sis

MOTH ORCHIDS

Moth orchids
(*Phalaenopsis* hybrid)

MOTH ORCHIDS ARE NO MORE DIFFICULT to grow successfully in homes and offices than many other houseplants, since they prefer moderate light, comfortable room temperatures, and most grow to 15–24 in/37.5–60 cm when in full bloom. The broad green leaves spread outward, so the plants are wider than they are tall when not in flower.

Several blossoms appear on each flowering spike, and sometimes a second flower spike emerges when the first one is cut. Flowers last 6 weeks or longer. The flat blossoms with sensual centers may be white, pink, or yellow, or show intricate mottled patterns. Moth orchids develop sturdy roots, including some that wander over the surface of the pot, perhaps in search of a convenient tree limb.

SPECIFICATIONS

Light: Moderate to bright. Try an east window where nights are cooler than days. Most growers keep these orchids indoors year-round.

Temperature: *At night,* 65°F/18°C, to near 80°F/27°C, *midday. In winter,* 2 weeks of cool temperatures (about 55°F/13°C) improve flowering.

Fertilizer: *In spring and summer,* add a balanced houseplant fertilizer, mixed at half the normal strength, to the water every third watering. *In fall and winter,* feed every 3 weeks, diluting fertilizer to one-fourth the normal strength.

Water: Allow soil to dry to 1 in/2.5 cm below the surface between thorough waterings. Moderate humidity is essential.

Soil: Orchid potting mix.

Repotting: Repot every 2 years to replace decomposed potting mix. These plants like to be somewhat rootbound.

Longevity: Five years or more; indefinitely when propagated from plantlets.

Propagation: Most moth orchids develop small plantlets, called keikis, on the flowering spike. After the plantlets have three leaves and 3 in/7.5 cm roots, they can be cut away and potted up.

Selections: Pedigrees on moth orchids can be quite long, indicating the extensive hybridizing that has been done with these plants. Price also varies widely, with the latest releases more costly than established varieties. You should have no trouble locating a reliable, tried-and-true strain in a color you like at a reasonable cost.

Display tips: Because of their easygoing nature, moth orchids often can be grown alongside other houseplants on a windowsill that cools at night and warms up in the day.

Plectranthus australis plek-TRAN-thus

SWEDISH IVY, CREEPING CHARLIE

Swedish ivy
(*Plectranthus australis*)

POPULAR AND EASY TO GROW, Swedish ivy is a wonderful houseplant for beginners. Average to cool room temperatures and acceptance of average humidity make Swedish ivy a good choice for both home and workplace. In addition to producing cascading stems studded with glossy, rounded leaves with scalloped edges, Swedish ivy often blooms in late spring or early summer. As with other members of the mint family, the white or pale mauve blooms appear on short spikes.

After the flowers fade, pinch back stem tips to encourage the plant to develop new branches. You can prune back individual branches anytime, and even severe pruning will not kill this exuberant plant. Stem tip cuttings taken in summer, after the plants have bloomed, are easy to root and grow into new plants. Swedish ivy can be grown indoors year-round, or you can move it outdoors in the summer. If indoor space for plants is limited in winter, prune back the plants by half their size and allow them to rest in a cool place until spring. As long as they are watered occasionally and protected from freezing temperatures, they will recover quickly when brought into a warm room and given good care in spring.

SPECIFICATIONS

Light: Moderate light year-round.

Temperature: Average room temperatures (60–75°F / 16–24°C) year-round. *In winter,* can tolerate low temperatures, to 40°F / 4°C, for short periods of time.

Fertilizer: *From late spring to late summer,* feed every 2 weeks with a balanced houseplant fertilizer. *In fall and winter,* feed monthly. Plants that are cut back in fall and allowed to rest through winter need no fertilizer during this period.

Water: Moderate. Keep soil lightly moist at all times, but avoid over-watering.

Soil: Any good potting soil.

Repotting: Annually in spring or midsummer.

Longevity: 3 to 5 years, or indefinitely when propagated from rooted stem cuttings.

Propagation: Stem tip cuttings root within a month in damp seed-starting mix, and sometimes in plain water. Plants also may be divided.

Selections: Most plants have green leaves, but the 'Variegata' variety features green leaves with lovely white markings along leaf edges. It is well worth seeking out.

Display tips: Swedish ivy can be grown in pots, but it is ideal for hanging baskets, in which the trailing stems can be allowed to cascade over the sides of the containers.

TROUBLESHOOTING

Leaves are dull and droopy.
CAUSE: Too much light.
REMEDY: Move to a shadier location, and increase fertilizer to help the plant recover from the stress of excessive light.

Plant does not bloom.
CAUSE: Excessive nitrogen fertilizer; insufficient light.
REMEDY: Switch to a high-phosphorous (low-nitrogen) plant food in spring. Position plant so that it is exposed to more natural light as days become longer and brighter.

White cottony masses on stems and leaf undersides.
CAUSE: Mealybug.
REMEDY: Swedish ivy is often among the first plants to be infested with this pest. Isolate plant, remove mealybugs by hand with a cotton swab, and treat with insecticidal soap. See page 272 for more information on managing mealybugs.

Leaves pale; webby material on leaf undersides.
CAUSE: Spider mites.
REMEDY: Identify this pest using the information on page 276. Once a positive diagnosis is made, prune plant back severely so that only 3–4 in/7.5–10 cm of stem remain. Clean remaining foliage carefully, and isolate plant. Spray with insecticidal soap if needed to kill surviving mites.

Entire plant wilts and does not recover when watered.
CAUSE: Root rot.
REMEDY: Take stem tip cuttings from healthiest branches and root them in damp seed-starting mix. Dispose of parent plant.

FAMILY: **PRIMULACEAE**   ORIGIN: **EUROPE AND ASIA**

Primula acaulis, P. polyantha, P. obconica, and hybrids PRIM-u-la

PRIMROSE

Primrose (*Primula polyanthus*)

PRIMROSES INCLUDE OVER 425 SPECIES of wildflowers and garden beauties, four of which are grown as fragrant flowering house-plants. The most popular primroses are inexpensive *P. acaulis* hybrids, which hold bright flowers very close to the crown on short stems; flowers often have contrasting yellow eyes. The flowers of hybrid English primrose (*P. polyantha*), fairy primrose (*P. mala-coides*), and German primrose (*P. obconica*) are held higher, on upright stems, and they tend to bloom a little longer than the little guys. Still, regard indoor-grown primroses as temporary invest-ments, rather like cut flowers with leaves and roots.

All species mentioned above are cool-natured plants that are grown from seed started in summer in cool greenhouses. They are ready for sale 4 to 5 months later, from December onward. Choose plants with buds that have just begun to open, and inspect them closely for any signs of insect activity. The most challenging aspect of keeping primroses happy is watering them frequently. Pinching off individual blooms helps extend the plants' bloom time. Many gardeners set plants outside in the garden in moist partial shade after the last spring frost passes. With luck, the plants will persist for several seasons.

SPECIFICATIONS

Light: Bright indoor light but no direct sun.

Temperature: Cool (50–70°F / 10–21°C).

Fertilizer: Little needed when plants are grown in pots.

Water: Constant moisture is critical, as plants wilt very quickly.

Soil: Any good potting soil.

Repotting: Generally not needed.

Longevity: A few weeks to 6 months when grown indoors. In frost-free climates, some selec-tions can be grown outdoors as winter annuals. In cooler climates, primroses often grow as short-lived perennials.

Propagation: Seeds started indoors in fall or late winter.

Selections: 'Libre' German prim-rose (*P. obconica*) does not irritate skin, which was a problem with earlier varieties of this species. Choose other primroses based on the color and form you want.

Display tips: Group several plants together in a basket, with the space between the pots filled with moss or another natural material. Slip small plants into more decorative ceramic pots for temporary display on a tabletop in a well-lit room.

TROUBLESHOOTING

Flowers open pink and turn darker over a period of days.
CAUSE: Flowers naturally darken as they age, especially on *P. obconica*
REMEDY: Use hue as a cue to flower age, and pinch off the oldest ones to promote the formation of new bud-bearing stems.

Flowers last only a couple of days.
CAUSE: Warm temperatures.
REMEDY: Keep plants in your coolest room at night or when you are not at home. Bring them to a warm, bright room when you are present to appreciate them.

Leaf edges appear crinkled and begin to turn brown.
CAUSE: Salt buildup in containers.
REMEDY: Flush containers with several changes of fresh filtered water, watering until water drips freely from the bottom of the pots each time. Trim off browned leaves to keep the plants looking neat.

Leaves and flowers wilt.
CAUSE: Too dry, or direct sunlight
REMEDY: Check to make sure soil in the pot is very moist. Keep a small pitcher near plants to make watering convenient. Place plants where they will not cook in direct sun.

Leaves are yellowish, with faint webbing on leaf undersides.
CAUSE: Spider mites.
REMEDY: Dispose of the plant. Otherwise, this pest can quickly spread to more long-lived houseplants.

Leaves wilt despite correct water and light.
CAUSE: Aphids or root rot.
REMEDY: Check leaf undersides for aphids, which also can hide in the plant's crown. Rinse plants thoroughly and spray with insecticidal soap. Dispose of plants affected by root rot, as it cannot be cured.

FAMILY: **ERICACEAE**   ORIGIN: **MAN-MADE HYBRID OF JAPANESE SPECIES**

Rhododendron hybrids row-doh-DEN-dron
AZALEA, FLORIST'S AZALEA

Azalea (*Rhododendron* hybrid)

INDOOR AZALEAS ARE SO BEAUTIFUL that they deserve their popularity as Mother's Day plants. When kept in a cool room, an azalea will hold its delicate blooms for 3 to 4 weeks, followed by a light flush of new leaves. Enjoy your azalea as a living bouquet, because florist's azaleas are difficult to rebloom unless you live where winters are short and mild. Unlike hardy garden azaleas, which shed their leaves in winter, the florist types are tender evergreens that cannot tolerate freezing temperatures. The plants also need bright light indoors, equivalent to dappled shade outdoors, if they are to stay strong enough to set numerous buds and blooms. That said, getting a florist azalea to rebloom is challenging but not impossible, especially if you have a place outside where the plant can be placed for several weeks in the fall. Cool fall weather, or mild winter weather, is needed to help the plant set buds that open in spring.

SPECIFICATIONS

Light: *Indoors*, bright. *Outdoors*, mostly shade.

◆ **Temperature:** Cool to average room temperatures (60–75°F / 16–24°C) while in bloom. *Outdoors*, above 40°F/4°C. Needs 6 weeks of 40–50°F/4–10°C fall weather to set buds.

Fertilizer: Twice yearly, feed plants with an acid-forming azalea fertilizer that contains iron, a necessary micronutrient.

Water: Keep soil lightly moist at all times, and prevent dryness in the center of the root mass by plunging pot into a larger container of water weekly. Keep it submerged until no bubbles appear, then allow pot to drain until dripping stops.

Soil: If you plan to keep the plant, repot it into a half-and-half mixture of peat moss and potting soil.

Repotting: Not necessary for a plant kept as a temporary bouquet. If you want to rebloom your plant, shift it to a larger pot after the last blooms have withered.

Longevity: A few months to several years.

Propagation: Rooted stem tip cuttings, though rooting is slow and the results seldom match the quality of plants produced by commercial growers.

Selections: Choose plants based on the flower color you like, which may be pink, red, white, or salmon. White flowers show imperfections more than other colors.

Display tips: Enjoy a potted azalea in very close quarters during the weeks it is in bloom.

TROUBLESHOOTING

Leaves turn brown while still attached to stems.
CAUSE: Root rot.
REMEDY: Several types of soil-borne fungi can cause azalea roots to rot. Infected plants will slowly (or quickly) die, and should be discarded.

Plant sheds many leaves.
CAUSE: Side effect of dry soil conditions, past or present.
REMEDY: Make sure plant is thoroughly watered, either by soaking container in a sink or bucket or by repeatedly watering it. The plant may have been allowed to dry out before it came to live with you, and is showing its displeasure. Discard a plant that has lost more than one-third of its leaves, as it will never recover.

Leaves turn yellow, while leaf veins remain green.
CAUSE: Iron deficiency.
REMEDY: Spray plant with a chelated iron product. You may also increase fertilizer after checking to make sure iron is present in the fertilizer you are using on your azalea.

Plant does not rebloom, or reblooms very lightly.
CAUSE: Lack of cold weather to help set buds.
REMEDY: In fall and winter, a florist azalea needs at least 6 weeks of temperatures between 40–55°F / 4–13°C in order to set buds. Keeping the plant outdoors in the fall and then moving it to an unheated garage where it will be chilled, but not frozen, is usually best.

Leaves appear parched, with webby material on leaf undersides.
CAUSE: Spider mites
REMEDY: Isolate plant and prune off badly infested stems. If more than one-third of plant is infested, disposing of it is usually better than attempting to get rid of the mites. See page 274 for more information about this pest.

FAMILY: **ROSACEAE**   ORIGIN: **CHINA**

Rosa chinensis hybrids RO-sa chi-NEN-sis
ROSE, MINIATURE ROSE, MICRO-ROSE

Miniature rose (*Rosa chinensis* hybrid)

MINIATURE ROSES THAT GROW less than 18 in/45 cm tall have recently won places on store shelves, especially in spring from Valentine's Day to Mother's Day. Varieties that grow to less than 14 in/35 cm tall are often called micro-roses. Although mini- and micro- roses are sold alongside other indoor plants, their true home is outdoors. Roses need 6 hours of direct sun daily in order to thrive, so they must be moved outside at the earliest possible time if they are to live long, happy lives. In spring, enjoy a new plant indoors until the last frost passes, and then repot it and place it outdoors on your porch or patio. Miniature roses will grow in pots, but they also make great garden plants. Tremendously hardy, miniature roses that are transplanted to the garden in late spring easily survive winter in cold climates when protected with a mound of mulch or loose soil. Allow container-grown plants to become dormant in winter, and keep them in a garage or other protected place in winter so their roots will not freeze.

SPECIFICATIONS

Light: Bright light, including as much direct sun as possible.

Temperature: Average room temperatures (60–75°F/16–24°C). Outdoors, plants adapt to temperature extremes, provided they are well rooted.

Fertilizer: Fertilize monthly with a balanced fertilizer that contains micronutrients.

Water: Allow soil to dry to within .5 in/1.25 cm of surface between thorough waterings.

Soil: Any good potting soil.

Repotting: When initial flush of flowers fades, remove plant from pot and soak roots in water to separate plants (frequently there are more than one). Tease apart roots and transplant to individual 6 in/15 cm pots.

Longevity: A few months indoors, to many years when grown outdoors in open sun.

Propagation: Root stem tip cuttings taken in early summer as described on page 299. Use rooting powder and maintain high humidity.

Selections: There are more than 100 named varieties, which vary in size, color, fragrance, and bloom type. Pink 'Cupcake' is a top choice. Other award-winning miniature rose varieties are listed at the website of the American Rose Society (www.ars.org).

Display tips: Enjoy a gift plant indoors while the blooms last, which is usually 4 to 6 weeks. Then move plant outdoors.

TROUBLESHOOTING

Buds shrivel before they open.
CAUSE: Very dry air.
REMEDY: After being grown in humid greenhouses, plants often go into shock when moved to dry indoor rooms. Clip off failed buds and mist plant daily for 2 weeks. Plant may not fully recover until it is repotted and moved outdoors.

Plant appears healthy but does not bloom.
CAUSE: Not enough light.
REMEDY: Miniature roses need very bright light before they will produce buds and flowers. If you do not have a place where they can receive 6 hours of sun daily, grow them within 2 in/5 cm of fluorescent lights.

Leaves develop black spots, with yellow between the spots.
CAUSE: Rose blackspot, a common fungal disease.
REMEDY: Clip off affected leaves as soon as you see them. Try to keep leaves dry when watering, as blackspot spreads on damp leaf surfaces. Plants that lose most of their leaves to this disease often recover when given good care. Resistance varies greatly with variety.

Leaves appear bleached, with faint webbing on leaf undersides.
CAUSE: Spider mites.
REMEDY: Roses are very susceptible to this pest, described on page 274. Isolate plant, prune off badly infested branches, and thoroughly clean plant with plenty of warm water. Spray plant with insecticidal soap, and move it to a shady spot for a few days. Increasing humidity often helps prevent spider mite problems.

Leaves turn yellow and fall off.
CAUSE: Environmental stress.
REMEDY: When roses are kept in the dark too long while they are shipped to stores, allowed to dry out, or exposed to high temperatures, they often shed their leaves and enter a state of semi-dormancy. Allow plant to rest in a cool place for 2 weeks, then repot and resume normal care. Assuming the plant receives bright light, it may recover. Roses naturally shed their leaves in winter.

Rosmarinus officinalis

ros-MAR-i-nus o-fis-in-AL-is

ROSEMARY

Rosemary
(*Rosmarinus officinalis*)

SEVERAL POPULAR CULINARY HERBS can be grown outdoors in summer and kept indoors in winter, but rosemary is the best one to grow indoors year-round. Strong light is needed to grow compact plants, but even a plant that stretches toward the light will bear plenty of flavorful leaves for cooking. Varieties vary in their size and growth habit. Very compact strains grow into bushy plants less than 18 in/45 cm tall, while those with a trailing habit make fine subjects to train onto a hoop or other topiary form. Varieties also vary in their willingness to bloom. All bloom best when given a cool rest period in winter. The strongest bloom season is late spring. After plant blooms, trim back old stems to encourage the emergence of plenty of stocky new side branches.

If you begin with a plant that has been pruned into the shape of a Christmas tree, expect it to become bushier over time. These are usually 2-year-old plants, which will begin to deteriorate after another year. Stem tip cuttings propagated from tree-form plants will not have the same shape as their parent unless they are grown in full sun and trained by meticulous pruning.

SPECIFICATIONS

Light: *Spring through summer,* bright light, including 4 hours or more of direct sun. *In fall and winter,* can adapt to less light. In any season, turn plant weekly to give all sides a turn at directional light.

Temperature: *From late spring to late summer,* warm (60–80°F/16–27°C). *In fall and winter,* cool (45–70°F/7–21°C).

Fertilizer: *From spring through summer,* feed every 2 weeks with a balanced all-purpose plant food. *In fall and winter,* feed monthly.

⬥ **Water:** Allow soil to dry to within 1 in/2.5 cm of the surface between waterings. Be careful not to overwater, as this plant needs somewhat dry conditions. However, it should not be allowed to dry out completely.

Soil: Any good potting soil, with a small amount of sand added to provide a gritty texture. Cactus potting soil, which contains a lot of perlite, is also a good choice.

Repotting: Annually in spring. Clay pots, which help the roots dry out between waterings, are ideal for rosemary.

Longevity: About 4 years for individual plants, which can be kept indefinitely when propagated from stem tip cuttings.

Propagation: In summer, take 3 in/7.5 cm stem tip cuttings and root them as described on page 299. Roots develop in about a month.

Selections: 'Blue Boy' and a few other varieties are very small and compact, making them ideal for growing in pots. Trailing varieties such as 'Lockwood' and 'Santa Barbara' can easily be trained to grow as topiary.

Display tips: Plenty of warm sun brings out the best in rosemary's flavor. Keep your plant near the kitchen so it will be convenient to use in cooking.

TROUBLESHOOTING

Little new growth; some yellowing of old leaves.
CAUSE: Too little fertilizer; acidic growing conditions.
REMEDY: Repot plant in fresh potting soil. Mix ½ teaspoon/ 2.5 ml of lime into the soil. Increase frequency of feeding, but do not fertilize rosemary with a very strong fertilizer solution.

Stems floppy, with spaces between leaves.
CAUSE: Not enough light.
REMEDY: When grown outdoors, rosemary enjoys baking in full sun. Indoors, give plants as much direct sun as possible in summer, when most new growth is produced. If you cannot place plant in a south or west window, shift it outdoors for the summer.

Plant does not bloom.
CAUSE: Not a heavy-blooming variety, or lack of cool winter temperatures.
REMEDY: Rosemary blooms best when it feels seasonal changes cooler in winter and warmer in summer. Some varieties bloom much more enthusiastically than others. To encourage flowering, give plant a cool winter rest and switch to a high-phosphorous plant food for a few weeks in spring.

FAMILY: **GESNERIACEAE**   ORIGIN: **EASTERN AFRICA**

Saintpaulia hybrids saynt-PAW-lee-a

AFRICAN VIOLET

African violet (*Saintpaulia* hybrid)

THE CHEERY BLOSSOMS AND DOWNY LEAVES of African violets have won them the number one spot among flowering houseplants, and they are quite easy to grow. Always dainty in demeanor, African violets are excellent plants to grow on a windowsill that receives light filtered through the leaves of outdoor trees. They are at their best when kept indoors year round. African violets can be damaged by overwatering, chilling, or placement in harsh sun, but otherwise these stalwart little plants seldom complain. Don't be reluctant to buy plants that are in bloom, because African violets bloom again and again when given reasonable care. Do pinch off old flower stems to keep the plants looking neat.

SPECIFICATIONS

Light: Bright indirect light or fluorescent light.

Temperature: Average room temperatures (65–75°F / 18–24°C) year-round.

Fertilizer: Feed every 2 weeks with a high-phosphorous plant food, or use a balanced houseplant food mixed at half the rate recommended on the package.

Water: Keep soil lightly moist at all times. Water thoroughly with lukewarm water, and then pour off any excess water that accumulates in the pot tray. In summer, leach pots once or twice to remove accumulated salts (see page 263). Avoid wetting the leaves when watering.

Soil: A peaty potting soil or African violet mix.

Repotting: Repot once a year to refresh soil but keep plants in small pots. When repotting, prune off up to one-third of the roots and set the plant slightly deeper in the pot.

Longevity: With attentive care, plants have been known to live 50 years.

Propagation: Root healthy, medium-sized leaves with 1–2 in/ 2.5–5 cm of stem attached as described on page 299. Leaves develop roots in about a month, and plantlets form within 4 to 6 weeks after that.

Selections: Choose plants based on flower colors you like. Collectors grow African violets that have unusual flower forms, including doubles, bells, and star-shaped blossoms, and there are variations in leaf type, too.

Display tips: A single plant in a pretty ceramic pot makes a lovely desktop accent. Group small plants together in a shallow basket, using Spanish moss or sphagnum moss to fill the crevices between the containers.

TROUBLESHOOTING

Plant does not bloom.
PROBLEM: Too little light; lack of darkness.
REMEDY: African violets sometimes stop blooming in winter, when light levels are low. Move plants to a bright south or west window in winter to keep them in bloom. In spring and summer, keep them where light is less intense and switch to a high-phosphorous fertilizer. Some people add a light pinch of Epsom salts to water to push balky plants into bloom. Plants also may fail to bloom if they do not receive 8 hours of darkness each night.

Old leaves shrivel to brown.
PROBLEM: Normal for African violets.
REMEDY: Pinch off old leaves as they fail and dispose of them. Plants that are underfed shed leaves more quickly than those that are adequately fertilized.

Plant grows lopsided, curving to one side.
PROBLEM: Natural response to directional light.
REMEDY: In the wild, African violets grow between rocks, curving as needed to get the best light. To correct this shape requires renovating the plant. Remove all leaves except seven or eight in the central crown, then remove the old roots, leaving a 3 in/7.5 cm trunk. Use a knife to peel the lowest 2 in/5 cm of the trunk, like a carrot. Set the groomed plant to root as if you

were rooting a stem cutting (see page 299). When new growth appears, transplant into African violet soil.

Brown spots on leaves.
PROBLEM: Cold water on leaves; any water on leaves when plant is in bright light.
REMEDY: Avoid wetting leaves when watering. If leaves need to be cleaned, either brush them lightly with a dry paintbrush or rinse them with lukewarm water on a warm, dry day. Place plant in a shady spot until the leaves are dry.

Leaves bleached and wilted; tiny insects on leaf undersides.
PROBLEM: Cyclamen mites.
REMEDY: This pest is very difficult to control. Dispose of infested plants, and isolate any others that were growing nearby.

FAMILY: **SAXIFRAGACEAE**   ORIGIN: **EASTERN ASIA**

Saxifraga stolonifera saks-i-FRA-ja sto-lon-IF-er-a
STRAWBERRY BEGONIA, ROVING SAILOR, MOTHER OF THOUSANDS

Strawberry begonia
(*Saxifraga stolonifera*)

IF YOUR SPACE FOR HOUSEPLANTS IS LIMITED and you want only plants that grow and change quickly, strawberry begonia is an excellent choice. Often grown outdoors as a groundcover in Zones 6 to 9, this tough little saxifrage makes a pleasing, carefree houseplant. Growing to 6 in/15 cm tall and 12 in/30 cm wide, strawberry begonia produces rounded leaves in rosettes with hairy red leaf undersides and stems. In spring, plants may produce sprays of tiny white flowers, especially if the plant is allowed to rest for a few weeks in winter in a cool place (50–55°F/10–13°C). Strawberry begonia's leaves and petite form are attractive, and robust crops of little plantlets borne on dangling runners to 24 in/60 cm long add to its charm. These are easily grown into new plants to keep or share. Should the plantlets become so numerous that the plant appears unkempt, thin them by clipping off unwanted runners close to the plant's crown.

SPECIFICATIONS

Light: Bright, from an east or west window.

Temperature: Cool to average room temperatures (50–75°F/10–24°C).

Fertilizer: *In spring and summer,* feed monthly with a balanced plant food. *In fall and winter,* feed every 6 weeks.

Water: Allow soil to dry to within 1 in/2.5 cm of the surface between waterings. Water more in summer than in winter, when plant often rests.

Soil: A fast-draining potting soil that contains perlite or sand, with pebbles added to the bottom of the container for enhanced drainage and extra weight.

Repotting: Repot each spring until the plant's third year, when the crowns often become woody and prone to rot. Replace old plants with rooted plantlets.

Longevity: 3 years for individual plants, or indefinitely when plantlets are propagated.

Propagation: Use a bent paper clip to pin plantlets into small pots set around the parent plant, where they will quickly grow roots. Detach from parent plant after three weeks. Transplant three rooted plantlets into a shallow, 6-inch pot.

Selections: The 'Tricolor' variety features green leaves with splashy cream margins, delicately edged with red. It requires more exacting care than species selections, which have green leaves with silver markings along the veins.

Display tips: Young plants can be grown in small pots for a year. In the second year, shift them to hanging pots or baskets, so the plantlets can arch downward.

TROUBLESHOOTING

Leaves are pale and brownish.
CAUSE: Too little light; too much sun.
REMEDY: This plant needs some direct light, but strong sun can bleach the leaves. Try it in an east window, which is usually an ideal setting.

Plant droops or collapses.
CAUSE: Chronic overwatering; acute dryness.
REMEDY: Waterlogged roots can cause plant to droop, but it should perk up when the soil is allowed to dry out. Should plant become so dry that it collapses, rehydrate container as described on page 328.

Old leaves yellow and turn brown.
CAUSE: Plant is too old; roots may be rotting.
REMEDY: Propagate new plant by rooting a few plantlets. When they show strong growth, discard the parent plant.

Leaves shrivel; mold appears at soil line.
CAUSE: Root or crown rot, caused by botrytis or another soil-borne fungus.
REMEDY: If only one crown in the container is affected, use a sharp knife to cut it out. Meanwhile, propagate new plant by rooting plantlets, as other crowns in the container may become infected. Moist soil conditions favor this problem.

Small wedge-shaped insects are seen on new leaves.
CAUSE: Aphids.
REMEDY: Thoroughly clean plant with plenty of warm water. If problem persists, spray plant with insecticidal soap.

Leaves pale and bleached, with faint webbing on leaf undersides.
CAUSE: Spider mites.
REMEDY: Isolate plant, and snip off badly affected leaves. Thoroughly clean plant with plenty of warm water. Swish plantlets in a bowl of soapy water, then rinse and pin them in pots to grow new roots. Older plants that have suffered a serious infestation may never recover, but young plants free of mites often prosper when given good growing conditions.

Senecio × hybridus sen-EE-see-oh hi-BRID-us

CINERARIA

Cineraria (*Senecio × hybridus*)

INSTEAD OF THINKING OF CINERARIA as a houseplant, regard it as a living cut flower. These lovely bloomers are grown as annuals that begin their lives as seeds sown in greenhouses in summer. Four months later, after a strict regimen of controlled temperatures that start out warm and are made progressively cooler, the seedlings are poised to explode with dense trusses of starry, daisy-shaped flowers. Cinerarias are usually sold from January through April, so they are perfect plants for providing late-winter color indoors.

Cinerarias hold their blossoms best if they are kept in a cool room where temperatures never rise above 65°F/18°C. If you have a cool porch, move your plants there at night, because cinerarias find cool (50°F/10°C) nights quite pleasing. Don't worry if temperatures dip to 40–50°F/4–10°C, because cool nights do the plants no harm. Cinerarias will wilt quickly should they become dry, so watch them closely for signs of drought stress. Seriously wilted plants may never recover from the trauma. Use scissors to snip off individual blossoms as they fade. When the blooming period ends, discard the plants.

SPECIFICATIONS

Light: Bright diffuse sunlight.

Temperature: Cool (50–65°F/ 10–18°C).

Fertilizer: None needed.

Water: Keep constantly moist at all times, but avoid overwatering. Plants benefit from high humidity.

Soil: Any potting soil.

Repotting: Not needed, unless you want to shift a purchased plant to a more decorative container.

◈ Longevity: 1 bloom season that usually lasts 4 to 6 weeks.

Propagation: Seeds sown in late summer.

Selections: Choose plants by color of the blooms. Most of the cinerarias offered for sale are of the 'Jester' variety, which comes in five colors and grows to 10 in/ 25 cm tall.

Display tips: Place pots inside wicker baskets to display on tabletops when the plants are in full bloom. Three pots, placed together in an oblong planter, make a great indoor windowbox for a cool north window.

TROUBLESHOOTING

Leaves appear pale and limp.
CAUSE: Too much direct sun.
REMEDY: Move plants to filtered light. Light from south or west windows is often too bright, with warmer temperatures than these plants like.

Plants wilt daily.
CAUSE: Uneven watering. The interior of the root mass may have become extremely dry, so that it sheds water rather than absorbing it.
REMEDY: Water plants thoroughly, then set the containers in a pan of water for half an hour to rehydrate them. Remove and allow excess water to drain away.

Flower colors are pale.
CAUSE: Too little light.
REMEDY: Move plants to a brighter spot, where they will receive filtered sun for a few hours each day.

Blossoms fade within a few days after buds open.
CAUSE: Warm temperatures.
REMEDY: Move plant to a cooler place. Cineraria blossoms last much longer when plants are kept in a place where temperatures stay below 65°F / 18°C.

Plants collapse and will not perk up after watering.
CAUSE: Root rot.
REMEDY: Discard plants.

Small insects are present on plants.
CAUSE: Aphids, whitefly, or thrips.
REMEDY: Discard plants, because these pests can spread to other, more long-lived houseplants.

FAMILY: **GESNERIACEAE**   ORIGIN: **BRAZILIAN RAIN FORESTS**

Sinningia speciosa hybrids

sin-IN-gee-a spe-see-OH-sa

GLOXINIA

Gloxinia (*Sinningia speciosa* hybrid)

NOT SO LONG AGO, these African violet cousins were grown as perennial plants that died back and became dormant for 3 months each year. The tuberous root was then replanted in fresh soil, and it promptly regrew, delighted its owners with big, velvety flowers, and gradually faded back to dormancy again. This story has changed, in that most gloxinias sold in florist shops and retail stores these days are hybrids grown as annuals. Bred to grow quickly from seed, today's gloxinias are so focused on flowering that they don't invest energy in a serviceable storage root. Their ability to rebloom is therefore seriously compromised, and plants that do come back after a period of dormancy are not likely to show good vigor.

An annual houseplant can still be a great houseplant, however, so don't be afraid to invest a few dollars in a pretty gloxinia. Choose plants with buds that are just beginning to open. Each blossom will last about a week, and the bloom period should last about 2 months. Should serious insect problems arise — for example, an outbreak of spider mites, cyclamen mites, or thrips — it is best to discard the plant rather than working with pesticides or soap sprays, which usually ruin gloxinia blossoms.

SPECIFICATIONS

Light: Bright filtered sunlight.

Temperature: Average room temperatures (60–75°F/16–24°C).

Fertilizer: Feed every 2 weeks with high-phosphorous plant food.

⬧ Water: Keep soil moderately moist. Dryness induces dormancy. When watering, avoid wetting the leaves.

Soil: Light-textured potting soil with extra peat, or African violet soil.

Repotting: Not needed for short-lived plants. When handled as perennials, repot in late winter, as plants emerge from dormancy.

Longevity: 2 months to several years.

Propagation: Seeds sown indoors in late winter.

Selections: Gloxinias come in three sizes. Regular gloxinias feature huge flowers to 3 in/7.5 cm across, and the plants are usually sold in 6 in/15 cm pots. Smaller, compact gloxinias, sold in 4 in/10 cm pots, have smaller flowers, but they are often in big clusters.

Mini gloxinias are sold in 4 in/10 cm pots, or they may be the color plants in preplanted tabletop gardens. Of these three, regular gloxinias have the best chance of coming back after a 2 to 3-month dormancy period.

Display tips: Place blooming gloxinias on a tabletop or bookshelf where the velvety blossoms are easy to see. Use small pieces of statuary or decorative containers to showcase gloxinias in full bloom.

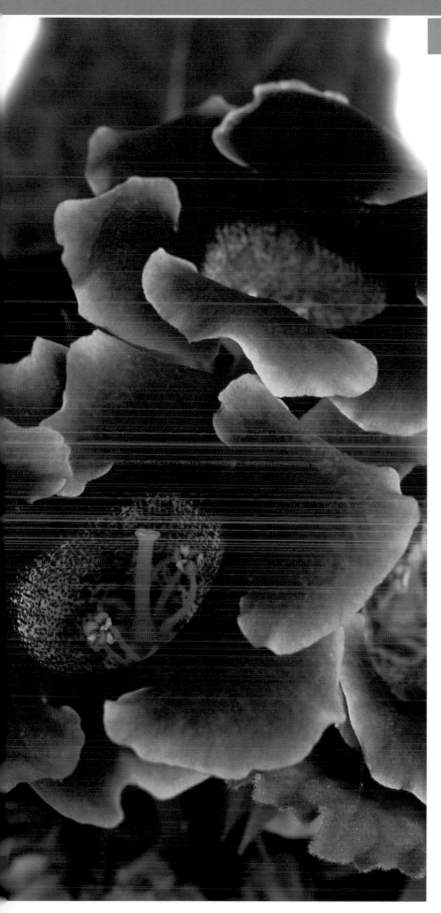

TROUBLESHOOTING

Brown spots on leaves.
CAUSE: Water spots.
REMEDY: Water plants in the morning so that any water that gets on the leaves dries quickly. Avoid wetting the leaves when watering the plants.

Bleached rings on leaves.
CAUSE: Cold water.
REMEDY: Use warm water (above 55°F/13°C) when watering gloxinias.

Twisted, cupped, or curled new leaves.
CAUSE: Too much nitrogen fertilizer.
REMEDY: Reduce feeding, and be sure to use a high-phosphorous plant food rather than a balanced one, which may contain too much nitrogen.

New leaves appear eaten around the edges.
CAUSE: Boron deficiency.
REMEDY: Drench plants with a boron solution made from Epsom salts, as described on page 18.

Leaves are yellow, or mottled with yellow.
CAUSE: Too much direct sunlight. If only oldest leaves are yellow, the plants may be entering their dormant period.
REMEDY: Move to filtered light, or allow plant to dry out and become dormant.

Leaves appear pale and bleached.
CAUSE: Spider mites or cyclamen mites (page 274).
REMEDY: Discard plants.

Flowers are deformed, appear chewed.
CAUSE: Thrips (page 276).
REMEDY: Discard plants.

FAMILY: **SOLANACEAE**   ORIGIN: **SOUTH AMERICA**

Solanum pseudocapsicum

so-LAN-um su-doh-CAP-se-cum

JERUSALEM CHERRY, CHRISTMAS CHERRY, CHRISTMAS PEPPER

Jerusalem cherry
(Solanum pseudocapsicum)

A TOUGH LITTLE SUBSHRUB, Jerusalem cherry is related to tomatoes and edible peppers. However, the fruit is toxic, so advise children not to pick them, and keep them out of the reach of pets. These safety precautions aside, Jerusalem cherry makes a versatile indoor plant in fall and winter. After a quiet show of starry white flowers, round, cherry-sized fruits start out dark green, then become Halloween yellow, and slowly ripen to red as Thanksgiving gives way to Christmas. In spring, the plant can be pruned back and placed in a cool place to rest. After the last spring frost passes, move it outdoors and it should regrow without delay.

Plants more than 2 years old often become brittle, so it's a good idea to propagate stem cuttings from year-old plants. Easier still, gather the ripe fruits and plant them in a pot or on any piece of moist ground in spring. Seedlings will almost certainly appear, and these can be dug, potted up, and adopted as replacements for aged specimens.

SPECIFICATIONS

Light: Bright, including direct sun for up to 4 hours a day.

Temperature: Average to warm room temperatures (65–75°F / 18–24°C).

Fertilizer: *From spring to early winter,* feed monthly with a balanced houseplant food or a water-soluble tomato fertilizer. *In late winter,* no feeding necessary.

Water: Allow soil to become dry to within 1 in/2.5 cm of the surface between waterings, but do not let soil become so dry that the plant wilts.

Soil: Any good potting soil.

Repotting: Repot young plants as they become rootbound until the roots fill a 6 in/15 cm pot. In spring, repot year-old plants to refresh soil.

Longevity: 2 to 3 years, or indefinitely when propagated from seeds or rooted stem cuttings.

◈ Propagation: Take stem cuttings in spring and root them as described on page 299. Plants are also easily grown from seed gathered from shriveled fruits. Seedlings started outdoors in early summer bloom and set fruit the following fall.

Selections: In addition to this species, less shrubby ornamental peppers (*Capsicum frutescens*) are sometimes sold as holiday plants. These are not as long lived as Jerusalem cherry, and should be discarded after their fruits are no longer attractive.

Display tips: Use sharp scissors to shape plant before displaying it in a sunny window. A cloth wrapping placed over the pot can change with the fall and winter holidays, keying the plant to the most appropriate theme. This plant makes a great sidekick for a larger calamondin orange.

TROUBLESHOOTING

Plant blooms but does not set fruit.
CAUSE: Poor pollination.
REMEDY: When grown outdoors, wind helps move pollen to where it is needed, but indoors there may not be enough air movement. Jiggle the plants a few times a day when they hold many open flowers, or use a small dry paintbrush to dab the centers of the blossoms, which spreads the tiny grains of pollen.

Leaves are small and light green.
CAUSE: Insufficient fertilizer.
REMEDY: Plants grown in pots need regular feeding. Increase frequency of fertilizer application.

Plant does not bloom.
CAUSE: Insufficient light; too much supplemental light at night.
REMEDY: These plants look best in winter when they enjoy strong outdoor light during the summer. They also fruit best in response to days becoming shorter in the fall. To support this process, leave your plant outside as long as possible, but do bring it in before temperatures drop to freezing.

Leaves sticky; small insects are present.
CAUSE: Aphids, whiteflies, or spider mites.
REMEDY: Gather fruits for replanting and dispose of plant. This plant is short lived by nature, and it is easier to grow replacements than to restore the health of an infested plant.

FAMILY: **ARACEAE**   ORIGIN: **INDONESIA AND CENTRAL AMERICA**

Spathiphyllum species spa-thi-FY-lum
SPATH, PHYLLUM, PEACE LILY

Peace lily (*Spathiphyllum species*)

SPATHIPHYLLUMS ARE PRESENT in most offices, malls, and homes for good reason. They are easy to grow, produce showy, spoon-shaped flowers, and tolerate low light and average humidity. In NASA studies, spathiphyllums were found to help remove formaldehyde, benzene, and carbon monoxide from tainted indoor air. Small varieties grow to only 16 in/40 cm tall, with the largest ones often reaching 6 ft/1.8 m in height and width.

When purchased or received as gifts, spathiphyllums usually hold several flowers. Cut off these flowering stems when the blossoms ripen to green. Use a soft, damp cloth to wipe dust from the foliage, and do not expect a fresh crop of blooms until the following summer. Once plants have been nicely situated in a home or office for several months, they usually resume their natural bloom cycle. In addition to a flush of flowers in early summer, many cultivars continue to bloom intermittently throughout the year.

SPECIFICATIONS

Light: *In fall and winter,* low to moderate. *In spring and summer,* moderate to bright.

Temperature: Average room temperatures (65–75°F/18–24°C) year-round.

◆ Fertilizer: *From spring through fall,* feed monthly with a balanced plant food that includes micro-nutrients, diluted to half the normal strength. *In winter,* feed every 6 weeks.

Water: Keep soil lightly moist at all times, and avoid overwatering. Use room-temperature water.

Soil: Any good potting soil.

Repotting: Repot annually in spring to refresh soil. This plant likes to be slightly rootbound.

Longevity: Many years, if divided every 5 years or so.

Propagation: Propagate older plants by dividing them in spring. Trim off leaves that fail in the weeks following division.

Selections: Dozens exist, varying in size, leaf color, and flowering habits. The giant peace lilies seen in malls and airports are usually 'Sensation', which grows to 6 ft/1.8 m tall. 'Supreme' is the most common variety sold in 10 in/25 cm pots. 'Lynise' has textured leaves and often grows to 36 in/90 cm tall.

Display tips: The dark leaves of peace lily appear most refined when the plant is grown in a plain pot with a glossy finish. Display blooming plants on a low pedestal where the flowers can be easily seen.

TROUBLESHOOTING

Leaf tips are brown; stems droop.
CAUSE: Overfertilization and/or overwatering.
REMEDY: Allow soil to become nearly dry before watering. Water lightly yet frequently, and avoid soaking the soil. Use a very dilute fertilizer.

Leaves are pale and curled, with brown leaf margins.
CAUSE: Excessive light.
REMEDY: Peace lily cannot tolerate direct sun. Move it to a place that gets filtered light, or near an east window. In winter, peace lilies can accept light levels that are quite low.

Plant does not bloom.
CAUSE: This plant usually blooms in cycles, with flowers produced mostly in spring and summer. Low light levels suppress blooming. Plants that are more than 5 years old may not bloom unless they are rejuvenated by dividing them.
REMEDY: In spring, move plant to a slightly brighter location and feed and water it regularly. Divide old, overgrown plants.

Yellow margins on lowest leaves, or yellow edges on all leaves.
CAUSE: Too dry; micronutrient deficiency.
REMEDY: Increase water and fertilizer. Use a dilute fertilizer that contains magnesium and iron, because peace lily is sensitive to deficiencies of these nutrients.

Small, dark-colored insects on flowers.
CAUSE: Thrips.
REMEDY: Large-flowered peace lilies in particular are attractive to thrips. Isolate plant from other blooming houseplants and implement control measures described on page 276.

Streptocarpus × hybridus

stretp-toh-KAR-pus hi-BRID-us

STREPTOCARPUS, CAPE PRIMROSE

Cape primrose
(Streptocarpus × hybridus)

A CLOSE RELATIVE TO AFRICAN VIOLETS, streptocarpus is a larger plant, with long, strap-shaped leaves that arch outward, making it wider than it is tall. Full-sized plants grow to 12 in/30 cm tall and up to 30 in/75 cm wide. Dwarf varieties are smaller. Most streptocarpus are complex hybrids that have been bred to produce big, showy trusses of flowers that may be pink, purple, white, or red, depending on variety. Many have contrasting white or yellow throats.

A delightful plant to grow near a large window, streptocarpus needs somewhat cool temperatures to thrive. It is a wonderful plant for offices lit by fluorescent lights, and the increasing availability of vigorous hybrids have contributed to its growing popularity. Superior varieties are sold by many suppliers that specialize in African violets (see 'Plants and Supplies' on page 337).

SPECIFICATIONS

Light: Moderate to bright light, or 15 hours of fluorescent light daily.

Temperature: Cool room temperatures (60–70°F/16–21°C).

Fertilizer: Feed every 2 weeks with a high-phosphorous plant food diluted to half the usual strength.

Water: Keep soil lightly moist at all times spring through summer. Water slightly less in winter, but do not allow soil to become so dry that plant wilts.

Soil: African violet potting soil.

Repotting: Repot annually in spring, being careful not to set the plant too deeply in the pot. Streptocarpus has many surface roots that should be barely covered with soil. Keep streptocarpus in small containers, because overpotting can lead to problems with root rot.

Longevity: To 10 years or more.

Propagation: Grow plantlets from rooted petiole leaf cuttings as described on page 302. Plants that develop multiple crowns can be divided.

Selections: There are dozens of named hybrids in a range of colors and bicolors. Two that are easy to grow are 'Bristol's Blue Bonnet', which produces trusses of blue flowers, and 'Dibley's Falling Stars', which is pale lavender with a white throat.

Display tips: Keep plant near a sunny south window where it gets abundant indirect light. Pinch off old flower stems to keep plant looking neat.

TROUBLESHOOTING

Plant does not bloom.
CAUSE: Too little light; nights too long.
REMEDY: Streptocarpus is sensitive to day length, and will not bloom unless days are at least 15 hours long. If needed, place plants beneath a fluorescent light 15 hours each day. Plants grown in natural light bloom best in late spring and early summer.

Leaf edges turn brown.
CAUSE: Overwatering; fertilizer burn.
REMEDY: Water plants lightly yet frequently to keep the soil uniformly moist. Do not feed plants that have

dried out. Instead, water them until the soil is lightly moist before adding fertilizer to the water.

Outer leaves shrivel to brown.
CAUSE: This is the natural growth habit of streptocarpus.
REMEDY: Use sharp scissors or a razor blade to trim off old leaves as soon as they begin to fail.

Plants grow poorly, appear limp despite regular watering.
CAUSE: Stem or root mealybugs; root rot.
REMEDY: Check stems for white cottony masses. If mealybugs are present, remove them with tweezers. Also check for root mealybugs by pulling plant from pot and

inspecting roots. Remove any mealybugs by hand, swish roots through clean water, and repot in fresh soil in a clean container. Roots that appear black have rotted. Trim them off and repot the plant in fresh soil.

Leaves show faint yellow specks and appear parched.
CAUSE: Spider mites.
REMEDY: Isolate plant and trim off badly infested leaves. Spray leaf undersides with water to dislodge mites, and repeat after three days. If problem persists, spray with insecticidal soap or a neem-based insecticide. See page 274 for more information about this pest.

PART 2

FOLIAGE HOUSEPLANTS

FAMILY: ARACEAE   ORIGIN: SOUTHEAST ASIA

Aglaonema commutatum and hybrids ag-la-oh-NEE-ma ko-mu-TAH-tum

·CHINESE EVERGREEN

Chinese evergreen
(Agalaonema commutatum)

ONE OF THE EASIEST FOLIAGE PLANTS to grow, Chinese evergreen tolerates low light better than most other houseplants. It features glossy, often variegated leaves that bend outward in an elegant arch. Very small plants, such as those included in dish gardens, will grow in plain water, or in a container filled with clean pebbles or marbles, until you are ready to pot them up. Large aglaonemas can reach 36 in / 90 cm in height, but they normally stay much smaller.

This plant has long had one weakness: a low tolerance for cold air. But newer cultivars are much less likely to be injured by low temperatures. Newer varieties also form thicker clumps, so mature plants stay bushy rather than growing upright. New growth of all aglaonemas emerges from the crown, so plants that grow too tall cannot be pruned back without killing them.

SPECIFICATIONS

Light: Low indoor light near a north or east window.

Temperature: Normal room temperature (65–75°F / 18–24°C).

Fertilizer: *From spring through summer,* feed monthly with a balanced fertilizer. *In winter,* feed every 6 weeks.

Water: Keep soil lightly moist at all times. Do not overwater nor keep so dry that the leaves droop. This plant tolerates dry air better than most, but still benefits from misting every day or so when indoor air is very dry.

Soil: Any good potting soil.

Repotting: Every 2 years is normally sufficient, as these plants like to be slightly rootbound. Repot in any season.

Longevity: 10 years or more.

Propagation: When a plant grows too tall, cut off the tip and root it like a stem tip cutting as described on page 299. Aglaonemas also may be propagated by division, but this operation should not be undertaken until plants become quite rootbound.

Selections: Newer varieties that are less likely to be injured by temperatures below 50°F / 10°C include 'Emerald Star', with white speckles on bright green leaves, and 'Silver Bay', in which each leaf center is generously splashed with cream, and several others.

Display tips: When small, aglaonema is an ideal tabletop plant for dim living rooms or cozy reading areas. Larger plants show best when combined with dark-leafed plants with a similar tolerance of low light, such as pothos or sanseveria.

TROUBLESHOOTING

Leaves develop gray, greasy splotches that turn yellow.
CAUSE: Cold injury.
REMEDY: Remove damaged leaves, and keep plant in a place where it will not be chilled by cold windows or blasts of cold from entryways. This plant needs temperatures above 60°F / 16°C at all times.

Leaves are stiffly upright rather than arching; pale in color with paler leaf tips.
CAUSE: Too much light.
REMEDY: Move plants to a shadier location. Chinese evergreens are native to the jungle floor, so they need low light. Commercial growers grow them in 70 to 90 percent shade.

Plants appear weak despite watering; small disc-shaped creatures on stems and leaf undersides.
CAUSE: Scale.
REMEDY: This is the most serious insect pest of aglaonema. Dispose of badly infested plants. If infestation is light, isolate plant and follow control procedures given on page 273.

New leaves are yellow and small, deformed with kinked edges.
CAUSE: Copper deficiency.
REMEDY: Root temperatures below 65°F / 18°C can limit the plants' uptake of copper, or the soil may be deficient. Treat plant with a micronutrient spray (see page 262), keep in a warm place, and repot if appropriate to refresh the soil.

White cottony insects on stems or leaf undersides.
CAUSE: Mealybugs.
REMEDY: Isolate plant and follow control directions given on page 273.

FAMILY: **ARAUCARIACEAE**   ORIGIN: **NORFOLK ISLAND, EAST OF AUSTRALIA**

Araucaria heterophylla

ar-a-KAR-ee-a he-ter-oh-FEE-la

NORFOLK ISLAND PINE, NORFOLK PINE

Norfolk Island pine
(*Araucaria heterophylla*)

THIS PLANT'S ELEGANT HORIZONTAL BRANCHES studded with soft needles have made Norfolk Island pine a favorite parlor plant for more than 100 years. However, it can be difficult to please in dry indoor rooms unless you are willing to mist it daily to increase humidity. And, because this plant needs abundant light, it's also important to monitor it closely for problems with dry soil. Any type of stress, from dry soil to overfertilization, can cause the needles to drop. Once shed, they are never replaced.

That said, if you have a suitable place for Norfolk Island pine, such as a large south or west window or cool sun porch, it can become a beloved green companion. Turn the plant regularly to encourage even growth, and never trim it from the top or sides. Do remove low branches that die, which is normal with this plant. When grown indoors, plants usually stop growing at 5–6 ft/ 1.5–1.8 m tall. In its ancestral home, this species can reach 200 ft/ 60 m. If you move your Norfolk Island pine outdoors in summer, be sure to place it where it will get a half day of shade.

SPECIFICATIONS

⬥ Light: High light, near a west or south window where the plant will get 1 to 2 hours of direct sun each day.

Temperature: Cool (55–75°F/ 13–24°C).

Fertilizer: *From March to September,* feed monthly with a balanced fertilizer. Spray twice yearly with a micronutrient spray.

Water: Water often enough to keep soil lightly moist at all times.

Soil: Any good potting soil, with additional gravel in the bottom of the pot to add weight and enhance drainage (see pages 259-60).

Repotting: Repot young plants yearly, increasing pot size by 1 in/ 2.5 cm inch, until plant is in a 12 in/30 cm pot. Repot large plants every 3 years. Handle gently, as the roots are scant and fragile.

Longevity: Many years.

Propagation: Seeds, though starting with a purchased plant saves several years of growing time.

Selections: Sold by species name.

Display tips: This plant needs a stable location and plenty of room. When well grown, it becomes a focal point in any light-filled room.

TROUBLESHOOTING

Branches droop downward.
CAUSE: Too little light.
REMEDY: Move plant to a brighter location.

Older leaves are yellow; needles fall from plants.
CAUSE: Overly wet roots often cause leaves to turn yellow before they are shed, but too little water or low humidity also can cause needles to drop. Overfertilization can make new needles at stem tips appear yellow and scorched.
REMEDY: Check the soil before watering, and water often enough to keep it constantly moist. Use a dilute fertilizer, and feed plants only when you are certain that they have not been stressed by overly dry soil. Mist plants daily to maintain high humidity.

New growth is pale and slow.
CAUSE: Too little fertilizer; micronutrient deficiency.
REMEDY: Increase frequency of feeding, and spray plant with a micronutrient spray as described on page 262.

Small round bumps on stems; needles pale and limp.
CAUSE: Scale.
REMEDY: Isolate plant and treat with insecticidal soap or horticultural oil as described on page 275. If plant is outdoors, drench roots with a pesticide that contains imidacloprid.

White cottony creatures on leaves and stems.
CAUSE: Mealybugs.
REMEDY: Isolate plant, and remove mealybugs with a cotton swab dipped in alcohol. See page 273 for other control measures.

Leaves pale; webby material between needles.
CAUSE: Spider mites.
REMEDY: Severe infestations are very difficult to control. Isolate plant, and move it outdoors as soon as possible. Spray weekly with soap-oil spray as described on page 275.

FAMILY: CONVALLARIACEAE   ORIGIN: CHINA

Aspidistra eliator as-pi-DIS-tra ee-lee-AT-tor

ASPIDISTRA, CAST IRON PLANT, BARROOM PLANT

Cast iron plant *(Aspidistra eliator)*

AN IDEAL FOLIAGE PLANT FOR LOW LIGHT, aspidistra is often grown as a groundcover in warm-climate shade gardens. Indoors, this plant will put up with much neglect, though it responds to good care by producing numerous 24 in/60 cm leaves, up to 4 in/10 cm wide, with a waxy coating that makes them naturally glossy. In Victorian times, aspidistra earned the name of barroom plant because of its ability to tolerate the dank and polluted air of taverns.

Green-leafed aspidistras tend to be the most vigorous selections, though there are varieties with leaves speckled with pale yellow, and a third group with irregular cream stripes down the leaves. The striped aspidistras are a bit unstable, as they often revert to green. To keep the green leaves from outcompeting the variegated ones, remove some of the green ones as they appear. Aspidistra produces small inconspicuous brownish flowers near the soil line, which are thought to be pollinated by snails.

SPECIFICATIONS

Light: Low light from a north window, or artificial light.

Temperature: Adaptable to changing temperatures, which can range from 45–85°F/7–29°C.

Fertilizer: *From late spring to early fall,* feed every 2 to 3 weeks with a balanced houseplant fertilizer. *In winter,* feed once or twice.

Water: *In late spring and early summer,* keep soil lightly moist. *In midsummer and fall,* allow soil to become nearly dry between waterings. *In winter,* be careful not to overwater, as plants grow very little during this time.

Soil: Any potting soil.

Repotting: Usually needed only every 3 years, to refresh the soil.

Longevity: Many years; indefinitely when propagated by division.

Propagation: Divide a crowded clump by pulling it apart into halves and repotting in containers only slightly larger than the root masses of the divided clumps. Division is usually not necessary more often than every 5 years.

Selections: There are many named varieties, and the same plant may go under several names. For example, 'Ginga' and 'Starry Night' are the same speckled variety, and 'Variegata' and 'Okame' are the same striped one. An aspidistra with unusually stiff, narrow green leaves, *A. capitosa* 'Jade Ribbons', is becoming increasingly available.

Display tips: Use aspidistra as a floor or table plant in dim rooms, or in offices, schools, and other commercial areas where plants are needed that thrive in low light and require no skilled care.

TROUBLESHOOTING

Leaves develop open cuts, or slits, between leaf veins.
CAUSE: Too much fertilizer.
REMEDY: Leach pots to remove excess fertilizer (see page 263). Do not feed plants again for a month, then resume feeding with a more dilute fertilizer. Wait until new leaves develop to gradually remove the ones that show slits. Even though they are imperfect, they continue to gather solar energy that benefits the plants.

Leaves turn yellow.
CAUSE: Possible overwatering.
REMEDY: It is normal for aspidistra to shed outer leaves from time to time, but yellowing of any but the oldest, outermost leaves indicates overwatering. Check drainage holes to make sure they are not plugged with debris, and water plant less, allowing soil to dry between waterings.

Leaf tips pale and yellow.
CAUSE: Spider mites.
REMEDY: Check plants regularly for this pest, which tends to infest leaf tips first. Isolate plant, remove badly infested leaves, and clean thoroughly. See page 274 for more information on this pest. Do not use oil-based sprays on aspidistra, as oils penetrate the waxy coating on the leaves and cause slight mottling.

Pale dots on leaf surfaces; disc-shaped bumps on stems and leaf undersides.
CAUSE: Scale.
REMEDY: Remove scale by hand using your fingernail or a toothpick. If tiny white larvae are present, spray with insecticidal soap. The same species of scale that infests ferns can feed on aspidistra, so if one type of plant becomes infested, be sure to check others kept nearby.

FAMILY: **AGAVACEAE**   ORIGIN: **MEXICO**

Beaucarnea recurvata, syn. *Nolina recurvata* bow-KAR-nee-a re-kur-VAT-a

PONYTAIL PALM, BOTTLE PALM, ELEPHANT FOOT

Ponytail palm
(*Beaucarnea recurvata*)

LONG LIVED AND EASY TO PLEASE, beaucarnea makes a wonderful long-term green companion. Often called ponytail palm because of the way its narrow, 36 in/90 cm-long leaves spew from a central topknot like a ponytail, beaucarnea is not a palm at all. Rather, its true nature as a semi-succulent is revealed by the bulbous shape of its lower trunk, which serves as a water reservoir. A slow grower, beaucarnea may take 2 decades to reach its mature indoor height of about 8 ft/2.4 m. Plants more than 4 ft/1.2 m tall become extremely heavy, making them difficult to move. If you keep a large beaucarnea, it will need to be equipped with a wheeled platform.

The only challenge to growing beaucarnea is learning its water needs. Overwatering in winter is a common mistake, so be careful. Beaucarnea leaves tend to collect dust, so a thorough midwinter cleaning of the leaves with a pump spray bottle of water and a soft cloth, followed by moderate soaking of the soil, may be the only attention this plant requires from November to March.

SPECIFICATIONS

Light: Bright. Can adapt to lower light in winter provided it receives plenty of light from spring through fall.

Temperature: Average room temperatures (65–75°F/18–24°C) year-round.

Fertilizer: *In spring and summer,* feed monthly with a balanced houseplant fertilizer. *In fall and winter,* do not feed.

◆ Water: *From spring through fall,* allow soil to dry to within 2 in/5 cm of the surface between waterings. *In winter,* water only occasionally. Plant likes low humidity.

Soil: A fast-draining soil, such as cactus potting soil.

Repotting: Every other year, or when the base of the trunk expands to within 2 in/5 cm of the edge of the pot.

Longevity: To 30 years or more when grown indoors.

Propagation: Seeds; potting up offsets that occasionally appear near the base of the plant. To propagate an old plant, the only option is to cut off its head, which may force out two or three buds a few inches below the cut; these buds can then be cut away and rooted. The operation, best undertaken in summer, requires a bit of luck.

Selections: Sold by species name, upon which plant taxonomists do not agree. Long accepted as *Beaucarnea,* details of this plant's flower structure (blooms never appear on indoor-grown plants) have led some experts to reclassify it as *Nolina* (family Liliaceae).

Display tips: This plant is almost always grown as a solitary table or floor specimen. It is a fine companion for smaller flowering houseplants.

TROUBLESHOOTING

Leaf tips turn brown.
CAUSE: Overwatering; under-watering.
REMEDY: Plants kept outdoors on shady balconies and patios, or those grown in a bright sunroom, are not as likely to show this symptom as are indoor-grown plants, which almost always show a few brown leaf tips. The low metabolic rate that results when plants are kept in low light, with little moisture moving through their systems, often causes modest browning of leaf tips on otherwise healthy plants. Snip them off with sharp scissors (see page 257). Avoid overwatering. When in doubt, do not water, but also do not allow plant to dry out completely. Should the soil become extremely dry, rehydrate it gradually rather than all at once.

Base of plant shows dark, shriveled areas.
CAUSE: Stem rot, bacterial soft rot
REMEDY: Whether caused by fungi or bacteria, the rotting of the base of a beaucarnea usually leads to the plant's demise. Overwatering contributes to the problem. It is possible that by withholding water, a plant with a small amount of stem rot will seal off the injury internally and continue to grow. However, a badly affected plant should be discarded.

Leaves appear pale, with pinprick dots and webby material of leaf undersides.
CAUSE: Spider mites.
REMEDY: Isolate plant, and wipe leaf undersides with a soft cloth dipped in soapy water. Repeat after 5 to 7 days. See page 274 for more information about this pest. Periodic cleaning of beaucarnea leaves is the best way to prevent mite infestation.

FAMILY: **MARANTACEAE**   ORIGIN: **BRAZIL AND CENTRAL AMERICA**

Calathea species and hybrids

ka-LATH-ee-a

CALATHEA, PEACOCK PLANT, ZEBRA PLANT

Peacock plant *(Calathea hybrid)*

IF YOU HAVE A PLANT THAT SEEMS like a prayer plant (*Maranta*, see page 210) but is not a prayer plant, it is probably this prayer plant cousin. Several *Calathea* species are valued as houseplants, though all demand high humidity levels in order to flourish. Small specimens often are included in dish gardens, where their feathery, parallel leaf stripes on velvet-textured leaves have an enchanting effect. Some calatheas have narrow, lance-shaped leaves to 16 in/ 40 cm long, while others feature oval leaves, 9 in/22.5 cm long and 6 in/15 cm wide. New leaves are curled as they emerge, and most selections have distinct reddish color on leaf undersides. Mature plant size is usually less than 18 in/45 cm high and wide.

In winter, use every practical method for keeping humidity above 60 percent for your calathea (see page 266). In summer, you can set the plant outdoors in a shady spot provided temperatures stay above 65°F/18°C and below 90°F/32°C. Check leaves often for pests, particularly when bringing plants indoors that have been outside. Calatheas love regular warm showers, indoors or out.

SPECIFICATIONS

Light: Bright indirect light, but no direct sun.

Temperature: Average to warm room temperatures (70–85°F/ 21–29°C).

Fertilizer: *From spring through summer,* feed with a high-nitrogen foliage plant fertilizer every 3 weeks. *In fall and winter,* feed monthly.

⬥ Water: Keep soil lightly moist at all times, and maintain high humidity. Use distilled water or rainwater, as calathea is sensitive to fluoride and salts.

Soil: Fast-draining potting soil that contains peat and perlite.

Repotting: Repot annually in spring to refresh soil and provide a clean container.

Longevity: 5 to 8 years, or longer when propagated by division.

Propagation: Calathea is not easy to divide, so wait until the plant is quite large to attempt it, and expect the plant to be set back by the operation. You can also try rooting stem cuttings under very warm, moist conditions (see pages 299-302). Most calatheas are grown from tissue culture.

Selections: There are numerous named varieties, of which 'Corona', with broad, pale green leaves with dark margins, is quite popular. Lance-leafed calatheas, such as *C. rufibarba*, are not as showy, but tend to be easier to grow.

Display tips: Group calatheas with other plants that need humid conditions, such as ferns, orchids, and bromeliads. A single well-grown calathea makes a beautiful specimen plant for any room.

TROUBLESHOOTING

Leaf tips and edges turn brown.
CAUSE: Low humidity; excessive fertilizer; hard water; fluoride in water.
REMEDY: Plants often develop a few burned leaf tips as they acclimate themselves to a new home. Keep humidity high, and leach pots periodically to prevent root damage from salts from fertilizer or water (see page 263).

New leaves are lighter green than older ones.
CAUSE: Insufficient nitrogen or iron.
REMEDY: Increase frequency of feeding. Check fertilizer label to make sure it includes iron. If not, and increased feeding does not solve the problem within a few weeks, treat plant with an iron spray (available at garden centers).

Leaves yellow and speckled with sticky undersides.
CAUSE: Spider mites.
REMEDY: Calathea is easy prey to mites if high humidity is not maintained. It is important to detect this problem very early, at which time you can try a systemic pesticide (see page 272). If faint webbing is present on leaf undersides, the infestation is very advanced and the plant should be discarded. Never use any type of oil spray on calathea, as serious leaf burn can result.

Cottony creatures on stems and leaves.
CAUSE: Mealybugs.
REMEDY: Isolate plant and remove mealybugs by hand, using a cotton swab dipped in alcohol. Repeat after 3 days, and continue to monitor plant for a month. Never use any type of oil spray on calathea, as serious leaf burn can result.

FAMILY: **ANTHERICAEA**   ORIGIN: **TROPICAL AFRICA AND SOUTH PACIFIC**

Chlorophytum comosum

klor-oh-FY-tum ko-MO-sum

SPIDER PLANT, AIRPLANE PLANT

Spider plant
(Chlorophytum comosum)

POPULAR AND EASY TO GROW, spider plant is an excellent house-plant for beginners. Its strap-shaped leaves, which grow to 15 in/37.5 cm long, arch outward from a central crown. Spider plant also does an admirable job of cleaning the air of airborne pollutants, though its roots are sensitive to tainted water. The brown leaf tips often seen on this plant sometimes are the result of fluoride and other minor contaminants present in many public water supplies.

Spider plant is phenomenally prolific. When less than a year old, plants eagerly produce small, white flowers on the tips of upright stems, which gradually arch outward and develop plantlets on their ends. Sometimes the plantlets themselves produce plantlets. However, when a spider plant is kept in a room where lights are used at night, the urge to flower is likely to be weak. If you want your spider plant to propagate itself, either place it outdoors in the fall so it can respond to days that are becoming shorter, or move it to a room that is not used at night, for 3 weeks in fall or winter, when days are naturally short.

SPECIFICATIONS

Light: Bright to moderate year-round.

Temperature: Average room temperatures (65–75°F/18–24°C) year-round. Avoid chilling below 55°F/13°C, or temperatures warmer than 80°F/27°C.

Fertilizer: *In spring and early summer,* feed every 2 weeks with a balanced houseplant fertilizer mixed at half the normal rate. *In fall,* feed monthly.

Water: *In spring and summer,* keep soil lightly moist. *In fall and winter,* allow the surface to dry 1 in/2.5 cm deep between waterings.

Use rainwater or distilled water if your tap water is fluoridated.

Soil: Any good potting soil.

Repotting: Repot young plants annually in spring. Mature plants grown in 6 in/15 cm pots need repotting every other year.

Longevity: 5 years or more; indefinitely if plantlets are propagated.

Propagation: Set plant in a place where you can put several small pots filled with damp potting soil next to it. Sink the young plantlets into the soil in the smaller pots, so the root buds are barely covered, and use a bent-out

paper clip or small stone to hold the plantlets in place as they root, if necessary. They should root in 2 to 3 weeks. After that time, sever them from the parent plant. Discard excess plantlets.

Selections: The very common 'Vittatum' selection features a white stripe down the center of each leaf. All-green spider plants are increasingly difficult to find.

Display tips: This is an ideal plant for a hanging basket, though it grows equally well in a pot placed on a table or windowsill.

TROUBLESHOOTING

Leaf tips turn brown.
CAUSE: Tainted water;
overfertilization.
REMEDY: Snip off brown tips with
sharp scissors (see page 257).
Leach soil using rainwater or distilled water (see page 263). Use
rainwater or distilled water to water
this plant. Dilute liquid fertilizer to
half strength or less.

**Plant does not bloom or produce
plantlets.**
CAUSE: Too-large pot; too much
light at night; too much fertilizer.
REMEDY: Keeping plants slightly
rootbound increases flowering.
Plants bloom and produce offspring
in response to short nights. In fall
or winter, keep plant in a room
where no supplemental lights are
used at night for 3 weeks. After
3 weeks, it can be brought back
into living areas used at night.
Overfertilization also can cause
plants to produce lush leaves
but no offspring.

Brown discs on leaves.
CAUSE: Scale.
REMEDY: Use your fingernail to
remove the scale. Repeat every
few days. Isolate plant until problem is controlled.

**Plantlets die when transplanted
to pots.**
CAUSE: Plantlets too old.
REMEDY: Plantlets root best when
they are small to medium sized.
Older plantlets often develop dry
calluses over their roots, so they
root very slowly. Plantlets also may
fail when suddenly severed from
the parent plant. For best results,
secure young plantlets in pots for
2 weeks before detaching them
from the parent plant.

FAMILY: **VITIDACEAE**   ORIGIN: **AUSTRALIA, SOUTH AMERICA**

Cissus rhombifolia, C. antarctica, C. discolor

SIS-us rom-bi-FO-lee-a

GRAPE IVY, KANGAROO VINE, BEGONIA VINE

Grape ivy (*Cissus rhombifolia*)

EASY TO GROW IN MOST HOMES and offices, evergreen vines of the *Cissus* genus come equipped with curling tendrils that easily cling to a stake, post, or any shape of trellis. Plant size varies with selection, but most can be kept to less than 24 in/60 cm tall with regular spring pruning. Grape ivy (*C. rhombifolia*) is the most durable species, with hairy brown branches and fuzzy new leaves, which become glossy as they mature. It adapts well to low light, and has a more refined texture than the once-popular kangaroo vine (*C. antarctica*). Begonia cissus (*C. discolor*) has showy variegated leaves that resemble those of fancy-leafed begonia. However, it is a slow-growing plant that requires constant warmth and high humidity, making it challenging to grow.

SPECIFICATIONS

Light: Moderate light from an east window, or fluorescent light.

Temperature: *In fall and winter,* cool room temperatures (55–70°F / 13–21°C). *In spring and summer,* warm (65–80°F/18–27°C range).

Fertilizer: Feed monthly with a balanced houseplant food.

Water: *From spring through summer,* water frequently to keep soil lightly moist at all times. *In fall and winter,* allow soil to dry to within 1 in/2.5 cm of the surface between waterings.

Soil: A porous, fast-draining mix such as peaty potting soil amended with perlite, or African violet planting mix.

Repotting: Repot annually in early summer. Use a heavy pot, and train plant to grow on a stake or trellis.

Longevity: To 10 years; indefinitely if propagated from rooted stem cuttings.

Propagation: In early summer, set 3 in/7.5 cm-long stem tip cuttings to root in sand or perlite, as described on page 299. Use rooting powder, maintain high humidity, and keep temperatures around 75°F/24°C.

Selections: The 'Ellen Danica' variety of oak leaf grape ivy is very easy to grow and adapts to most home and office situations. 'Mandiana Compacta' is dwarf, leafy, and compact, and easily trained to a short post.

Display tips: Grow a young plant in a hanging basket. In its second or third year, shift it to a larger pot where it can be trained to a post and employed as an upright room divider.

TROUBLESHOOTING

Leaf tips turn brown.
CAUSE: Soil and air too dry.
REMEDY: Increase frequency of watering, but avoid overwatering plant. Mist every day to increase humidity. In spring, prune off branches that hold damaged leaves.

Leaves shrivel and fall.
CAUSE: Soil too wet or too dry.
REMEDY: Water as often as needed to keep soil moist, which can be every 2 to 3 days in warm summer weather. Plant needs less water in winter, when little new growth is produced.

Powdery white patches on older leaves.
CAUSE: Powdery mildew.
REMEDY: Prune off affected leaves or branches. Increase air circulation around the plant. This problem is easy to prevent by pruning off older branches in spring, which stimulates the production of healthy new foliage. Older leaves are most likely to show symptoms of this disease.

Small wedge-shaped insects on new leaves and stem tips.
CAUSE: Aphids.
REMEDY: Rinse off aphids with a fine spray of water, and repeat daily until they are gone. See page 269 for more information on this pest. Always test a pesticide on a sample

leaf before using it on cissus, which is sensitive to pesticides, oils, and some soap sprays.

Leaves are pale and stippled with yellow, with faint webbing on leaf undersides.
CAUSE: Spider mites.
REMEDY: Isolate plant. Prune off badly infested leaves and branches. Use a soft cloth dipped in warm water to carefully clean the undersides of remaining leaves. Shift plant to a shady spot and mist often. See page 274 for more information on this pest. Always test a pesticide on a sample leaf before using it on cissus, which is sensitive to pesticides, oils, and some soap sprays.

Codiaeum variegatum pictum

ko-dee-AY-EE-um var-I-ee-GA-tum PIK-tum

CROTON, JOSEPH'S COAT

Croton
(*Codiaeum variegatum pictum*)

TECHNICOLOR CROTONS HAVE BEEN GROWN outdoors in Florida and southern California for many years, but as houseplants they proved difficult to satisfy. Then crotons went to Europe, where greenhouse growers gave them a makeover, selecting varieties that are much better adapted to low light. Today crotons are one of the most widely sold foliage plants, and because they are easily propagated in greenhouses, they are quite affordable as well.

Bold leaf colors that include yellow, orange, and yellow-and-green combinations are the hallmarks of crotons. Leaf color is most vivid when plants get plenty of light. Crotons also have a high transpiration rate, so they need frequent watering. Should you purchase a pot that contains more than one plant (which is not uncommon), plan to keep it as a cluster for a year. The second year, in early summer, separate the plants by cutting through the roots with a serrated knife, repot them, and keep them outdoors where they can bask in warm dappled shade for several weeks. Anytime a croton becomes tall and lanky, you can cut off the top and root it like a stem tip cutting.

SPECIFICATIONS

Light: Bright. Plants benefit from spending summer outdoors in dappled shade. Three weeks before bringing plants indoors in the fall, move them to a shadier spot to acclimate them to lower light.

Temperature: Warm (60–85°F / 16–29°C).

Fertilizer: *In spring and summer,* feed every 2 weeks with a balanced houseplant food. *In fall and winter,* feed monthly.

Water: Keep soil lightly moist at all times. Crotons like moderate humidity, and benefit from regular misting in winter, when indoor air is often very dry.

Soil: Any good potting soil.

Repotting: Repot annually in late spring. Keeping plants slightly rootbound helps to control their size.

Longevity: Several years to indefinitely if propagated from tip cuttings every few years.

Propagation: Root stem tip cuttings as described on page 299. When kept constantly moist at 70–80°F / 21–27°C, croton cuttings root in less than a month.

Selections: Many named varieties are available with varying leaf shapes and colors. The croton most commonly sold in stores is 'Petra'.

Display tips: Wipe leaves often with a damp cloth to keep them glossy. Crotons are lovely when backlit by a sunny window.

TROUBLESHOOTING

New leaves are small and green; lack color.
CAUSE: Too little light; too little fertilizer.
REMEDY: Move plant to a brighter location and increase frequency of fertilization.

Leaf tips turn brown.
CAUSE: Too much water.
REMEDY: Water lightly yet frequently, and do not allow plants to sit in saucers of standing water.

Older leaves drop off.
CAUSE: This is normal, but plants also may shed leaves if they are too cool, too wet, or too dry.
REMEDY: No action needed if plants otherwise appear healthy

and show new growth in spring and summer.

Plant is bare at the base; lacks lateral stems.
CAUSE: This growth pattern often develops with indoor crotons.
REMEDY: Prune off the top in late spring and root the cutting. Meanwhile, the parent plant should produce lateral stems provided it is given plenty of light and warm temperatures.

White cottony masses on stems or leaf veins.
CAUSE: Mealybugs, which are common on crotons.
REMEDY: Isolate plant, and follow control measures described on page 273.

Leaves pale and limp; faint silky webbing on leaf undersides
CAUSE: Spider mites, which infest crotons that are stressed by dryness, particularly dry air.
REMEDY: Isolate plant, and follow control measures described on page 274. Increase humidity by misting plant often, and by keeping the plant on a tray of damp pebbles.

Dark discs on stems and leaf undersides.
CAUSE: Scale.
REMEDY: Follow control measures described on page 273. Inspect new plants closely for scale. If the infestation is severe, move plant outdoors for treatment if possible. If the problem arises in winter, consider disposing of the plant.

FAMILY: **LILIACEAE**   ORIGIN: **SOUTHEAST ASIA AND PACIFIC ISLANDS, INCLUDING HAWAII**

Cordyline terminalis KOR-di-leen ter-mi-NAL-is

TI PLANT, HAWAIIAN TI, GOOD LUCK TREE

Ti plant *(Cordyline terminalis)*

ON SOME PACIFIC ISLANDS, it is thought that growing a ti plant near an entryway brings good luck. It certainly brings a tropical touch, along with plenty of color. There are all-green ti plants, but more colorful varieties with red, orange, and pink streaks in the leaves are preferred houseplants. Plenty of light is needed to maintain good color. In low light, variegation patterns become much less pronounced. Ti plant also needs above-average humidity, especially in summer.

Ti is a slender plant comprised of long, strap-shaped leaves that emerge from a narrow stalk. Young plants are much fuller than mature specimens, which become leaner as they grow to 5 ft/1.5 m tall indoors. As they gain height, they naturally shed their lowest leaves. The stalk becomes a sturdy trunk topped with a cluster of colorful leaves. If a midsized ti is cut down, new branches often sprout from near the base. And, in addition to rooting the leafy tip like any other tip cutting, new plants can be grown from 2 in/5 cm pieces of the stalk, barely buried on their sides in warm, moist potting soil.

SPECIFICATIONS

◆ **Light:** Bright, including up to 4 hours of sun daily.

Temperature: Warm (60–85°F/ 16–29°C).

Fertilizer: *In spring and summer,* feed plants every 2 weeks with a balanced houseplant food that includes micronutrients. *In fall and winter,* feed monthly.

Water: Moderate even moisture, so that roots stay lightly moist at all times. Mist plant every day or so to increase humidity. This plant can suffer badly in extremely dry air.

Soil: Any good potting soil that drains well.

Repotting: Every 2 years in spring. Even tall plants are often happy in smallish pots.

Longevity: 10 years or more.

Propagation: Every few years, root a tip cutting as described on page 299. Ti also may be air layered.

Selections: Many named varieties are available that show different leaf patterns. One of the most popular ones, 'Tricolor', features red, pink, and cream streaks in dark green leaves.

Display tips: Use treelike older plants as floor plants. Even young plants have tall, linear lines that work well when displayed near blue bloomers that need abundant light, such as streptocarpus and exacum.

TROUBLESHOOTING

Color in leaves changes to all green.
CAUSE: Too little light.
REMEDY: Intense light for at least half of the day is needed to maintain good leaf color in a variegated ti plant. Grow near a south or west window, in a bright room with light-colored walls that reflect light.

Leaf margins and tips turn brown.
CAUSE: Insufficient humidity or fluoride in water.
REMEDY: Remove badly affected leaves. Begin misting plant daily, but not when the sun is shining brightly. Place a few pinches of garden lime or wood ashes in the pot to raise the pH, which helps with the fluoride problem. If you know your water supply is fluoridated, switch to distilled water for this plant.

Yellowing of leaves, especially near edges of older leaves.
CAUSE: Magnesium deficiency.
REMEDY: Switch to a plant food that contains this micronutrient. If plant has not been repotted for more than a year, replant in fresh soil. Add a pinch of Epsom salts to water two to three times a year.

Leaves parched; webby material on leaf undersides.
CAUSE: Spider mites.
REMEDY: Isolate plant, clean leaves by hand using a sponge dipped in warm, slightly soapy water. See page 274 for more control measures for this pest. Regular misting of leaves helps prevent problems with spider mites.

Small brown bumps on leaf undersides.
CAUSE: Scale.
REMEDY: Remove scale with a toothpick or fingernail if possible. Spray plant with insecticidal soap to control newly hatched scale. Keep plant in subdued light for 2 days following application of insecticidal soap.

FAMILY: **ARACEAE**   ORIGIN: **CENTRAL AND SOUTH AMERICAN RAIN FORESTS**

Dieffenbachia hybrids di-fen-BAK-ee-a

DIEFFENBACHIA, DUMB CANE

Dumb cane
(*Dieffenbachia* hybrid)

THIS POPULAR FOLIAGE PLANT is often called *dumb cane* because the plant's sap contains calcium oxalate crystals that are potent irritants of human and animal mucous membranes, and chewing the leaves causes the tongue and throat to swell, making speech impossible (and suffocation a possibility). The sap is poisonous to cats, too, so they should not be allowed to play with the leaves.

As for the "cane" part of the name, older dieffenbachias typically grew quite tall until they became tufts of leaves atop a canelike stalk. Some still do, though modern hybrids are more compact and bushy than were their forebears. Many grow to only 12 in/30 cm tall. Numerous hybrids are available that feature different variegation patterns in the leaves, and you may occasionally find all-green dieffenbachias as well. When breeders evaluate new dieffenbachias, they look for a low incidence of leaf burn due to fluctuations in fertilizer and light levels — the most common problem with dieffies.

SPECIFICATIONS

Light: Moderate filtered light. Turn plant often to encourage even growth.

Temperature: Average to warm room temperatures (65–80°F/ 18–27°C).

Fertilizer: *In spring and summer,* high-nitrogen foliage plant food or balanced plant food every 2 weeks. *In fall and winter,* feed monthly.

Water: Keep soil lightly moist, never waterlogged, with moderate humidity. Plant adapts easily to most homes and offices.

Soil: Any good potting soil.

Repotting: Every other spring.

Longevity: 3 to 15 years; indefinitely when propagated from rooted cuttings.

Propagation: When a dieffenbachia grows too tall, use a sharp knife to lop off the top of the plant so that a 6 in/15 cm-tall trunk remains. When pups emerge from the lower stem, cut them away and plant them in small pots. In addition, you may have luck trimming the excised top to about 6 in/ 15 cm long, while removing all but the three or four topmost leaves. Set the groomed tip in a jar of water to root for 3 weeks, and then transplant to a new pot.

Selections: Choose varieties based on your personal preferences, because they're all good.

Display tips: Dieffenbachias work well in formal rooms when grown in brass or ceramic containers. In mixed containers, they combine well with arrowhead vine, pothos, and prayer plant.

Leaves droop and fall without yellowing first.
CAUSE: Plant is being chilled.
REMEDY: Move plant to a warmer place where temperatures will stay above 60°F/16°C.

New growth is lopsided or uneven.
CAUSE: Plant is stretching toward light.
REMEDY: Turn the plant a quarter turn every 3 days. If plant still appears lanky, increase light level by moving it to a brighter spot.

Little or no new growth.
CAUSE: Insufficient light or not enough fertilizer.
REMEDY: Provide supplemental light or move to a brighter location; feed plant every 2 weeks with a high-nitrogen foliage plant food.

Leaf edges turn brown and curl.
CAUSE: Too much fertilizer.
REMEDY: Flush soil with clean water to wash away any accumulated fertilizer and salts. After 2 weeks, resume feeding with a dilute solution of water-soluble houseplant food.

Lowest leaves turn yellow and drop.
CAUSE: This is the normal growth pattern of this plant.
REMEDY: Snip off failing leaves during regular grooming.

White, cottony masses on stems and leaf undersides.
CAUSE: Mealybugs.
REMEDY: Clean off with swabs dipped in alcohol. Repeat every 3 days until the mealybugs are gone.

TROUBLESHOOTING

Drooping leaves.
CAUSE: Too little water.
REMEDY: Water plants lightly yet frequently so that the soil never dries out completely.

Brown tips on leaves.
CAUSE: Uneven watering.
REMEDY: Provide water frequently, but never force the roots to sit in water. Learn to judge moisture level in container by tipping it to assess its weight as well as by checking for moisture in the top inch of soil.

Leaves appear pale and bleached, with webby material on leaf undersides.
CAUSE: Spider mites.
REMEDY: Isolate plant and treat the problem immediately. See page 274 for detailed information about this pest.

FAMILY: **ARALIACEAE**   ORIGIN: **SOUTH PACIFIC**

Dizygotheca elegantissima

di-zee-GOTH-ee-ka el-i-gan-TIS-i-ma

FALSE ARALIA, FINGER PLANT

False aralia
(Dizygotheca elegantissima)

CLOSELY RELATED TO SCHEFFLERA, this plant is also called spider aralia or threadleaf aralia, because of its narrow, dark green leaves with sawtoothed edges. And, although the leaves resemble those of marijuana, the two plants are not related. New aralia leaves emerge copper colored, and darken to blackish green as they are exposed to light. In the wild, false aralia grows into a 20 ft/6 m-tall tree, but when grown indoors plants slowly grow to 5–6 ft/1.5–1.8 m, with a lean, upright form.

This plant likes to stay put, and may shed leaves when moved from one location to another. Despite its height, false aralia flourishes in a rather small pot, and its bushiness depends in large part on the quality of light it receives. Warm temperatures and moderate to high humidity are important to avoid problems with leaf drop and spider mites. Regular misting also helps to keep the leaves clean.

SPECIFICATIONS

Light: Moderate to bright indirect light.

Temperature: Warm room temperatures (65–85°F/18–29°C). Plants are damaged by chilling below 60°F/16°C.

Fertilizer: *From spring through summer,* feed every 2 weeks with a balanced liquid plant food. *In fall and winter,* feed monthly.

◆ **Water:** Drench plants and then allow soil to dry to at least 1 in/2.5 cm below the surface before watering again. Avoid overwatering, but never allow the soil to become completely dry.

Soil: Any good potting soil.

Repotting: Repot annually in spring, but keep plant in a smallish pot. As plant gains height, use a heavy ceramic or clay pot to help avoid toppling.

Longevity: 10 years or more.

Propagation: Commercial growers often start this plant from seed, but the best propagation methods to use at home are rooting stem tip cuttings or air layering. Use rooting powder with either method (see page 299) and be patient. Warm temperatures and high humidity are important to successful propagation.

Selections: This plant is usually sold by common or species name. Small plants may be included in dish gardens.

Display tips: The dark green leaf color and upright, linear posture of this plant work well when grouped with foliage plants with lighter green leaves, such as variegated dracaena or Chinese evergreen.

TROUBLESHOOTING

Leaves become dry and drop off.
CAUSE: Dry air; underwatering.
REMEDY: Increase humidity by misting every morning or keeping plant in a room with a humidifier. Water more often, so that the soil in the pot never dries out completely.

Healthy leaves drop off.
CAUSE: Change in environment.
REMEDY: This plant often sheds leaves when moved to a new place. To minimize trauma, protect plant from chilling and avoid moving it in winter, when recovery from change is likely to be slow.

Leaf edges turn brown.
CAUSE: Excessive exposure to sun.
REMEDY: Aralia can take abundant light, but direct sunshine causes stress, in part due to root restriction in small pots. If plant is moved outdoors in summer, keep it in a shady spot.

New leaves are very small.
CAUSE: This is aralia's normal growth pattern, but plant may need more frequent feeding if leaves fail to gain size as they mature.
REMEDY: This plant produces two types of leaves. Juvenile leaves, produced by young plants or branches near the base of older ones, are small and narrow compared to mature leaves. If new leaves at the tops of older plants are quite small, increase frequency of feeding.

Leaf undersides sticky; leaves pale and stippled.
CAUSE: Spider mites.
REMEDY: Isolate plant, and wipe leaf undersides with a soft cloth dipped in a solution of insecticidal soap. Mist plant twice daily for a week. If the infestation is severe, discard plant, as it will never fully recover.

Small, cottony masses on stems, especially near base of leaflets.
CAUSE: Mealybugs.
REMEDY: Isolate plant. Thoroughly clean plant by hand, using a cotton swab dipped in alcohol. Repeat after 5 days. See page 273 for other ways to control persistent problems with this pest.

FAMILY: AGAVACEAE   ORIGIN: TROPICAL AFRICA AND MADAGASCAR

Dracaena species dra-SEE-na

DRACAENA, CORN PLANT, RAINBOW PLANT

Rainbow plant (*Dracaena marginata* 'Tricolor')

SEVERAL SPECIES OF DRACAENA MAKE excellent, easy-to-grow houseplants, and they are especially useful where you want a strongly upright form. Most dracaenas have long, strappy leaves variegated with white or red. The familiar corn plant, *D. fragrans* 'Massangeana', grows to 6 ft/1.8 m tall, as do some selections of *D. deremensis* such as 'Janet Craig' and 'Warneckei'. However, controlling the height of a dracaena is as simple as lopping off its head. Even the red-margined rainbow plant (*D. marginata* 'Tricolor') can be handled this way. Within weeks after the old topgrowth is removed, a pair of new shoots will appear to take its place. Dust tends to accumulate on dracaena leaves, which can be rinsed off with water or gently wiped away with a soft cloth.

SPECIFICATIONS

Light: Moderate to bright indirect light.

Temperature: Average room temperatures (65–75°F/18–24°C).

Fertilizer: *In spring and summer,* feed every 2 weeks with a balanced houseplant fertilizer. *In fall and winter,* feed monthly.

Water: Keep lightly moist at all times, but avoid overwatering.

Soil: Any good potting soil.

Repotting: Repot young plants every 2 years. After plants reach desired size, repot every 2 to 3 years.

Longevity: 10 years or more; indefinitely when propagated from cane cuttings.

Propagation: When plants become too tall, cut off the cane at any height. New leaf clusters will grow from just below where the cane was cut. You can cut sections of the cane into 6 in/15 cm pieces and root them like stem cuttings (see page 299).

Selections: Numerous cultivars are available, with slight variations in leaf patterns and size. Variety name is often not as important as choosing healthy plants that have received good care.

Display tips: Young plants can be kept on tabletops, but as dracaenas gain height they are best used as floor plants. Two or three plants grown together in a pot create an interesting silhouette when their canes are cut at different levels.

TROUBLESHOOTING

Brown spots on leaves.
CAUSE: Sun scorch.
REMEDY: Place where plant will not receive direct sun, especially midday or early-afternoon sun.

Leaves droop and turn yellow.
CAUSE: Root rot from over-watering.
REMEDY: Check the bottom of the pot to make sure the drainage holes are clear. Allow soil to dry slightly between waterings, and never allow the base of the plant to sit in standing water.

Leaves pale, with faded variegation patterns.
CAUSE: Too little light or not enough fertilizer.
REMEDY: Move plant to a brighter location, and increase frequency of fertilization. In some situations, such as warm, well-lit offices, plants need to be fed every 2 weeks year-round.

Lowest leaves fall off.
CAUSE: Sudden environmental change, or too cold.
REMEDY: It is not unusual for newly purchased plants to shed a few leaves after the trauma of being moved to a new place. Be patient. If leaves continue to fall after 2 months of attentive care, consider repotting the plant.

Leaves pale, turning yellow, with webby material on leaf undersides.
CAUSE: Spider mites.
REMEDY: Isolate plant and place it in a low-light situation where it can be sprayed with insecticidal soap and then misted with water twice daily. If the infestation is severe, it is usually best to cut off the top of the plant, dispose of it, and propagate new plants from the old cane.

Brown discs on leaf undersides.
CAUSE: Scale.
REMEDY: Remove by hand, using your fingernail or a toothpick. Recheck plant weekly. Cleaning leaves with a soft cloth twice a year usually prevents problems with scale.

FAMILY: **ARACEAE**   ORIGIN: **SOLOMON ISLANDS**

Epipremnum aureum (formerly known as *Pothos aureus*) ep-i-PREM-num AW-ree-um

POTHOS, DEVIL'S IVY

Pothos (*Epipremnum aureum*)

POTHOS HAS A WELL-DESERVED REPUTATION as the easiest house-plant to grow. Long, vining stems trail over the sides of the pot, often reaching 8 ft/2.4 m or more unless they are trimmed back. The glossy, heart-shaped leaves unfurl constantly, usually emerging green and becoming more variegated as they age. Bright light increases the growth rate of this vigorous plant. Once or twice a year, prune pothos to keep it bushy and full. Clip back some vines to within 2 in/5 cm of the soil, and shorten others by cutting them off at any point. Overwatering is the only serious mistake you might make with this forgiving plant, because pothos cannot stand water-logged soil. Be especially careful with freshly repotted plants, which appreciate somewhat dry conditions as they recover from the change.

Vigorous, fast-growing pothos plants are ideal low-maintenance plants for offices or new houses, where formaldehyde from carpet, plywood, or other materials may be a contaminant. Cats who play with the dangling vines quickly learn to avoid pothos, because the poisonous (but nonlethal) sap causes a burning sensation in the mouth.

SPECIFICATIONS

Light: Moderate to bright light or fluorescent light.

Temperature: Average room temperature (60–80°F/16–27°C).

Fertilizer: *From spring through fall,* feed every 2 weeks with a balanced houseplant food. *In winter,* feed monthly.

Water: Allow soil to dry to within 1 in/2.5 cm of the surface between waterings. Tolerates dryness better than overwatering.

Soil: Any good potting soil that drains well.

Repotting: Repot annually in spring, shifting plant to a slightly larger pot. Control the size of very large plants by clipping off up to a third of the vines along with some of the roots, and do not increase container size.

Longevity: 10 years or more; indefinitely when propagated from rooted stem tip cuttings.

Propagation: Cut back a long stem near the soil, and wait for a new shoot to emerge from the base of the plant. When the new shoot is 4 in/10 cm long, root it as described on page 299. Stem tips also may be rooted, though they are slower to develop roots.

Selections: Inexpensive plants with leaves marbled with yellow or white are widely available. 'Neon' has nearly chartreuse leaves, while 'Marble Queen' is so heavily variegated with white that green is the secondary leaf color. Plants may be labeled with obsolete botanical names, including *Pothos aureus* or *Scindapus aureus*.

Display tips: Make the most of the way pothos stems drape downward by displaying the plant atop a tall piece of furniture or file cabinet.

TROUBLESHOOTING

Leaves are mostly green and lose variegation.
CAUSE: Too little light; weakly variegated variety.
REMEDY: Move plant to a brighter location. Also be patient, as new leaves often emerge green and develop variegation as they age.

Leaves turn yellow and fall.
CAUSE: Too much water; transplant trauma.
REMEDY: A few weeks after repotting, pothos plants often shed a few leaves. Continued yellowing of leaves is usually due to too much water or inadequate pruning. Stems allowed to grow more than 4 ft / 1.2 m long often shed most of their leaves. Check drainage holes to make sure they are free of debris, and water plant less frequently.

Brown spots on leaves surrounded by yellow halos.
CAUSE: Bacterial leaf spot.
REMEDY: Clip off affected leaves, or entire branches that hold many spotted leaves. Keep leaves dry when watering the plant.

Yellow or wilted leaves; soft mushy stems.
CAUSE: Root rot, caused by several types of soil-borne fungi.
REMEDY: Propagate a few stem tip cuttings if possible, then dispose of the plant and soil. Thoroughly clean container before using it to grow another houseplant.

White, cottony masses on stems or leaf undersides.
CAUSE: Mealybugs.
REMEDY: This pest only occasionally infests pothos, which is normally a remarkably pest-free plant. Remove mealybugs with a cotton swab dipped in alcohol. If necessary, repeat after 1 week.

FAMILY: ARALIACEAE   ORIGIN: HYBRID DEVELOPED IN FRANCE IN 1910

× *Fatshedera lizei* fat-sha-DER-a LIZ-ee-i

TREE IVY, FAT-HEADED LIZZY, ARALIA IVY, BOTANICAL WONDER

Tree ivy (× *Fatshedera lizei*)

IN NATURE, IT IS QUITE UNUSUAL for plants of different genera to cross, which is exactly what happened with this plant. One parent, *Fatsia japonica,* is a broad shrub occasionally grown as a houseplant, but more often planted outdoors in mild winter climates. Fatshedera's other parent is a strain of familiar English ivy. The result is a lanky semi-climber that lacks rootlets, so it must be tied to its support. Some people train fatshedera to wander up a window frame, in which case stems can reach 8 ft/2.4 m in length. Or, you can prune back the top of the plant yearly to keep it as a leafy, 24–36 in/ 60–90 cm-tall shrub. To create a very lush plant, grow two or three fatshederas together in the same container.

Fatshedera's beautiful five-lobed leaves, which are often 8 in/ 20 cm across, make this a very dramatic foliage plant. Floral designers often polish the leaves and use them in cut-flower arrangements.

SPECIFICATIONS

Light: *In spring and summer,* bright, filtered light. *In fall and winter,* more moderate natural light or fluorescent light.

Temperature: *In spring and summer,* average room temperatures (65–75°F/18–24°C). *In fall and winter,* cool to average (55–70°F/13–21°C).

Fertilizer: *From spring through fall,* feed every 2 weeks with a balanced houseplant fertilizer. *In winter,* feed monthly.

Water: *From spring through fall,* keep soil lightly moist, allowing it to dry to within .5 in/1.25 cm of surface. *In winter,* water slightly less, but mist daily to discourage spider mites.

Soil: Any good potting soil.

◆ Repotting: Annually in spring. Three plants can be grown together in a 10 in/25 cm pot and tied to a central upright post. Keep newly repotted plants in cool shade for a week to minimize post-repotting collapse, which is common with fatshedera.

Longevity: About 10 years; indefinitely when propagated from rooted stem tip cuttings.

Propagation: Root stem tip cuttings as described on page 299. Use rooting powder, and enclose cuttings in a plastic bag to maintain high humidity.

Selections: A common variegated form has showy cream-to-yellow splotches in the centers of the leaves. It goes by various names, including 'Aureamaculata' and 'Annemeike'. However, green-leafed varieties are often easier to grow.

Display tips: Tie primary stems to a pillar, and use fatshedera as a floor plant or room divider in a place with plenty of filtered and reflected light.

TROUBLESHOOTING

Leaves turn yellow and drop.
CAUSE: Poor drainage; overwatering; transplanting trauma.
REMEDY: Check drainage holes to make sure they are not blocked by debris. Water less, allowing soil to dry slightly between waterings. This plant often sulks for a few weeks after repotting.

Variegated leaves gradually become all green.
CAUSE: Not enough light.
REMEDY: Variegated varieties need a little more light and warmth than fatshederas with all-green leaves. Move plant to a brighter location, or consider shifting it outdoors for a few weeks in summer.

Leaves appear pale and parched, with faint webbing on leaf undersides.
CAUSE: Spider mites.
REMEDY: See page 276 for ways to clearly identify this pest. If spider mites are present, isolate plant and prune off badly infested leaves or branches. Clean remaining leaves by hand, wiping leaf undersides with a soft cloth dipped in soapy water. In spring, prune plant aggressively to force out healthy new growth.

New growth distorted; small wedge-shaped insects present.
CAUSE: Aphids.
REMEDY: Pinch back any badly damaged stem tips. Remove light infestations with a spray of water. If problem persists, follow up with an application of insecticidal soap.

White, cottony masses on stems or leaves.
CAUSE: Mealybugs.
REMEDY: Remove by hand with tweezers or a cotton swab dipped in alcohol. Repeat every 3 days until mealybugs are gone.

Ferns

Bird's nest fern (*Asplenium nidus*) shatters the myth that all ferns are finicky houseplants.

THE SOFT, DELICATE APPEARANCE OF FERNS brings a surge of green vitality to any place where you want a tropical touch. And, although ferns are not difficult to grow, most of them do need higher levels of humidity than humans consider comfortable. Indeed, once-popular ferns such as the maidenhairs (*Adiatum* species) are seldom seen in homes and offices today because of their need for very moist air. The ferns profiled in this section are happy with moderate levels of humidity, which can be achieved by misting the plants once a day (or less frequently), double-potting them with sphagnum moss, or setting them on a tray of damp pebbles. These and other techniques for raising the humidity level around plants are explained in detail on page 266. Today's roomy bathrooms are ideal spots for small ferns, which love to be bathed in steam each time you shower. You can also grow small ferns in a terrarium, as described on page 321.

Exactly how attentive you must be to the matter of humidity depends on whether a fern has thin, feathery leaves or thick, leathery ones. The thinner the leaves, the more essential high humidity becomes. This is why holly ferns, bird's nest ferns, and brake ferns often succeed in the same place that a feathery asparagus fern sheds into a withered mess. Three of the more challenging ferns are described on the facing page, but working with these species is best undertaken only after you are sure you have a site that provides the high humidity levels they require. Begin with an easy fern before moving on to the more demanding ones.

Caring for Ferns

Ferns have shallow, fibrous roots that quickly fill the surface soil in containers. Pots should be as wide as they are deep. Clay pots darken a shade when they are well dampened, so they make good containers that double as moisture indicators. Ferns with attractive surface roots, such as squirrel's foot ferns and hare's foot ferns, are ideal plants for moss-lined hanging baskets.

Light: The natural habitat of most ferns is the shady forest floor, though some grow in the crotches of tree limbs in damp forests or jungles. All grow best in moderate light and are easily burned by full sun. Indoors, near a north window, is the first place to try placing a

The dainty nodding leaflets of maidenhair ferns (*Adiantum capillus-veneris*) are beautiful, but they require humidity levels that seldom drop below 50 percent, which is not practical in most homes. They can, however, be grown in terrariums or in minimally ventilated bathrooms.

Staghorn ferns (*Platycerium bifurcatum*) need high humidity, too, along with an unusual planter — a wad of sphagnum moss attached to a piece of wood. A staghorn fern is difficult to water unless you have a greenhouse or sunroom where drips aren't a problem.

Asparagus ferns (*Asparagus densiflorus*) often do well in shady outdoor settings, but they have trouble in dry indoor environments. High humidity is required, and because the leaflets are so small, shedding is often a problem. Asparagus ferns are not true ferns, but members of the lily family.

fern in summer. In winter, move the plant to an east window if you have one. Offices lit by fluorescent lights are usually bright enough for ferns. If your office is dim, a fern placed on a pedestal, lit with an energy-saving fluorescent bulb, will become a dramatic focal point.

Some ferns, especially Boston ferns, respond well to being moved to a shady spot outdoors in the summer. In any season, do not move ferns more often than necessary, because they often react poorly to a change of location. If a fern is doing well where it is, limit its movement to rotating it a quarter turn every few days to make sure that all sides get exposed to directional light.

Temperature: Despite their tropical demeanor, most indoor ferns grow best in normal or cool room temperatures. A temperature difference of about 10°F/3°C between day and night is beneficial, since this mimics the conditions they might enjoy in the wild. Slight chilling of ferns, to about 50°F/10°C, is much less stressful than overheating. Dry heat is a fern's worst enemy.

Fertilizer: Ferns are not heavy feeders, but they do need a little plant food to support new growth. From mid-spring through summer, feed ferns with a balanced houseplant food mixed at half the rate given on the package. How often you feed a fern depends on the season, the species, and the age and vigor of the plant. Monthly feedings may be sufficient, but ferns that show strong seasonal growth in early summer will benefit from more frequent doses of fertilizer. Feed ferns less often in winter. Suspend feeding of ferns for a few weeks after dividing them, or after a repotting operation that involves pruning the roots. Resume feeding after a 6-week recovery period. This break gives new or damaged roots time to develop protective outer layers, which reduces the risk of chemical burning from fertilizer.

Water: Water ferns lightly yet often. Overwatering can cause roots to rot, while underwatered ferns will not grow and may wilt. In summer, it's a good practice to check ferns daily, though you may need to add water only every other day. In winter, check ferns twice a week. Keep a small pump spray bottle filled with water near your ferns, and mist them each time you check the soil's moisture. (See page 326 for more information on moisture-monitoring methods.) Dribble a little water from the bottle into the containers whenever they seem dry. Room-temperature water is best for misting and watering ferns.

If a fern dries out too much, the peat moss in the soil mixture — combined with a tight mass of surface roots — may make it difficult to reestablish even moisture in the container. To rehydrate a very dry fern, fill a tub or sink with room-temperature water and submerge the pot to just over the rim. Hold the pot in the water for about 2 minutes, until bubbles stop floating to the surface. Remove the pot and allow it to drain until it stops dripping. Never leave a fern sitting in standing water for more than a few minutes.

Soil: When planting ferns, amend packaged potting soil with peat moss. A half-and-half mixture of potting soil and pulverized peat moss is perfect for most ferns. Dry peat moss absorbs a lot of water, so it's best to mix the potting soil and peat moss together in a pail and dampen it well before using the mixture to pot up a fern. Do not use potting soil that contains fertilizer. Fertilizer that dissolves too fast can burn delicate fern roots.

Repotting: Like most plants, ferns develop more new growth in summer than in winter, so spring is the best season to repot them. If you want to encourage a small fern to grow larger, move it to a slightly larger pot when the roots have filled the container. To control the size of large ferns, remove the plant from the container and use sharp scissors to prune off about a quarter of the roots. Then replant it in the same size container it grew in before. Except for big Boston ferns, there is seldom a need to use a pot more than 8 in/ 20 cm wide.

When repotting any fern, take a moment to check the health of the roots. Healthy fern roots have light brown to whitish growing tips. If the roots are black, they are dead. Trimming away dead roots will help protect the health of those that remain by limiting the number of fungi, which regard struggling roots as a delicious lunch.

Propagating: Some ferns, such as Boston ferns, multiply by sending out shallow roots, which develop buds that grow into new plants. These ferns can be propagated by division. Use a sharp knife to cut away little plants that grow near the edge of the container, with roots attached; promptly pot them up, and then refill the hole left behind with a mixture of potting soil and peat moss. Alternatively, in spring when new fronds begin to unfurl, remove the entire plant from the pot and use a sturdy serrated knife to cut the root mass into two or three chunks. Also cut back old fronds and discard them. Repot the divisions and be patient as they slowly recover from surgery.

Sheer curtains are an ideal way to make sure that light-loving ferns, such as polypody ferns (*Polypodium aureum*), enjoy plenty of light yet are shielded from direct sun.

The furry "feet" of *Davallia* and other ferns have earned them pet names such as rabbit's foot fern and squirrel's foot fern.

Ferns that develop furry creeping rhizomes, such as *Davallia* and *Polyodium* species, can be propagated by severing surface roots and planting them in a fresh container. Use a piece of wire or a bent-out paper clip to pin them securely on the surface of the potting mixture. To maintain high humidity while the rhizomes develop roots, enclose the container in a translucent plastic bag until tiny new fronds appear.

Most other ferns reproduce by sporolation, an ancient reproductive process that evolved 200 million years ago, when Earth was a world of water. You will often see round to oblong brown spore cases arranged symmetrically on the undersides of fern fronds in spring and summer. These structures contain single-celled spores, which are the size of dust particles. Unlike seeds, spores contain no food reserves. If they fall onto a very moist medium, they divide into specialized cells that become eggs and sperm. A watery environment is needed for the sperm to unite with the eggs, but if fertilization is successful, the fertilized zygote grows into a new fern.

The fronds of brake ferns (*Pteris* species) often show unusual shapes or frilled edges. They are frequently called table ferns because they are so easy to grow indoors.

Depending on the species, the transition from spore to new plant may take weeks or months, so it is a difficult process to manage indoors. However, it may occur quite spontaneously in a humid terrarium. Should you see a greenish mass growing on the soil's surface beneath a fern in your terrarium, it may be evidence of spores that have successfully reached their sexual stage. Continue to watch, but do not attempt to transplant baby ferns until the little fronds are at least 1–2 in/2.5–5 cm tall.

Small details: Chemically speaking, ferns are delicate plants. Never use any type of leafshine product on ferns, because they can cause severe damage. Ferns are sensitive to pesticides, too, so it's best to control any pests by removing them by hand or by rinsing the plants in a gentle shower. Tobacco smoke can harm ferns, as can other chemical air pollutants. Ferns that show excellent health are a welcome indicator of clean, uncontaminated air.

TROUBLESHOOTING

Fronds turn yellow and wilt.
CAUSE: Overwatering.
REMEDY: Reduce amount of water given at a time. Clip off damaged leaves. Check roots to make sure they have not rotted. Dispose of plants if roots are mostly black or dark brown.

Fronds droop and appear wilted.
CAUSE: Underwatering.
REMEDY: Increase water. Rehydrate pot to eliminate badly dried-out pockets (see page 328).

Leaflets are light green and dull.
CAUSE: Excessive light.
REMEDY: Move to a shadier location. Leaf color should stabilize in a couple of weeks.

Leaves turn brown.
CAUSE: Low humidity; natural aging of fronds.
REMEDY: Clip off brown leaves; increase humidity (see page 266).

Leaves bleached and pale, webby material between fronds or on leaf undersides.
CAUSE: Spider mites (see page 274).
REMEDY: Clip off badly infested fronds, then take the plant into the shower and clean it to dislodge mites. Repeat twice weekly for 2 weeks. Do not use pesticides, which easily damage fern leaves.

Hard brown discs on leaves or stems, especially leaf undersides.
CAUSE: Scale (see page 273).
REMEDY: Clip off badly infested fronds. Use tweezers to remove individual scales. Do not use pesticides, which easily damage fern leaves.

Brown patches on leaves.
CAUSE: Conditions too cold and wet.
REMEDY: Reduce watering and move to a warmer location.

Leaf tips yellow with brown streaks.
CAUSE: Shock from change of location, especially from change of temperature.
REMEDY: Avoid moving plant unless necessary; avoid overheating and chilling.

Getting to Know Your Ferns

In the following pages, six of the most popular, easy-to-grow ferns are described in detail. They are listed in alphabetical order by botanical name, but you may not know a fern's botanical name if it came to you in a dish garden, or if you bought it without benefit of an identification tag. The chart below will help you identify which fern you have. Then turn to the appropriate plant profile to get to know your fern better.

Botanical Name	Common Names	Description	Ease of Culture
Asplenium nidus	Bird's nest fern	Flat, upright fronds with dark veins near the base; vase-shaped with twiglike hairs in central "nest"	Adapts well to dry air
Cyrtomium falcatum	Holly fern, Japanese holly fern	Glossy, dark green fronds on arching stems; leaflets have serrated edges.	Tolerates cold; good for drafty entryways
Davallia species	Squirrel's foot fern, rabbit's foot fern, deer's foot fern	Furry rhizomes at the soil surface; frond shape and texture varies with species.	Needs high humidity; great in baskets
Nephrolepis exaltata	Boston fern, sword fern	The classic fern; lush clusters of long, green, arching fronds	Better outdoors than indoors; tends to shed
Polypodium aureum	Polypody fern, hare's foot fern	Broad, deeply divided, pointed green leaflets, often with wavy edges	Easy small fern; responds well to good care
Pteris species	Brake fern, ribbon fern, table fern	Small, compact ferns with showy fronds that may be variegated or frilled	Lovely little ferns; great for beginners

When well pleased, spreading ferns such as *Davallia* grow into a thick jungle of fine-textured foliage.

Asplenium nidus as-PLEN-ee-um NY-dus

BIRD'S NEST FERN

Bird's nest fern
(*Asplenium nidus*)

THE BROAD, APPLE GREEN FRONDS of the bird's nest fern are arranged in a vase shape, which gives this fern a bold, upright appearance. Frequently the fronds have prominent leaf veins that darken to chocolate brown near the base of the plant. The bird's nest name comes from the hairy central crown, which resembles a bird's nest. Ferns of this genus were once called *spleenworts,* since it was believed that they could cure illnesses associated with the spleen.

The bird's nest fern is easy to grow in homes and workplaces. It tolerates dry air better than many other ferns, but raising humidity a little by placing the pot atop a dish of damp pebbles is beneficial. A healthy plant will grows to 18 in/45 cm tall, or taller when it is very well pleased. New fronds unfurl from the plant's center. It is normal for the oldest, outer fronds to turn brown. When this happens, simply clip them off with scissors. If the broad leaves of bird's nest fern collect dust, rinse them with a light spray of water, and then wipe clean with a soft damp cloth.

SPECIFICATIONS

Light: Near a north window or in bright fluorescent light.

Temperature: Cool to average (55–75°F/13–24°C).

Fertilizer: *From spring through fall,* feed monthly with a balanced houseplant fertilizer mixed at half the normal strength. *In winter,* dilute fertilizer to quarter strength for monthly feedings.

Water: *In spring and summer,* maintain constant moderate moisture. *In fall and winter,* keep soil slightly drier.

Soil: Half-and-half mixture of peat moss and potting soil.

Repotting: Every 2 years, in early spring.

Longevity: Many years.

Propagation: Spores.

Selections: The fronds of 'Antiquorum' have ruffled edges.

Display tips: In the wild, this fern grows in the crotches of trees, so it has a very shallow root system. Small plants can be mounted on pieces of driftwood, which can then be "planted" in broad containers.

Cyrtomium falcatum sir-TOH-mee-um fal-KAT-um

HOLLY FERN, JAPANESE HOLLY FERN

Holly fern (*Cyrtomium falcatum*)

HOLLY FERN LOOKS MORE LIKE a small shrub than a fern. Like a holly, the leathery, dark green fronds have a glossy finish, with toothed edges. Tremendously cold tolerant, holly ferns are often grown as a shade-tolerant groundcover in mild winter climates, where they easily survive temperatures as low as 30°F/-1°C. Indoors, take advantage of holly fern's cold tolerance by growing it in drafty entryways. Holly ferns also tolerate dry air well, and they greatly enjoy spending the summer outdoors in a shady spot.

Holly ferns grow to about 24 in/60 cm tall, and multiply by division. When repotting, make sure the crown sits slightly high; it should not be buried. The roots of holly ferns are tougher than those of other ferns, and not nearly as likely to burn when grown in potting soil that includes natural or synthetic time-release fertilizer. Early spring is the best time to repot a holly fern, because plants make most of their new growth in early summer. Keep the glossy leaves clean by rinsing them from time to time in a warm shower.

SPECIFICATIONS

Light: Moderate light from a north or east window.

Temperature: In spring and summer, average to warm (65–80°F/18–27°C). In fall and winter, cool to average (50–70°F/10–21°C).

Fertilizer: In spring and summer, feed with a balanced houseplant fertilizer diluted to half the normal strength weekly. In fall and winter, use the same strength fertilizer monthly. Plants grown in a planting mix that includes fertilizer require less frequent feeding.

Water: Constant light moisture; tolerates occasional dryness.

Soil: Any good potting soil.

Repotting: Annually, in early spring.

Longevity: 5 to 7 years; indefinitely when propagated by division every 4 to 5 years.

Propagation: Division of mature plants in spring (see pages 306–07).

Selections: Sold by species name.

Display tips: The dark green of holly fern foliage makes it a top background plant in groupings that include plants with variegated leaves or light-colored flowers.

FAMILY: **DAVALLIACEAE**   ORIGIN: **SOUTHWESTERN EUROPE**

Davallia species da-VAL-ee-a

DEER'S FOOT FERN, SQUIRREL'S FOOT FERN, RABBIT'S FOOT FERN, BALL FERN

Rabbit's foot fern (*Davallia species*)

ALL OF THE DAVALLIA FERNS develop creeping surface rhizomes covered with furry scales so that they resemble animal's feet. The foliage of various species varies as well. Deer's foot fern (*D. canariensis*) features large, thick rhizomes and sturdy, leathery fronds. Squirrel's foot fern (*D. trichomanoides*) has smaller rhizomes and more feathery fronds. Rabbit's foot fern (*D. fejeensis*) has very furry feet and light, airy fronds. Davallias with fine foliage need more humidity than those with thicker fronds.

These ferns grow 12–18 in/30–45 cm tall, and are at their best in hanging baskets. When given ample moisture, the creeping rhizomes will grow out of the container and over the side of the pot. These furry rhizomes are more than decorative; they take up moisture and nutrients for the plant, and work best when allowed to crawl over a damp surface. Never bury them, or they will rot.

Davallias are sensitive to salt buildup. In early summer, purge out excess salts by soaking the container in a tub of warm water. Then allow it to drip dry. Slight shedding of old leaflets is normal, especially in winter.

SPECIFICATIONS

Light: North or east window, or in good fluorescent light.

Temperature: *At night,* cool (60°F/16°C). *During the day,* warm (75°F/24°C), year-round.

Fertilizer: *Year-round,* feed every 2 weeks with a balanced houseplant food mixed at half the normal strength.

Water: Water lightly yet often; mist daily to keep rhizomes from drying out.

Soil: Half-and-half mixture of potting soil and peat moss.

Repotting: Every 2 years, preferably in spring.

Longevity: Many years; indefinitely when propagated from rhizomes.

Propagation: Spores, division, and propagation of rhizomes (see page 335).

Selections: Sold by species or common names.

Display tips: Grow davallias in a moss-lined hanging basket or broad clay pot so that the furry rhizomes can easily be seen.

Nephrolepis exaltata nef-ro-LEP-sis eks-al-TA-ta

BOSTON FERN, SWORD FERN

Boston fern
(Nephrolepis exaltata)

THESE ARE THE LARGE, INEXPENSIVE FERNS often sold in hanging baskets in the spring. Many people buy them to hang on a porch or patio in summer. When shopping, look for plants with new fronds unfurling from the plant's center.

Boston ferns are descended from a mutation that turned up growing in a parlor in Boston around 1890. The fronds may grow from 12–36 in/30–90 cm long, depending on selection and growing conditions. Although Boston ferns are great outdoors in summer, keeping them healthy through winter can be a challenge because they need bright light and high humidity. Mist them daily when keeping them indoors, and try to find a good place where they receive plenty of light but no direct sun. Indoors or out, some shedding of old fronds and browning of frond tips is normal. Keep scissors handy for clipping off fronds that break or turn brown.

New plants grow from the outside of the parent clump. These can be cut away and replanted, or you can allow the plants to develop into a large mass and then cut them into smaller clumps before replanting them.

SPECIFICATIONS

Light: Filtered light from a south or west window.

Temperature: *Indoors. At night, below 60°F/16°C; during the day, about 70°F/21°C. Outdoors:* Adapts to a range of 60–70°F/16–21°C nights and 80–85°F/27–29°C days.

Fertilizer: *Year-round,* feed every 2 weeks with a balanced house-plant food mixed at half the normal strength.

Water: Constant light moisture. In warm summer weather, large baskets often need to be rehydrated (see page 328).

Soil: Half-and-half mixture of peat moss and potting soil.

Repotting: Annually, in late spring or early summer.

Longevity: 2 years or so; indefinitely when propagated by division.

Propagation: Division of clump preferably in spring.

Selections: 'Compacta' grows to only 18 in/45 cm tall and 30 in/75 cm wide. 'Bostoniensis' is larger, with long cascading fronds that may reach 36 in/90 cm in length. 'Fluffy Ruffles' is stiffly upright. Numerous other cultivars are available.

Display tips: Hanging baskets are the ideal way to grow Boston ferns.

Polypodium aureum pa-lee-POH-dee-um AW-ree-um
POLYPODY FERN, HARE'S FOOT FERN

Polypody fern
(*Polypodium aureum*)

THIS LITTLE 12-INCH-TALL FERN is easy to grow, and makes a lovely small specimen when grouped with other plants that like moderate to high humidity. A single handsome polypody fern makes an elegant addition to any well-lit room. Polypody fern's fronds, comprised of flat, pointed leaflets with wavy edges, are much less prone to shedding than ferns with more feathery foliage. In addition to attractive, deep green leaves that often have a gray-blue cast, polypody ferns develop furry creeping rhizomes on the soil's surface. However, the fronds often become so lush and thick that the rhizomes are hidden from view.

Grow these plants in broad clay pots that provide room for the rhizomes to spread. Because of their small size and creeping roots, polypody ferns are also good plants to mount on a moss-covered stone or log in a terrarium. When grown in open rooms, keep in mind that polypody ferns need more light than other ferns. They are also at their best when misted daily and fertilized weekly from spring through summer.

SPECIFICATIONS

Light: Bright indirect light.

Temperature: *At night,* cool (60–65°F/16–18°C). *During the day,* warm (70–80°F/21–27°C).

⬥ Fertilizer: *In spring and summer,* weekly applications of a balanced houseplant food mixed at half the normal strength. *In fall and winter,* feed monthly with the same solution.

Water: Constant light moisture year-round.

Soil: Half-and-half mixture of peat moss and potting soil.

Repotting: Every 2 years, in spring.

Longevity: 4 to 5 years; indefinitely when propagated by division.

Propagation: Spores; rhizome division (see page 335).

Selections: 'Mandaianum' has bluish green fronds with twisted and toothed edges. Some selections have grayish leaf undersides, giving them a silvery appearance.

Display tips: The fronds of mature plants often arch outward to form nearly horizontal layers, which gives them a refined, formal appearance.

Pteris species TER-is

BRAKE FERN, RIBBON FERN, TABLE FERN

Brake fern (*Pteris cretica*)

FERNS OF THIS SPECIES ARE SO DAINTY that you may think they are difficult to grow, but in fact they are excellent ferns for beginners. Many cultivars have unusual frilled frond tips or variegated leaflets. For example, various forms of brake fern (*Pteris cretica*) feature white stripes down the centers of the leaflets, or lacy edges lining lime green fronds. Tiny ribbon ferns (*P. ensiformis*), sometimes called Victoria ferns, have silvery fronds with dark green edges. Other ferns within this genus develop frills at the ends of the leaflets. All make fine tabletop plants for any room. Avoid placing them in high-activity areas, because the foliage is somewhat brittle and easily damaged by physical contact.

Most table ferns grow only 6–12 in/15–30 cm tall, but a few can reach 36 in/90 cm. Cool nights are important, but these ferns tolerate neglect better than most others. Do mist table ferns daily in winter when indoor humidity is likely to be very low. These are generally slow-growing ferns that rarely need dividing.

SPECIFICATIONS

Light: *From spring through fall,* moderate light near a north window. *In winter,* bright light near an east window, or fluorescent light.

Temperature: Average to cool (60–70°F/16–21°C).

Fertilizer: *In spring and summer,* weekly applications of a balanced houseplant food mixed at half the normal strength. *In fall and winter,* feed monthly with the same solution.

Water: Keep soil very lightly moist at all times, but avoid over-watering. Needs slightly less water than other ferns.

Soil: Half-and-half mixture of potting soil and peat moss. Do not pack it around roots too tightly.

Repotting: Annually or as needed, preferably in spring.

Longevity: 5 to 6 years; indefinitely when propagated by division every 4 to 5 years.

Propagation: Spores; division every fourth spring.

Selections: 'Albo-lineata' Cretan brake fern has a cream stripe in the center of each leaflet. 'Victoriae' sword brake fern has silvery white fronds edged with dark green. 'Cristata' crested spider brake fern has long slender leaflets with frilled tips. Many more are available.

Display tips: Place these showy ferns on tabletops where the fine details of the leaflets can be viewed up close. Small plants make pretty centerpieces.

Ficus

The weeping fig (*Ficus benjamina*) is the most popular tree to grow as a houseplant.

SEVERAL VERY DIFFERENT HOUSEPLANTS are called ficus, including the four profiled here: weeping fig *(Ficus benjamina)*, rubber plant *(F. elastica)*, fiddle-leaf fig *(F. lyrata)*, and creeping fig *(F. pumila)*. More than a dozen additional species are occasionally grown as houseplants.

Like other members of the Moraceae family, houseplant ficus have a sticky, latex-type sap, which is in such abundant supply in the rubber plant that actual rubber can be made from it. Found on every tropical and temperate continent, plants of this genus feature unusual, fig-type flowers *(ficus* is Latin for fig). Fig flowers line the inside of a fruitlike cavity, which has an opening through which insects can enter. After the flowers are fertilized, the cavity develops into a fruit. Ficus species grown as houseplants very rarely show this characteristic, a shortcoming for which they can be forgiven considering how willingly they adapt to indoor growing conditions in homes and offices.

Caring for Ficus

With the exception of the tough little creeping fig vine, houseplant ficus have a well-deserved reputation for coping poorly with change. They tend to perform best when kept in a spot they like and moved as little as possible. Do rotate your plant to ensure that all sides get their turn to absorb directional light, but do not mistake the shedding of leaves as a sign that a ficus should be moved or repotted. Ficus plants will adjust to any space that suits them, but the process often takes a few weeks. Be patient.

Attentive watering is also required, and with practice you will learn the preferences of your plant. Tip containers slightly to feel their weight before and after watering. Because most ficus are trees, they are grown in large pots. Once the soil in the containers becomes compacted with roots, water applied from the top may run out through the drainage holes before it thoroughly moistens the roots. Occasionally it may be necessary to rehydrate pots in which rubber plant or fiddle-leaf ficus are grown in order to restore moisture to the innermost sections of the container (see page 328.)

People often become quite attached to their ficus plants, which have quirky yet agreeable personalities. With a good understanding of your plant's nature, you should have wonderful success growing the ficus of your choice.

TROUBLESHOOTING

Leaves drop from any large-leafed ficus.
CAUSE: Common response to environmental stress; or, in weeping fig, usually a normal yearly occurrence.
REMEDY: Many new owners of ficus plants are alarmed when their plants begin shedding leaves as soon as they get them home. Resist the temptation to repot, feed, or overwater a shedding plant. Instead, allow them about 6 weeks of recovery time. Plants may show no new growth until spring, but they should stop shedding leaves within a few weeks. Weeping fig often sheds leaves yearly, in the fall, even when the plant is perfectly happy and has not been subjected to stress.

Leaves of weeping fig or fiddle-leaf fig feel sticky and fall while still green.
CAUSE: Scale, which appears as very small beige bumps on bark, stems, and leaves.

REMEDY: Prune out badly infested branches. Take plant outdoors if you can, and spray it thoroughly with a soap-oil spray (see formula on page 275). Two days later, wash plant with warm water, wiping leaf undersides by hand. After a week, inspect plant closely and repeat treatment if needed.

Leaf tips of fiddle-leaf fig turn brown.
CAUSE: Improper watering or magnesium deficiency.
REMEDY: When watering, make sure the entire root mass becomes well moistened, as water is prone to run down the sides of the pot before it soaks in. Once a year, mix a teaspoon of Epsom salts into the water to provide magnesium, which is sometimes absent in fertilizers.

Leaves appear pale and parched, with webby material on leaf undersides.
CAUSE: Spider mites.

REMEDY: All ficus are moderately susceptible to spider mites, though they are seldom the first plants in a diversified collection to become infested. See pages 274–75 for information on making a positive identification of this pest. If a large-leafed ficus becomes infested, gently wash leaves with a sponge dipped in soapy water, rinse it well, and then treat with insecticidal soap. Ficus tolerates the soap oil spray described on page 275.

Rubber plant ficus has large, dark-colored leaves but shows little new growth.
CAUSE: Insufficient light.
REMEDY: Once acclimated to low light, rubber plant will remain healthy, but moderate to bright light is needed to coax out new growth. If necessary, move plant outdoors to a shady porch or patio in summer. It should respond to warmth and increased light by producing a nice flush of new leaves.

The broad leaves of fiddle-leaf fig (*Ficus lyrata*) make it a fine sculptural plant that can help structure space in large rooms.

FAMILY: **MORACEAE**   ORIGIN: **INDIA AND ASIA**

Ficus benjamina FIY-kus ben-ja-MEEN-a
WEEPING FIG, WEEPING CHINESE BANYAN

Weeping fig *(Ficus benjamina)*

THE MOST POPULAR TREE GROWN as a houseplant, weeping fig often goes into crying fits by shedding its leaves. In late summer and fall, the loss of up to 20 percent of the leaves is quite natural. To keep leaf loss to a minimum in any season, mist plant daily to increase humidity, and withhold fertilizer until the leaf drop stops. Also, resist the temptation to overwater a shedding plant, which makes the problem worse. With good care, new leaves will appear in spring and summer to replace those that were lost. Weeping figs are slow growers. Dwarf cultivars grow to only 36 in/90 cm tall, but most weeping figs grow to 10 ft/3 m or more when they are happy. Prune large plants by thinning out tall branches.

You can keep your weeping fig indoors year-round, or move it to a shady place outdoors for the summer. Before bringing the plant inside, check it carefully for sticky leaves, caused by feeding of scale insects. See page 273 for more information on this pest.

SPECIFICATIONS

Light: *Indoors*, bright indirect light. *In summer outdoors*, shade.

Temperature: Average (65–75°F /18–24°C), but can adapt to a broader range (60–85°F/16–29°C).

Fertilizer: *In spring*, sprinkle time-release fertilizer granules over the surface of the soil. Or, *from spring through fall*, feed monthly with a balanced house-plant food. *In winter*, do not feed.

Water: Allow soil to dry to within 2 in/5 cm of the surface between waterings. Water less in winter, when light levels are low.

Soil: Any good potting soil that drains well.

Repotting: Repot only when necessary, usually every 3 years. The best time to repot is late spring, just before new growth begins.

Longevity: 20 years, more or less.

Propagation: Air layering is difficult, requiring up to 4 months of exacting conditions. Most people just start over with a new purchased plant.

Selections: 'Starlight' has green leaves variegated with white, and tends to grow slowly. Dark-leafed varieties, such as 'Midnight' and 'Indigo', adapt to changing light levels more easily than many other strains.

Display tips: Grow as a floor plant positioned in a place where it will not be moved more than absolutely necessary.

Ficus elastica FY-kus ee-LAS-ti-ka

RUBBER PLANT, INDIA RUBBER TREE

Rubber plant *(Ficus elastica)*

THE STICKY LATEX SAP OF RUBBER PLANT does dry into a low-quality rubber, but indoors this species is valued for its smooth, glossy leaves that often grow more than 8 in/20 cm long. In the wild, this large evergreen can grow to 40 ft/12 m or more, but indoor plants require years to reach 12 ft/3.6 m. Wipe the leaves periodically with a damp cloth to keep them shiny, and avoid environmental changes, which often cause rubber plant to shed its lower leaves. If you want to encourage a plant to branch, lightly nicking the bark just above where a low leaf detached itself will mobilize new growth from the latent node. Rubber plants also may send out aerial roots near the base, which should be tucked down into the soil or wound around the soil's surface inside the pot.

SPECIFICATIONS

Light: Bright to moderate light but no direct sun.

Temperature: Average to warm room temperatures (65–80°F/18–27°C).

◆ **Fertilizer:** Feed three to four times a year with a balanced houseplant food that includes micronutrients. Twice yearly, add ½ teaspoon/2.5 ml Epsom salts to a quart of water, and soak the roots with this solution.

Water: *From spring through summer,* keep lightly moist, but do not overwater. *In fall and winter,* water less, allowing soil to dry to 1 in/2.5 cm below the surface.

Soil: Any peaty potting soil that drains well.

Repotting: Every other year, or more often if plant sends out numerous aerial roots. Do not repot a plant that is shedding leaves, as a shedding plant benefits from a stable environment.

Longevity: 15 years or more.

Propagation: When plants outgrow their space, propagate by air layering as described on page 304.

Selections: Several varieties with reddish leaves are named after wines, such as 'Burgundy' and 'Cabernet'. The 'Decora' series of patented rubber plants have showy variegated leaves except for 'Melany', which features a compact, branching form with glossy green leaves.

Display tips: This is a great floor plant, capable of showing exuberant growth in good light. Plants in low light tend to grow broad and bushy. If needed, provide supplemental overhead light to keep a large plant growing upright.

FAMILY: **MORACEAE**   ORIGIN: **WESTERN AFRICA**

Ficus lyrata FY-kus leer-AH-ta

FIDDLE-LEAF FIG, BANJO FIG

Fiddle-leaf fig *(Ficus lyrata)*

WITH HUGE, SLIGHTLY WAVY, GREEN LEAVES in the shape of a fiddle, this tropical fig is actually a tree capable of growing 40 ft/12 m tall in its jungle home. Indoors, plants grow very slowly, and can be kept for many years before they outgrow their space. The large, light-catching leaves grow to more than 12 in/30 cm long and 6 in/15 cm wide. When kept clean, they impart a lush, serene elegance to any indoor space.

Fiddle-leaf fig is easy to grow, and can be trained into various shapes. To promote bushiness, prune off the top of a young plant. If you prefer a more treelike shape, allow the plant to grow tall, then clip off all leaves and branches from the lowest section of the trunk. Plants with braided trunks are available, too, and they are as simple to grow as single plants. This species produces edible fruits when grown outdoors, but indoors it is strictly a foliage plant.

SPECIFICATIONS

Light: Bright to moderate indirect light or fluorescent light.

Temperature: Average to warm (60–85°F/16–29°C).

Fertilizer: Feed three times a year (spring, midsummer, and fall) with a high-nitrogen foliage plant food that includes micronutrients.

Water: Keep soil lightly moist at all times, but avoid overwatering. This ficus needs more water than other species.

Soil: Any good potting soil that drains well. A heavy, soil-based mix amended with peat moss is ideal.

Repotting: Repot every other year in spring, but try to keep plant in a small pot to control its size. Use a heavy container to help prevent toppling.

Longevity: 10 years or more, or until plant becomes too large to keep indoors.

Propagation: Air layer a healthy stem as described on page 304. Most commercially available plants are grown from tissue culture.

Selections: In addition to the species, a few compact varieties are available. An exemplary patented variety, 'Little Fiddle', produces leaves half the size of regular fiddle-leaf figs, and grows less than 6 ft/1.8 m tall over a period of many years.

Display tips: An excellent floor plant for homes or offices, fiddle-leaf fig is at its best when the leaves are kept clean and polished.

Ficus pumila (also known as *F. repens*)

FY-kus pu-MEE-la

CREEPING FIG

Creeping fig *(Ficus pumila)*

YOU CAN GROW THIS PETITE VINING FICUS in a pot, but its climbing talents are better put to use clinging to a topiary form. The stems develop rootlike holdfasts, similar to those of English ivy, which attach tightly to wood, brick, or other solid surfaces. The heart-shaped leaves, to 1 in/2.5 cm long, give creeping fig a fine texture, and it often flourishes when grown in terrariums with other small-leafed plants. With regular trimming, it can also be used as a groundcover in large containers in which upright plants such as Norfolk pine are grown. Creeping fig likes constant light moisture, but the plants will yellow or rot if overwatered. Often grown as an outdoor groundcover or wall plant in Zones 8 and 9, creeping fig can survive 30–40°F/-1–4°C temperatures, but not hard freezes.

SPECIFICATIONS

Light: Adapts to low, moderate, or bright light, but cannot tolerate direct sun. Bright light is needed to support fast growth.

Temperature: Withstands temperatures to freezing, but grows best with average to warm room temperatures (55–85°F/13–29°C).

Fertilizer: *From spring through summer,* feed monthly with a balanced houseplant food. *In winter,* when light levels are low, do not feed.

Water: *From spring through summer,* keep soil lightly moist at all times, with moderate to high humidity. *In winter,* water less, allowing the surface of soil to dry between waterings.

Soil: Any good potting soil that drains well.

Repotting: Every 2 years when grown as topiary; yearly, in terrariums.

Longevity: To 5 years for individual potted plants; indefinitely when propagated.

Propagation: Root stem tip cuttings in spring as described on page 299.

Selections: In addition to the species, some cultivars feature quilted green leaves similar in shape to tiny oak leaves. 'Snowflake' and a few other cultivars are variegated with white. The leaves of 'Minima' are quite small, which makes them work well in terrariums.

Display tips: Grow on a moss-filled wire form as topiary, or allow stems to crawl over rocks in a terrarium. Creeping fig also grows well in a small pot, kept on a table-top near a lamp or other light source.

FAMILY: **ACANTHACEAE**   ORIGIN: **COLUMBIA AND PERU**

Fittonia verschaffeltii

fi-TOW-nee-a ver-sha-FEL-tee-i

NERVE PLANT, SILVER NET LEAF

Nerve plant
(*Fittonia verschaffeltii*)

EACH LEAF OF A FITTONIA PLANT is a living work of art. Against a background of deep olive green, leaf veins of white, pink, or green branch and flow in symmetrical patterns. The finely etched leaves of fittonia have earned it a prominent place in small dish gardens and terrariums, where it usually grows beautifully with the help of constant moisture and very high humidity. However, the plants often do not fare as well when planted into individual pots and handled as regular houseplants. Dry indoor air and strong light easily stress fittonia, and the plant cannot tolerate dry soil. However, when kept in an ideal spot and watered attentively, nerve plant's new growth becomes so vinelike that regular pinching is needed to keep it bushy and full. Also pinch off small flower spikes should they appear, because they will weaken the show of leaves. Full-sized fittonias grow about 6 in/15 cm tall and 12 in/30 cm wide, with miniature forms smaller.

Despite their temperamental nature, fittonias are very easy to propagate from stem tip cuttings. In a terrarium, stem tips tucked into any vacant spot of soil often show new growth within 2 weeks.

SPECIFICATIONS

Light: Moderate indirect light or fluorescent light.

Temperature: Average room temperatures (65–75°F/18–24°C).

Fertilizer: *From spring through summer,* feed monthly with a balanced houseplant food. *In winter,* feed every 6 weeks.

◆ Water: Provide water as needed to keep plant constantly moist. Plant will collapse if it dries out.

Soil: Any peaty potting soil that holds moisture well.

Repotting: Annually in spring, or as needed to rearrange plants in a dish garden or terrarium.

Longevity: Several years; indefinitely when propagated from stem tip cuttings.

Propagation: In spring or summer, root stem tip cuttings as described on page 299. Under warm, humid conditions, cuttings develop roots in 2 to 3 weeks.

Selections: Vein color varies with selection, and may be white, pink, or red. Selections also vary in leaf size. Miniature forms are ideal for small terrariums.

Display tips: This plant requires high humidity, so it is best grown in a terrarium or dish garden. Combine it with small ferns, prayer plant, and other foliage plants that need humid conditions.

TROUBLESHOOTING

Entire plant collapses.
CAUSE: Dry soil.
REMEDY: Fittonia is famous for having fainting spells when its roots fail to keep the succulent stems supplied with water. If promptly watered, the plant will recover with no ill effects, but dehydration for more than a few hours can be fatal

Leaves turn yellow.
CAUSE: Too much water; poor drainage.
REMEDY: Check drainage holes in bottom of pot to make sure they are not plugged with debris. Fittonia needs light moisture at all times, but roots suffer when all oxygen is forced from the soil by water. Pinch back stems to remove yellow leaves, and allow slightly more drying time between waterings.

Small white gnats hover over the soil.
CAUSE: Fungus gnats.
REMEDY: The moist, peaty soil conditions fittonia needs favor fungus gnats, which require ongoing management once established. See page 270 for detailed information on the life cycle and control measures for this pest.

White cottony masses on stems or leaves.
CAUSE: Mealybugs.
REMEDY: Isolate plant, and remove mealybugs with tweezers or a cotton swab dipped in alcohol. Repeat every few days until mealybugs are controlled. Do not use pesticides, oils, or soap sprays on this plant, as the thin leaves are easily damaged.

New growing tips are wilted; small wedge-shaped insects present on stems or new leaves.
CAUSE: Aphids.
REMEDY: Pinch off badly infested stem tips. If possible, place plant over a sink of lukewarm water and gently wash off aphids. Watch plant closely, and repeat after a few days. Do not use pesticides, oils, or soap sprays on this plant, as the thin leaves are easily damaged.

FAMILY: ASTERACEAE   ORIGIN: INDONESIA

Gynura aurantiaca,
G. sarmentosa gy-NUR-a aw-RAN-ti-ah-ka

VELVET PLANT, PURPLE PASSION

Velvet plant
(Gynura sarmentosa)

IF YOU LIKE HOUSEPLANTS THAT GROW RAPIDLY, velvet plant should be on your most-wanted list. Whether grown in pots or hanging baskets, velvet plant wastes no time developing stocky stems studded with dark red or green leaves covered with a down of purple hairs. Stems may grow to 20 in/50 cm tall. Easy to grow provided you have a brightly lit spot, velvet plant has been popular in homes for 200 years.

Year-old velvet plants often produce small yellow-orange flowers in spring, but they emit an unpleasant smell, so most people clip them off. Should your plant bloom, take it as a sign that the plant has reached maturity, and expect it to begin to decline. Before that happens, root stem cuttings. Use the method described on page 299, but remove any covering of the cuttings each night so that the leaves get a break from constant dampness. The hairs on velvet plant leaves trap moisture, which makes them prone to rot when they are not allowed to dry out. Still, this is one of the easiest of all indoor plants to propagate from stem cuttings.

SPECIFICATIONS

Light: Most comfortable in moderate light; bright light intensifies leaf color.

Temperature: Cool to average room temperatures (60–75°F/16–24°C).

Fertilizer: *From spring through fall,* feed with a balanced houseplant food every 2 weeks. *In winter,* feed monthly.

Water: Keep soil lightly moist at all times. Plant will wilt quickly if it becomes dry, but makes a fast recovery when rehydrated.

Soil: Any good potting soil.

Repotting: Repot annually in spring. Propagate plants more than 2 years old instead of repotting them.

Longevity: 2 to 3 years; indefinitely when propagated by rooting stem cuttings.

◈ Propagation: Root 3 in/7.5 cm-long stem cuttings as described on page 299.

Selections: Plants sold under the variety name 'Purple Passion' tend to be upright and very dark purple. Trailing forms, suitable for hanging baskets, are often classified as *G. sarmentosa.*

Display tips: The dark foliage of velvet plant is useful in containers planted with several houseplants, especially hanging baskets. Or, you can keep it in its own pot and display it alongside plants that have chartreuse leaves or blooming houseplants with pink flowers. The downy leaves look great when backlit by a sunny window.

TROUBLESHOOTING

Leaves are more green than purple.
CAUSE: Too little light.
REMEDY: Move the plant to a slightly brighter place for a few days, and then to a spot that receives a little direct sun. Leaf color should darken within 2 weeks.

Plant wilts daily even when watered.
CAUSE: Pocket of dry roots and soil in middle of pot; plant may be extremely rootbound.
REMEDY: First try rehydrating the pot (see page 328). If problem persists and plant is more than 2 years old, prune back the plant

by half its size, set three of the best stem tips to root (see page 299), and repot the mother plant. (Wait until you know you have successful rooted cuttings before you discard the mother.)

Leaves show dark patches.
CAUSE: Water damage from water that remained on leaves for long periods after watering; water droplets on leaves that heated up from sunlight.
REMEDY: When watering, try to keep leaves dry. Should you wet the leaves on purpose to clean them, shake off excess moisture and set the plant in a shady place to dry.

Leaves puckered or curled, with small insects clinging to leaf undersides.
CAUSE: Aphids.
REMEDY: If only a few leaves are infested, pick them off and dispose of them. Then take plant outside or into a warm shower and rinse it off thoroughly. Recheck after 3 days, and "paint" any aphids found with a cotton swab dipped in soapy water.

Plant collapses and does not respond to rehydrating.
CAUSE: Root rot, which can be made worse by overwatering or cold conditions.
REMEDY: Discard plant. Allow new plants to become almost dry between waterings, and keep them in a place where temperatures stay above 60°F/16°C.

FAMILY: **ARALIACEAE**   ORIGIN: **EUROPE AND WESTERN ASIA**

Hedera helix he-DER-a HEE-liks

ENGLISH IVY

English ivy *(Hedera helix)*

THIS VERSATILE PLANT HAS A DAINTY demeanor that works well in pots or hanging baskets, as well as trained as topiary or employed as a groundcover in containers occupied by large, upright houseplants. There are hundreds of varieties, including many with small, finely cut leaves, often called needlepoint ivies. Small-leafed ivies are the most popular houseplants, though dozens of other varieties deserve consideration. Ivy enjoys spending part of the year outdoors, particularly spring and fall, when days are mild and nights are cool.

When planted outdoors, English ivy can become a pest by running up trees and buildings, but indoors it needs help holding onto support. Pin stems in place when training ivy on a moss-filled topiary form. Some people develop slight dermatitis from exposure to ivy's sap, and the leaves are poisonous if eaten.

SPECIFICATIONS

Light: *In spring and summer,* moderate light. *In fall and winter,* bright or fluorescent light.

◆ **Temperature:** Average to cool room temperatures (50–70°F / 10–21°C); temperatures should be 10°F/6°C cooler at night than during the day.

Fertilizer: Feed monthly year-round with a high-nitrogen foliage plant fertilizer.

Water: Allow surface of soil to dry between waterings, but do not let soil dry out completely.

Soil: Any good potting soil that drains well.

Repotting: Every 1 to 2 years, in spring or fall, when roots show through the drainage holes. Shift to a slightly larger pot, but avoid very large containers, which may contribute to problems with root rot.

Longevity: Many years; indefinitely when propagated from stem tip cuttings.

Propagation: Root stem tip cuttings in damp perlite or plain water.

Selections: There are more than 500 named cultivars, which vary in leaf shape, size, and variegation. Cultivars honored by the American Ivy Society include 'Golden Ingot' and 'Duck Foot'. A variegated form of Algerian ivy (*H. canariensis*), 'Floire de Marengo', is a good choice for warmer growing conditions.

Display tips: Place ivy in pots near the edge of a mantle or other surface where the stems can cascade over the edge. Ivy topiaries are a fine accent for formal rooms and outdoor sitting areas.

TROUBLESHOOTING

Leaves of variegated varieties change to mostly green.
CAUSE: Insufficient light.
REMEDY: In winter, move plant close to an east or west window or provide supplemental fluorescent light. Place plant outdoors for a few weeks in spring and fall, when temperatures are cool. Moderate light conditions are appropriate in summer, when plants are best kept indoors to protect them from excessive heat.

Leaves look parched, with yellow pinpricks near the base of affected leaves.
CAUSE: Spider mites.
REMEDY: Perhaps the most susceptible of all plants to these tiny pests, ivy must be watched closely for early symptoms. Prevent this problem by thoroughly washing plant once a month with cool water. If mites are confirmed to be present (see page 276), isolate plant and prune off severely infested leaves or branches. Fill a deep sink with cool water, and wash plant to dislodge mites. Repeat after 5 days before trying additional remedies as described on page 274. Always wash plants before bringing them indoors.

Leaves wilt; plant shows little or no new growth.
CAUSE: Too much or too little water.
REMEDY: Ivy needs constant light moisture, but roots will rot if plant is overwatered. Check drainage holes to make sure they are free of debris, and switch to frequent light waterings for a few weeks to see if the plant improves.

Tan or brown discs on stems and leaf undersides.
CAUSE: Scale.
REMEDY: Scale insects are seldom seen on ivy kept indoors yearround, but sometimes appear on plants that are kept outdoors. Carefully check plant for scale and other insects before bringing it indoors. Remove scale with your fingernail, or consider other remedies described on page 273.

White cottony deposits on stems.
CAUSE: Mealybug.
REMEDY: Wash plant, then remove any mealybugs that remain with a cotton swab dipped in rubbing alcohol. Repeat after a week if problem persists.

FAMILY: **ACANTHACEAE**   ORIGIN: **MADAGASCAR**

Hypoestes phyllostachya

hy-po-ES-tes fy-lo-STAK-ee-uh

POLKA DOT PLANT, FRECKLE FACE, MEASLES PLANT

Polka dot plant
(Hypoestes phyllostachya)

THE BEAUTIFULLY VARIEGATED LEAVES of polka dot plant have become much more painterly in recent years. Plant breeders have produced varieties that show much more color in their leaves, including some in which the base color of the leaves is red rather than green. And, although pink remains the most popular choice in polka dot plants, white and red variegated forms often are available in spring.

Polka dot plant is grown from seeds, and commercial growers customarily set three seedlings in each pot. This plant can be grown outdoors in summer, or you can keep it as a houseplant year-round. Pinch back stems that grow more than 10 in/25 cm long to encourage the development of bushy branches. Polka dot plant is an excellent color plant to display among ferns and other foliage plants, and it benefits from the increased humidity that results when plants are grouped together. Occasionally, year-old plants produce spikes of purple flowers in late winter. After blooming, plants quickly deteriorate. Bloom or no bloom, it is best to replace plants in spring with vigorous young seedlings.

SPECIFICATIONS

Light: Bright light or filtered sun from a south or west window.

Temperature: Average to warm (65–80°F/18–27°C).

Fertilizer: Feed every 2 weeks with a balanced houseplant fertilizer mixed at half the normal strength.

Water: Keep lightly moist at all times, but avoid overwatering.

Soil: Any good potting soil.

⚠ Repotting: Shift new plants to larger containers as soon as they are purchased. Repot again in midsummer if plants become rootbound.

Longevity: Up to 2 years for individual plants.

Propagation: Seeds started in late winter or rooted stem cuttings. Even when rooting powder is used, rooting is slow.

Selections: Two series, 'Splash' and 'Confetti', are widely available as seedlings in the spring. In addition to the traditional pink-speckled forms, both series include varieties with deep rose, red, and white variegation. In the red forms, the green parts of the leaves are blushed with deep burgundy.

Display tips: Grown in a ceramic or brass container, the variegated leaves of polka dot plant appear quite clean and formal.

TROUBLESHOOTING

Variegation fades and leaves become mostly green.
CAUSE: Too little light.
REMEDY: Strong light is needed to keep the leaves of this plant nicely colored. Pinch back leggy growth and shift to a brighter location.

Leaves curl inward.
CAUSE: Too much light.
REMEDY: Hot sun for more than an hour each day can stress plants, resulting in slow growth and curled leaves. Shield plant from direct sun with a sheer curtain.

Leaves turn yellow and drop off.
CAUSE: Overwatering.

REMEDY: Reduce watering, and consider repotting plant to improve drainage.

Leaves drop off without turning yellow.
CAUSE: Drought stress.
REMEDY: Pinch off leggy stems and increase frequency of watering. New stems will emerge within a few weeks.

Small white flying insects congregate on plant.
CAUSE: Whitefly.
REMEDY: Thoroughly clean plant with tepid water, then isolate it from other houseplants. See page 277 for control measures for persistent infestations of whitefly.

Leaves pale and parched; webby material on leaf undersides.
CAUSE: Spider mites.
REMEDY: Pinch off badly infested stems and dispose of them. Clean plant with tepid water, then isolate it from other houseplants. Mist daily to increase humidity. See pages 274-76 for control measures for persistent infestations of spider mites.

Small brown bumps on stems; plants grow slowly.
CAUSE: Scale.
REMEDY: Remove scale by hand, using a fingernail or toothpick. Pinch off badly infested stems. Consider disposing of badly infested plant.

Maranta leuconeura ma-RAN-ta lu-kon-UR-a

PRAYER PLANT

Prayer plant
(*Maranta leuconeura*)

PRAYER PLANT HAS THE REMARKABLE ABILITY to fold its leaves, prayer-like, in response to darkness. Light causes the leaves to resume their horizontal posture, which you can watch if you keep a lamp near the plant and turn it on after dark. Accepting of moderate light, including most types of office lighting, a prayer plant can be a long-lived green companion if given good care. In 2 or 3 years, a small plant received in a dish garden will grow to 12 in/30 cm tall and 16 in/40 cm wide.

Prayer plants produce small, white, tubular flowers when kept in conservatories, but they rarely bloom when handled as houseplants. Indoor-grown prayer plants excel at producing dramatic leaves, and they benefit from being trimmed back periodically, which keeps them shapely and promotes new growth. Prayer plants often rest in winter, and then produce a flush of new leaves in spring. To keep the showy leaves in top viewing condition, wipe them periodically with a damp cloth. In summer, give your prayer plant a thorough outdoor shower on a warm day. This will clean the plant and leach accumulated salts from the soil.

SPECIFICATIONS

Light: Moderate light from a north or east window, or fluorescent light.

Temperature: Average to warm (65–80°F/18–27°C).

Fertilizer: *In spring and summer,* feed every 2 weeks with a balanced houseplant fertilizer mixed at half the normal rate. *In fall and winter,* feed monthly with the same solution.

Water: Keep soil lightly moist at all times, and raise humidity by misting plant every few days or keeping it on a bed of damp pebbles.

Soil: Any good potting soil.

◆ Repotting: Prayer plant likes well-aerated soil, which is the main reason to repot annually in spring. Do not pack the potting soil tightly around the roots.

Longevity: Many years.

Propagation: When plant becomes too large, divide it in spring by cutting the roots into two large chunks. Plant may need several weeks to recover from this operation.

Selections: 'Erythroneura' and 'Fascinator' are called red prayer plants or herringbone plants because of their bright red leaf veins. 'Kerchoveana', or green prayer plant, is sometimes called "rabbit tracks" because of the square, brownish marks between the leaf veins. 'Massangeana', also called silver prayer plant, has blackish green leaves with silvery gray midribs.

Display tips: Grow prayer plant in a shallow container or combine it with other foliage plants in a tabletop garden. Prayer plant benefits from having close neighbors, which usually increases humidity.

TROUBLESHOOTING

Leaves pale and slightly curled.
CAUSE: Too much light.
REMEDY: Prayer plant does not need direct sunlight and grows best with filtered or indirect light.

No new growth.
CAUSE: Insufficient fertilizer or stunting from fertilizer burn or accumulated salts.
REMEDY: Repot plant in a clean container with fresh soil. A month later, begin feeding it with a dilute balanced plant food. Expect most of the plant's new growth to appear in late spring and summer.

Plant appears weak and floppy despite regular watering.
CAUSE: Root mealybugs.
REMEDY: Remove plant from pot and inspect the roots. If mealybugs are present, swish the root ball in a pail of warm water and remove any hangers-on by hand. Repot in a clean container with fresh soil, and isolate plant until you are sure it has recovered.

Small brown discs on leaves and stems.
CAUSE: Scale.
REMEDY: Isolate plant and treat for scale as described on page 273.

Leaves dry and pale; faint webbing on leaf undersides.
CAUSE: Spider mites.
REMEDY: Prune off badly affected leaves and isolate plant. Clean thoroughly with warm water and begin misting daily. Spray with insecticidal soap if problem persists, or try another remedy described on pages 274–76.

Monstera deliciosa mon-STER-a de-lis-ee-OH-sa

MONSTERA, SWISS CHEESE PLANT, SPLIT-LEAF PHILODENDRON

Swiss cheese plant
(*Monstera deliciosa*)

EASY TO GROW AND TOLERANT of occasional neglect, this handsome foliage plant produces dramatically perforated leaves to 12 in/ 30 cm long, or sometimes larger. A climber that attaches itself to a post with aerial roots, monstera makes a bold, vertical accent plant in large spaces. Over a period of 7 years it can grow to 6–8 ft/ 1.8–2.4 m tall. Mature plants develop rounded slits, or windows, in their leaves that resemble the holes in Swiss cheese. In the wild, these holes help the plant withstand strong winds. When grown outdoors in tropical areas, monstera produces an edible fruit, but plants seldom flower and fruit when grown indoors.

Healthy plants produce a steady parade of pencil-thick aerial roots, which gather moisture from the air. Secure roots that emerge near the base of the plant into the soil, and train others to cling to the plant's post. The leaves of this plant are poisonous, and can cause a severe burning sensation in the mouth if eaten by people or pets.

SPECIFICATIONS

Light: Moderate to bright light, but no direct sun.

Temperature: Average to warm (65–85°F/18–29°C).

Fertilizer: *From spring through summer,* feed every 2 weeks with a balanced houseplant fertilizer. *In winter,* feed monthly.

Water: Allow the soil to dry to within an inch of the surface between waterings. Water less in winter than in summer.

Soil: A heavy mix comprised of 2 parts clean, bagged topsoil, 2 parts peat moss, and 1 part sand or perlite.

Repotting: Repot every other spring. Keep plant in a large pot that provides room for planting of the aerial roots that emerge near the base of the plant. Mature plants require the support of a stout wood post.

Longevity: Many years.

Propagation: When the plant outgrows the space you have for it, propagate a vigorous stem tip by air layering or by rooting it as a stem tip cutting. Air layering is the easiest and most reliable method.

Selections: Most plants have glossy, dark green leaves, but variegated forms are available. Over time, these may revert to all-green leaves. Young plants without windows in their leaves are sometimes sold as *Philodendron pertusum*.

Display tips: This is an ideal floor plant for large spaces. It can fill the corner of a brightly lit room, or you can use it to divide space in large, open corridors. Clean leaves often to keep them vibrantly glossy.

TROUBLESHOOTING

Leaves turn brown at the tips.
CAUSE: Soil too dry.
REMEDY: Water more frequently, using rainwater or distilled water. If plant dries out completely, rehydrate pot as described on page 328.

New leaves are small or lack perforations.
CAUSE: Too little light; too little fertilizer.
REMEDY: It is normal for young plants to develop leaves without holes or slits, but when new leaves on older plants fail to develop perforations, the plant needs more light and fertilizer.

Old leaves turn yellow and shrivel to brown.
CAUSE: Natural in winter when temperatures and light levels are low. In summer, yellowing leaves are caused by uneven watering, which makes the soil too wet or too dry.
REMEDY: Clip off failing leaves with sharp scissors. Water more frequently to keep soil evenly moist.

White colony deposits on stems and leaf undersides.
CAUSE: Mealybug.
REMEDY: Isolate plant, and remove mealybugs with tweezers or a cotton swab dipped in alcohol. Repeat every few days until mealybugs are gone. The open growth habit of this plant makes it easy to remove mealybugs by hand.

Leaves pale, with faint webbing on leaf undersides.
CAUSE: Spider mites.
REMEDY: Isolate plant, and thoroughly clean leaf undersides with a soft cloth or sponge dipped in soapy water. Repeat after a week. Regular cleaning of leaves will prevent this problem, as will keeping plant in a moderately humid place. Monstera is less likely than other houseplants to become infested with spider mites.

Palms

Upright palms evoke a tropical mood in the starkest of surroundings.

FOSSILS OF PALMS DATING BACK 65 MILLION YEARS have been found, though some may be much older, possibly existing in the time of the dinosaurs. They are thought to be among the first plants that began reproducing by producing flowers and seeds — a major turning point in plant evolution. In the history of civilization, drawings from ancient Egypt make it clear that the date palm was regarded as a symbol of longevity 5,000 years ago. The date palm is also mentioned numerous times in both the Bible and the Koran.

Palms are mostly plants of the tropics, though some grow outdoors in semitropical climates. However, the same palms that grow into 30 ft/9 m-tall trees in warm regions stay much smaller when grown indoors. Still, a palm that grows too tall presents a problem, because a palm cannot be pruned back from the top without weakening or killing it. It is much safer to choose a palm that fits the space you have in which to grow it.

In terms of interiorscaping, palms are almost always "floor" plants, employed as architectural specimens in roomy spots where they impart a strong tropical mood. Grow large palms in tubs set on wheeled platforms so they can be rotated easily to expose all sides of the plants to good directional light. Small palms, such as dwarf lady palms, can be used as tabletop plants.

The boldly textured foliage of palms comes in two basic forms: fan and feather. Palms with fan foliage have leaflets that radiate from a stem in a circular pattern, while those with feathery foliage have leaflets that emerge from a central vein in parallel lines. The two most popular indoor palms — areca palms and parlor palms — feature feathery foliage. Of palms with fan-type foliage, the lady palms are usually the easiest ones to grow.

Caring for Palms

After consulting the general guidelines given here, refer to the plant profiles on the pages that follow for advice about the best potting soils and fertilization practices for specific palms. You may find that your palm collects dust on its leaves more noticeably than do other houseplants. This is uncomfortable for both you and the plant, so it's a good idea to clean plants from time to time in a warm shower. Leafshine products will make palm leaves glossy, but not all palms can tolerate them. To be safe, try this old way of polishing palm leaves: Mix 1 tablespoon of milk with 1 cup of warmed rainwater, and use this mixture to wipe down the leaves with a soft cloth. Although this process sounds laborious, it gives good satisfaction as well as the opportunity to closely examine each leaflet for the presence of spider mites, scale, or other pests.

Light: Some palms, such as date palms, require bright light, while parlor palms will accept low light provided they are properly acclimated. Palms can adapt to changes in light, but this process is very slow, sometimes taking as long as a year. Palms grown for indoor use are gradually moved to 70 to 80 percent shade for 3 to 12 months before they are offered for sale. If moved quickly from sun to shade, many palms simply die. Keep this in mind if you live in a mild winter climate where palms are often planted outdoors. Never buy a palm that's accustomed to sun and attempt to grow it indoors.

Palms enjoy spending the warmest part of summer outside on a porch or patio, but again, it's important to keep them in a shady spot. Otherwise, they may have a difficult time adjusting to reduced light levels when you bring them back inside in the fall. Palms grown in shade grow more slowly than those that grow in sun, but the fronds of shade-grown palms have a rich, dark green color.

Temperature: Because they are tropical plants, palms are well equipped for coping with temperatures as high as 100°F/38°C. They grow very little in temperatures below 65°F/18°C, though some can withstand slight chilling with no problems. Warmer is generally better where palms are concerned.

Fertilizer: Most houseplants are easily fed with a steady diet of liquid plant food — but not palms. Liquid plant foods leave behind salts, which often injure palms. Palms do not need much fertilizer, and what they do need is best provided by sprinkling a teaspoon of coated, time-release fertilizer granules into the top of each container in spring. Supplement this feeding with micronutrients, which are in good supply in any well-rotted compost. A light sprinkling of approximately ½ cup/118 ml of compost, spread over the top of the soil in the pot twice each year, is usually sufficient. You can also provide micronutrients by drenching the leaves with a micronutrient spray, as described on page 262. Yet another option is to use a high-quality rose fertilizer, which often contains a nutrient balance that is ideal for these plants.

If it's summer, the prime growth season for palms, and you suspect that your palm needs more fertilizer, you can use two light applications of a balanced houseplant food, made 2 weeks apart, to see if the plant perks up. If your palm responds favorably, you can either give it more time-release fertilizer or continue with the liquid for a few more weeks, provided you flush the container monthly to wash out excess salts.

Water: Palms are sensitive to salt accumulation in the soil, which can come from water or fertilizers. They also can be damaged by fluoride and other chemicals present in many public water supplies. Whenever possible, use distilled water or clean rainwater to water your palms. Water filters remove many contaminants, so filtered water is a good second choice. Most palms grow best when the soil is kept lightly moist at all times. They can be damaged by having their roots exposed to standing water for even short periods of time.

The biggest water-related problem you are likely to have is salt. Managing potential salt problems in the soil requires a three-pronged approach. First, add some sand to the potting soil to help it drain quickly. Second, use a coated, time-release fertilizer rather than a liquid plant food as your primary means of feeding your palm. Third, leach the container two to three times a year by flooding it with water, allowing the water to drain away, and then flooding it again. Repeat three times in the course of a day. Indoors, this is best done in a roomy bathtub. In summer, you can leach pots outdoors using warm water from a hose.

The plants profiled here can tolerate dry air, but it's always a good idea to mist them from time to time. In addition to raising humidity levels, misting may discourage spider mites, which love the foliage of palms.

Soil: Think *beach* when considering soil for palms. Although palms may grow well enough in ordinary potting soil, most are happiest with a soil mix composed of 2 parts peat, 1 part pine bark, and 1 part sand. Some species respond to fine-tuning the mix with additional sand; date palms like the heaviness brought about by the addition of a bit of clay soil. See the plant profiles for specific suggestions, and turn to page 314 for more information on creating customized soil mixtures. If you do not want to make a custom soil for a palm, the next best choice is to use packaged African violet soil amended with a little sand.

Repotting: It is usually not necessary to repot palms more often than once every 3 years. Crowded roots help limit a palm's size, which is generally a good thing with indoor-grown palms. The main reasons to repot palms are to relieve very severe root crowding, to promote growth of small, young plants, and to provide the plants with clean containers that are free of salt deposits, along with a fresh supply of soil. Watch planting depth closely, and try to replant palms at the same depth they grew in their previous container. Palms can be damaged by planting them too deeply. Also, do not attempt to spread out the roots of potted palms as you repot them. The brittle roots break easily and should be kept as intact as possible. After repotting palms, make sure that the soil is well packed around the roots by repeatedly tamping the container and then flooding it with water.

Propagating: Most palms are grown from seed, though a few species, such as lady palms, grow into clumps that can be propagated by division. Commercial growers often plant three seedlings in a pot to produce a fuller-looking plant. Separating them often injures so many roots that the operation is not successful, though it's worth trying with very young plants, such as little parlor palms that come to you in a dish garden.

It's possible to grow palms from seeds, provided you have a very warm place for them to sprout and grow. To test a palm seed to see if it is good, drop it into a pail of water. Seeds that float lack sound endosperms, the organs that grow into a seedling, so they are best discarded. Fresh palm seeds germinate much better than old ones.

Most palm seeds germinate best when they are planted very near the surface so that the seed is barely covered. Germination

Among indoor palms, lady palms (*Rhaphis excelsa*) are unique in their tendency to grow low and broad rather than tall and upright.

times range from a few days to several months, and temperatures must be kept in the 75–80°F/24–27°C range. Enclosing the seeded container in a plastic bag, and keeping it on top of a refrigerator or hot-water heater is a good method to try at home. Use a small, 2 in/ 5 cm pot, and do not attempt to transplant the seedling until it has two or more leaves. Young palm seedlings need abundant light, so planting seeds in early spring, so the plants can spend their first summer outdoors, tends to give the best results.

Small details: Several potential problems with palms, including dust on leaves, salt accumulation in the soil, and infestations of spider mites, can be prevented by taking the plants outdoors and treating them to a long, warm shower. Indoors, you can do this in a roomy bathtub. In the fall, 2 weeks before bringing in palms that have spent the summer outdoors, check them very carefully for evidence of scale, mealybugs, or spider mites. Hand-pick any pests that you find, and then spray plants thoroughly with plenty of warm, clean water. Some palms tolerate insecticidal soap, while others do not (see below). If mite problems become severe, treat a test leaf and wait 3 days before spraying the entire plants.

TROUBLESHOOTING

Brown discs on leaf undersides; round spots on tops of leaves.
CAUSE: Scale.
REMEDY: Gently remove by hand if possible. Repeat every few days, then spray plants with insecticidal soap after testing plant for tolerance. See page 273 for more information on these pests.

Leaves have faint yellow specks; leaves appear stressed; webby material on leaf undersides.
CAUSE: Spider mites.
REMEDY: Isolate infected plant, and remove badly infested leaves. Clean plants using one of the methods described on page 274. Increase humidity by misting at least once a day. Spray plants monthly with insecticidal soap after testing plant for tolerance.

White woolly patches on stems or where leaflets join stems.
CAUSE: Mealybugs.

REMEDY: Remove with cotton swab dipped in alcohol; repeat every 3 days until the plants are clean.

Brown or black patches on leaves.
CAUSE: Fungal leaf spot diseases, which include *Cercospora* leafspot on lady palms, and anthracnose on several other species.
REMEDY: Remove affected leaves; wash off plant and place it where air can circulate freely through the foliage.

Leaf tips are brown.
CAUSE: Too little water; water tainted by fluoride or chlorine.
REMEDY: Snip off brown tips; gradually increase water; switch to rainwater or distilled water.

Old fronds turn brown.
CAUSE: Normal for most palms.
REMEDY: Use a sharp knife, pruning shears, or a small saw to cut off old fronds near the trunk.

Yellow spots or streaks on leaves.
CAUSE: Nutrient deficiency.
REMEDY: A shortage of potassium, magnesium, or manganese can cause this problem. Drench plants with a micronutrient spray, and topdress the pot with an inch of good compost. Change to a fertilizer that includes abundant potassium and micronutrients. Occasionally add a pinch of Epsom salts to water.

New leaf is smaller than older leaves.
CAUSE: Too little fertilizer; not enough light.
REMEDY: Feed plant more often; increase light slightly. Corrective measures are best taken in spring.

Leaves are yellowish green.
CAUSE: Too much sun; iron deficiency.
REMEDY: Move plant to a shadier spot. Feed with a micronutrient foliar spray that includes iron.

Getting to Know Your Palms

In the following pages, six of the most popular, easy-to-grow palms are described in detail. They are listed in alphabetical order by botanical name, but you may not know a palm's botanical name if it came to you in a dish garden, or if you bought it without benefit of an identification tag. The chart below will help you identify which palm you have. Then turn to the appropriate plant profile to get to know your palm better.

Botanical name	Common names	Description
Chamaedorea species	Parlor palms	Elegant, feathered fronds with rich, dark green color; best palms for low light
Chamaerops humilis	European fan palm, Mediterranean fan palm	Stiff, fan-shaped gray-green leaves; black hairs on trunk; needs some sun
Chrysalidocarpus lutescens	Areca palm, feather palm	Large, architectural plants for big spaces; generally easy to grow
Howea forsteriana	Kentia palm, sentry palm	Long, feathery fronds droop slightly; slow growing and easy to keep
Phoenix roebelinii, P. canariensis	Pygmy date palm, Canary Island date palm	Long, arching fronds with thin, pointed leaflets; needs warmth and good light
Rhapis excelsa	Lady palm	Fans of broad, dark green or variegated leaves; tolerates limited light, easy to keep small

European fan palm (Chamaerops humilis)

Chamaedorea elegans, C. seifrizii, C. radicalis, and hybrids kam-eh-DOOR-ee-a EL-e-gans

PARLOR PALM

Parlor palm
(Chamaedorea elegans)

POPULAR SINCE VICTORIAN TIMES, parlor palms adapt beautifully to low light. You can place them near an east window or grow them in a room illuminated with fluorescent lights. Very young plants are sometimes grown in dish gardens or terrariums. Fully mature parlor palms *(C. elegans)* are 3–4 ft/.9–1.2 m tall and 3 ft/.9 m wide. Other *Chamaedorea* species may grow slightly taller. All have strappy, green leaflets on fronds that grow from 9–24 in/22.5–60 cm long. Exposure to sun can cause leaves to develop brown tips, so be careful where you place a parlor palm if you shift it outdoors in the summer. And, although parlor palms tolerate dry indoor air, they are healthier when misted regularly to increase humidity.

Parlor palms are famous for flowering after they are more than 3 years old. However, the seeds that follow the beadlike sprays of flowers are seldom fertile and should be clipped off when they begin to turn brown. Watch parlor palms closely for infestations of spider mites. Cleaning the leaves by hand from time to time is the best preventive measure.

SPECIFICATIONS

Light: Moderate natural light or fluorescent light.

Temperature: Average to warm room temperatures (65–80°F/ 18–27°C).

Fertilizer: Needs a little more fertilizer than other palms, especially in summer.

Water: Keep soil lightly moist at all times; will recover from occasional dryness better than from extremely wet conditions.

Soil: African violet soil amended with extra sand.

Repotting: Repot young, actively growing plants yearly in spring. Mature plants need repotting only every other year.

Longevity: 10 years or more.

Propagation: Seed.

Selections: Small parlor palms sold as 'Bellas' are young specimens of *C. elegans*. Plants labeled 'Florida Hybrids' are crosses between *C. erumpens* and *C. seifrizii*. They tend to grow lean and tall.

Display tips: Parlor palms make excellent office plants. In the home, use one to fill an empty corner behind a sofa or other large piece of furniture.

Chamaerops humilis KAM-er-ops HEW-mil-is

EUROPEAN FAN PALM, MEDITERRANEAN FAN PALM

European fan palm
(*Chamaerops humilis*)

Sunroom

IF YOU HAVE A SOLAR SPACE that gets at least 4 hours of bright sunlight during the day but cools off at night, it will make a perfect home for a European fan palm. Hardy enough to grow outdoors in Tucson and Texas, this plant's natural habitat is dry, rocky mountain slopes. The stiff, fan-shaped fronds up to 24 in/60 cm across have a silvery sheen; it is normal for the ends of the leaflets to split as they mature. When grown indoors, European fan palms will slowly grow to about 4 ft/1.2 m tall. Old, outer fronds wither and new ones are produced from the plant's crown. As the plant ages, the trunk develops numerous black hairs, giving it a rugged appearance.

Commercial growers produce European fan palms from seed, yet this is one of the few palms that often produces suckers, which can be carefully cut away and transplanted to new pots. European fan palms of any age grow very slowly and make the most of their new growth in summer. If you move them outdoors in summer, clean them thoroughly before bringing them inside in the fall.

SPECIFICATIONS

🔆 **Light:** Direct sun 4 hours daily, with bright filtered light the rest of the day.

Temperature: Cool nights (50–60°F/10–16°C) and warm days (70–80°F/21–27°C) are ideal. Fertilizer: *In spring,* fertilize with a time-release fertilizer. *In summer,* feed once or twice with a balanced houseplant food. *In fall and winter,* do not feed.

Water: *In spring and summer,* keep constantly moist. *In fall and winter,* allow to dry to within 2 in/5 cm of surface between waterings.

Soil: Peaty mix amended with compost and sand.

Repotting: Deep roots are fragile, so repot only as necessary, about every 2 to 3 years.

Longevity: 20 years or more.

Propagation: Seeds; division of suckers.

Selections: European fan palm is sold by species name. A different fan palm, Chinese fan palm (*Livistonia chinensis*), features fronds that droop slightly. It is grown the same way as its European counterpart.

Display tips: Plant in a deep tub, and use this exotic-looking palm as an anchor plant in a bright sunroom.

Chrysalidocarpus lutescens

kris-a-lid-oh-CAR-pus lu-TES-ens

ARECA PALM, FEATHER PALM, GOLDEN CANE PALM, YELLOW BUTTERFLY PALM

Areca palm
(Chrysalidocarpus lutescens)

THE **MOST POPULAR PALM** for bright indoor spaces, areca palms feature feathery, medium green fronds, with 80 to 100 leaflets on each arching frond. The lowest parts of the stems are yellow to yellow-orange.

Although areca palms grow to nearly 30 ft/9 m tall in the wild, when grown indoors they typically grow 6–7 ft/1.8–2.1 m tall. This is quite large for most homes, though you can trim off the tallest frond or two without seriously harming the plants. Small areca palms often grow 6–10 in/15–25 cm per year, making the most of their new growth in summer. Areca palms can be grown outdoors only in frost-free areas. In temperate climates, they enjoy spending the summer outside in a shady spot.

Areca palms are grown from seed, though they rarely produce drooping panicles of yellow flowers, followed by seeds, when they are grown indoors. Seed starting is best left to greenhouse growers; germination time ranges from 2 to 6 months at 80°F/27°C. Purchased plants that are 24–36 in/60–90 cm tall are usually about 18 months old, so they tend to be somewhat costly.

SPECIFICATIONS

Light: Bright, indirect light from a south or west window.

⚠ Temperature: *During the day,* warm (above 75°F/24°C). *At night,* no cooler than 65°F/18°C.

Fertilizer: *In spring,* feed with a time-release fertilizer. *In summer,* this palm benefits from a micro-nutrient spray. *In fall and winter,* do not feed.

Water: *In spring and summer,* constant light moisture. *In fall and winter,* slightly drier.

Soil: Peaty yet porous mix amended with sand.

Repotting: Every 2 to 3 years.

Longevity: 10 years or more.

Propagation: Seeds. Although areca palms can be propagated by division, this is very difficult to do at home.

Selections: Sold by species name.

Display tips: Plant in large tubs set on the floor in a warm, well-lit spot. Placement near a white wall will reflect extra light, which helps keep the plants full.

Howea forsteriana, H. belmoreana

HOW-ee-a for-ster-ee-AN-a

KENTIA PALM, SENTRY PALM

Kentia palm (*Howea forsteriana*)

SEEDS OF THE KENTIA PALM were first collected in 1870 on Lord Howe Island, which is northeast of Australia. For the next hundred years, this palm steady grew in popularity since it adapted well to the dim interiors of European parlors. Kentia or sentry palms remain fine choices for rooms with tall ceilings, as they can reach 8 feet in height. However, they grow so slowly in limited light that many years pass before they outgrow their space. Because of their slow growth, kentias often cost more than other palms. A kentia that fills a 10 in/25 cm pot is 3 to 5 years old.

The fan-shaped leaflets of kentia palms droop slightly, and usually have a dark green color that shows best in rooms with light-colored walls. All palms of this species grow from single trunks, but commercial growers often plant several in a pot to make it appear more lush and full. Kentia palms benefit from spending the summer outdoors and from regular cleaning of their leaves during the winter.

SPECIFICATIONS

Light: Bright light, near a south or east window.

Temperature: *During the day, average to warm (75–80°F / 24– 27°C). At night, 60–65°F / 16–18°C.*

Fertilizer: *In spring and summer, feed with a lime-release fertilizer. In fall and winter, do not fertilize.*

Water: *In spring and summer, keep soil lightly moist at all times. In fall and winter, allow soil to become almost dry between waterings.*

Soil: Peaty potting soil amended with sand, or African violet potting soil with a little sand added.

◆ Repotting: Repot only when necessary, no more often than every 2 years. Handle the fragile roots with great care.

Longevity: 20 years or more.

Propagation: Seed.

Selections: These two species are very similar. Kentia palm (*H. forsteriana*) has wider spaces between the leaflets; the leaflets of sentry palm (*H. belmoreana*) often show a slight curl.

Display tips: These palms are ideal for growing in tubs in bright rooms with cathedral ceilings.

FAMILY: **ARECACEAE**   ORIGIN: **VIETNAM, CANARY ISLANDS**

Phoenix roebelinii, P. canariensis

FEE-niks row-bel-EE-nee-i

PYGMY DATE PALM, CANARY ISLAND DATE PALM

Pygmy date palm
(Phoenix roebelinii)

COUSINS TO THE DATE PALMS of the Bible, both the pygmy date palm and Canary Island date palm produce edible fruits when grown outdoors. Plants grown indoors seldom flower, but they do feature flashy, arching fronds studded with thin, delicate-looking leaflets. The bases of the leaflets are armed with sharp spines, and older trunks develop thorns as well. Wear gloves when trimming off old fronds that droop below horizontal level.

These little date palms aren't so little when grown outdoors in Florida, Texas, Arizona, and California, where they mature into thick-trunked trees. Indoors, the plants stay much smaller, often growing to less than 36 in/90 cm tall. The Canary Island palm is a little taller than the pygmy date palm. These palms have heavy roots that make for heavy containers. When grown near an east window where they will get strong morning light, they seldom require moving.

Date palms are sensitive to shortages of micronutrients. Yellow splotches on leaflets is a typical symptom of too little magnesium or manganese. Use an annual drench of Epsom salts, made by mixing 1 teaspoon/4.93 ml of the salts into a quart of water, to provide magnesium. Or, use a good rose fertilizer that contains micronutrients to fertilize these palms.

SPECIFICATIONS

Light: Bright filtered light.

Temperature: Warm. *During the day,* 75–85°F/24–29°C. *At night,* 65–70°F/18–21°C.

⬥**Fertilizer:** *In spring,* feed with a time-release fertilizer that includes micronutrients, such as a rose fertilizer. *In summer,* repeat this dosage one more time. Sensitive to deficiencies of magnesium and manganese, so apply a micronutrient spray annually in summer. *In fall and winter,* do not feed.

Water: *In spring and summer,* water often, allowing soil to dry to within 1 in/2.5 cm of surface between waterings. *In fall and winter,* water slightly less.

Soil: Amend standard potting soil with compost, sand, and a small amount of clay soil.

Repotting: Repot young plants annually in spring to promote new growth. Mature plants have heavy, brittle roots and are difficult to repot.

Longevity: Many years.

Propagation: Seeds.

Selections: These palms are sold by species name.

Display tips: Place out of high-traffic areas, as the fronds are delicate yet armed.

Rhaphis excelsa RAY-fis ek-SEL-sa
LADY PALM

Lady palm (*Rhaphis excelsa*)

OVER 300 YEARS AGO, the Japanese fell in love with the fresh, clean lines of lady palms. Each frond is comprised of 5 to 9 glossy, 1 in/2.5 cm-wide leaflets arranged in a fan pattern. Although plants often grow to 10 ft/3 m or more outdoors, small containers dramatically limit their size. When handled as bonsai, plants may be maintained as 14 in/35 cm-tall miniatures for many years.

Lady palms are easy to grow indoors, adapting readily to limited light. Too much light, particularly direct sun, can cause the leaves to turn yellow-green. Lady palms also need a lean diet. Too much fertilizer can cause the variegation patterns of the showiest varieties to fade. These factors make lady palms excellent choices for people who want a formal, easy-to-keep plant that evokes an Oriental mood. However, like most other palms, lady palms are sensitive to fluoride and other chemicals in water, as well as soil-borne salts. Periodic leaching of the pots will help prevent serious problems.

A few other *Rhaphis* species are sold as indoor plants, but none are as adaptable and easy to grow as the lady palm.

SPECIFICATIONS

◆ Light: *Indoors,* filtered light from an east window. *Outdoors,* 80 percent shade.

Temperature: Average to warm (60–80°F/16–27°C).

Fertilizer: *In summer,* feed monthly with a balanced houseplant food mixed at half the normal strength, or provide a light sprinkling of time-release plant food. *In fall through spring,* do not feed.

Water: *In summer,* water plants by soaking them often, then allow soil to dry to within 1 in/2.5 cm of surface. *In winter,* allow soil to dry to within 2 in/5 cm of the surface between waterings.

Soil: African violet mix amended with sand.

Repotting: Repot young plants every 2 years. When plants reach desired size, repot only as needed to refresh soil.

Longevity: Many years.

Propagation: Seeds; division.

Selections: More than 100 cultivars exist, most with Japanese names. 'Koban' is a popular greenleafed variety. 'Zuikonishki' has cream-and-green variegated leaves.

Display tips: These elegant plants are traditionally grown in shallow bonsai pots or ceramic urns.

Pandanus veitchii pan-DAN-us ve-ECH-ee-i

SCREW PINE, VEITCH SCREW PINE

Screw pine (*Pandanus veitchii*)

A STRONG ARCHITECTURAL PLANT, pandanus adapts well to life in homes and offices, though it does need plenty of elbow room. The arching, strap-shaped leaves can grow to 36 in/90 cm long, and the edges tend to be prickly. To avoid brushing against it, allow a pine a 5 ft/1.5 m space in which to grow. Over a period of several years, a healthy pandanus will grow to 4 ft/1.2 m tall. Aerial roots emerge near the base of the plant as it ages. In the wild, these "stilt" roots would help hold the plant firm in strong winds, common in the seaside locations where it likes to grow. Indoors, simply tuck the roots into the pot, and bury them during routine repotting.

Pandanus is not a pine. The "pine" part of its common name was earned because the leaves resemble those of pineapple. As for the "screw" part, pandanus's leaves spiral around the base of a central rosette, like the frets on a screw.

SPECIFICATIONS

◆ **Light:** Bright, including up to 3 hours of direct sun. Plant can be moved outdoors in summer provided it is placed in partial shade.

Temperature: Average to warm room temperatures (65–80°F/ 18–27°C).

Fertilizer: *From spring through summer,* feed every 2 weeks with a balanced, all-purpose houseplant food. *In winter,* feed monthly.

Water: Allow soil to dry to within an inch of the surface between thorough waterings. Plants need more water in summer, less in winter.

Soil: Any good potting soil with a small amount of sand added.

Repotting: Annually in spring, moving plant to a pot one size larger. Between repottings, push aerial roots into the soil so they help anchor the plant.

Longevity: 10 to 15 years.

Propagation: When older plants produce basal shoots, or pups, cut them off and root them as you would stem tip cuttings, as described on page 299.

Selections: Variegated forms are most popular, but *P. utilis,* with solid green leaves, is a handsome plant with a palmlike demeanor.

Display tips: Use as a floor plant in a large, open room with other high-light plants. Smaller plants with daintier foliage make good companions.

TROUBLESHOOTING

New leaves are small.
CAUSE: Needs repotting to larger container; not enough fertilizer.
REMEDY: When roots become extremely cramped, pandanus shows its displeasure by straining to make new growth. Shift to a slightly larger pot and keep plant well fed in summer, when warm temperatures encourage new growth.

Leaves turn all green.
CAUSE: Not enough strong light.
REMEDY: Increase light by moving plant to a brighter location or by providing supplemental fluorescent light.

Leaf edges turn brown.
CAUSE: Air too dry.
REMEDY: Plant needs average to high humidity. Place plant on a tray of damp pebbles or keep it in a room with a humidifier.

Leaf tips curled and parched, with webbing on underside.
CAUSE: Spider mites.
REMEDY: See page 276 for ways to identify this pest. If present, clean leaves thoroughly by hand, wiping each leaf underside with a soft cloth dipped in soapy water. Repeat weekly until mites are controlled.

Peperomia caperata, P. argyreia, P. obtusifolia

pep-er-OHM-ee-a kap-er-AH-ta

PEPEROMIA

Peperomia (*Peperomia caperata*)

THREE SPECIES OF PEPEROMIA have made the journey from South American rain forests to modern homes and offices. All grow nicely in moderate light and make few demands on their keepers. The smallest and most popular peperomias have heart-shaped leaves with a waffle texture. Growing to only 8 in/20 cm tall and wide, the corrugated leaves of *P. caperata* may be green, reddish, or silvery gray with green leaf veins, depending on variety. Occasionally, the plants produce slender flower spikes that resemble rat's tails. A second small species, *P. argyreia,* is often called watermelon peperomia because of the arching stripes of silver-gray that mark its nearly elliptical leaves. Both of these species are sensitive to overwatering, but generally make fine tabletop plants, or they can be grown with other small foliage plants in a dish garden.

A third species, *P. obtusifolia,* commonly called baby rubber plant, has a more upright posture. The rounded leaves are usually deep green, though there are varieties with gold-and-white variegated leaves. Because of its easygoing nature, this peperomia is often recommended for workplaces.

SPECIFICATIONS

Light: Low to moderate light from an east or north window, or bright fluorescent light.

Temperature: Average room temperatures (65–75°F/18–24°C).

Fertilizer: *Spring to fall,* feed twice monthly with a balanced houseplant fertilizer mixed at half the normal rate. *In winter,* feed monthly.

Water: Allow the soil to dry to within .5 in/1.25 cm of the surface between light to moderate waterings. In summer, leach the pots once or twice to remove excess salts that may have accumulated in the soil.

Soil: A light-textured potting soil that includes perlite or coarse gravel. Peperomias need some air around their roots.

Repotting: Repot in spring to refresh the soil, but keep peperomias in rather small pots.

Longevity: 6 years or more.

Propagation: Propagate *P. caperata* and *P. argyreia* from petiole leaf cuttings, as is done with African violets (see page 302). Propagate *P. obtusifolia* by rooting stem tip cuttings taken in spring.

Selections: 'Emerald Ripple' is the standard green-leafed variety among rippled peperomias. 'Red Luna' and several others have reddish leaves; the leaves of 'Metallica' are marked with silvery gray. Names vary among smooth-leafed peperomias. Choose plants with leaf colors and patterns you find attractive.

Display tips: All peperomias are fine tabletop houseplants. Small ones are ideal for desktops or shallow windowsills.

TROUBLESHOOTING

Plant appears slightly wilted despite regular watering.
CAUSE: Roots are deprived of oxygen.
REMEDY: Allow plant to dry slightly, remove it from the pot, and make sure the drainage holes are not blocked by debris. Use a toothpick to make a dozen or so small holes in the bottom and sides of the root ball. If problem persists, repot the plant using a light-textured potting mix.

Raised, scablike swellings on leaf undersides.
CAUSE: Corky scab or oedema, caused by overwatering.
REMEDY: This problem is most likely to develop in cool, cloudy weather, when peperomia needs less water. Water lightly in winter, and avoid heavy watering when temperatures and light levels are low.

Older leaves shrivel and die.
CAUSE: Normal in most cases, but sudden leaf losses can be due to salt damage or fertilizer burn.
REMEDY: Clip off damaged leaves. Leach the soil to remove any accumulated salts (see page 263). Always dilute fertilizer to half of the strength recommended on the label.

White cottony masses on leaves or stems.
CAUSE: Mealybugs.
REMEDY: Isolate plant, and remove mealybugs by hand, using a cotton swab dipped in alcohol. If problem persists, see other control measures for this pest on page 273.

Philodendrons

Bird's nest philodendrons feature leaves that change color as they age, and they are as easy to grow as other philodendrons.

FOR GENERATIONS, PHILODENDRONS HAVE SERVED as backbone plants in indoor gardens, and for good reason. Easy to grow and comfortable in the same environments that suit people, philodendrons show enough steady growth to keep them interesting. Should they outgrow their space, most philos are easily propagated.

Although the word *philodendron* loosely translates as "tree-loving," not all philodendrons are vining in habit, and those that do climb need help holding onto a support post. However, when secured to a post with florist's tape or pins, vining types like heartleaf philodendron and blushing philodendron do attach themselves, albeit slowly, with aerial roots. Those that do not climb, often called *self-heading philodendrons,* grow into rounded, spreading plants that need a bit of elbow room.

Caring for Philodendrons

Philodendrons are very responsive plants, which makes caring for them all the more rewarding. Within weeks after repotting in late spring, philodendrons often reward their keeper with a fast flush of new growth. But don't expect your philodendrons to produce flowers when grown indoors. These members of the Araceae family produce spade-shaped flowers and tiny seeds when grown outdoors in tropical climates, but it's extremely rare for philodendron houseplants to bloom.

Some people are allergic to philodendron sap, which can cause an itchy rash in susceptible individuals. When repotting plants, wear gloves and a long-sleeved shirt should you have this problem. Philodendron leaves are poisonous to pets and people, though large amounts must be ingested to cause serious illness.

You can keep your philodendrons indoors year-round, or treat them to summer outdoors in a shady spot. Even indoor-grown philodendrons like to be taken outside once or twice during the summer for a thorough cleaning with plenty of fresh water. Unlike some other houseplants, moving philodendrons from place to place causes them no noticeable distress. The few problems you are likely to have with philodendrons are detailed on page 231.

TROUBLESHOOTING

Older leaves turn yellow.
CAUSE: Cold temperatures, excessive light, or inadequate nutrition.
REMEDY: While it is normal for philodendrons to shed older leaves from time to time, when several turn yellow at once it is usually due to stress. Containers kept on cold floors in winter may lead to serious chilling of the roots, which can cause this symptom. Yellowing of otherwise healthy leaves is usually due to too much light, while pale new growth is likely to be due to insufficient fertilizer or use of a plant food that lacks essential micronutrients such as magnesium and calcium.

Stems are long and leggy, with several inches between leaves.
CAUSE: Insufficient light.
REMEDY: Philodendrons can tolerate low light for a short period in winter, but they grow best with bright indirect light. Consider moving them outdoors to a shady spot in summer, and possibly provide supplemental fluorescent light in winter.

New growth slow, leaf size small.
CAUSE: Insufficient fertilizer.
REMEDY: Philodendrons are moderate feeders, and how much and how often you fertilize them depends on the age of the plants and the growing season. In summer, when days are long and warm, feed philodendrons every 2 weeks if they lack vigor. Philodendrons often produce little new growth in winter.

New growth rumpled, with yellow specks.
CAUSE: Aphids.
REMEDY: Rinse off plants, then spray new growing tips with insecticidal soap. Plants usually outgrow problems with aphids once they are eliminated. Aphids are most likely to be seen on plants that have been kept outdoors.

White cottony deposits on stems or leaves.
CAUSE: Mealybug.
REMEDY: Remove mealybugs with tweezers or a cotton swab dipped in alcohol. Repeat after 5 days. Mealybugs are usually more common on other houseplants. Should a philodendron become infested, carefully check your other houseplants for signs of this pest. More information about mealybugs is given on page 272.

Recently repotted plant droops.
CAUSE: Too much water.
REMEDY: Roots are always damaged when plants are repotted, and modest root pruning is often necessary when repotting philodendrons. Use moist potting soil when repotting, but water newly repotted plants very lightly for two weeks. Use of a heavy, soil-based potting mix also can cause this problem. Philodendrons prefer a light, pealy mix that drains well.

Getting to Know Philodendrons

There are dozens of philodendron species kept as cultivated plants, but the four types summarized in the chart below and included in the following plant profiles are the most common ones.

Botanical name	Common names	Description
Philodendron bipinnatifidum	Lacy-tree philodendron, anchor philodendron	Deeply cut green leaves spread from a central crown; nonclimbing
Philodendron erubescens	Blushing philodendron, climbing philodendron	Vining plant; leaves green on upper sides, reddish below
Philodendron hybrids	Bird's nest philodendron, mounding philodendron	Glossy spade-shaped leaves in various colors, radiating from a bushy base; nonclimbing
Philodendron scandens oxycardium	Heartleaf philodendron	Small heart-shaped green or variegated leaves on vining stems

Philodendron bipinnatifidum

fil-oh-DEN-dron by-pin-a-ti-FY-dum

LACY-TREE PHILODENDRON, ANCHOR PHILODENDRON

Lacy-tree philodendron
(*Philodendron bipinnatifidum*)

LONG LIVED AND EASY TO GROW, this philodendron has so much personality that it deserves the space it requires. Newly arrived from the nursery, plants are often quite upright, but they gradually assume a more relaxed posture. Plants eventually become twice as wide as they are tall, so a mature lacy-tree philodendron needs 6 ft/ 1.8 m of elbow room in which to stretch its leaves.

This species is also called anchor philodendron because of its tendency to produce long, ropelike aerial roots near the base of the plant. Tuck these back into the pot when possible, or wind them around the soil in the top of the container. Cutting off a few won't hurt the plant, but retain as many anchor roots as you can if you plan to divide the plant within a few months. When repotting, the anchor roots can be shortened with clean pruning shears. Keep newly repotted plants slightly dry for a few weeks to allow cut and injured roots to heal.

SPECIFICATIONS

Light: Moderate light. This plant enjoys increased light outdoors in summer.

Temperature: Average to warm (60–80°F/16–27°C); warmer in summer.

Fertilizer: *Year-round,* feed monthly with a balanced house-plant food.

Water: Allow soil to dry to within an inch of the surface between thorough waterings. Large plants tend to dry out in the middle and benefit from occasional rehydrating, as described on page 328.

Soil: Any good-quality potting soil that drains well.

Repotting: Annually in spring to set anchor roots in the soil and loosen compacted roots.

Longevity: 10 years; indefinitely when divided every few years.

Propagation: Division every 3 to 5 years, which requires cutting through the woody roots with a serrated knife.

Selections: Two improved named varieties are often sold. 'Hope' is a full-sized plant that withstands shipping better than the regular species. 'Xanadu' has smaller leaves and grows only 36 in/90 cm wide, so it is a good choice where space is limited.

Display tips: Use as a floor plant in a large, well-lit spot where the leaves can be allowed to sprawl a bit, such as near a large window or sliding patio doors.

Philodendron erubescens fil-oh-DEN-dron er-u-BES-ens

BLUSHING PHILODENDRON, CLIMBING PHILODENDRON

Blushing philodendron
(Philodendron erubescens)

AN OLD FAVORITE, blushing philodendron is a determined climber with elongated heart-shaped leaves borne on reddish stems, often with red leaf undersides. Easy to grow in a warm, brightly lit room, blushing philodendron can reach 6 ft/1.8 m in height over a period of several years. It must be trained to a post, which can be bark-covered wood or a moss-filled pole. The plant cannot attach itself well without help, so you will need florist's tape and pins (made from bent paper clips) to train the stems and aerial roots where you want them to go. To help keep the base of the plant well clothed with leaves, propagate a stem tip using the air-layering method when the plant has reached 4 ft/1.2 m in height. After the dominant stem tip is removed, a new branch usually emerges near the base of the plant.

SPECIFICATIONS

Light: *In summer,* bright light. *In winter,* moderate light.

Temperature: Average to warm room temperatures (65–80°F / 18–27°C). Can be moved outdoors in summer.

Fertilizer: *In spring and summer,* feed every 2 weeks with a high-nitrogen foliage plant food that includes micronutrients. *In fall and winter,* feed monthly.

Water: *From spring through fall,* keep lightly moist at all times. *In winter,* water less, allowing soil to dry to within 1 in/2.5 cm of the top of the pot. Especially in winter, mist moss-covered support pole to provide moisture to aerial roots.

Soil: Any peaty potting soil that drains well, such as African violet soil.

Repotting: Annually in spring until plant fills a heavy 12 in/30 cm pot. When repotting, keep plant attached to its support pole.

Longevity: To 10 years; indefinitely when propagated by air layering.

Propagation: This is one of the easiest houseplants to propagate by air layering, as described on page 304.

Selections: A hybrid form, 'Red Emerald', has glossy, heart-shaped leaves that emerge red and ripen to green, with vivid red stems and leaf veins. An older variety with less red in its leaves, 'Burgundy', is still widely available.

Display tips: The pillar shape of this plant make it ideal to place near entryways or in corners that receive good light from nearby windows.

Philodendron hybrids fil-oh-DEN-dron
BIRD'S NEST PHILODENDRON, MOUNDING PHILODENDRON

Bird's nest philodendron
(*Philodendron* hybrid)

BOTH NATURE AND NURTURE play a role in the performance of these plants, which differ from other philodendrons in that they do not climb, yet they have broad, spade-shaped leaves. Complex hybrids developed in the 1980s, bird's nest or mounding philodendrons carry the genes of several species, including *P. auriculatum, P. bipinnatifidum, P. deflexum,* and *P. selloum.* Their branching habit results not from breeding or training, but from tissue culture propagation, which is how all of them are produced. So, this is one houseplant that owes its existence and success to modern science.

Bird's nest philodendrons are typically sold by variety name (see Selections, below), and they require a little less light than other large philodendrons. Lush, compact plants that need no pinching or training, these hybrids grow to less than 24 in/60 cm tall and wide. Beyond routine watering and feeding, the only maintenance they require is periodic leaf cleaning, which is easily done with a soft, damp cloth or sponge.

SPECIFICATIONS

Light: Moderate natural or fluorescent light.

Temperature: Average to warm room temperatures (70–85°F/ 21–29°C).

◆**Fertilizer:** *From spring through fall,* feed monthly with a high-nitrogen foliage plant food that includes magnesium and other micronutrients. *In winter,* feed every 6 weeks.

Water: Keep lightly moist, but allow soil to dry to within .5 in/ 1.25 cm of surface between waterings. Moderate humidity is beneficial, especially in winter when indoor air may be very dry.

Soil: Any peaty potting soil that drains well.

Repotting: Annually in spring, to shift plant to slightly larger pot. These plants grow best with somewhat restricted roots.

Longevity: 7 to 10 years.

Propagation: Can be propagated by air layering, but the resulting plants will not have the basal branching habit of plants grown from tissue culture.

Selections: 'Prince of Orange' and 'Autumn' feature leaves that emerge copper to orange and ripen to green as they age. The foliage of 'Moonlight' is medium chartreuse green. 'Black Cardinal' has slightly wavy leaves heavily blushed with dark burgundy and set off by deep violet-red stems.

Display tips: Keep leaves clean to show off their lustrous finish. Containers should be short and stout to help prevent toppling.

Philodendron scandens oxycardium

fil-oh-DEN-dron SKAN-dens oks-ee-KAR-dee-um

HEARTLEAF PHILODENDRON

Heartleaf philodendron (*Philodendron scandens oxycardium*)

EVERY DISH GARDEN INCLUDES a tendril or two of this familiar plant, which is more versatile than you might think. Small plants always look dainty in a pot, and the naturally waxy leaves need no help to show their natural luster. Keep young plants compact and bushy by pinching back stem tips from time to time. If desired, snip out the paper sheaths that cover leaf buds after they turn brown.

After a year or two, shift young plants to a hanging basket or begin training them up a moss-covered post. You will need to attach the stems with floral tape, but eventually they will sink aerial roots into the support post. After this happens, leaf size may enlarge from the usual 2 in/5 cm to more than 4 in/10 cm from base to tip. Heartleaf philodendron can be kept to any size desired by pruning the long stems, which will grow to 4 ft/1.2 m or more if allowed to wander.

SPECIFICATIONS

Light: Moderate light, with good tolerance of lower light in winter.

Temperature: Average room temperatures (60–75°F/16–24°C).

Fertilizer: *From spring through fall,* feed monthly with a high-nitrogen foliage plant food that includes micronutrients. *In winter,* feed every 6 weeks.

Water: Allow soil to become slightly dry between waterings, but never allow it to dry out completely. Requires less water than other philodendrons.

Soil: Any peaty potting soil that drains well, such as African violet soil.

Repotting: Repot every other year, in spring or early summer.

Longevity: 10 years or more; indefinitely when propagated from rooted stem cuttings.

Propagation: Easy to root from stem tip cuttings as described on page 299.

Selections: In addition to plants with green leaves, variegated forms are available. These grow best in cool conditions; warmth can cause creamy tones to turn green. A slightly different subspecies, *P. scandens micans,* has a velvety leaf texture with bronze tones in new foliage.

Display tips: Treat plants to a tepid shower from time to time to keep the leaves clean. This is an ideal table plant when grown in a pot, or it can be maintained in a hanging pot or basket or trained to a post.

FAMILY: **URTICACEAE**   ORIGIN: **VIETNAM**

Pilea cadierei py-LEE-a ka-dee-ER-ee-i
ALUMINUM PLANT, WATERMELON PILEA

Aluminum plant *(Pilea cadierei)*

THE MOST GIFTED ARTIST would have difficulty creating a painting as beautiful as the leaves of aluminum plant. Each leaf is marked with slightly raised silver splotches between green leaf veins, so that they appear to have been decorated with silver paint. The patterning of the splotches has earned this plant the nickname of watermelon pilea, since its markings are reminiscent of those present on watermelon rinds.

Pilea is grown as an outdoor groundcover in tropical areas, and indoors it makes an easy houseplant in moderately humid surroundings. Young stems are tinged with pink, while older ones become slightly woody. Tiny white flowers sometimes appear in summer, but they are hardly noticeable and not at all showy. Pilea greatly benefits from being pinched back in early summer to stimulate the production of new branches. When you pinch tips from plants more than 2 years old, set some to root in damp seed-starting mix. The new plants grown from cuttings will probably grow more vigorously than their parent plant, which may then be discarded.

SPECIFICATIONS

Light: Moderate to bright light from an east or west window.

Temperature: Average room temperatures (60–75°F / 16–24°C).

Fertilizer: *In spring and summer,* feed plants weekly with a balanced houseplant food diluted to half the recommended rate. *In fall and winter,* feed monthly.

Water: Keep soil lightly moist at all times, but do not allow roots to stand in water. Aluminum plant likes moderate to high humidity.

Soil: Any good potting soil.

Repotting: Annually in spring.

Longevity: Individual plants remain in good condition up to 5 years, but the plant may be kept indefinitely if propagated from rooted stem tip cuttings.

❖ **Propagation:** Root stem tip cuttings in spring or early summer as described on page 299. Under warm, humid conditions, cuttings root within a month.

Selections: The 'Minima' variety is dwarf, and it is often seen in dish gardens.

Display tips: Pilea is great in hanging baskets, where it often grows quite lush and full with ample light. In a terrarium, a single stem of this plant with its lower leaves pinched off resembles a miniature palm tree.

TROUBLESHOOTING

Leaves have brown splotches; lower leaves drop off.
CAUSE: Too cold; too wet.
REMEDY: Pilea cannot tolerate chilling, which often occurs when it is kept near a cold window in winter. Move to a warmer spot and reduce watering. In spring, cut back old stems to help plants develop flawless new growth.

Growth is leggy, with few leaves near base of plant.
CAUSE: This is normal for plants more than 2 years old. In a younger plant, it can signal too little light.
REMEDY: Pinch back plant to encourage the emergence of new branches. Locate plant where it gets bright filtered light for at least 4 hours each day.

Plant wilts despite regular watering.
CAUSE: Root rot.
REMEDY: Aluminum plant needs ongoing moisture, but too much leads to this problem, which often cannot be cured. Take tip cuttings and try to root them, and dispose of the parent plant.

Leaves pale and wilted, webby material on leaf undersides.
CAUSE: Spider mites.
REMEDY: Clip off and dispose of badly infested leaves or branches. Thoroughly clean plant with luke-warm water, and isolate it from other plants. Mist daily for a week. If problem persists, see other control measures for this pest on page 274. Aluminum plant can tolerate insecticidal soap, but it is easily damaged by other pesticides.

New growth puckered; small insects on stems.
CAUSE: Aphids.
REMEDY: Clip off badly damaged tips, and clean plant thoroughly. If needed, spray with insecticidal soap. Do not use chemical insecticides on this plant.

Schefflera species shef-LER-a

DWARF SCHEFFLERA, UMBRELLA TREE

Umbrella tree
(*Schefflera* species)

TWO PLANTS OF DIFFERENT SIZE go by the common name of schefflera, and they require identical care. Umbrella tree (*S. actinophylla*) is a large, treelike plant with glossy green leaflets to 10 in/25 cm long that spiral out, like spokes on a wheel. Dwarf schefflera (*S. arboricola*), is a smaller, bushier plant, with leaflets 4 in/10 cm long. There are variegated forms of dwarf schefflera, as well as some with wavy, slightly ruffled leaf edges.

In either size, a schefflera can be a very long-lived plant when given casual care and protected from extreme heat and cold. Scheffleras do not like being moved about, and they may shed leaves if subjected to cold drafts or blasts of hot air from heating vents. Be careful not to overwater these plants, and check the leaves every few weeks for signs of pests. In winter, raise the humidity for a schefflera by keeping a humidifier operating nearby. Leafshine products will not hurt a schefflera when used properly, but you can keep schefflera leaves glossy by cleaning them regularly with a soft cloth.

SPECIFICATIONS

Light: Bright filtered light or indirect light from fluorescent light and light-colored walls.

◆ **Temperature:** Average to warm room temperatures (*at night:* about 65°F/18°C; *during the day:* 75– 80°F/24–27°C).

Fertilizer: *Year-round,* feed monthly with a balanced houseplant food. Or, use a time-release granular fertilizer that includes micronutrients.

Water: Allow the top inch of soil to become nearly dry between thorough waterings. Leaves often droop when the soil becomes too dry.

Soil: Any good potting soil that includes peat moss.

Repotting: Repot young plants each spring. After 5 years or so, repot only every 2 to 3 years.

Longevity: Many years.

Propagation: Air layering is the best method to use at home, though small stem tips may also be rooted. See directions for air layering on page 304.

Selections: Among large scheffleras, 'Amate' is resistant to spider mites. Several varieties of dwarf schefflera, such as 'Green Gold', are splashed with yellow variegation. A third species, *S. elegantissima,* more commonly classified as *Dizygotheca* and known as false aralia, is profiled on page 176.

Display tips: Grow tall or large plants in very heavy pots to prevent toppling. Tall plants often need to be staked.

TROUBLESHOOTING

Older leaves turn yellow and drop off.
CAUSE: Overwatering.
REMEDY: Check the top of the soil with your finger, and do not water plant until the top 1 in/2.5 cm feels dry. Pour off any water that accumulates at the base of the pot after watering the plant.

New leaves are pale and limp.
CAUSE: Plant needs more fertilizer.
REMEDY: Feed plant with a water-soluble plant food that includes micronutrients. If the plant responds well, begin feeding it every 2 weeks with a liquid fertilizer mixed at half the normal strength.

Variegation fades, or stems become long and leggy.
CAUSE: Too little light.
REMEDY: Move plant to a brighter spot. All scheffleras tend to become lanky as they age. Propagate plants that have lost their shape and are impossible to stake.

Leaves parched, with faint webbing on leaf undersides.
CAUSE: Spider mites.
REMEDY: Isolate plant, and initiate control measures as described on page 274. Maintaining high humidity helps prevent problems with this pest.

White cottony masses on stems.
CAUSE: Mealybugs.
REMEDY: Isolate plant, and remove mealybugs with a cotton swab dipped in alcohol. Repeat every 5 days until all mealybugs are gone.

Dark disks on leaf undersides, leaves appear limp with dark, powdery patches.
CAUSE: Scale.
REMEDY: Clean leaves by hand with a soft cloth and warm, soapy water to remove scale and sooty mold. Repeat weekly until problem is controlled. When buying a new plant, inspect leaf undersides to make sure you are not accidentally importing this pest.

FAMILY: **ARACEAE** ORIGIN: **CENTRAL AMERICA**

Syngonium podophyllum

sin-GO-nee-um poh-doh-FY-lum

ARROWHEAD PLANT, NEPTHYTIS, GOOSEFOOT PLANT

Arrowhead plant
(Syngonium podophyllum)

HERE IS AN EASY-CARE FOLIAGE PLANT that has changed dramatically in the last twenty years. The species was originally a vine that needed to be secured to an upright support. However, it has been intensively selected for compact growth habit, leaves in varying shades of green and bronze, and improved resistance to disease. The selection process became more intense in the early 1990s, when commercial growers turned to tissue culture as the primary method of propagation. As a result, today's syngoniums are more colorful, easier to grow, and less expensive than they have ever been. Most grow into lush plants less than 15 in/37.5 cm tall when kept in a 6 in/15 cm pot, and they are often labeled with their original botanical name, *Nepthytis,* which was changed back in 1879. Syngonium's sap contains calcium oxalate crystals that can irritate skin and are toxic to pets and people.

SPECIFICATIONS

Light: Moderate.

Temperature: Average room temperatures. Plant can tolerate temperatures ranging from 60–90°F/16–32°C; around 70°F/21°C is ideal.

Fertilizer: *From spring through fall,* feed every 2 weeks with a balanced houseplant food diluted to half the normal strength. *In winter,* feed monthly.

Water: Keep soil slightly moist at all times, and use room-temperature water. Err on the dry side rather than overwatering this plant. Average room humidity is fine.

Soil: Any good potting soil.

Repotting: Every 2 years, preferably in spring.

Longevity: Many years.

Propagation: When old plants begin to vine, they can be tied to a pillar or you can cut them back and propagate a new plant by rooting the tip as described on page 299.

Selections: Numerous named varieties, including some that are patented, feature various leaf colors, from lime green to copper red, with many showing strong white variegation. Choose plants based on foliage colors that you find appealing.

Display tips: Small plants mix well with other foliage plants in tabletop gardens, and they make excellent additions to hanging baskets. This plant grows well alongside small philodendrons (to which is it distantly related) and compact dieffenbachias.

TROUBLESHOOTING

Leaves appear pale and limp.
CAUSE: Excessive light from direct sun.
REMEDY: Modern arrowheads do best in moderate light, and they do not adapt well to direct sun. Move to a shadier place.

New leaves turn brown and wither.
CAUSE: Drought stress.
REMEDY: Arrowheads constantly produce new leaves, and if they run short of water, they often drop the new leaf before it unfurls. Snip off the dead leaf, and water more attentively, so that the soil never dries out completely.

Several leaves shrivel and turn brown at once.
CAUSE: Chemical damage.
REMEDY: The thin leaves of arrowhead plant are easily injured by pesticides, leafshine products, gaseous fumes, and other pollutants. Should the leaves become dirty, clean them with a fine spray of water. Before using any pesticide on this plant, apply a small amount to a single leaf and observe it for 3 days before treating the entire plant.

Small cottony masses on stems.
CAUSE: Mealybugs.
REMEDY: Remove by hand, using a cotton swab dipped in alcohol. Repeat every few days until the mealybugs are gone.

Small disk-shaped creatures on stems or leaf undersides.
CAUSE: Scale.
REMEDY: Remove by hand, using your fingernail or a cotton swab dipped in oil. Repeat often until infestation is under control.

Leaves appear pale; webby material on leaf undersides.
CAUSE: Spider mites.
REMEDY: Consider discarding the plant. Should you decide to save it, remove badly infested leaves, even if severe pruning is required, and use a lightly oiled cloth to clean remaining leaves by hand. Enclose the pruned plant in a roomy plastic bag that will keep the remaining leaves quite humid for several days. Then rinse the plant thoroughly and monitor it closely for continued problems.

# Tolmiea

FAMILY: SAXIFRAGACEAE   ORIGIN: PACIFIC COAST FROM ALASKA TO NORTHERN CALIFORNIA

Tolmiea menziesii tol-MEE-a men-zee-ES-ee-i
PIGGY-BACK PLANT, YOUTH-ON-AGE, THOUSAND MOTHERS

TOLMIEA IS ONE OF THE FEW houseplants that is native to North America. It grows wild on damp streambanks in the shady forests of the Pacific Northwest. A hardy perennial, piggy-back plant can be grown in shady gardens, where it slowly spreads via creeping roots. When kept indoors in containers, piggy-back plant provides refreshing green color and features a very unique leaf pattern. On mature leaves, plantlets spontaneously arise from the point where the leaf stem attaches to the leaf. This special talent has earned the plant fitting nicknames, such as "youth-on-age" and "thousand mothers." It is also known as "hedge nettle," as the leaf and stem hairs can cause minor dermatitis. To avoid possible discomfort, wear gloves when repotting or trimming your piggy-back plant.

Piggy-back plant
(*Tolmiea menziesii*)

SPECIFICATIONS

Light: Moderate. Do not expose the plant to full sun.

Temperature: Cool to average room temperatures; can tolerate substantial chilling, but grows best in temperatures between 50–75°F / 10–24°C.

Fertilizer: *In spring and summer,* feed every 2 weeks with a balanced houseplant fertilizer. *In winter,* feed monthly.

Water: Keep soil lightly moist at all times. Piggy-back plant needs moderate humidity, and benefits from occasional misting if indoor air is very dry.

Soil: Any good potting soil.

Repotting: Repot annually for 2 years, moving plant to a slightly larger pot. Because this plant spreads naturally, it does well in a wide pot or hanging basket. In the third year, propagate several leaf cuttings and either set the parent plant outdoors in a shade garden or discard it.

Longevity: When grown in pots, plants lose vigor in only 3 years, but they can be kept indefinitely due to ease of propagation.

◆ Propagation: Root petiole leaf cuttings as described on page 302. Wait until the parent leaf withers to cut it away from the new rooted plantlet.

Selections: Piggy-back plants are available with chartreuse leaves, and some are mottled with white. However, this plant is most valued for its interesting growth pattern.

Display tips: Grow piggy-back plant in a hanging basket. As the plantlets form on large, older leaves, they add weight and cause the stems to bend downward. Use the apple green color of piggy-back plant to good advantage by growing it near plants that have very dark green or reddish foliage.

TROUBLESHOOTING

Leaf margins turn brown.
CAUSE: Low humidity; too much sun.
REMEDY: Mist plant daily, or keep it in a room with a humidifier. Water frequently to keep soil constantly moist. Protect from exposure to direct sun.

Plant is straggly and leggy.
CAUSE: Low light.
REMEDY: Pinch back old leaves to encourage the plant to assume a more compact shape. Low light causes stems to lengthen, so moving the plant to a slightly brighter location should make new growth stockier, too.

Leaves pale; faint webbing on leaf undersides.
CAUSE: Spider mites.
REMEDY: Isolate plant, and clearly identify this pest (see page 276). If spider mites are present, prune back plant by half its size to remove the most seriously infested leaves. Move plant to a shady place, and spray daily with a fine spray of water. Try insecticidal soap as a last resort.

Small wedge-shaped insects on new stems and leaves.
CAUSE: Aphids.
REMEDY: Rinse plant thoroughly to dislodge aphids. Spray with insecticidal soap if problem persists. See page 269 for more information on this pest.

COMMELINACEAE   ORIGIN: **MEXICO AND BRAZIL**

Zebrina pendula and *Tradescantia albiflora*

ze-BREEN-a PEN-du-la, tra-des-KAN-tee-a al-bi-FLOR-a

WANDERING JEW, INCH PLANT, WANDERING SAILOR

Wandering Jew (*Zebrina pendula*)

TWO VERY SIMILAR PLANTS — *Zebrina pendula* from Mexico and *Tradescantia albiflora* from Brazil — go by the name of "wandering Jew." They require the same care, so they will be discussed together here. These are extremely easy, fast-growing houseplants, valued for their colorful foliage striped with purple or white. Small pink flowers sometimes appear in spring, but they are rather insignificant.

The stiff stems root readily when nodes come into contact with soil, which makes wandering Jew simple to propagate. This is fortunate, since plants tend to become leggy and overgrown after a couple of years. Every other spring, root three or four stem tip cuttings in a 5 in/12.5 cm pot. Within a few weeks, the new cluster of plants will be ready to replace its parent, which can then be discarded.

SPECIFICATIONS

Light: Bright to moderate.

Temperature: Average room temperatures (60–75°F/16–24°C).

Fertilizer: *From spring through fall,* feed every 2 weeks with a balanced houseplant fertilizer. *In winter,* when new growth is usually much slower, feed monthly.

Water: Water thoroughly and then allow soil to dry until the top inch of soil feels dry before watering again. Water less in winter, when the plants often rest.

Soil: Any good potting soil.

Repotting: Because plants are best replaced in their second or third year, repotting is necessary only if you want to shift the plant into a hanging basket or decorative container.

Longevity: 3 years for individual containers; indefinitely when propagated from tip cuttings.

Propagation: Root 3 in/7.5 cm-long stem tip cuttings in spring or summer, as described on page 299. Even without the use of rooting powder, cuttings usually root within 3 weeks.

Selections: Choose plants based on colors you like. Those with green-and-white leaves, such as 'Quicksilver', have a more formal demeanor than those that are heavily striped with purple.

Display tips: After keeping young plants for a year in pots, shift them to hanging baskets for their second year so that the long stems can dangle freely in the air.

TROUBLESHOOTING

Variegation fades and leaves turn mostly green.
CAUSE: Too much fertilizer; too little light.
REMEDY: Continue to feed every 2 weeks, but dilute fertilizer to half the strength recommended on the package. Move plant to a slightly brighter location.

Leaf tips turn brown.
CAUSE: Air too dry; erratic watering.
REMEDY: Increase humidity by keeping plant on a tray of damp pebbles, using a humidifier, or by misting every other day. Keep soil lightly moist. Pinch off affected leaves if they are unsightly.

Entire stem withers.
CAUSE: Root rot.
REMEDY: Remove affected stem, and reduce watering. As soon as possible, propagate stem tips. Root rot is usually caused by fungi that proliferate in the potting mix.

Stems become long and brittle, with widely spaced leaves.
CAUSE: Too little light.
REMEDY: Pinch back leggy stems to encourage new branches to form, and move plant to a brighter spot. Brittle, overgrown plants can be rejuvenated by cutting back a third of the stems to about 4 in/10 cm long.

Small, wedge-shaped insects on stems or new leaves, often with sticky residue.
CAUSE: Aphids.
REMEDY: Pinch off badly affected stems. Rinse plant with a fine spray of water, and spray with insecticidal soap if problem persists.

Leaves pale and curled, with webby material on leaf undersides.
CAUSE: Spider mites.
REMEDY: Isolate plant and prune off badly affected parts. Thoroughly clean plant with water, and mist daily. See page 274 for other methods for controlling persistent populations. If the infestation is severe, attempt to root stem tip cuttings and discard the parent plant.

PART 3

HOUSEPLANT CARE

The difference between people who claim that "houseplants hate me" and those who possess "green thumbs" is simple. Success with houseplants — or any other plants, for that matter — requires a basic understanding of the environments plants need to flourish, as well as respect for their talents and limitations. If you are one of the thousands (or perhaps millions) of people who have watched too many houseplants perish under your care, you need only to acquire some practical knowledge of how plants grow to change your brown thumb into a green one.

You will be wise to begin with plants that are easy to please, such as pothos, spider plant, or Swedish ivy, before advancing to more challenging houseplants. Yet even these and other "easy" plants need appropriate care based on a good understanding of their needs. This is the purpose of the following pages, in which topics relevant to thoughtful plant care are arranged alphabetically and discussed in detail. Use the information here to learn what plants need from their environments and from you. From choosing containers to troubleshooting pest problems, this section is intended not only to tell you what to do, but to explain why and how houseplants respond to the attention provided by their human keepers.

Acclimatization

See also Light (page 284), Wind (page 330)

The gradual process of adapting to changing environmental conditions, such as light, temperature, or even wind, is called acclimatization. Plants can best adapt to changes when they are gradual rather than sudden. Plants that are moved outdoors in spring and brought back indoors in fall often need to be acclimatized to the attendant changes in light, temperature, and wind.

African Violet Food

See also Fertilizer (page 261)

Plant foods high in phosphorous are often preferred for blooming houseplants, because plenty of phosphorous (the middle number in the fertilizer analysis, printed on the label) supports plants' efforts to produce buds and flowers. African violet fertilizers are the most widely available high-phosphorous houseplant foods; three popular African violet fertilizers have analyses of 1-3-2, 8-14-9, and 12-36-14. However, some African violet fertilizers are balanced, with equal amounts of the three major nutrients. When shopping for a high-phosphorous plant food, be sure to read the label.

Botanical Name

Almost 300 years ago, a Swedish botanist named Carl Linnaeus (1707–1778) came up with the idea of giving plants Latin names consisting of two words, representing the plant's genus and species. In his lifetime, Linnaeus managed to classify and name 7,700 plants, and the process he began continues today. Botanical names are used worldwide, so they comprise a universal language of plants.

One way to understand botanical names is to think of them as English proper names in which the last name comes first. For example, "Jones, John," tells you that the person is a Jones (a large, somewhat similar group of people), but that he is the specific guy known as John. In parallel form, *Ficus* identifies a plant as a member of the genus that includes figs, and *benjamina* — the species name — clarifies that the plant in question is weeping fig. A third, nonitalicized word in single quotes in a botanical name is the variety name, for example, *Ficus benjamina* 'Starlight'. An × within a botanical name tells you that the plant is a hybrid created by crossing different species. Some hybrids are so complex that no attempt is made to identify their species. This is often the situation with hybrid orchids, tulips, and many other flowering plants that have long, complicated pedigrees.

Botanical names are useful if you do additional research on a favorite houseplant, or if you plan to shop for a certain plant you want to add to your collection. The pronunciation of botanical names is often variable, which is not surprising when you consider that Latin, the language of the Roman Empire, is considered "dormant," and is rarely spoken outside religious and scientific circles. The pronunciations given in this book are commonly used, but it's important to realize that there is no absolute right or wrong where pronunciation is concerned. Regardless of pronunciation, you can depend on botanical names to accurately identify specific plants.

Cleaning

See also Grooming (page 265), Pruning (page 308)

Beyond regular grooming, one of the simplest ways to improve the appearance of your plants is to keep them clean. Like other indoor surfaces, plant leaves often collect dust, though they also filter dust from the air through their transpiration processes. Removing this dust helps the plants by improving photosynthesis and transpiration. Once-popular leafshine products make leaves extra glossy, but, like dust, they can block the leaf pores, making it difficult for plants to exchange gases and release moisture. Instead of using commercial waxes, try using a half-and-half mixture of milk and water to bring out the sheen in naturally shiny plant leaves.

Wait until after your plants are clean and dry to wipe containers with a soapy cloth to remove dirt and fingerprints. This is also a good time to rinse out drainage trays — the final step in giving your entire indoor garden an orderly facelift.

Fine-foliaged plants. Plants with finer foliage can be cleaned with a gentle spray of water. In summer, it is usually easiest to take plants outdoors, set them in a shady spot, and spray them from all sides with a very fine spray of water. (If the pots need to be leached to remove excess salts, both tasks can be accomplished at the same time.) To allow time for especially nasty deposits of dirt to soften, wait 10 minutes or so after the first shower and then spray plants again. Gently shake off water and allow the plants to dry in a place protected from strong sun before returning them to their usual place.

If you must clean plants indoors, you can invite them into your shower or set them in a bathtub or sink and clean them with water from a spray bottle. Direct spray from a bathroom shower is often too harsh for houseplants, so the spray bottle method is usually best. Adding a few drops of dishwashing liquid to a quart of water in

To clean the foliage of plants with hairy or finely cut leaves, tape a plastic produce bag over the pot and soil, then swish the foliage in a pan of warm water. It helps to loosen the dirt if you mix a few drops of dishwashing liquid into the water.

the spray bottle helps loosen dirt and dust so it floats off easily. Be sure to rinse cleaned plants well with lukewarm water before shaking off water droplets and returning plants to their places.

With some plants, such as ferns or others with fine leaf hairs that trap dust (velvet plant [*Gynura*] and piggy-back plant [*Tolmiea*] are two examples), you may want to submerge the foliage in warm, soapy water to get them clean. To avoid unnecessary mess, enclose the container and the base of the plant in a plastic bag, firmly taped in place. Fill a deep sink with lukewarm water with a small amount of dishwashing liquid added, and hold the plant upside-down while swishing it through the water. Allow the plant to drip dry before shifting it back into bright light.

Hairy-leafed plants. African violets and other plants with hairy leaves can be submerged, or you can use a soft paintbrush to sweep dust and debris from the leaves. African violets and some other hairy-leafed plants will develop leaf

spots if water droplets do not dry promptly, or if the plant is exposed to bright sunlight while the leaves are wet. After cleaning, shake off excess moisture and turn on a gentle fan, which will circulate air and speed drying time.

Cacti. To clean spiny cacti, use a cotton swab to remove dirt and dust that persists after the plants have been sprayed with water.

Large-leafed plants. Although it's a slow process, the best way to clean large-leafed plants is to do it by hand, one leaf at a time. Use a soft cloth or sponge and a pail of warm, soapy water, and support one side of the leaf with one hand while you wipe over the surface with the other. Clean both the top and undersides of each leaf. Along with dust and dirt, you may find yourself wiping up light infestations of spider mites and other tiny insects from leaf undersides. Don't hurry, because this can be a very enjoyable chore that gives amazing results. Scientists have pointed

To prevent bruising of leaves, and to do a better job of cleaning leaf crevices, support the back of a leaf with one hand while sponging or wiping the other side. Be sure to clean both sides, because many pests hide on leaf undersides.

out that such intimate contact between plants and their keepers benefits both parties. As you gently work them over, your plants are bathed in your breath, which is rich in the carbon dioxide they crave.

Containers

See also Interiorscaping (page 280), Repotting (page 309), Soil (page 314), Terrariums (page 321)
The containers you choose for your houseplants are the only home they know, but they are part of your home, too. This balancing act — providing containers that meet the needs of your plants while also pleasing you with their presence — is not difficult if you keep a few fundamental guidelines in mind. These include size, drainage, and material. When interior decor is your priority, it is usually best to choose the container before you choose the plant. Once the container and plant are in place, you may find that a third element, such as a small piece of statuary, works magic in bringing the composition to life.

Keep in mind that flat surfaces, such as floors, tabletops, and windowsills, are not the only places to keep plants. Various types of hardware — including hooks, chains, and fiber hangers — can be used to turn almost any container into a hanging basket, or you can use a container designed to be suspended from a hook. This is often a great way to give a plant bright light that might otherwise be wasted. When installing a hook in the ceiling or mounting hanging hardware on a wall, make sure it is firmly anchored into a joist (the solid pieces of wood behind sheetrock). Otherwise, only very light plants, such as tillandsias (air plants), will be suitable for hanging.

Size. Regardless of the material from which a container is made, its size should be proportional to that of its occupant. As a rule of thumb, measure the height of the plant from the soil line to the highest leaf. Divide this number by 3, and you

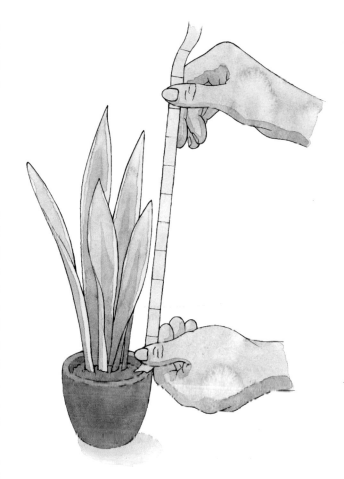

Choose containers in propor proportion to the size of the plant. A container that is about one-third as tall as the plant often works best.

have a good guess as to the ideal diameter of the container, measured in inches.

This equation won't work with low-growing, vining plants or small, squat cacti, so the next size-wise guideline is to choose the smallest container that will accommodate the roots of the plant. There are two reasons to go small with containers. One is that small containers have a dwarfing effect on plant size, which is usually desirable under indoor conditions. Second, soil that is not employed in the service of roots tends to hold onto excess moisture, which in turn sets a tempting table for fungi that cause roots to rot.

The diameter of the top of the pot (the measurement between opposite edges) is usually about the same as its depth. However, some plants with shallow surface roots do better in a low, squat container. Notice, too, that pots that narrow toward the base are prone to toppling over when planted with tall plants, though they are fine for small ones. Heavy pots with attached drainage dishes are often ideal for top-heavy plants. If a tall plant insists on tipping over, move it into a square planter that sits solidly in place.

Drainage. Whatever their size or shape, containers for plants must have drainage holes in the bottom through which excess water can escape. Several midsized drainage holes are better than one large one. Many gardeners place a piece of screen over the holes to keep soil from coming out along with excess water, but it is better to leave the holes unobstructed. That way, you can check for the presence of roots growing out of the bottom of the pot, and if drainage problems develop you can reopen the holes by poking them with a skewer, awl, or pencil. If soil loss is a big concern, simply line the bottom of the pot with a thin layer of pebbles or broken crockery when repotting your plants (see page 309). A half inch of loose pebbles or broken crockery improves drainage too.

Unfortunately, many beautiful brass, ceramic, or hand-thrown pottery planters do not include drainage holes. Holes can be drilled into plastic or fiberglass, but don't try this with fine ceramic or pottery. Instead, use these as *cachepots,* the term used to describe "containers for your containers." Place an inch of clean pebbles in the bottom of the cachepot, and set your plant in a container that can be slipped inside the drainless one. (It's common to use a thin plastic pot for the inner one.) As long as water is not allowed to form a deep puddle that keeps plant roots too wet, this double-potting system works quite well. If you accidentally overwater, be sure to drain off any excess that pools up in the bottom of the cachepot.

If a decorative container has no drainage holes, line the bottom with a layer of pebbles, and grow your plant in a well-drained container that can be slipped inside the prettier one and set on the pebble bed.

Materials. When purchased, most plants are growing in plastic containers. Plastic is lightweight, holds moisture well, and seldom breaks as plants are packed and shipped. There certainly are attractive plastic containers, but those supplied by greenhouse growers are more practical than pretty. Once a plant has had a few weeks to adjust to conditions in its new home, a container upgrade is usually in order. Possible materials include clay, better plastic, fiberglass, and ceramic.

TERRA-COTTA CLAY POTS. It is hard to criticize the handsome good looks of a healthy houseplant situated in the favorite choice, a clean clay pot set atop pebbles in a matching tray. Earth-toned clay pairs well with plants, and in the interest of uniformity, some people grow all of their plants in clay pots. Because it dries quickly, clay is the preferred container material for plants that like periods of dryness between waterings, such as bromeliads and orchids. If you find that clay pots dry out too fast, you can paint their insides with paraffin or any color of latex paint. Or you can shop for dense Italian clay pots, which usually have "Made in Italy" stamped on the bottom. These cost more than comparatively porous Mexican-made pots and are usually a shade darker in color.

PLASTIC POTS. Always supplying superior moisture retention, plastic pots come in a variety of colors and finishes. Those with a dull matte finish often must be tapped with a finger to see if they are ceramic or plastic! Many plastic pots also have snap-on trays, which do a great job of capturing water that drips from the bottoms of the pots (an especially desirable feature for hanging baskets). If you want a container in an unusual shape, such as an oblong box or a certain size of pedestal, you are most likely to find it in plastic.

GLAZED CERAMIC CONTAINERS OR FIBERGLASS CONTAINERS. Designed to look like fine clay or ceramic, these are usually the pots of choice for formal living rooms. Good-quality fiberglass containers can be costly, but with a little care they will last a lifetime. Some contain enough metal to create a burnished finish, and fiberglass containers can be painted or antiqued if you want to make them fit a certain color scheme. Fiberglass containers are also quite lightweight, which makes them a top choice for large houseplants. Better garden shops carry fiberglass pots in a range of sizes and colors, including many that are replicas of classic Mediterranean styles. Select these with the same care you might put into choosing a piece of furniture.

Smaller plants are most appropriate for ceramic containers, particularly pots that include an attached or matching drainage tray. When protected from abuse, ceramic containers often outlive the plants they are partnered with, so keep versatility in mind when investing in ceramic pots. Neutral grays and browns are easy to work with, and do not compete with plants for attention.

Regard plant containers as a long-term investment. Choose containers that work well with your interior décor, suit your personal taste, and include drainage holes through which excess water can escape.

Grouping matching containers together is a good way to display plants with different forms, textures, and foliage colors.

THE MORE STRIKING THE FOLIAGE, the plainer the container should be. A glossy dark-leafed peace lily *(Spathiphyllum)* would look great in a gilt-trimmed Oriental pot, but a prayer plant *(Maranta)*, with its dramatic, vividly marked and veined leaves, calls for a simple, single-colored container.

- Grow bulbs and other short-lived bloomers in plain plastic pots until they form buds. Then, to bring out their best, slip them into a decorative wicker basket and hide the interior container from view with moss.

- When a clay or ceramic pot breaks, pick up the larger pieces and then use a hammer to smash it into smaller pieces that can then be used to line the bottoms of containers. (You should always wear protective eyewear to avoid injury from flying pieces.)

- Clean your plant containers between uses. Scrub pots with plenty of hot, soapy water and let them soak, if needed, to remove salt deposits around the rims.

Diseases and Disorders

See also Fertilizer (page 261), Insect Pests (page 268), Pruning (page 308)

Unlike plants that live in the wild world of the outdoors, houseplants enjoy a comparatively clean environment, so they tend to have few problems with disease. However, their confinement in pots, with no way to escape stressful conditions, puts them at high risk for several common disorders. These disorders often look like diseases, and you are wise to consider both possibilities when working with a distressed houseplant.

Disease. Most houseplant diseases — including leaf spots and diseases that cause stems and roots to rot — are caused by fungi. Fungi some-

what resemble plants in their life cycle. Microscopic spores germinate and use enzymes to penetrate plant cells. Using the cells as food, the fungus spreads until it becomes mature, at which time it releases thousands of new spores.

LEAF SPOTS CAUSED BY FUNGI may have a sunken middle or a dark place in the center of the spot — the "fruiting" site that produces the next generation of spores. Removing leaves that show suspicious spots interrupts the life cycle by removing multitudes of potential spores. When a leaf-spotting disease is afoot, it also helps to keep leaf surfaces dry, because most of these fungi need damp leaf surfaces in order for spores to germinate and grow.

FUNGI THAT CAUSE ROOTS AND STEMS TO ROT are more secretive, and by the time the plant wilts or becomes brown and mushy near the base it is very close to death. Overwatering often contributes to this problem, especially when combined with cool temperatures. Root rot also can become established when roots are damaged during repotting, because some root rot fungi can enter a host plant only through open wounds. Contaminated potting soil or dirty containers set the stage for disaster when roots are pruned during routine repotting.

Whatever the cause, it is often futile to try to revive a plant that has suffered from rotting of its roots or basal stems. If a plant is shriveled or collapsed and you suspect root rot, remove it from its container and inspect the roots. Rotted roots are black or nearly disintegrated. Some soil-borne diseases destroy the fine root hairs and root sheaths, leaving only fragile, stripped fibers behind. Other fungal diseases leave roots intact until they have destroyed the plant by girdling stems near the soil line. Dark brown spots near the base of wilted stems are usually caused by fungal diseases. Some fungi coat the base of affected stems with fuzzy gray mycelium.

Roots that are noticeably darker than others often have been damaged by fungi. Clip them off when repotting your plants.

Plants plagued with rotting roots can sometimes be saved by propagating a healthy stem cutting, or you can simply discard the affected plant. Before using the container to grow a new plant, scrub it well with hot, soapy water, then dip it in a solution of ½ cup/118 ml chlorine bleach per gallon of water and let it dry in the sun.

What about Fungicides?

FUNGICIDES ARE CHEMICALS that kill or inhibit the growth of fungi, so it makes sense that using a fungicide might cure a disease problem. Unfortunately, this rarely works, for two reasons:

- Fungicides are best used preventatively, before a disease becomes serious, because they are more useful for stopping fungal spores from germinating than for routing out an established infection.

- Leaf tissues do not regenerate once they have been devastated by a fungal disease, so stopping the progress of the fungus does little to restore the health of the plant.

Save your use of fungicides for outdoor plants at high risk of developing fungal diseases, and use them to prevent, rather than cure, fungus problems.

Disorders. Much more frequently than they are weakened by disease, houseplants show symptoms of physiological disorders. One of the most common is brown leaf tips (described below); most other disorders are easier to prevent.

When you suspect that a plant is plagued by a disorder, go back to the basics. Make sure the plant is being given a fair chance in terms of light and temperature, and pay closer attention to watering and feeding. If you cannot provide suitable growing conditions for a certain plant, either discard it or give it to someone who can. Relieved of this needless aggravation, you can spend your energy nurturing plants that are more easily satisfied by the sites you have to offer.

"WEEPING." Occasionally pothos and other houseplants weep droplets of moisture when they are overwatered. Increasing air circulation while reducing watering solves this problem.

OEDEMA. Peperomia and some succulents actually suffer ruptured tissues when overwatering coincides with low light conditions. This condition, called *oedema,* causes corky bumps or ridges to form on stems and leaf undersides. Affected leaves may eventually turn yellow and fall from the plant. Keeping the plant warmer and watering less stops the damage.

LEAF SHED. Plants shed leaves for a number of reasons, including over- or underwatering, changes in light or temperature, or as part of their normal growth pattern. Many plants shed a few leaves in the weeks immediately after they are moved, but if a plant continues to shed leaves despite good care, it should checked to see if it needs repotting. The combination of rootbound growing conditions and scant fertilizer often causes plants to turn yellow and shed their oldest leaves.

FAILURE TO THRIVE. Air pollution can cause plants to fail to thrive, and plants, like people, tend to slow down as they reach old age.

BROWN LEAF TIPS. One of the most common physiological disorders is the browning of leaf tips, which can be caused by tainted water, erratic watering, overfeeding, or a combination of factors. Plants with long, strappy leaves are most likely to develop brown leaf tips because moisture and nutrients must make such a long trip to keep cells at the leaf tips well supplied with moisture and nutrients.

When forced to take up too much water, some plants develop bumpy ruptures in their leaves or stems, a condition called *oedema.*

In many plants, brown leaf tips is a symptom of tainted water, uneven watering, or overfeeding.

Disposal of Plants

See also Interiorscaping (page 280), Propagation (page 298), Pruning (page 308)

Diamonds may last forever, but houseplants seldom do. Sometimes their life spans are measured in mere weeks, while others may stay with you for decades. How do you decide when to give up on a struggling houseplant? Disposing of a houseplant often feels like a small death — the price we pay for our attachments to our green companions. Yet it is always best to allow plants to die when their time comes, and often even to hasten their death by pulling them from their pots, scattering the soil in an outdoor flowerbed, and then cleaning up the container to get it ready for a new tour of duty.

Of course, you don't want to throw in the towel too soon. Some plants seem to be dead when they are merely dormant, so check the plant profiles in Parts 1 and 2 to see if your plant sometimes rests in a dormant state. Many plants that develop tuberous roots do rest between growth cycles, and it can be great fun to coax them back to life when they are ready.

Plants may also respond to your help should they become overgrown and woody. Pruning them rather aggressively — and propagating some of the prunings as rooted stem cuttings — can accomplish two purposes: rejuvenating the parent plant, and creating vigorous young offspring. Plant propagation does involve time and trouble, so it is most appropriate for plants you truly like and want to keep around for future seasons of enjoyment.

Be honest with yourself about this, because sometimes you may not like a plant, or perhaps you feel that it does not like you. This is a valid reason to let it go. If the plant is in good health, find it a new home (see "Adoption Options for Homeless Houseplants," on page 258). Its new owner may be delighted, and you can follow your heart to a better plant choice for you — a win-win

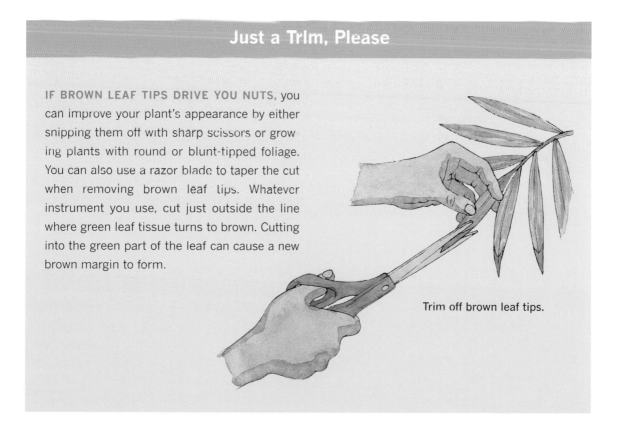

Just a Trim, Please

IF BROWN LEAF TIPS DRIVE YOU NUTS, you can improve your plant's appearance by either snipping them off with sharp scissors or growing plants with round or blunt-tipped foliage. You can also use a razor blade to taper the cut when removing brown leaf tips. Whatever instrument you use, cut just outside the line where green leaf tissue turns to brown. Cutting into the green part of the leaf can cause a new brown margin to form.

Trim off brown leaf tips.

PERHAPS YOU ARE MOVING to a state that has plant quarantines, or to a house or apartment where there is not enough room for all of your plants. When you've cared for a plant for a long time but must give it up, keep a positive attitude as you explore options. You might give special plants to friends or neighbors, donate them to a thrift shop operated by a local charity, or offer them to a church or nursing home. If the plant can be propagated (but you don't feel motivated to do it), perhaps a horticultural education program at a local high chool or technical college would like to have the plant as a project. Open yourself to possibilities, and your good houseplants will never be homeless.

situation. Take what you learned from the plant about the site and care you have to offer, and use that knowledge to select a new plant that's a perfect match to the place and its keeper.

You are under no obligation to keep a plant that refuses to thrive or is long past its prime. Plants received as gifts associated with landmark events such as marriages, births, and deaths carry an emotional charge for their keepers. Should the plant lose vitality, we may worry that the event it symbolized has become tainted or lost its meaning. This is rather silly, and it is a drama of which the plant is completely unaware. A little grieving for the plant may be in order, but then let bygones be bygones and move on. Get a healthy new plant, perhaps of a species or variety that you have admired in other places, and your sorrow will be short lived. Houseplants should be pleasures rather than burdens.

As much as we might like to live free of our tendency to judge others (and be judged as well), it happens. Unhealthy or decrepit houseplants can be the basis of negative judgments, which may be no big deal if the poor things are in your home. But in a business setting, stressed-out plants are simply unacceptable. You and your coworkers may be accustomed to sharing space with feeble, misshapen plants, but strangers may find their presence shocking or even depressing. People who know healthy houseplants find it painful to encounter distressed ones, so do yourself and the world a favor by getting rid of them. This can be a

very positive move! Even if the office budget — or time constraints — do not allow for refurbishment projects, discarding feeble plants and replacing them with vigorous new ones may be the next best thing. At home or at work, a revitalized interiorscape infuses the space with vibrant new energy. Even though you may resist the idea at first, you'll likely be amazed at the difference when shabby old plants are removed.

When you let go of old plants, consider the new opportunities that await you. If you enjoyed having a pot of dainty daffodils on your kitchen table in spring, perhaps a Persian violet *(Exacum)* is just the thing to take its place. But don't rush to replace a departed plant with the first candidate you see. When a vacancy opens up in a good plant-growing space, shop around and consider a range of prospects before you settle on the next houseplant you will call your own.

Double Watering

See also Fertilizer (page 261), Watering (page 326)

The process of flushing out the soil in a container by drenching it with water to remove excess salts is sometimes called *double watering*. And, in situations where a container has dried out completely, watering the plant twice will restore the moisture level in the pot. See "Flushing Out Excess Salts" on page 263 and "Rehydrating Parched Plants" on page 328 for more details about these watering procedures.

Drainage

See also Containers (page 251), Repotting
(page 309), Soil (page 314)

The process through which water moves through
roots and soil is called *drainage*. When drainage is
slow, roots are often forced to sit in water, which
causes them to run short of oxygen and possibly
rot. When drainage is very fast, roots may not
have time to take up water before it disappears.
How fast or slow a container drains depends on
the size and number of drainage holes present in
the bottom of the container and how well they are
working, as well as on the texture of the potting
medium and the density of plant roots. The size
and shape of the container affects drainage, too.
Tall, narrow containers tend to drain quickly near
the top, though the bottom section of the container may still be very moist. Low, broad containers usually drain in a more uniform fashion.

All houseplants require containers that have
holes in the bottom through which excess water
can escape, or drain away, yet they vary in their
drainage requirements. Plants that grow best
when they dry out between waterings — for
example, most cacti and succulents, and some
bromeliads and orchids — benefit from a planting
system that provides fast drainage. Such a system
is comprised of small containers with numerous
drainage holes, filled with a very porous potting
mix. Plants that prefer constant moisture around
their roots fare better with moderate drainage,
which is created by growing them in containers
with fewer drainage holes and a dense, moisture-
retentive potting mix.

Your choice of container size and potting mix
can be tailored to meet the needs of each plant,
but with all plants it is important that the
drainage holes remain open. The simplest way to
do this is to line the bottoms of containers with a
layer of coarse pebbles, shards of broken clay
flowerpots or old dinner plates, or a few small
stones, set so that water can flow around them

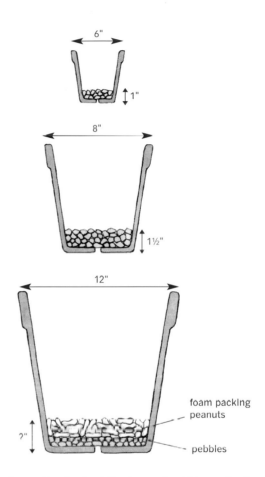

foam packing
peanuts

pebbles

Gauge the depth of the layer of pebbles or broken
crockery placed in the bottom of the container to
the size of the pots. When using very large pots,
you can increase the depth of the drainage layer
without increasing weight by using foam packing
peanuts atop a thin layer of pebbles.

and then out through the holes below. In addition
to enhancing drainage, a loose layer of rocky fill
keeps the potting medium from crumbling out
through the bottoms of the pots. Small containers are fine with a thin layer of drainage material
(or none at all), but larger pots need more help in
the drainage department. In a 6-inch container,
include 1 inch of rocky fill at the bottom, increasing to 2 inches in a 12-inch pot. To limit the weight
of very large containers, you may include only
1 inch of rocky fill, covered with a couple of inches
of foam packing peanuts.

Despite the use of rocky fill, sometimes soil or roots block the drainage holes. If you thoroughly water a plant and little or no water drains out through the bottom, there is likely a problem with blocked drainage holes. Lay the pot on its side, and open any blocked holes with a slender skewer, awl, or pencil. Check the pot again the next time you water. If drainage is still slow, or if roots are emerging from the drainage holes, make plans to repot before root rot becomes a problem.

Note also that the use of rocky fill in the bottom of the pot is not mandatory if you set pots atop trays filled with damp or dry pebbles, which accomplishes the same purpose in terms of

Fixing Floral Wrappings

MANY BLOOMING HOUSEPLANTS include decorative wrappings over plain plastic pots. These wrappings also cover the drainage holes, which can cause serious problems for the plant. You can have the pretty wrappings and a healthy plant, too, if you take a few minutes to make necessary renovations. Choose among the options below for fixing this looming drainage problem.

- Place a rubber band around the bottom of the pot, and use your fingers to locate the drainage holes in the bottom. Use a small pair of scissors to cut holes in the paper or plastic wrapping, or cut away the bottom section of the wrapping altogether. Set the plant in a transparent plastic tray lined with a thin layer of pebbles or color-coordinated aquarium gravel.

- Carefully remove the wrapping, setting aside the ribbon that holds it together. Cut a round from a disposable plastic plate, fit it into the bottom of the wrapping, and top it with a thin layer of pebbles, aquarium gravel, or sand. Place the plant back into the wrapping and resecure the ribbon.

- Moss-lined baskets usually include a plastic liner to keep water from seeping out onto tabletops or other furniture. This is fine for short-lived forced bulbs, but for more long-lived plants it is best to disassemble the basket, cut out the plastic liner, and dispose of it. If seepage is a problem, set the container on a plate or plant tray.

Insert a plastic plate filled with pebbles under the pot to correct the situation when purchased plants include a decorative wrapping that blocks drainage holes. When you're done, you can re-wrap the plant if you like.

drainage and provides an easy way to increase humidity near the plants. Some plants need every bit of space within the pot for roots, and little or no rocky fill gives them the room they need, while making it easier for you to examine the plant's root situation through the drainage holes.

Fertilizer

See also Repotting (page 309), Soil (page 314), Watering (page 326)

The primary energy force for plants is light, but they also need nutrients that support strong growth. Here are some fertilizer guidelines:

- As a general rule, fertilize plants whenever they are actively producing new growth, which for most plants is spring to fall, when light levels are high. Plants kept under lights should also be fed in winter, but feeding plants that are resting in weak winter light can do more harm than good.

- Feed plants when the soil is moist. Plants that have been stressed by dry soil conditions may take up more nutrients than they can use when fertilized before they have a chance to rehydrate roots, leaves, and stems.

- Withhold fertilizer from newly purchased plants or plants that have been moved to a new place, because the task of adjusting to new conditions is difficult enough without the additional pressure to produce new growth.

- As a broad general rule, wait at least 6 weeks after repotting plants in fertilizer-enriched soil before you begin feeding them again. Plants usually need no fertilizer for several weeks after they are repotted into potting soil that includes fertilizer. Most potting soils do include a bit of starter fertilizer, and it is best to allow

plants time to make use of these nutrients before giving them additional food. Knowing when to begin feeding freshly repotted plants is part of the grower's art, because several factors influence the rate at which the plants use the fertilizer, including light, temperature, frequency of watering, size of the root mass, and overall growth rate of the plant.

Choosing plant fertilizers. Feeding your plants need not be complicated. A few plants respond best to special fertilizers, but most houseplants are easily fed with a balanced houseplant food, a high-phosphorous houseplant food, or a high-nitrogen foliage plant food.

The differences between these three types of fertilizer is based on the *fertilizer analysis*, which is represented by the three hyphenated numbers on the fertilizer label. These numbers stand for nitrogen, phosphorous, and potassium. Here is what each nutrient does:

NITROGEN, the first number, supports the production of new stems and leaves. Young plants and foliage plants benefit from plenty of nitrogen, which is especially important for foliage plants that are growing rapidly, as many do in spring and early summer. In addition to a high first number in the fertilizer analysis, *high-nitrogen* houseplant foods usually say something about "foliage" plants on the label.

PHOSPHOROUS, the second number, is essential for all plants, but particularly important for flowering houseplants. Plants are encouraged to produce buds and blossoms by plant food rich in phosphorous. Many (but not all) African violet foods are high in phosphorous. When looking for a *high-phosphorous food* for blooming houseplants, look for an African violet food in which the middle number (phosphorous) is approximately twice as big as the first one (nitrogen): for example

Big Numbers, Little Numbers

IN THE EXAMPLES HERE, there is often a big spread in the actual numbers in the same kind of fertilizer. What does this mean? The product with larger numbers (20-30-20) is more concentrated, so less is required. Lower numbers (6-5-6) mean that more drops or granules will be needed per quart of water. Always read a product's label to make sure you are mixing it at the recommended rate. Many plants grow best when fertilizer is mixed with water at half the strength recommended on the label, or sometimes less. The plant profiles provide specific suggestions for fertilizing individual houseplants.

1-3-2 or 8-14-9. Fertilizers with extremely high middle numbers are often called "bloom start" fertilizers. These are more appropriate for using outdoors for feeding plants that are growing in open soil than for feeding houseplants. Because their roots are restricted to pots, even houseplants that grow best with a high-phosphorous fertilizer need a bit of balance in their diet.

POTASSIUM, the third number, improves the functioning of roots and supports plants' ability to move moisture and nutrients to all of their tissues.

In *balanced houseplant fertilizers,* which are often called all-purpose plant foods, the three numbers are roughly the same, indicating a balance of the three major nutrients. The three most popular balanced houseplant foods show these nutrient analyses on their labels: 8-7-6, 6-5-6, and 20-30-20; other balanced fertilizers show analyses of 7-7-7, 20-20-20, and so forth. As long as the numbers in the analysis are close, the product qualifies as a balanced fertilizer. Most of your houseplants will grow best using this type of fertilizer.

Understanding micronutrients. As well as nitrogen, phosphorous, and potassium, plants need small amounts of other nutrients, often called *micronutrients*. Micronutrients such as calcium, copper, iron, and magnesium are present in fresh, good-quality potting soils, but plants that are repotted infrequently benefit from plant foods that replenish their micronutrient supply. When buying houseplant fertilizer, try to choose a product that includes at least a short list of micronutrients.

Don't discard a plant food because you see no micronutrients listed in the fine print, however. Magnesium can be provided by adding a pinch of Epsom salts to water, or you can mix up a micronutrient buffet by making compost tea. Buy a small amount of bagged compost at any garden center, swirl a gallon of it with 2 gallons/7.5 liters of water, let it settle for an hour or so, and then pour off the brown "tea" and use it to water your plants.

Alternatively, you can filter the tea through a strainer lined with a paper towel, pour it into a pump spray bottle, and spray it onto plant leaves. Treating plants to compost tea twice a year, in spring and late summer, ensures that plants get all the micronutrients they need, along with naturally occurring enzymes, which often have an invigorating tonic effect on plants.

Making compost tea can be messy, but there is an alternative. Look for micronutrient fertilizers that are mixed with water and sprayed onto plant leaves. These are sold at most garden centers (or by mail order). Many of these products are made from dried, powdered seaweed, or kelp. A few are rich sources of iron, which is often needed by azaleas, gardenias, and other plants that grow in acidic soil. If you grow a variety of houseplants, consider adding one of these products to your fertilizer collection.

A word on fertilizer form. So far we've been discussing the chemical side of fertilizer, but you also have a choice of fertilizer forms — liquid concentrates, powders, crystals, tablets that dissolve in water, spikes that are pushed into the potting soil, or time-release fertilizers, which are coated granules that slowly release nutrients as they dissolve.

For most plants, the best choice is a liquid or mix-with-water powder or crystal form, which gives you tight control over how much fertilizer goes into the pot. One is no better than another, though liquids dissolve very quickly, and do not clump or melt when exposed to high humidity as powders and crystals sometimes do. Both liquids and soluble powdered fertilizers are available as organic products, derived from natural materials, or you can use synthetic forms (plants don't seem to be able to tell the difference). Spikes are quite unpredictable, and should be used only when you anticipate a long absence when you must leave your plants in the hands of an inexperienced plant-sitter.

Very large, long-lived houseplants such as palms, Norfolk pines, and others that grow into small trees can easily be fed by scratching 1–2 tsp/5–10 ml of coated *time-release fertilizer* into the top .5 in/1.25 cm of soil. You can also use a balanced organic fertilizer, which releases nutrients slowly as it decomposes. With either organic or time-release fertilizer, a small amount of fertilizer dissolves and moves down into the soil each time the plant is watered. Commercial growers use these products extensively, and you will often see a few round yellowish or greenish pellets on the soil's surface of newly purchased plants. It is fine to leave these alone until you repot the plant. When you replace the soil, simply discard them along with the old potting soil in any convenient outdoor bed.

Flushing Out Excess Salts

PLANTS RARELY TAKE UP every last bit of fertilizer, particularly in the top 1 in/2.5 cm or so of soil. In that area, moisture tends to evaporate, leaving behind accumulated salts. Frequently, you can see these salts as whitish deposits on the inner rim of the container, and sometimes on the soil's surface, too. Few plants are immune to the effects of these salts, which destroy root tissues and interfere with a plant's ability to take up nutrients and water. Make a practice of flushing out pots every 4 to 8 weeks. Sometimes called *double watering*, or *drenching*, the procedure goes like this:

- Water plants thoroughly with plenty of clean, tepid water.

- Allow excess water to drip out through the drainage holes for 30 minutes, then drench the pots again.

- For plants that are especially sensitive to salts, a third drenching may be helpful. Be sure to pour off all excess water that accumulates in pot trays when you are finished.

- Resume regular watering and feeding when the soil reaches the appropriate level of dryness for the plant.

- **SIGNS OF TOO LITTLE FERTILIZER.** Weak new growth, in which new leaves are small and pale, is a classic sign of too little fertilizer. Plants suffering from micronutrient deficiencies often show unusual yellowing of tissues between leaf veins, or pale leaves with darker leaf veins. When starved plants are given one or two feedings with an appropriate plant food, their leaf color usually improves quickly, becoming greener in a matter of days.

- **SIGNS OF TOO MUCH FERTILIZER.** Very dark, lush leaves with some browning or curling of leaf edges suggests too much fertilizer. Blooming houseplants may refuse to produce buds when given too much nitrogen.

Very dark-colored leaves with slightly curled edges are often signs that the plant is receiving too much fertilizer.

Very light-colored leaves often indicate that a plant is underfed, or that it is being stressed by too much light.

Troubleshooting fertilizer problems.

Plants give you clear signs when they are receiving just the right amount of plant food. For instance, when older leaves have good color, and new leaves steadily appear, gradually attaining a size that compares with that of the older leaves, you've got the fertilizer routine just about right.

The common indicators listed above, as well as many other nutritional disorders, are described in the troubleshooting sections of commonly affected plants in Parts 1 and 2. Before deciding that a plant is over- or underfed, evaluate other variables such as light, temperature, and proper watering practices. The closer each of these conditions comes to a plant's ideal, the better its prospects for living a long, productive life.

Fungus

See also Diseases and Disorders (page 254), Insect Pests (page 268)
Most of the diseases that give rise to leaf spots on otherwise healthy leaves are caused by various fungi, and fungi also cause diseases that result in root rot. These problems are discussed in detail on page 255. However, plants that show dark, dirty-looking deposits on their leaves are probably not suffering from a fungal disease. Blackish "dirt" is usually sooty mold, which grows on the honeydew excreted by sucking insects. You can rule out fungus as the problem if you can wash off the deposits with lukewarm, soapy water. As you clean away the sooty mold, look for its cause, which is likely to be scale, mealybugs, or another insect that sucks plant sap. See page 268 for more information on these pests.

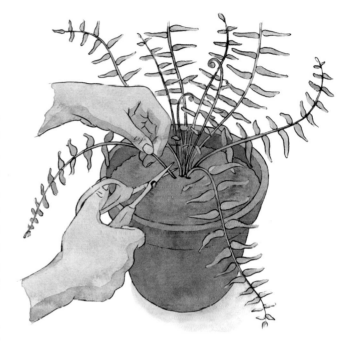

Never pull on plants when removing withered foliage. Use small pruning shears or sharp scissors instead.

Grooming

See also Cleaning (page 249), Pruning (page 308)
To keep your houseplants looking their best, take time every 2 to 3 weeks to relieve them of old leaves, while taking stock of their general condition. You might think of these grooming sessions as wellness patrols — the time when you practice good preventive health care while improving the appearance of your plants. You can use your fingertips to pinch off failing leaves from many plants, but a small pair of scissors makes a cleaner cut and avoids any twisting of stems.

Health patrol. As you remove withered or yellowed leaves, check your plants carefully for evidence of insect pests or diseases. Insect pests often hide on leaf undersides, while leaf spots with circular or halo-type patterns are often caused by fungal disease. When entire branches show signs of pest problems, go ahead and snip them off. Pest-damaged foliage never recovers its vigor, and it does no good when left on the plant. Pick up withered leaves that lie crumpled on the soil's surface as well, because they can harbor diseases and insect pests, too.

Precautions. Most leaves that are shed by plants are not troubled by pests. Shedding leaves is more often the plant's way of letting go of the old and making way for the new. As you aid in this process, the plant benefits from improved air circulation and light exposure, and of course the plant looks better, too. Plants that have shed most of their lower leaves and become unattractive in the process can be staked, prepared for propagation, or possibly discarded.

Humidity

See also Terrarium (page 321), Watering
(page 326)

Before your green companions' ancestors became houseplants, every one of them enjoyed life outdoors, many in extremely humid jungle environments. On their way to your home, the progeny spent weeks, months, or years in humid greenhouses. Compared to these settings, modern homes and offices are quite arid, especially in winter when heated air becomes extremely dry. When you take a plant that's accustomed to a very humid environment and force it to grow in dry air, it may not be able to adequately replenish moisture lost through its leaves. Leaf tips and edges may become dry and turn brown, or the plant may shed many of its leaves. Plants with thin leaves or those with long, strap-shaped foliage tend to suffer most from low levels of humidity.

You always have a choice between altering indoor humidity to meet the needs of plants or changing your plant choices in keeping with prevailing humidity. Several ways of raising indoor

humidity are described below, or you can stick with plants that adapt to low humidity, such as cacti and succulents. Another option is to grow plants that need high humidity in a terrarium — a perfect solution to providing a humid place for plants in dry offices, or for enjoying the company of plants if you suffer from numerous allergies. See page 323 for details on planting and caring for a terrarium.

Humidity means the amount of water vapor present in the air, and it is measured with an instrument called a *hygrometer*. But you do not need a hygrometer to know some basic things about prevailing humidity. Rooms in which water is often used, such as the bathroom and kitchen, tend to be more humid than other areas of the house. If you keep plants that crave high humidity, try to place them near sources of running water.

Plants are constantly taking up moisture through their roots and releasing it through their leaves, so to some extent, they create their own humidity. In a study done at Washington State University, simply adding several plants to a computer lab increased humidity by about 10 percent

In winter, when indoor air is quite dry, group high-humidity-loving plants together on a pebble-lined tray that can be filled halfway with water. To further raise humidity, place glasses or bowls of water among the plants.

Plants under Cover

TO PROVIDE EXTRA HUMIDITY for a small, special plant, keep it on a bed of damp pebbles and cover it with a glass cake cover at night. If you keep your plants on lighted shelves, see if you can find a way to fashion plastic flaps that can be let down over the sides at night. Many collectors of fancy-leafed begonias or small ferns use such humidity tents at night to capture humidity within the enclosure. In the daytime, the flaps are raised to admit plenty of fresh air. Such an enclosure need not be made of clear plastic; cloth or roll-type window shades will do just fine.

while reducing the amount of dust floating in the air. However, plants that need high humidity cannot turn a very dry environment into a comfortably humid one without a little help. One very simple strategy for increasing humidity is to place plants close together, because groups of transpiring plants form pockets of humidity on their own. There is some natural symmetry here, in that we tend to fill our brightest indoor spots with closely spaced plants. Placing bowls or glasses of water between plants increases humidity while keeping water handy for dribbling into containers.

To further increase humidity, you can place plants on watertight trays filled with clean pebbles, which are then covered halfway with water. The water should not be so deep that it reaches the bottoms of the containers, which can cause roots to rot. The trays also need to be rinsed every few weeks to keep them from becoming a secret haven for fungus gnats or other pests. Regular cleaning also limits the amount of salts that accumulate on the pebbles as water evaporates.

Misting plants, by spraying them with a fine spray of water, is helpful for plants that need unusually high humidity, but for some plants it can do more harm than good. Plants with hairy leaves, such as African violets, dry very slowly, and leaves that stay damp for long periods of time can develop problems with disease. However, a few plants, such as bromeliads, actually take up moisture through specialized scales on their leaves, so misting them accomplishes two things — the plants absorb moisture, and they enjoy increased humidity.

Misting plants from time to time when the air is very dry is a sound practice, but you should not mist heavily without a specific purpose in mind. Do mist plants that are at high risk of developing problems with spider mites, which often follow on the heels of very dry conditions. Keep in mind that misting is not a substitute for a thorough rinse, which is the best preventive measure for this pest. Misting is also helpful in early winter, when humidity levels fall in keeping with an increase in indoor heating, or as a way to ease the adjustment of new plants that are accustomed to greenhouse conditions. Once plants have 2 to 3 weeks to adjust to such changes, it is best to allow humidity to gradually drop to levels that are comfortable for both you and your plants as opposed to continuous heavy misting. Most people and plants are comfortable in rooms where the humidity level ranges between 40 and 50 percent. Running a humidifier in rooms where a number of plants are kept is usually the best solution in buildings with extremely dry indoor air.

Insect Pests

See also Cleaning (page 249), Diseases and Disorders (page 254), Grooming (page 265), Moving Houseplants (page 291), Propagation (page 298). Like other plants, houseplants are occasionally bothered by insects. When houseplants are moved outdoors in the summer, a number of insects, including various caterpillars, earwigs, and other critters that are seldom seen indoors, may breakfast on plant leaves or buds. Taking appropriate precautionary steps when bringing plants in following their outdoor summer vacation, as outlined on page 291, will greatly reduce the likelihood that you will see insects on your houseplants.

Yet a few insects, including the eight described in detail here, have no trouble colonizing plants that never move from the places you select for them. In alphabetical order, these include aphids, earwigs, fungus gnats, mealybugs, scale, spider mites, thrips, and whiteflies. On page 278 you will find five insecticides that can be safely used to treat insect problems on houseplants.

The most common way for any of these insects to gain entry to your home or office is by hitching a ride on new plants, where they may be hidden in crevices, or there may be one or two microscopic eggs attached to the underside of a leaf. For this reason, many people keep new plants separated from others for 3 to 4 weeks, during which time any lurking insect problems have ample time to become apparent. Isolating plants does not mean that you need to keep them in a separate room. A distance of 10 ft/3 m or so is sufficient to keep minor insect populations from moving from one plant to another, because insects seldom seek new host plants when they are satisfied with the one they have.

The diversity of species among houseplants also gives you a degree of protection from insect epidemics. The insects described here can infest a number of different plants, but insects vary in their ability to digest the juices of specific plants. For example, if you have a dish garden in which the English ivy becomes infested with spider mites, you may find that dieffenbachia grown only a few inches away remains unaffected. So, when you must take steps to control insects that turn up on a certain species, it is seldom necessary to subject all of your plants to washing or spraying. Do, however, watch neighboring plants closely. If a new outbreak is going to occur on a previously unaffected plant, it will usually do so within a month.

In addition to looking for insects, look for what they leave behind, which is tactfully referred to as *honeydew*. Most insects that infect houseplants suck plant juices, and their excrement is usually this sticky liquid. Leaves that show shiny patches or the presence of a sticky residue on surfaces near plants are evidence of feeding by sucking insects including aphids, mealybugs, scale, and some other species. If the insects have been present on the plant for some time, the honeydew darkens to what is called sooty mold. Both honeydew and sooty mold can be cleaned off with warm, soapy water and a soft cloth, but controlling the insects that created the mess often requires more extensive efforts.

Plants that have had more than half of their leaves damaged by insects are often not worth saving. However, if the plant can be propagated from a stem cutting and you find a stem that appears insect free, you can try rooting the cutting as described on page 299. This is often the best way to retain a beloved plant that has been ravaged by insects.

A–Z Guide to Specific Insect Pests

Aphids

Description. Where there is one aphid, there are many more, because these tiny sucking insects always appear in groups. They can hitch rides indoors on plants, people, or pets, and because female aphids are born pregnant, they quickly form colonies when they find a suitable host plant. Many plants can host aphids, which are most commonly found on tender young leaf tips, the undersides of new leaves, or the buds of blooming houseplants. Because aphids suck plant juices, infested stems and leaves often are curled or distorted.

Most aphids are less than ½₂ in / .3 cm long, round or oval in shape, with colors that range from green to yellow to red. Some aphids develop

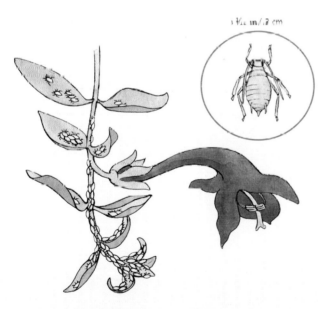

¹/₁₂ in/.3 cm

Aphids are usually found in dense colonies, feeding on tender new growth at stem tips. Pinch off heavily infested stems before trying other control measures.

Share Your Breath

IN ADDITION TO USING your eyes to inspect plants for insect activity, you can also use your breath. Breathing on plants sometimes causes still insects to move in response to the carbon dioxide in your breath. And, since carbon dioxide is used by plants (they convert it to oxygen), blowing on them gently is a nurturing gesture as well.

wings, while others do not. When many aphids feed on a plant, they leave behind a sticky residue that makes leaves shiny and often causes gummy specks to form on tabletops and floors beneath infested plants.

Control. Fortunately, aphids are not difficult to control. The first thing to do is clip off stem tips that are heavily infested. If only a few aphids are present, you can remove them with a cotton swab dipped in alcohol. For more serious infestations on large plants, clean the plants thoroughly in a lukewarm shower or take them outdoors and spray them with a fine spray from the hose. The spray will dislodge many aphids, though some will survive hidden away in leaf crevices. You can get these stowaways by repeating the procedure after a few days. Very small plants can be cleaned by dipping them in a sink of soapy water after first enclosing the container and soil in a tightly wrapped plastic bag. (See "The Dope on Soap" on page 271.) Insecticidal soap kills aphids quickly and easily, so it is a good idea to make a practice of spraying all plants kept outdoors in summer with a dilute soap spray before you bring them indoors in the fall.

SOME HOUSEPLANT PESTS can gain entry to your home or office on people or pets. Once inside, they may get lucky and settle in on hospitable plants. Never give them a helping hand by dusting plants with a feather duster, which can be like a rapid-transit system for spider mites or baby mealybugs. Instead, clean dusty plants by hand or spray them off in a shower. Clean plants one at a time, rinsing your cloth or sponge and replacing water in your pail between plants. This is the best way to avoid transferring insects or eggs from one plant to another.

Earwigs

Description. The pincers found on these prehistoric-looking insects look scary, but they are much too weak to penetrate human skin. There is also no truth to the old superstition that earwigs crawl into sleeping people's ears and eat their brains. It *is* a fact that earwigs are attracted to the cool dampness on the undersides of flower pots. They are most often seen on plants shifted outdoors in summer, but sometimes earwigs sneak

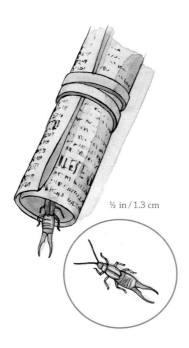

½ in / 1.3 cm

A cigar-sized roll of damp newspaper placed next to plants is an easy way to capture earwigs, which are most active at night.

indoors and find safe havens beneath houseplant containers. Earwigs rarely cause serious damage to plants, though they will eat roots and leaves rather than starve to death.

Control. Indoor conditions are usually too dry for earwigs, so they do not reproduce indoors. You can gather them with a vacuum cleaner if you don't want to touch them, or you can trap them. Roll a piece of newspaper into a hollow, cigar-sized roll held tight with rubber bands, dampen it well, and place it where earwigs have been seen. At night, the earwigs will crawl inside the tube, and you can dispose of it first thing in the morning. Earwigs are also easy to trap in small sticky traps, such as those used to capture ants, roaches, spiders, and other small insects. Sticky traps are widely available at supermarkets and discount stores. Be sure to place them out of the reach of children and small pets.

Fungus Gnats

Description. When you notice slender, dark gray $\frac{1}{16}$–$\frac{1}{8}$ in / .2–.4 cm long flies flitting about atop the soil in a houseplant, or when tiny flies congregate in warm windows or near your favorite reading light, you know you have a problem with fungus gnats. Often fungus gnats sneak indoors through open doors or windows and then breed in the damp soil of houseplant containers. Adults may lay 300 eggs at a time, which hatch a week later into tiny, threadlike larvae. The larvae feed on rotting vegetation in the soil as well as on tiny plant

The Dope on Soap

SOAP SPRAYS AND DIPS, or gently wiping leaves with warm, soapy water, is the least toxic way to control most houseplant insects. Soap controls insects by coating them with fatty acids. It has no residual effect, so repeat applications often are needed. Most commercial insect control sprays marketed for use on houseplants are based on soap, or you can use the same insecticidal soap you use to control insects in your vegetable garden.

Many people use dishwashing liquid mixed with lukewarm water at the rate of 1 tsp/5 ml per 1 qt/.946 l of water. While dishwashing liquids may do a good job, they can also pose risks, since they include fragrances, antibacterial agents, and other chemicals that may damage plant leaves. Never use laundry detergent or detergents made for use in dishwashers in homemade plant sprays, because they are much too harsh for plants.

A few plants are sensitive to soap (see page 278 for a list of high-risk plants). If plants droop a few hours after being sprayed with a soap solution, immediately rinse them off with lukewarm water. Never allow plants that have been sprayed with soap to sit in bright sun. Soap sprays may temporarily interfere with the protective cutin layer on leaf surfaces, making them more susceptible to leaf scorch.

roots. After feeding for 2 weeks, they pupate into adults. Plants growing in severely infested soil appear weak, grow poorly, and often shed older leaves.

Control. The first thing to try is to allow the soil to dry out between waterings, because fungus gnats need constant moisture. If problems persist, try trapping the adults and larvae. Adults are attracted to yellow sticky traps placed near lights. Attach a piece of yellow plastic or poster board to a wooden skewer or stick, coat it with petroleum jelly, and install it in an infested houseplant placed near a lamp, like a gnat-catching flag. An old remedy for trapping the larvae involves pushing slices of raw potato into the soil, which attract the larvae. Gather the potato pieces and dispose of them every 2 days. As a last resort, repot the plant in fresh soil.

Fungus gnats that defy these control measures can be quickly eradicated by drenching the soil with a special strain of *Bacillus thuringiensis* (Bt *israelensis*), which is sold as Gnatrol. This product is widely used in commercial greenhouses, and it is safe and effective.

⁵⁄₁₆–⁵⁄₈ in / .2 –.4 cm

Make sticky traps for fungus gnats by coating a small piece of yellow plastic or poster board with petroleum jelly.

Mealybugs

Description. Numerous houseplants are subject to attack by these strange sucking insects, which are often brought into homes and offices on infested plants. Mealybugs are experts at hiding in small nooks where leaves join stems, and some species feed on plant roots. Adult mealybugs are ⅛–⅜ in/.2–.9 cm across, and look like whitish cottony blobs, which loosely attach themselves to stems, leaves, or roots. They weaken plants by sucking plant juices. The white coating on the adults, nymphs, and eggs protects them from sprays with water or pesticides, so the best way to control them is by hand.

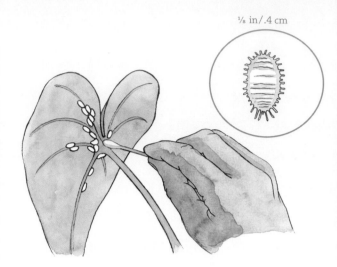

⅛ in/.4 cm

Mealybugs are easily removed by hand. Use a cotton swab dipped in rubbing alcohol, which usually kills the uncollected mealybugs. Or, pick them from plant stems and leaves with tweezers.

What about Systemics?

PESTICIDES that are placed in the soil and then taken up by plants are called *systemic pesticides*, because they introduce a toxin into the entire plant system. Insects that feed on treated plants are poisoned as they take in the plant's juices. Systemic pesticides are an effective way to treat scale problems that do not respond to simpler strategies, and they are sometimes used to control other sucking insects, too. However, when you use a systemic pesticide, you are bringing a toxic substance into a closed indoor environment. It is therefore important to read the product's label carefully.

Older systemic pesticides often used as their active ingredient disulfoton, which is extremely toxic. Most newer products are based on imidacloprid, which is much less toxic to people, earthworms, and birds. It is included in some potting soils and combination ready-to-use pest control sprays that are safe to use indoors. Read the label, because concentrated forms of imidacloprid-based pesticides should be applied outdoors rather than indoors. Move the plant outdoors for treatment, and allow the spray to dry completely before bringing the plant back inside. Also remember that *systemic pesticides should never be used on edible plants.*

Control. Begin by using a fingernail, toothpick, or cotton swab dipped in rubbing alcohol or vegetable oil to dislodge and collect all the mealybugs you can find. Pay close attention to the places where leaves are attached to stems, which is a favorite place for mealybugs to hide. Repeat this procedure weekly until the plant is free of mealybugs. If the plant tolerates insecticidal soap, a thorough spray will often kill any mealybugs you missed.

African violets, cacti, and some other houseplants are attacked by mealybugs that feed on plant roots. Sometimes you can find root-feeding mealybugs on the bottom of the pots, or you can allow the roots to dry a bit and then tap the plant out to inspect its roots. If mealybugs are present, gently repot the plant in clean soil and then take it outdoors and drench the roots (but not the leaves) with an insecticide such as carbaryl.

When any type of mealybug problem develops in greenhouses, a natural predator called the *mealybug destroyer* is often released, and it does a good job of hunting down and killing mealybugs. However, using this small black lady beetle is not practical in homes and offices unless a large collection of plants is seriously infested with the pest.

Scale

Description. Scales are bizarre little insects that attach themselves to plants and suck plant juices. Most species are exclusively female. When males do occur, they do not have mouths, and therefore live but for a short time. Once a juvenile scale attaches itself to a leaf or stem with its needlelike mouthparts, it seldom moves. Instead, it grows larger, exudes a waxy coating that forms a helmet-like shell, and bears hundreds of young, all in one place.

Several species of scale infest houseplants, including a few that normally live on outdoor trees and shrubs in mild climates. Others are tropical species that inhabit greenhouses where houseplants are grown commercially. Wherever they come from, scales are formidable houseplant pests. They can infest hundreds of different types of plants, but tend to be most troublesome on ficus and ferns.

The evidence of scale infestation is easy to detect. Affected leaves or stems may be weak and slightly yellow, and there is often a sticky substance on the table or floor beneath the plants. This is honeydew excreted by the scale as they feed on plant juices. Most scale are found on stems or leaf undersides, especially near the central leaf vein. They may be brown, gray, or black bumps, which are often shaped like flattened discs. Fully grown adults range from $1/16$–$1/8$ in/ .2–.4 cm in diameter. Juvenile scales, called crawlers, do move about, but they are so small that they are very difficult to see.

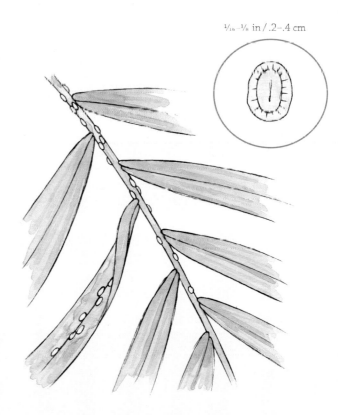

$1/16$–$1/8$ in / .2–.4 cm

Use a soft cloth dipped in warm, soapy water to remove scale from leaves and stems.

Cyclamen Mites

ANOTHER MITE PEST, much smaller than spider mite, sometimes causes leaves and flowers of African violets, begonias, cyclamens, and gloxinias to become dwarfed and distorted. Cyclamen mites are very difficult to see, and extremely hard to control. When new leaves and flowers of any of these plants appear streaked, curled, and distorted, isolate the plant immediately and consider disposing of it. The best way to kill cyclamen mites is to submerge the plant's foliage in 110°F water for 15 minutes — but keep in mind that this sometimes kills the plant as well.

Control. Practice prevention of this pest by thoroughly cleaning any ferns or ficus that spend the summer outdoors before moving them back indoors for the winter. Treating plants with insecticidal soap a week or two before they are brought indoors is an excellent preventive practice. Some ferns are damaged by soap, so test a sample frond before treating the entire plant.

Should you discover scale on any houseplant, your first line of defense is to attempt to clean it by hand using a soft cloth dipped in warm, soapy water. Although this is laborious, it is worthwhile if the infestation is light and you value the plant. On cactus and other untouchable plants, use a cotton swab dipped in soapy water or oil to remove scale.

After removing as many scales as you can, treat the plants with insecticidal soap, and then place them in a shady place to rest. Another option is to use horticultural oil, which smothers scale insects. Whether you use soap or oil, repeat the application 10 days later to kill scales that may have escaped the first treatment. If you tried to clean away scale by hand and were unsuccessful, you will probably have better luck after you have given the plants a thorough spray with insecticidal soap. You'll find that dead scale are easier to remove than live ones.

Several chemical insecticides can be used on scale that persists despite treatment with insecticidal soap or oil and hand cleaning, but be sure to check a sample leaf first to make sure that the plant can tolerate the chemical. Soap sprays cannot be used on palms, so when a large palm becomes infested with scale, a systemic insecticide containing *imidacloprid* is often the best solution (see "What about Systemics?" on page 272).

Spider Mites

Description. Perhaps the most dreaded pests of houseplants, spider mites are not true insects, but are more closely related to spiders and ticks. Spider mites damage plants by piercing the leaves with needle-sharp mouthparts and then sucking out plant juices. They congregate on the undersides of plant leaves, where they may not be seen until the plant is seriously infested. Mite-laden leaves may show numerous yellow pinpricks, or they may be dry and limp while still green. Left uncontrolled, spider mites can kill their first victim and then spread to other nearby plants.

Spider mites cannot hurt people or pets, however, because they are so very tiny. Most adults are only ⅕₀ in/.05 cm long, so you would need a 15× magnifying glass to see them. Under magnification, spider mites may be green, yellow, red, black, or colorless. Without a magnifying glass, you can usually see faint silky webbing on the undersides of badly infested leaves. Also, if you tap or brush the underside of an infested leaf over a white piece of paper, you may be able to see miniscule moving dots.

Control. Spider mites usually gain entry to homes and offices on new plants, so it's always a good idea to keep new plants isolated from others for a couple of weeks. In dish gardens, sometimes

Soap-Oil Treatment for Spider Mites

THIS SIMPLE MIXTURE gives good control of light to moderate infestations of spider mites. First, give the plants a shower, which will dislodge and remove many of the mites. When spraying the mixture, be sure to thoroughly cover leaf undersides.

With small plants, such as African violets, it is often more practical to use this solution as a dip. To do this, fill a sink or roomy bucket with the solution, making sure that the water you use is warm. Wrap the container and soil snugly in a plastic bag, taping the edges around the base of the plant with cellophane tape, in order to keep the soap and oil from getting into the potting soil. Hold the plant by the base and swish it through the solution gently until the entire plant is thoroughly soaked. Shake off the excess, and allow the plant to dry before removing the plastic.

INGREDIENTS

1 tablespoon / 15 ml dishwashing liquid (do not use laundry detergent or dishwasher detergent)

1 tablespoon / 15 ml vegetable oil, such as canola or corn oil

2 quarts / 2 l lukewarm water

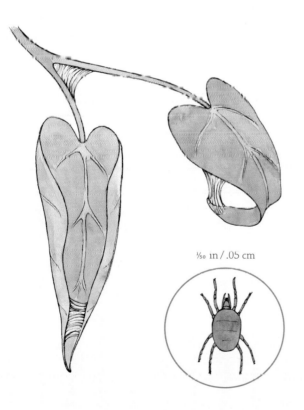

⅟₅₀ in / .05 cm

Early control is crucial with spider mites, which can infest a broad range of houseplants. By the time you see faint webbing on leaf undersides, the mite population is dangerously high.

one plant will have spider mites, but the others will be okay. This is usually because the infested plant was stressed in some way, which left it easy prey for the mites. Weak plants have more problems with spider mites than healthy ones.

Early detection is a challenge, but light infestations of spider mites are much easier to treat than severe ones. Spider mites multiply rapidly, with eggs hatching only 3 days after they are laid. A complete life cycle, from egg to egg-laying adult, can pass in only 2 weeks. Very dry conditions encourage spider mites, so they are often seen in winter, when plants struggle in dry, heated rooms. Misting plants regularly or setting them on beds of pebbles that are kept damp helps to prevent problems with spider mites.

How you control spider mites depends on the size and value of the affected plant, and how much you want to keep it. Small, inexpensive plants that have come into your life casually are best disposed of, because in the time it takes to bring the mites under control they could spread to more significant houseplants. However, if only some parts of the plant are infested, promptly

THE DAMAGE TO PLANT LEAVES caused by thrips and spider mites often looks similar, but only spider mites create a webby habitat on leaf undersides. Tap an infested leaf over a piece of white paper to correctly identify these pests. Thrips are dark slivers, while spider mites are tiny moving dots. If spider mites are present, use insecticidal soap only, and do not use chemical pesticides, which can make the problem worse. See page 274 for the best ways to handle spider mites.

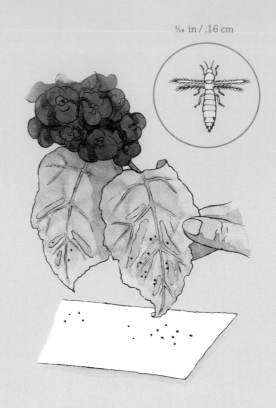

¹⁄₁₆ in / .16 cm

To confirm the presence of thrips, shake the suspicious leaf or blossom over a piece of white paper, and look for tiny, moving, shard-shaped creatures.

clip them off and dispose of them in a sealed plastic bag. Then treat the remainder of the plant with insecticidal soap or the soap-oil spray described on page 275. Repeat at least twice at 5-day intervals to make sure you kill new mites that hatch from eggs hidden in leaf crevices or beneath bits of webbing.

Do not attempt to control spider mites with pesticides. They often do not work, and mites rapidly become resistant to them. If you have a very large collection of houseplants that are affected by spider mites, you might consider releasing beneficial mite predators to bring spider mites under control. This solution is often used in greenhouses, and it is very effective. See Resources on page 337 for companies that sell beneficial mites.

Thrips

Description. These tiny, sucking insects are not extremely common on houseplants, but occasionally they manage to proliferate into bothersome populations. Generalized feeders commonly seen on garden flowers, thrips can come indoors on plants, people, and pets. Once confined to your house, they have no choice but to feed on the only food available to them, your houseplants.

Thrips are quite tiny, seldom growing to more than ¹⁄₁₆ in / .16 cm long. Adults look like dark-colored shards or bits of thread, while young thrips are usually yellowish brown. Thrips feed on both leaves and flowers. Leaves that are infested with thrips often show silvery streaks where the thrips rasp into leaf tissue before inserting their straw-like mouthparts to suck plant juices. When an infestation is severe, the leaf may pucker or curl around the thrips, and you often can see sprinklings of black feces, which look like finely ground black pepper. When thrips feed on flowers, the petals show dark spots or blotches.

To positively identify thrips, shake the plant over a piece of white paper and look for tiny moving slivers. With a very strong magnifying glass (16x or better), you may be able to see feathery wings on the largest thrips.

Control. The easiest way to control thrips is to wash them off plants with a fine spray of water. This is best done outdoors or in the shower, and it's a good idea to rinse the plant again after a few days. Should the problem persist, spray the plant with insecticidal soap (see page 278). Several widely available pesticides kill thrips, including carbaryl. Sticky traps are also a good option. You can make your own sticky trap by coating a piece of blue cardboard or plastic with petroleum jelly or motor oil and installing it in an infested plant like a little flag. While many other pests are attracted to yellow sticky traps, thrips are drawn to bright blue.

Whitefly

Description. When you are faced with an infestation of whiteflies, you usually know it, because little gnatlike creatures swarm into the air when you water your plants. These are adult whiteflies, which usually grow to about ¹⁄₁₆ in/.16 cm long and have four powdery wings. If you then use a magnifying glass to inspect leaf undersides, you may find barely visible eggs, crawlers (larvae), and pupae, all of which are very tiny and yellowish in color. Infested leaves are often pale and drooping from having their juices removed by feeding whiteflies.

Whiteflies that infest houseplants can feed on more than 60 species of plants. They may find your plants while the latter are outdoors in the summer, or you may accidentally bring them in when you adopt a new plant. Early intervention is important, because whiteflies reproduce and spread quickly. A complete life cycle can pass in only 40 days.

Control. Begin treatment by removing badly infested leaves, which probably will not recover from the feeding done by these sucking insects anyway. Then rinse the plant thoroughly, and follow up with a spray of insecticidal soap if the plant can tolerate soap sprays. Very delicate plants can be sprayed with a mixture of 4 parts water to 3 parts rubbing alcohol. Repeat this treatment every 7 to 10 days to make sure that no whiteflies survive.

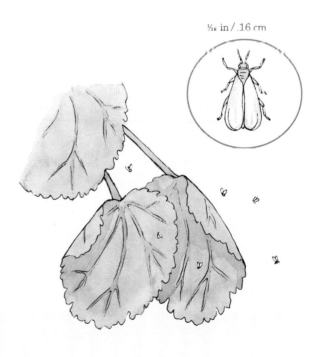

¹⁄₁₆ in /.16 cm

Whiteflies feed by sucking plant juices, so infested leaves often appear pale or limp.

Once you have had whiteflies, it's a good idea to monitor all plants for several months by using yellow sticky traps. Whiteflies are attracted to yellow. You can buy yellow sticky traps made for use with houseplants, or you can make your own by cutting yellow margarine tubs or other yellow plastic containers into 2 in/5 cm pieces, or you can use yellow cardboard. Attach the traps to wood skewers and coat them with motor oil or petroleum jelly. Either of these substances is sticky enough to catch tiny whiteflies. If even a few are detected, inspect all plants thoroughly and immediately take steps to bring them under control.

A–Z Guide to Houseplant Pesticides

Before using any pesticide on a houseplant, carefully read the product's label to make sure it is appropriate for both the pest and the plant. When any houseplant is treated with a pesticide, be sure to keep the plant in a shady place, as pesticides and bright light often combine to cause injury to plant leaves. Use the following lists as general guides; obscure houseplants are often not listed on pesticide labels. If you are unsure about a plant's tolerance of any chemical, apply it to a test leaf and wait 3 days before treating the entire plant.

Imidacloprid

What it is. Imidacloprid is the least toxic pesticide that works on contact with insects as well as systemically, by mixing with plant sap. Insects that subsequently feed on plants are poisoned as they take up small amounts of the pesticide.

Plants with delicate leaves that may be injured by this or other types of sprays can be treated by soaking the roots with this pesticide, or by repotting into soil that has been amended with

imidacloprid. This insecticide is owned by the Bayer company; products containing imidacloprid are widely available under the Bayer brand name.

Precautions. Do not apply imidacloprid concentrates indoors, and do not use this pesticide on edible plants such as rosemary or calamondin orange.

Insecticidal Soap

What it is. Insecticidal soaps, as well as homemade soap sprays, kill insects by cutting through their protective coatings, causing them to dry up. The spray must actually coat the insects to be effective.

Precautions. Insecticidal soaps are safe to apply indoors, but they can cause leaf injury to some plants, including those listed below. Never use insecticidal soap on newly rooted cuttings, which cannot have the functioning of their sparse leaves compromised in any way.

> **DO NOT USE ON:**
>
> Begonia
> Crown of thorns
> Ferns (not all are sensitive)
> Jade plant
> Palms

Neem

What it is. Neem is a natural pesticide made from a tree that makes pests stop feeding, and also interferes with maturation processes. Neem also deters several fungal diseases.

Precautions. It can safely be applied indoors. Products often have neem in their name, or you can check the label for azadirachtin, the active ingredient.

PLANTS OFTEN SENSITIVE TO NEEM:

African violet
Begonia
Crown of thorns
Ferns (not all are sensitive)
Geranium
Ivy
Jade plant and other succulents
Palms
Schefflera

Carbaryl

What it is. Carbaryl (best know as sevin) is a synthetic pesticide that kills a wide range of insects.

Precautions. Carbaryl should *not* be applied indoors. When applied outdoors, it has been known to damage leaves of some plants (see below).

PLANTS SENSITIVE TO CARBARYL:

Aluminum plant
Arrowhead plant
English ivy
Ferns
Peperomia
Schefflera

Orthene

What it is. Orthene (acephate) is a synthetic pesticide that is toxic to most insects.

Precautions. It can be applied indoors. Still, check the label, because it can cause leaf damage to some plants (see below).

PLANTS SENSITIVE TO ORTHENE:

African violet
Chrysanthemum
Ferns
Ficus
Geranium
Nerve plant
Palms
Piggy-back plant
Poinsettia
Prayer plant
Schefflera

Interiorscaping

See also Cleaning (page 249), Containers (page 251), Grooming (page 265), Light (page 284)

Using plants to make indoor rooms look and feel more inviting is called *interiorscaping*. Plants always provide a green link to the outdoor world, and there is no room that does not benefit from the presence of plants. The challenge is to choose sites that suit the needs of the plant and the design needs within the room. At the same time, you may want to use plants to support a particular decorating style. Cacti and succulents evoke a southwestern flavor; dainty African violets have the ornate appeal associated with plush Victorian interiors; and numerous foliage plants bring warmth to otherwise stark contemporary decors. For any style of decor, plants become comforting focal points that naturally draw attention wherever they are placed. They also soften sharp

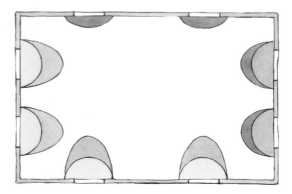

Light is always most abundant near south and west windows, with more subdued light available from the north and east.

angles, making rooms feel less confining and box-like. Homes and offices that might otherwise seem cold and sterile feel warm and inviting when interiorscaped with living plants.

As you organize your ideas, think about how plants will relate to the room, and to each other. Consider also the direction from which plants will be viewed, which is often the opposite from the light source that sustains them. The best interiorscapes include some flexibility, so that plants can be rotated from one place to another to change the look of the room, while giving plants opportunities to avail themselves of excellent light. If you work with flowering houseplants, set aside one of your most prominent, brightly lit locations to showcase plants at their peak of bloom.

You can analyze potential plant sites within a room by making a bubble drawing that identifies puddles of light from windows or overhead light fixtures. Furniture does not need light, so many plant lovers plan their furniture placement around the spots within the room that are most useful to plants. And some types of furniture partner well with particular plant shapes. Small plants that are attractive when viewed from above are best for tabletops, while cascading or vining plants work well when placed atop tall mantels,

There are containers in every color and style to complement any decor.

Bright windows serve as a stage for displaying the varied colors and textures of houseplants, as well as their sculptural qualities.

china closets, or file cabinets. Long sofas often appear more anchored in place when they are flanked on one side by a tall, vertical floor plant. Where floor space is limited, install wall shelves or hangers in places where good light is available for plants. Adding a shelf equipped with supplemental lights to an otherwise dim room creates an instant indoor oasis. In terms of interior design, a shelf upon which pretty plants are illuminated serves the same purpose as a fine piece of art.

Interiorscape basics.
Just as is true in outdoor gardens, every interiorscape is unique. However, a few simple guidelines are useful for creating orderly interiorscapes in which the plants appear to belong exactly where they have been placed.

ENTRYWAY ACCENTS. One of the most potent places for a plant is just inside the door, or at the closest location to the entry where light is available. Entryway plants are natural greeters, and they help ease the transition between the outdoor and indoor worlds. Select tough plants for this job over species that are easily injured when they are touched.

COMPANIONABLE GROUPINGS. Collections of differing types of houseplants often look best when they are arranged in groups of three or five plants, with the tallest plant placed behind or to the side of the smaller ones. This is an excellent way to capitalize on differences in plant color and texture among various houseplants.

LITTLE LANDSCAPES. In spaces where a single plant tends to get lost, try multiples instead. For example, you might locate two or three matching pots of the same plant together in the same place, which makes a strong textural statement. Or conjure up the feel of a forest by filling an indoor windowbox with different plants of similar size (they can be kept in individual containers slipped inside the planter). Dish gardens, in which several small plants are grown together in a low, broad container, can be moved from the windowsill to the dining table when you need a fast centerpiece.

Cascading plants, such as English ivy, pathos, or heartleaf philodendron, can be allowed to drape themselves over the edges of tables, mantels, tall cupboards, or file cabinets.

REPETITION. One plant is better than none, but most rooms appear better furnished when three or more plants are located where they can "balance" one another in terms of visual punch. When a diverse collection of plants is used, it is helpful to standardize containers to one type — an easy way to provide constancy of color and texture.

FRAMES. You can use plants to frame a view from a window or to draw attention to a comfortable chair or other piece of furniture inside a room. In your office, you might even frame yourself by placing an attractive plant behind you, so that people enjoy a little green scene from the other side of your desk. Plants speak softly, but they always say, "Look here."

FOCAL POINTS. Spotlight blooming plants or specimens with variegated leaves by placing them where they can be seen up close, the same way you might do with a vase of fresh-cut flowers. But don't overdo it; Use plain containers, and limit the number of showy plants within a scene so colors and intricate leaf patterns don't compete with one another.

ORNAMENTS. Tabletop plants often appear more refined in the company of small statuary, paperweights, candles, or a bowl of fresh fruit. To add more color and texture, you can use a decorative placemat to make the setting complete. In narrow passageways, mirrors work magic maximizing the presence of plants.

EXPANDING HORIZONS. You can get more interiorscaping ideas by visiting places where plants are artfully used. This happens automatically when you become interested in houseplants, because you suddenly notice plants that were there all along in malls, airports, hotel lobbies, plant and floral shops, cafés, and other people's homes and offices. When you find yourself marveling at the genius of the human who came up with a lovely

Clockwise from top: Triangles always work well as a general guideline for positioning plants. Dish gardens often benefit from small ornamental touches that help to refine the garden's theme. Blooming plants create a miniature garden when displayed together.

Time after time, marketing surveys show that the presence of healthy plants makes people perceive a business as respectable and prosperous, which explains why more and more businesses deck their halls with plants. In large cities, it's easy to locate professional interiorscaping firms that design, install, and maintain interiorscapes in commercial settings, or you can try it on your own. This is an excellent idea if your budget is limited, because you can redecorate with plants for much less than it would cost to refurbish an entire office. Here are some important considerations to keep in mind.

BRIGHT STOREFRONT WINDOWS. This situation calls for high-light plants. Many plants sold as "large foliage plants" have been acclimated to low light. Even if the species is a high-light plant, give it a few weeks to become accustomed to increased light levels.

RESPONSIBILITY. Put one motivated employee in charge of plant care responsibilities, and take into account that plant care requires valuable time.

A HEALTHY LOOK. Replace struggling plants with healthy ones. Stressed or sickly plants are worse than no plants at all. Send unhappy plants home with employees or customers who want them.

PROFESSIONAL INTERIORSCAPING. Include at least some professional interiorscape services in your budget if you have large spaces to furnish with plants. Aspire to a fine interiorscape the same way you aspire to a plush office.

---

interiorscape, consider this alternative interpretation: We may think we are in charge of plants, since we decide where and how they will be grown, but they also control us, nudging us to do their bidding by prospering in hospitable places and cleverly using their beauty and health-enhancing talents to win our favor. In the most wonderful interiorscapes, plants have been given everything they need by caring human hands. In return, they give us clean air, invigorating views, and happy hearts. It is, in all the important ways, a very fair deal.

Light

See also Acclimatization (page 248), Moving Houseplants (page 291)

Light is the most important variable in growing happy, healthy houseplants. Because we humans run on food, we tend to think that plants depend on fertilizer (as "food") in a very fundamental way. Certainly they do, but plants derive most of their energy from light. When deprived of light, the availability of nutrients and moisture is meaningless.

Plants make use of light through the process known as *photosynthesis*. Special cells within the leaves, called *chloroplasts,* take in light and transform it into energy. It is a small stretch to regard all plants as solar collectors. They receive, process, and store up light in the form of leaves, stems, roots, and sometimes flowers.

Plants that prefer high light contain numerous chloroplasts, which assemble into thick layers within the leaf tissues. The chloroplast layers within the leaves of low-light plants are comparatively thin. Yet plants can adapt to changing light levels by altering the density and arrangement of their chloroplasts. This happens naturally as light levels change with the seasons, or when available

A robust Boston fern basks in the reflected light from white walls and furnishings.

When deprived of sufficient light, plants naturally stretch toward the closest window.

light changes because you move the plant to a lighter or darker location. When exposed to increased light, plants respond by lining up more chloroplasts so they can put to use a more abundant supply of light. When light is decreased, leaves let go of chloroplasts that are no longer needed.

These changes do not happen overnight. Rather, adapting to changing light levels is a gradual process, which brings us to what is called *acclimatization*. When a plant is moved to a place where light conditions are different from the place it was before, it immediately begins making changes in its chloroplast structures, and other cells get in on the act as well. If the plant is not receiving enough light, it may twist and bend toward the light source in order to reorient its solar collectors (leaves) so they can collect every ray. This process, called *phototropism,* is also evident when stems lengthen as a plant stretches toward light. Some plants respond more dramatically, by shedding light-starved leaves. Ferns and ficus are famous for their tendency to shed leaves in response to a radical reduction in their light supply.

On the other hand, if a plant accustomed to low light conditions is suddenly moved into bright light, its leaves may be so ill-prepared that they wither. Thin layers of chloroplasts are usually housed by thin leaves with meager moisture reserves. Houseplants can be damaged or killed when moved from dim to bright light if they are not given 2 to 4 weeks to adjust to the change — a common challenge when plants are moved outdoors for the summer (see page 291). Leaves that are scorched by sudden exposure to bright sun seldom recover from the trauma.

Keep these processes in mind as you discover or create the ideal light conditions for your plants. Finding the best spot in your house to grow a certain plant is a hunting expedition, but knowing the light preference of the plant, and where such light is likely to be found, simplifies the task. The light preferences of individual plants are given in the plant profiles in Parts 1 and 2. Below we will discuss using natural light from windows and supplementing natural light with various types of artificial fixtures.

Assessing natural light. Spaces near windows are logical places to grow houseplants. Natural sunlight includes a full spectrum of rays, and of course no electricity is needed to run a window. Large windows admit more light than small ones, but almost any window can accommodate some type of houseplant. Keeping windows clean is an easy way to maximize natural light. It also can help to trim limbs from outdoor trees and shrubs that block light as it enters your windows. If the light from unobstructed, squeaky-clean windows proves insufficient, you can easily add supplemental light. Similarly, excessive natural light can be filtered through a sheer curtain, making it more acceptable to both plants and people.

Get to know the compass orientation of your windows by watching where the sun rises (east) and where it sets (west). In North America, a

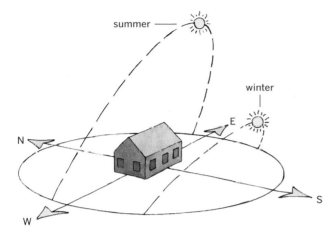

In the Northern Hemisphere, the sun's arc is much nearer to the southern horizon in winter, so north windows receive very little light. The sun's arc rises in summer, so all windows receive more light.

southern exposure always offers the strongest light because the sun arcs from east to west from a slightly southern spot in the sky. The arc is lower in winter and higher in summer, so even indoors there is a remarkable seasonal difference in how much light comes through a south-facing window. As a general rule, it is best to reserve space near south windows for high light plants.

Similar seasonal trends affect windows on the north side of your house. In summer, north-facing windows may provide enough light to grow low-light houseplants, but in winter few plants are satisfied with the weak light in a northern exposure. Yet there are exceptions. Many blooming houseplants need a cool rest in winter, which can coincide with low light conditions. If you have a room with a northern exposure that can be kept cool, at 55–60°F/13–16°C, it can become a valuable asset by providing space for resting cacti and other plants that need a cool, dry period of semi-dormancy. Should additional light be needed, you can use fluorescent fixtures (see also "Using Artificial Lights," page 289), which give off very little heat.

East windows typically get strong morning sun, while west windows are brightly lit from early afternoon until evening. Even low-light plants enjoy gentle morning sun, so east windows are often preferred places for plants that adapt to low to moderate light. Afternoon sun tends to be somewhat harsh and quite warm, so west windows are often good places for high-light plants that prefer warmer conditions.

Natural light from windows is always directional, meaning it comes from one primary direction. Plants respond by turning toward the light, often changing into a lopsided shape. To support good posture in your plants, make a habit of turning them a quarter turn about once a week. Plants grown in oblong boxes or dish gardens can be turned halfway, so that the front and back are given equal opportunities to bask in directional light.

Increasing interior light. Light from any direction becomes weaker as you move away from the window. Much of this decrease depends on the ability of interior walls to reflect light. White or light-colored walls reflect much more light than dark-colored walls, which are often said to absorb light. In rooms with dark walls, good plant-growing space is limited to 12–24 in/30–60 cm from the windowpane, while rooms with light-colored walls can accommodate larger plants, or plants placed more than 24 in/60 cm feet from the window. Mirrors hung so that they reflect light from windows can help illuminate any room.

In homes where good plant-growing windows are few, many plant lovers install a bump-out window with shelves in a south- or west-facing window, creating an ideal spot for houseplants. In addition to providing abundant light, such a window has the feel of a small greenhouse, and may help collect solar heat in winter that can be shared with the rest of the room.

A plant shelf, in which fluorescent light is maximized by reflective hoods, is a practical way to meet the light needs of a large collection of houseplants.

ONE OF THE MOST REMARKABLE INDICATORS of the changing seasons is day length, which horticulturists call *photoperiod,* or "light time." Plants that bloom in spring often use lengthening days as an important cue to develop buds and flowers, while those that bloom in fall and winter do so in response to days that are getting shorter and nights that are getting longer. In some plants, the photoperiod is such a strong trigger to flowering that they will not bloom unless they are provided with appropriate photoperiods. This happens naturally when plants are grown outdoors in their native habitats, but indoors you may need to manage the balance of light and darkness to promote strong bloom. For example, several popular, winter-blooming houseplants such as holiday cactus, kalanchoes, and poinsettias bloom when they sense that days are becoming shorter.

Rather than providing light to these "short-day" plants, the key is to deprive them of light daily for 14 continuous hours. You can do this by placing them in a room where no lights are used at night, and covering them with cardboard boxes for an extra few hours each morning or evening. Or place them in a dark closet outfitted with lights and a timer that will turn the lights on for only 8–10 hours a day. Three weeks of this light regimen is usually sufficient to induce flowering in short-day plants.

Using artificial lights. The ultimate way to increase interior light is to use supplemental lighting, which may work other magic for your home or office. Spotlights used to coax large plants to grow lush and full can be situated for maximum drama, and often make rooms look larger in the process. A shelf bursting with lush foliage that basks beneath a suspended light fixture becomes a refreshing indoor focal point. In your office, perhaps you can use a tall, linear floor lamp outfitted with compact fluorescent bulbs to transform a dull corner into a haven for air-purifying houseplants. When considering supplemental lights intended to benefit your houseplants, expect to be pleasantly surprised by the clean warmth they bring to any room.

There are many choices. Regular lightbulbs, called incandescent lights, can help supplement light a little, with two drawbacks. Incandescent lightbulbs give off heat, which may be undesirable for both you and your plants, and the light they provide is incomplete compared to natural light. Incandescent light is often called soft or "warm" light because it includes more red rays than blue ones. This is why it flatters human complexions.

Unfortunately, many houseplants, particularly foliage plants, prefer light with good saturation on the blue-to-green end of the spectrum.

Even inexpensive under-counter fluorescent lights are useful for providing light to plants.

What's a Foot-Candle?

HISTORICALLY, LIGHT FOR PLANTS has been rated in terms of foot-candles. Strictly speaking, a foot-candle is the amount of light cast by a candle 1 foot away. Plants that adapt to low light will grow with only 100–300 foot-candles of light, those that need medium light need 300–600 foot-candles, while high-light plants need a minimum of 700–1,200 foot-candles. In the interest of comparison, sunlight at noon on a clear summer day is usually in excess of 10,000 foot-candles.

Your plants will usually let you know when they are receiving too little or too much light, but if you like, you can calculate foot-candles using a camera with a built-in light meter, focused on a white piece of paper in the spot you want to measure. If the camera shows an f-stop of f2–f4, with a slow shutter speed to match, the foot-candle rating is probably less than 400, or low light. An f-stop of about 5.6 with a shutter speed above $1/125$ second suggests 400–600 foot-candles, or medium light. High light would give an f-stop of 8 or greater, which translates as more than 700 foot-candles.

You can also use the simple shadow test to evaluate light. When the shadow cast by your hand is barely discernable, the site receives low light. A well-defined shadow indicates moderate light, while a sharp, high-contrast shadow is created in high-light conditions.

This is exactly what you get with fluorescent light. Fluorescent light is a little short in red light waves, which is why it seems a bit "green." But compared to incandescent bulbs, fluorescent lights offer a broader light spectrum, the tubes are a bit more durable and give off less heat, and they are more energy efficient. New "compact fluorescent" bulbs (comprised of narrow, curved tubes) represent a huge advance in energy efficiency, requiring half the electricity of incandescent bulbs to put out the same amount of light. They also last much longer than incandescent bulbs. Compact fluorescent bulbs can be screwed into traditional lamps and light fixtures designed for incandescent bulbs, or they can be purchased as tubes that fit into tube-type light fixtures. In terms of the quality of light they provide, low heat output, energy efficiency, and long service life, compact fluorescent bulbs are well worth their cost, which is slightly higher than that of incandescent or traditional fluorescent bulbs.

When using artificial lighting, experiment with the distance between the light source and your plants. High-light plants respond well to having lights only 4–6 in/10–15 cm away, while plants that accept medium or low light thrive when the light source is 8–12 in/20–30 cm from the topmost leaves. Whenever it is practical, a reflective hood placed over the light helps capture and reflect light that would otherwise be lost to plants. Most light fixtures designed for plants include a hood. When using an under-cabinet-type light fixture, painting the mounting surface bright white has the same effect as a reflective hood.

Plants that have been struggling to make do with too little light often respond dramatically to supplemental artificial light. Once a fixture proves its worth, you will probably want to put it on a timer, so that the lights are turned on and off at regular times each day. Twelve to fourteen hours of continuous light is best for most houseplants, which also need regular periods of darkness. Some blooming houseplants will not set buds unless they are exposed to 12-plus hours of continuous darkness. See "Understanding Photoperiod," on page 289, for more information on handling light-sensitive plants.

High-intensity lights. Commercial growers, and some plant collectors, use special fixtures called high-intensity lights to simulate exposure to strong sunshine. Often abbreviated as HID lights ("high-intensity discharge"), these fixtures are costly and may require special wiring to accommodate the draw they make on electric circuitry. They are also not very pretty, and most require a ballast box to boost the power supply going to them. Still, if you develop a passion for cacti or other plants that need very bright light, eventually you may want to invest in HID fixtures.

There are two general types — metal halide and high-pressure sodium. Metal halide lights emit strong light at the blue end of the spectrum, so they are often used to encourage leafy growth of young plants. High-pressure sodium lamps do a better job of delivering red wavelengths, which encourage strong flowering. In commercial greenhouses, growers may use metal halide lights when blooming plants are young, and switch to high-pressure sodium lights when plants enter their flowering phase.

Both types of high-intensity lights are available from companies that provide equipment for hydroponic horticulture, which is the practice of growing plants in nutrient-enriched water that is continuously circulated around the plants' roots. Increasingly, these companies also offer compact fluorescent fixtures designed for plants, which are quite satisfactory for most houseplants. See Resources on page 337 for a list of suppliers.

Moving Houseplants

See also Acclimatization (page 248), Insect Pests (page 268), Light (page 284), Wind (page 330)
The most traumatic move a houseplant will ever make is its move to your home, so newly adopted houseplants should always be given special care. In the weeks prior to this move, they may have been shifted from greenhouse to truck to retail store, so they may already have been exposed to

Use a wheeled dolly to move very large houseplants, such as citrus trees or hibiscus. Extending the base of the dolly with a piece of scrap plywood will keep the plant from toppling in transit.

temperature or moisture stress. Whenever possible, choose plants that appear to have settled into the place where they are displayed for sale, which is usually evidenced by a little new growth. Make a mental note of the light and temperature conditions to which the plant is accustomed, and see if you can find a place with similar conditions in your home or office. It's a good idea to keep new plants isolated from others for a couple of weeks, so that any pests that may have been hiding in the foliage have a chance to reveal themselves. If you want to go ahead and put the plant to work in its permanent location, inspect it thoroughly for the presence of unwanted hitchhikers.

Be careful when moving very large plants, which are often surprisingly heavy. If you need to move a large plant only a short distance, you may be able to tip the container diagonally and roll it to its new place. Don't hesitate to get help with bigger moves, particularly those that involve going up or down steps, and make use of a rolling cart or dolly when moving your largest plants. Moving large plants when the soil is dry lightens their weight slightly. When broad plants must be moved through narrow doorways, angle them so you can bring them through bottom first, which usually results in fewer broken branches.

Indoor-outdoor houseplants. There are many houseplants that love to spend the summer outdoors, where warm temperatures and abundant light help support strong seasonal growth. Try to make this move an easy one by gradually acclimating the plants to increased light. Keep them in a very shady place for a week or more before shifting them to a spot that gets dappled or partial sun. Many houseplants should be kept in shade all summer. Outdoor shade is still brighter than most locations inside your house. However, a few plants (for example, hibiscus and miniature rose) bloom best when exposed to very bright summer sunshine. Make their transition from indoor light to sun as gradual as possible. Keeping plants in a wagon or on a wheeled cart that can be moved in and out of the sun quickly and easily will save you much time and worry.

As you choose outdoor locations for your plants, look for spots that are protected from

The top of a shady stone wall serves as a seasonal resort for plants that enjoy spending part of the summer outdoors.

Before You Bring Your Plants Indoors

EXAMINE ROOTS. Look for stowaway earthworms, earwigs, pillbugs, ants, and other unwanted critters. If you cannot pull the plants from the containers to make a visual check, soaking the roots (still in containers) in a tub filled with a weak insecticidal soap solution for 2 hours is a good idea.

CAREFULLY INSPECT LEAVES AND STEMS. Look for evidence of mites, aphids, mealybugs, and other small insects. If the plant tolerates insecticidal soap, as a safety precaution it's generally a good idea to treat plants before bringing them indoors.

CHECK POT RIM AND SOIL SURFACE. Look for white salt deposits inside the rim of the pot and on the soil's surface. If the container has not been leached for more than a month, do it before bringing the plant back inside (see page 263).

CLEAN UP. Wipe or scrub the outside of the pots to remove dirt and stains. In addition, wash out drainage trays.

wind. Houseplants are accustomed to still air, and twisting winds can quickly cause serious damage. Large plants can be dashed to the ground by wind, and heavy rain can be equally devastating. Covered sections of decks and patios are often better places for houseplants than locations that are open to the elements. If you do place houseplants where they will be rained upon, be sure to check the drainage trays following heavy rains, and dump out all accumulated water.

As days become shorter in late summer, plants will naturally adjust to less light, but it's still a good idea to move them to a very shady location for a week before bringing them indoors. Tropical plants should be brought indoors before nighttime temperatures dip below 55°F/13°C, but some plants, such as azalea, holiday cactus, and kalanchoe, benefit from staying outdoors through the short, cool days of autumn. However, hardy bulbs that are being forced into bloom are the only houseplants that can be left outdoors in freezing weather.

Every houseplant grower can recall a day when a sudden cold snap caused them to rush to get plants back indoors in one fell swoop, but ideally this should be a well-planned operation. Some plants will need repotting because they have responded to outdoor warmth and humidity by producing abundant new growth. Subject all plants to the checklist above, and take appropriate measures to fix any problems.

After moving a plant indoors, or when it is simply moved from one location to another, you may need to adjust your watering practices. Reduce watering a little after moving a plant, because it's always better to let plants become slightly dry than to drown their roots with too much water. In addition, watch for signs that the plant is getting too much or too little light. The retention of good leaf color or the appearance of new growth are signs that the plant has made any needed adjustments and is satisfied with its new home.

Plant Parts

Each part of a plant has a special job to do, and when they all work together as they should, you have a healthy, happy houseplant. Use the drawings on pages 294–297 to become familiar with common plant parts, including roots, stems, leaves, and flowers. Understanding various plant parts will deepen your appreciation for your plants and eliminate much of the mystery from routine maintenance activities. It will also improve the skill with which you care for your plants, and simplify complex tasks such as repotting and propagation.

Plant Parts

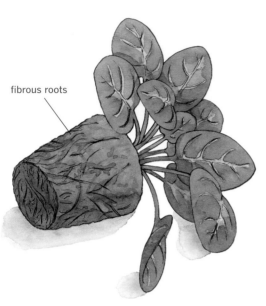

fibrous roots

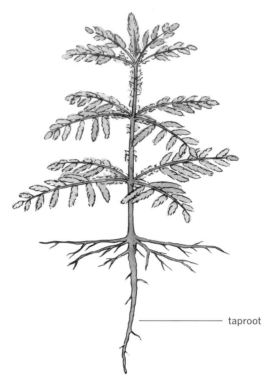

taproot

Fibrous roots may spread through the soil to form a thick network of thin fibers.

A taproot is a thick, vertical root that extends downward beneath the plant's crown. Smaller roots spiral outward from the taproot, which is often somewhat fragile.

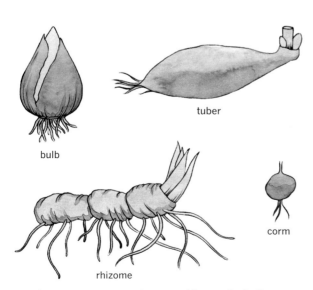

tuber

bulb

corm

rhizome

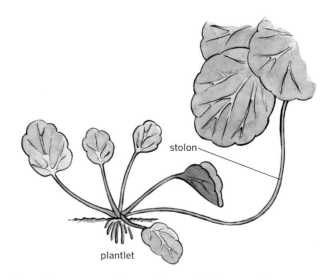

stolon

plantlet

Storage roots come in several forms, including **bulbs, corms, tubers,** and **rhizomes.**

Spreading roots such as **stolons** and rhizomes often include buds that grow into new **plantlets.**

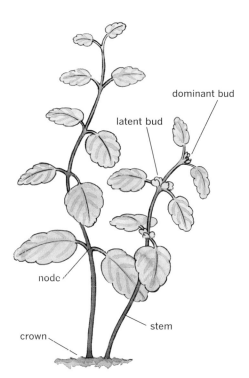

Stems attach to the roots at the plant's **crown.** The places where leaves attach to the stems are the **nodes.** The leaf bud at the tip of the stem is the **dominant bud.** Nodes further down the stems often include **latent buds,** which begin to grow when the dominant bud is removed.

Leaves attach to the stem, or to the plant's crown, with leaf stalks, or **petioles.** In some plants, the petiole also serves as a stem.

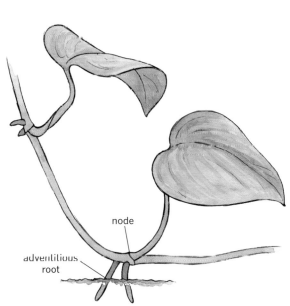

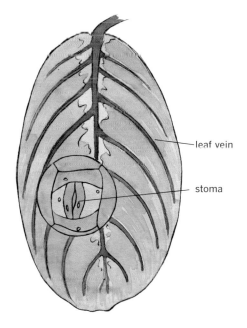

Nodes also may develop **adventitious roots,** which begin growing when they are in contact with damp soil.

Leaves receive moisture and nutrients, and transport energy synthesized by chloroplasts, through their leaf veins. **Stomata** are tiny pores in leaves that "breathe" by exchanging gases.

Leaf and Flower Forms and Parts

Simple leaves are singly attached to a stem or crown.

Compound leaves include several leaflets attached to a single petiole, or leaf stalk.

bract

Bracts are modified leaves that frame the true flowers. Bracts contain less moisture than petals, so they often persist for weeks rather than days.

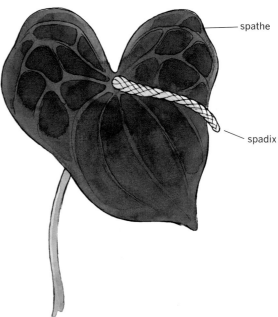

spathe

spadix

In some flowers, the bract is a fleshy **spathe.** The elongated finger-shaped structure inside the spathe is the flower.

A blossom or flower, sometimes called an **inflorescence**, is comprised of soft, fleshy petals that enclose the male flower parts *(stamen)* and the female flower parts *(pistil)*.

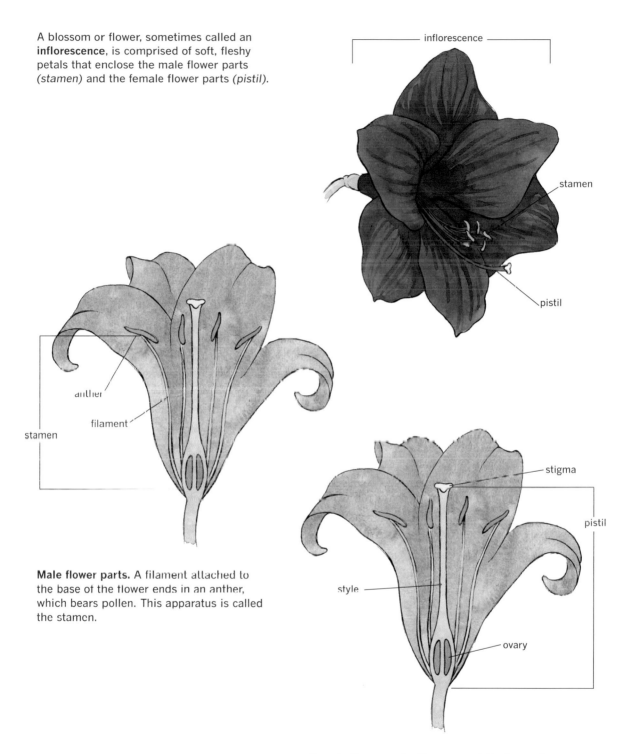

inflorescence

stamen

pistil

anther

filament

stamen

stigma

pistil

style

ovary

Male flower parts. A filament attached to the base of the flower ends in an anther, which bears pollen. This apparatus is called the stamen.

Female flower parts. The ovary at the base of the flower is the chamber where seeds form. It is attached to the stigma, the organ that receives pollen, by a tube called a style. The complete female flower structure is called the pistil.

Poisonous Plants

To defend themselves from leaf-eating predators, several houseplants are chemically equipped with toxic compounds that may taste extremely bitter, cause an acute burning sensation in the mouth, or trigger swelling of the mouth and throat when they are eaten by pets or people. People usually learn not to put these plants in their mouths instantly, but pets who are bored or too curious for their own good may not be trustworthy in the presence of some of these plants. You need not worry if you see evidence that a pet has casually played with the leaves of one of the plants listed below. Chances are good that during that play session, the plant will have taught the pet what it needs to know. However, if a puppy or kitten appears very sick after chewing one of these plants, your veterinarian will need to know which plant has caused the trouble, because the toxic compounds vary from one species to another.

Handle with Care

POISONOUS TO MAMMALS IF INGESTED
Some plants contain toxic chemicals that are poisonous to mammals when eaten:

- Anthurium
- Chrysanthemum
- Crown of thorns
- Dieffenbachia
- English ivy
- Jerusalem cherry
- Philodendron
- Poinsettia
- Pothos
- Swiss cheese plant
- Syngonium

POTENTIAL SKIN IRRITANTS
Other plants contain chemicals in their sap that can cause minor to severe skin irritation, depending on your individual susceptibility. To be safe, wear gloves when pruning or repotting them.

- Agave
- Anthurium
- Crown of thorns
- English ivy
- Philodendron
- Piggy-back plant
- Poinsettia
- Syngonium

Potting Up/On

See also Repotting (page 309)
When a plant needs more space for its roots, it is shifted to a container only slightly larger than the one it was growing in before. This procedure is called *potting up*. When potting up, take care not to move a small plant into a very large container, which can lead to problems with root rot. When a plant is repotted into a container the same size as the one it was growing in before, it is called *potting on,* or simply *repotting.*

Propagation

See also Repotting (page 309), Soil (page 314)
Many houseplants are so easily propagated that they can become your lifelong friends. It is also gratifying to propagate plants to share, and sometimes you may want to launch into a propagation project out of a sense of adventure. When you see roots emerging from stems looking for a place to go, or when you're pruning off stem tips to improve a plant's shape, it is fun to go to the next step and grow a new plant.

Understanding the botanical processes behind the transformation from stem or leaf to a nicely rooted new plant makes propagation less mystifying. In the course of normal growth, plants develop specialized cells that become roots, stems, leaves, and flowers. Along with these purposeful cells, plants lay down a safety cache of

MOST HOUSEPLANT GROWERS rarely, if ever, grow new plants from seed, but learning the basics of other means of propagation — especially rooting stem cuttings and division — is often necessary to prolong the lives of beloved plants. There are houseplants that are nearly impossible to propagate at home (for example, Norfolk pine and some palms), but most other houseplants need their keepers to take appropriate action when they become overgrown or are in need of a new mass of roots. Enter into any propagation project with a hopeful attitude and pay attention to small details, and you will probably be successful.

more versatile cells, which can morph into specialized cells should the plant's welfare be threatened. An excellent example is what happens when you propagate a new plant from the base of an African violet leaf. The base of the leaf stem, or *petiole*, is stocked with cells capable of developing into roots and leaf buds, and if conditions are right, this is exactly what happens.

With all plants, the art of successful propagation involves coaxing these latent cells to action. The individual plant's anatomy will suggest to you the best method to try; these anatomical features and the propagation methods that best suit them are discussed in detail in the following pages. Consult the plant profiles in Parts 1 and 2 as well to learn the best propagation methods for individual species. The six most common methods of propagating houseplants — rooting stem cuttings, rooting petiole leaf cuttings, simple layering, air layering, division, and seeds — are described in detail in the following pages.

None of these methods is extremely difficult, though patience is often required. And, although you may occasionally propagate a plant as an emergency measure to save its life, it is always best to get plants into the best possible condition before propagating them. If you want to propagate a plant that has been neglected, give it a few weeks of regular water, fertilizer, and appropriate light before beginning the propagation process.

As for timing, there are many exceptions, but spring is usually the best season to undertake propagation projects. Houseplants respond to the long, sunny days of spring and summer by producing new stems and leaves, so plants propagated in spring have the best opportunity to make fast, steady new growth. Propagate flowering houseplants when they are not in bloom, because plants in flowering mode are controlled by hormones that tell the plant to channel its resources toward the production of buds and blossoms, usually at the expense of new foliar growth.

Stem cuttings. Most plants that develop leaves attached to linear stems can be propagated by rooting 3–4 in/7.5–10 cm-long cuttings taken from the tips of the stems. You also can root sections of the stem other than the tips. This is often done with plants that develop canelike stems or that have stems liberally endowed with nodes, such as rosemary. Whether you are working with stem tips or stem sections, the places that will develop new roots and leaves are the *nodes* —

the places where the leaves attach to the stems. Nodes contain a good supply of cells that can grow into roots if needed to ensure the plant's survival.

The growth of these cells can be stimulated by plant hormones, called *auxins*, which are readily available in rooting powder. All garden centers sell rooting powder, usually packaged in small plastic jars. Stem cuttings that are set to root must quickly develop roots or they rot, and using rooting powder greatly increases the chances that the former, rather than the latter, will occur. With remarkably willing rooters, such as Swedish ivy, rooting powder is not necessary.

Rotting is also less likely if the cuttings are set into a medium that does not support the growth of fungi. Three such mediums are seed-starting mix, which is usually comprised of vermiculite and peat moss; plain perlite; or a half-and-half mixture of peat moss and sand (see page 314 for more information about these materials). A few plants prefer one medium over another, but most plants root equally well in any of the three.

The procedure for "sticking" cuttings is simple, but success is never guaranteed. It's a good idea to stick more cuttings than you need, because some of them may fail when microorganisms enter the cutting. Most plants with soft, fleshy stems root best when the cutting is set to root immediately after being taken from the parent plant, but succulents and semi-succulent plants sometimes root better if the cut surface is allowed to *callus* for one to several days before it is set to root.

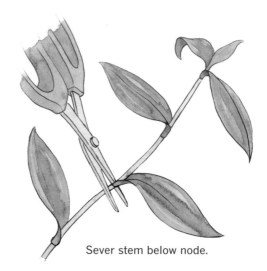

Sever stem below node.

2. Sterilize a sharp knife or pair of scissors by dipping it in boiling water for several seconds. Allow your cutting instrument to cool before severing a healthy stem just below a node.

Make a hole.

Dip end in rooting powder.

1. Cleanliness counts when handling cuttings. Wash your hands before filling small, clean containers with your medium of choice, dampen the medium well, and use a chopstick or skewer to make holes for the cuttings.

3. Remove all but the topmost leaves from the cutting. Dip the cut end in water, then dip it in rooting powder, tap off the excess, and poke it into its prepared hole. (To avoid contaminating the rooting powder in its original container, pour out the amount you'll need into a small saucer or cup, then dispose of any excess.)

Firm soil.

4. Use your fingers to make sure the medium is in good contact with the stem.

Cover with plastic.

5. For the first 2 weeks after setting any type of cuttings to root, enclose them in a plastic bag, container and all, and place them where they will receive no direct sunlight. A plastic bag or other humidity chamber is needed

because, until they develop roots, the cuttings have no way to replenish moisture lost through the leaves. A translucent plastic bag held aloft with sticks works great for individual containers, or you can place several containers together in a small box and cover the top with a piece of plastic.

Mist cutting.

6. Each morning, remove the plastic and lightly mist the cuttings. In warm weather, check them again in the afternoon. Add water to the containers only if the medium appears to be drying out. Try to keep it lightly moist but not extremely wet.

In the third week, take off the plastic cover, but continue to mist the cuttings daily and keep them out of bright light. Remove and dispose of any cuttings that have obviously died (the stems will be black or shriveled). By the third week, you may see signs of new growth in some of the cuttings. If so, move them to a place where they will get a little more light, and begin mixing a small amount of fertilizer into the water used to replenish the moisture in the containers.

Most stem cuttings will begin to root in 3 to 4 weeks, but some plants may need 2 months or more before they are ready to be potted into regular potting soil. Use the appearance of new growth as your guide. You can also test for the presence of roots by gently pulling on the cutting. A bit of resistance means that roots have anchored the cutting in the rooting medium. Ideally, stem cuttings set to root in late spring will show obvious new growth by midsummer, at which time they can be transplanted to small containers filled with an appropriate potting soil. Rapidly growing rooted cuttings may need to be repotted again after a few months.

Cane cuttings. Cut the cane into pieces that contain at least one node, and plant them on their sides, barely covered with rooting medium. With several plants with canelike stems (for example, dieffenbachia), you can trim the top cluster of leaves and attempt to root it like a stem tip cutting, set 2 in/5 cm-long cylinders of cane to root, and also preserve the parent plant, which may develop new stems that emerge from the base of the cane left behind.

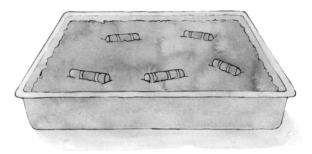

The latent nodes found on canes often can be coaxed into growing by planting small cane sections on their sides.

Petiole leaf cuttings. Some plants with very plump leaves that emerge from a central crown are best propagated from individual leaves. These include African violets, peperomias, rex begonias, piggy-back plants, and numerous succulents. The leaf stem, or petiole, is actually the plant part that develops roots. The procedure is similar to that used to root stem tip cuttings. Root several leaves, because not all of them will root successfully.

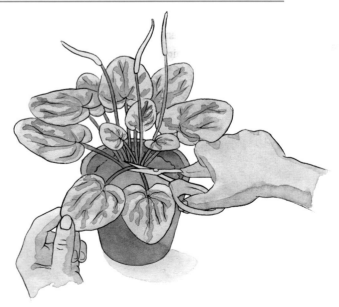

Remove petiole.

1. Choose healthy, medium-sized leaves rather than very large or very small ones. Using a sterilized knife or scissors, trim the petiole if necessary to make it 1–2 in/2.5–5 cm long. There is no need to trim succulent leaves, in which the leaf and petiole are merged into a single structure. However, you may need to let leaves taken from succulents dry overnight before setting them to root.

Plant leaf about ½ in/1.25cm deep.

2. Fill a clean, shallow container with dampened seed-starting mix, perlite, or a half-and-half mixture of peat moss and sand. Plant the prepared leaves diagonally, so the ends of the petioles are buried only about H in/1.25 cm deep.

3. Enclose the planted cuttings in a loose plastic bag to keep the cutting moist and humid, and place it in a warm place (75–80°F/24–27°C). Moderate light is usually best.

Check the cuttings daily to make sure the rooting medium has not dried out. If necessary, spray the cuttings and rooting medium with lukewarm water to maintain constant light moisture.

Petiole leaf cuttings usually root in 3 to 4 weeks. It then takes another month or so for small plantlets to form above the mass of new roots. When a plantlet has more than three leaves, it can be gingerly transplanted to a little pot, and the parent leaf may be snipped away and discarded. From this point on, plantlets will grow a little faster if a small amount of plant food is added to the water used to keep the growing medium moist.

Simple layering. Some plants readily produce roots (known as *adventitious roots*) at various places on their stems, most often in anticipation of the day when they find their way to a hospitable bit of soil, as might happen in the jungle if the stem were blown sideways in a storm, or perhaps stepped upon by a monkey. Spider plant provides an obvious example, with its habit of developing plantlets at the end of arching stems, each equipped with woody root buds. Other houseplants that have stems long enough to bend over and secure into a pot can reproduce in a similar way if given a little help. The big advantage of simple layering over rooting stem tip cuttings is that the cutting remains attached to the parent plant until roots have begun to grow. If you have tried rooting stem tip cuttings from a plant and failed, simple layering may prove to be a more successful method. Here's how to do it:

Pinch off leaves attached to node.

1. Position a small container filled with dampened rooting medium in a place where a stem can be secured. Ideally, the part of the stem to be layered should be a node 2–3 in/ 5–7.5 cm down from the stem's tip. Identify the section of stem that will be buried and pinch off any leaves attached to that node.

Secure the stem with a wire pin.

Sever the layered cutting
from the parent plant.

2. Wound the area right around the node by
scratching off the outer tissue with your fingernail or by making a tiny cut that goes not
quite halfway through the stem. This wound
will cue the plant to mobilize into survival
mode. Dust the wound lightly with rooting
powder and secure it in place with a stone or
piece of wire bent into a U. For the next few
weeks, keep the buried section of stem lightly
moist.

3. After 3 weeks or so, you can sever the layered cutting from the parent plant and treat
it as you would a rooted stem tip cutting, or
allow the layered stem more time to grow
roots. If the stem seems lazy at this task of
growing roots, a second wounding of the
layered stem, 1 inch above the soil, may
help it get started.

Air layering. Like simple layering (described
above), air layering coaxes a stem to develop roots
while it is still attached to the parent plant. This
method is most appropriate for upright plants,
such as schefflera. Air layering is the best method
to use when propagating upright plants that have
become top-heavy or outgrown their space.

In air layering, rooting medium is attached to
the plant stem, which is severed and treated like
a rooted stem tip cutting after roots have begun
to form. Although air layering takes time (usually
4 to 12 weeks), it is often surprisingly successful
with tall, leggy plants. With some plants, you can
air layer a primary stem, and after it is removed

and transplanted to its own container, new secondary stems will emerge farther down the plant.

As with other propagation methods, the first
step is to identify a place on the plant where latent
root cells are likely to be present. Nodes where
leaves attach are best, including the scarred areas
left behind after old leaves are shed. However, do
choose a spot with healthy green tissue over stem
areas that have gone woody with age. And,
because the stem will eventually be cut away as if
it were a stem tip, it's best if there are only a few
leaves growing above the air layering site. A scant
supply of new roots is incapable of supporting a
large number of leaves.

1. Once you have selected the place on the stem where you want a new tuft of roots to grow, remove any leaves that are present.

2. Lightly wound the stem with a clean, sharp knife, cutting no more than a third of the way through the stem.

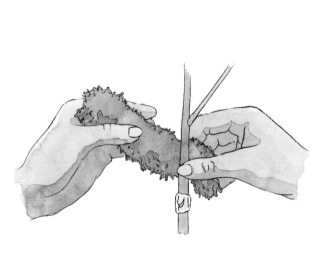

3. Dust the wound lightly with rooting powder and then wrap the wound with a "bandage" or dressing made from damp sphagnum moss (stringy, unmilled peat moss).

4. Cover it with plastic wrap and tape wrap in place with electrical or fabric bandage tape. You can also use clean potting medium packed into a small plastic bag firmly taped to the stem.

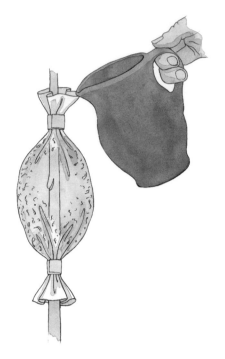

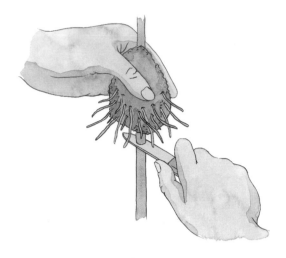

5. With either type of rooting pocket, leave a small opening in the top of the dressing where water can be added. Once the dressing is secure, add a few drips of water every few days to keep the moss or soil lightly moist.

6. Most air-layered plants begin producing roots in about a month, but wait until you see roots forming inside of the plastic to remove the dressing. When new roots are 2 in/5 cm long, cut the rooted section from the plant, remove the dressing, pot it up in clean potting soil, and treat it like a newly rooted stem cutting. Slowly increase light and fertilizer as new growth begins to appear. You are well on your way to having a robust new plant.

Division. Any plant that develops multiple growing crowns can be propagated by dividing the clump into smaller clumps. With most plants, division is a rather straightforward operation, consisting of teasing plants apart with your fingers and then using a clean knife or pruning shears to separate entangled clusters of roots.

With others, such as tree philodendron, adjoining crowns are held close by thick, woody roots that must be sawn apart with a small saw or stout serrated knife.

Since it is important to injure as few roots as possible, the best way to do this is to submerge the plant in a tub or dishpan filled with lukewarm water, where old potting soil can be gently floated away and roots can be untangled while well lubricated with water. When roots are so tight and tangled that you can't see what you're doing, feeling your way along with the root ball submerged in water makes the job easier.

Begin at the outside of the clump, dividing off crowns that are far from the mother clump. If the roots are so tangled or tightly attached that they will not come apart, it's best to grit your teeth and cut through the roots with a sharp serrated

Plants with Variegated Leaves

WHEN PROPAGATING PLANTS with variegated leaves, try division first, because rooted stem cuttings sometimes lose their variegation patterns and never recover them.

Tissue-Cultured Houseplants

SOME PLANTS ARE SO SLOW OR DIFFICULT to propagate using traditional methods that they are multiplied as test tube–grown clones. This process, called *tissue culture,* involves growing a new plant from a few cells placed in a special growing medium. When the tiny plantlets develop roots, they are transplanted to little wedges of soil, called *plugs,* which are then shipped to greenhouse growers to "finish." The tissue-culture process sometimes affects the shape of the plant, which is more likely to have basal branches than plants propagated by other means.

When thick roots make it impossible to pull plants apart, cut through the root mass with a serrated knife.

When dividing plants, soaking the roots in a pan of water often makes it easier to separate tangled roots.

knife. As a general rule of thumb, it is best to divide a crowded clump into halves. If desired, the halves can be cut in half again. Pot up the divided clumps, planting them at the same depth that they grew in their original container. Expect to see some shriveling of leaves in the days that follow. Trim off these damaged leaves close to the base, and allow the plant a little time to adjust to its new independence. If the plant does not show good vigor after a couple of months, take it up from the pot so that you can remove bits of decayed roots that were damaged when the plant was divided, then repot.

Seeds. Any plant that produces blooms eventually produces seeds, and seeds are the primary way that many houseplants propagate themselves when grown in the wild. However, because of insufficient pollination, seeds produced by indoor-grown plants may not be viable. And if the plants that produced the seeds are hybrids, the plants grown from the seeds will not be of the same quality and vigor of their parents. It is therefore not a good idea to save seeds from your own houseplants. However, you may want to try to grow some houseplants from high-quality purchased seeds.

SOME PLANTS COME TO US in crowded clumps that result when greenhouse growers plant several rooted cuttings together in a pot so that it appears lush and full. This is often done with jade plants and holiday cacti, as well as numerous other species. To give the plants room to grow, they must eventually be separated and replanted into individual containers. Follow the directions under Division on page 306 for implementing simple separations. It is best to wait until plants have settled into new surroundings to undertake this project, after which you may need to find new homes for an oversupply of plants.

This is usually a very slow process, and the vegetative propagation methods described above are always faster than starting from seed. Still, it can be done. Cacti, African violets, and even palms all can be grown from seed. Most young seedlings require very bright light, so do not attempt to grow plants from seed unless you have a greenhouse or a supplemental light fixture that can be suspended 2 in/5 cm from the tops of the plants.

The process itself is simple. Fill clean containers with damp seed-starting mix, and sow the seeds so they are covered to three times their diameter. Enclose the planted containers in loose plastic bags to create a moist, humid environment, and watch for the first emergence of tiny green sprouts. As soon as seeds germinate, move the containers to very bright light, and keep the planting medium lightly moist. The first leaves that emerge are often very simply shaped, but these seedling leaves soon give way to "true" leaves, which resemble those of a mature plant. When seedlings have more than three true leaves, gently transplant them to individual containers.

Pruning

See also Cleaning (page 249), Grooming (page 265), Propagation (page 298), Repotting (page 309)

You can prune a plant to remove dead or straggly branches, to improve the plant's posture, or to rejuvenate it by forcing it to push out new growth. It is always best to prune when plants are actively growing, though light trimming can be done at any time of year. Most plants that have lost their shape or are holding onto unhealthy branches are candidates for some type of pruning.

Before you take up your pruning shears (or scissors, which often work equally well), take a moment to study the natural shape of the plant and how and where it develops new growth. Many plants produce new growth from the tips of stems and branches. The tip of the stem is called the *dominant bud*. Farther down the stem, there are usually *latent buds* located at the *nodes* — the places where leaves are (or once were) attached to the stem. As long as the dominant bud, or growing tip, is intact, it sends chemical signals down the stem that tell the latent buds to remain at rest. When the dominant bud is pruned, this signal is turned off, and latent buds spring to action and begin to grow.

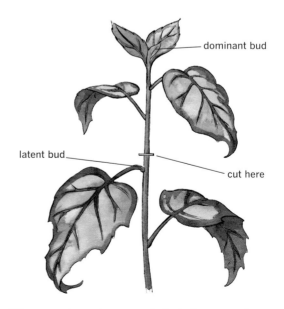

When pruning cuts are made just above a node, new stems will emerge from the latent node.

Bearing this in mind, try to make your pruning cut ⅛–¼ in / .3–.6 cm *above* a node or other branch junction. To keep a plant bushy and full, prune some branches "hard," cutting close to the base of the plant, and allow other branches to remain longer. Few plants benefit from a severe crew cut, though very vigorous houseplants such as geraniums and Swedish ivy respond well to aggressive pruning in the spring.

Most often, you will be doing light pruning to help plants grow into nicely balanced shapes or to snip off old blossoms from flowering houseplants. With many blooming plants, removing flowers as soon as they begin to fade encourages the plants to bloom again. If reblooming is not possible, trimmed plants will usually channel their energy toward the production of new leaves.

Some plants, such as Norfolk pine and most palms, cannot be pruned from the top, because they have no secondary buds. With these plants, keeping containers small helps control the size of the plants so pruning is not needed, except to remove unsightly old leaves. When plants become too large, it is best to find them a new home roomy enough to accommodate them.

Many people prune plants just before repotting them or prior to giving them a good cleaning. Be careful when watering pruned plants, because they need less water when they have fewer leaves to support. Finish up by cleaning your pruning shears or plant scissors so they will be ready for use when you next need them.

Repotting

See also Containers (page 251), Drainage (page 259), Soil (page 314), Top-Dressing (page 325)

When houseplants use up the soil and space in their containers, it's time to repot them. Some plants can go years between repottings, while others need to be repotted at least once a year. You can tell if a plant needs repotting by looking for the following five symptoms that a plant is suffering from crowded roots or exhausted potting mix.

- **LITTLE OR NO NEW GROWTH,** which occurs when roots become so crowded there is no room for them to grow, or when the potting medium breaks down so the plant's fine root hairs no longer have the physical structure they need to function properly. When plants are painfully rootbound, they often continue to produce new leaves, but the new leaves are small compared to the older ones.

- **ROOTS ARE SNEAKING OUT OF THE POT,** either through the drainage holes or by pushing the plant upward, so that it appears to be popping out of the pot. Some plants send anchor roots or aerial roots sprawling outside the container in a futile search for somewhere to go. At the same time, you may notice unusual yellowing of older leaves. While this is normal in some plants, and also can be a symptom of too little fertilizer, it is usually a sign that the plant needs more room around its roots.

From Pruning to Propagation

MOST PLANTS THAT BENEFIT from moderate to heavy pruning are easily propagated by rooting stem cuttings. Schedule pruning for the most promising propagation season, and get your propagation supplies together before you begin to prune. Often you will reap double benefits — a shapely, reinvigorated parent plant, and several healthy new offspring.

- **PLANT FREQUENTLY FALLS OVER** because it has become top-heavy with foliage. A plant that becomes a chronic toppler can be repotted into a heavy container with a broad base, and perhaps can be secured to a stake as well. If this does not solve the problem, prune the plant or propagate it to reduce its size, and/or start over.

- **PLANT IS CHRONICALLY THIRSTY**, even when regularly watered. When plants require constant watering, it is usually because the roots are compacted or have outgrown the container. Repotting into a slightly larger pot usually solves this problem.

- **SALT DEPOSITS HAVE FORMED** inside the rim of the pot and on the surface of the potting medium, which do not disappear when the container is thoroughly flushed (see page 263). In this case, it is only fair to provide the plant with a root zone that is not contaminated by high levels of salt.

Check mature plants yearly for signs that they are in need of repotting. At other times, if a plant shows one of the above symptoms, remove it from its container and examine the condition of the roots. When you see mostly roots and very little soil in the bottom half of the pot, repotting is probably in order. If the roots appear to have plenty of room to grow, pop the plant back into its pot and don't bother to repot.

The best time to repot any plant is when it is entering its most active season of new growth. For most houseplants this is spring, but some grow year-round, and others grow vigorously in fall or winter and rest in summer. Repotting is messy, so it's great to be able to do it outside in spring, summer, or fall.

Sometimes you may have an accidental opportunity to repot a plant out of season — for example, if it gets knocked to the floor or mangled by a pet. It is also not unusual to be surprised by the amount of new growth plants produce when they are kept outside during the summer. When you bring a plant indoors in the fall, you suddenly realize that the plant deserves roomier quarters if it is to prosper during the winter months. When you must repot a plant out of season, disturb the roots as little as possible, because full recovery from the event may be weeks or months away.

Plants that have been troubled by disease or poor growing environments are seldom saved by repotting, which is often so stressful that it adds to a plant's demise. Sometimes healthy plants respond to repotting by showing a fast spurt of new vigor, but it is also typical for repotted plants to sulk for a while as they adjust to their new container. Do not be alarmed if a plant sheds a few leaves in the weeks after it is repotted. This is a form of self-pruning, as the plant helps itself reach a good balance of roots and leaves. When given good care, repotted plants should recover completely within 2 months.

Repotting vs. Potting Up

WHEN A PLANT SEEMS TO NEED more space for its roots, you may decide to shift it to a larger pot, rather than simply repotting it in its original container. This technique is called *potting up*. Once the plant attains a size you find desirable, you can dispense with this operation and switch to top-dressing the plant rather than repotting it. See "The Top-Dressing Alternative," on page 325, and "Potting Up/On," on page 298.

Step-by-step repotting. If possible, cover a table or other waist-high work surface with newspapers or plastic sheeting. You can repot plants sitting on the ground, but the project will be easier on your back if you can work on a raised work surface. If you have trouble lifting heavy containers, get help (see "Two-Person Repotting Jobs," page 312). No plant is worth a permanent orthopedic injury.

1. Prepare plants to be repotted by thoroughly watering them a day or two ahead of time. Water again just before removing the plant from its old pot, because water acts as a lubricant, which is much needed when roots are tightly bound in the container.

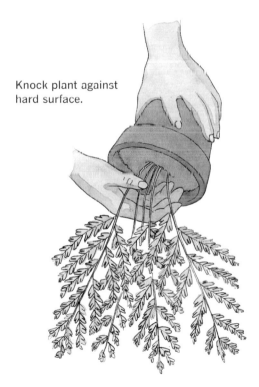

Knock plant against hard surface.

2. Tap the container to loosen the plant. If the plant can be picked up, you can knock the pot sharply against a table edge or other hard surface. With very large pots, it's more practical to tip the pot and knock against the high side with a rubber mallet, knife handle, or other blunt object. Regardless of the pot's size, make repeated blows to all sides of the pot. The idea is to break adhesions that often develop between roots, old potting medium, and the inside surface of the container. Pliable plastic pots can often be smashed slightly to squeeze the plant from its moorings.

3. Lay the plant on its side and see if it will jiggle free without your having to pull hard on the main stem (always a no no). If it is still stuck tight, use a knife to cut around the inside of the pot, the same way you might loosen a cake from a pan. Next, try to push the plant out from the bottom by poking upward through the drainage holes with a pencil or screwdriver. If it still refuses to budge, your only option is to break the pot. To break a plant out of a clay or ceramic pot, tap pot with a hammer until it shatters (save the pieces to use as drainage material). Thin plastic pots can be cut open with heavy-duty kitchen shears or a utility knife.

Use a knife to cut around inside of pot.

Root prune.

Trim plant
to a cube.

4a. Take a good look at what you have. If the roots form a solid mass, see if you can tease out a few that have wrapped into a tight spiral, and shorten them to the dimensions of the pot with a clean knife or pruning shears. This is often best done in a tub of water, or with the help of a hose and a gentle stream of running water. As you work, snip off any roots that appear black or dead, as well as those that unfurl into very long strands. There are exceptions, but most plants can be relieved of a quarter to a third of their roots as they are repotted. Don't worry about cutting the plant off at its knees, because root-pruned plants often rebound dramatically once they have settled into a new supply of fresh, clean potting medium.

4b. Alternatively, instead of trying to untangle the roots of houseplants that develop a dense network of fine, fibrous roots, remove the plant from its pot and stand it on a solid surface. Then use a sharp, serrated knife to slice four H-inch-thick slabs from the sides of the root mass, so that it is trimmed into a cube. Repot into the same size container or a slightly larger one.

5. Place at least 1 in/2.5 cm of fresh, moist potting mix in the bottom of the container, or line the bottom of the container with broken crockery or pebbles (see "The Drainage-Layer Controversy," on page 313). Set the groomed plant in the pot so that it will be planted at the same depth in grew in its

Two-Person Repotting Jobs

REPOTTING VERY LARGE PLANTS is a two-person job. If you have a huge plant that must be repotted, enlist the help of a friend or neighbor to help lift the container, pull the plant out, and hold the plant as you groom its roots. Another alternative is to call in an expert. Many companies that furnish and maintain large plants for businesses can be hired to do the job, or you may be able to take the plant to a friendly neighborhood nurseryman for professional repotting.

The Drainage-Layer Controversy

FOR YEARS, PEOPLE HAVE USED pebbles or pieces of broken clay pot (crockery) to line the bottom of containers. The primary purpose of this practice is to add an extra measure of drainage to the containers, which is not necessary if you place pots atop a bed of dry or damp pebbles, which has the same effect. However, if you are using self-watering plastic pots, where you cannot always tell if there is water sitting in the drainage tray, using a thin layer of crockery is a good idea. A drainage layer is also in order if you plan to set a container on a solid surface with no drainage tray below it. And some plants that require excellent drainage, such as cacti, benefit from having a layer of pebbles in the bottoms of their containers. Even when a drainage layer is not needed to protect roots from becoming waterlogged, it helps keep potting soil from leaking out through the bottom of the container. The choice is yours!

Repot plant at original depth.

Add soil.

previous container. Fill the space between the edge of the root mass and the container with potting mix, and then use a table knife or chopstick to gently press the soil inward toward the plant's roots.

6. Add more soil, and tamp the container on a firm surface to help settle the particles in place. As long as the potting soil is nicely moist when you repot a plant, it is best to wait a few days before giving it a thorough watering. This delay in watering gives

wounded roots a chance to wall off their injuries, and signals healthy roots to spread outward in search of water.

A few weeks after repotting, check the plant to look for spaces that may have developed between the edge of the pot and the soil by poking your finger into the potting mix. If needed, add a little fill soil to the top of the pot, but be sure to leave at least .5 in/ 1.25 cm of free space between the top of the potting mix and the rim of the pot.

Soil

See also Containers (page 251), Repotting (page 309), Watering (page 326)

The phrase "potting soil" is convenient yet misleading, because good potting soil for houseplants contains little, if any, actual soil. Instead, it is a mixture of growing media intended to do all the things soil does, without soil's negative side effects. Like soil, the medium should anchor the plant, provide particles to which tiny root hairs can cling, retain moisture until the plant needs it, yet not stay so wet that fungi and bacteria build up and cause roots to rot.

You cannot dig such a substance from your yard. True soil is made up of very small particles that are teeming with microorganisms. In the secret world of outdoor soil, these microorganisms form a dynamic community regulated by changes in temperature, moisture, the movement of earthworms and insects, and the constant inflow and decomposition of various types of organic matter. Conditions in containers kept indoors are much less lively, and if problem-causing microorganisms become established, there is no way for beneficial ones to gain entrance to set things right. This is why houseplants need special potting soil made of materials that naturally suppress soil-borne diseases and that have been further processed to rid them of microbial contaminants. Of equal importance is the texture of potting soil, which is noticeably light and fluffy compared to the soil outside your front door.

What is in the bag labeled "potting soil"? Ingredients vary from one brand to another, but most are blended from peat moss, composted bark or other plant material, and sand or perlite (see pages 315-16). They also may include shiny particles of vermiculite, and most have had their pH fine-tuned with lime (ground limestone) to bring it into the normal range. Many also contain small amounts of fertilizer to get plants off to a good start, but don't choose a potting soil based on its fertilizer content. Instead, look for dark color, a spongy texture, and little or no odor. You can easily provide plants with fertilizer on an as-needed basis.

These days, potting soils are better than they have ever been, so it is easy to satisfy your plants' need for good soil. The best potting soils are packaged in plastic bags with zipper-type closures, which helps keep them moist while keeping out unwanted microorganisms. After trying several brands, most houseplant growers settle on a favorite. Nationally marketed brands are usually safe bets, but you may get equal satisfaction with a "value" brand that costs less. If you keep only a few houseplants, a good all-purpose potting soil will probably meet your needs quite nicely. Buy no more than you think you will use in a few months, because opened bags of potting soil can become contaminated with microorganisms while also posing storage problems.

Unfortunately, even the best potting soil does not last more than a couple of years after it is put to work in a pot. Organic matter breaks down, minerals are taken up by plants, and the medium's ability to do its job gradually deteriorates. This is why plants need periodic repotting even when they have not outgrown their pots. As for your old, used potting soil, throw it outside in your garden, or if you have no garden, dump it in a bag and give it to someone who does. When potting soil has been used up or worn out by houseplants, it can serve a second tour of duty in outdoor beds, where millions of microorganisms know exactly what to do with the threads of root and holdout tidbits of bark present in tired potting soil.

Making adjustments. Some houseplants prefer or require potting mix that meets their special needs. Details on what to look for in specialty potting mixes for African violets, bromeliads, cacti and succulents, orchids, and palms are discussed in the prefaces to each of these plant groups in Parts 1 and 2. However, it can be interesting and rewarding to create specialty potting mixes yourself by changing the balance of the materials in the mix. You may also need to adjust the content of all-purpose potting mix to help a plant that stays thirsty, hungry, waterlogged, or just plain unhappy despite attentive watering and feeding. Become familiar with the following six soil amendments, and you will be ready to tailor potting mixtures to please plants in need of special attention.

PEAT MOSS. Harvested from bogs in Canada, Michigan, and a few other places, peat moss is made up of very small fibers that have a remarkable talent for taking up water. Peat moss also suppresses many types of fungi that can cause roots to rot. On its own, peat moss has an acidic pH, so it is a good addition to potting soil intended for use with azaleas, gardenias, and other plants that prefer acidic soil conditions. African violet soils often contain liberal amounts of peat moss (with lime added to offset its acidity) because of its moisture-holding talents. And the fine texture of peat moss makes it a valuable addition to seed-starting mixes, which are excellent for potting up newly rooted cuttings. On the down side, when a peaty soil dries out it can be difficult to remoisten (see "Rehydrating Parched Plants," on page 328). Before peat moss is packaged for sale or blended into potting soil, it is pulverized into a coarse brown powder. Unmilled peat moss, called *sphagnum peat moss*, is fibrous and stringy. When adding peat moss to another potting medium, be sure to moisten it first by mixing it with an equal measure of lukewarm water.

COMPOSTED PLANT MATERIALS. As you run your fingers through moist potting soil, and especially when you repot a plant grown at a nursery, you will probably encounter chunks of bark, bits of sticks, or other pieces of barely recognizable plant material. Although the outside of these tidbits will be black from natural decomposition, they are far from gone, which is good. The coarseness of these hard pieces aids drainage and helps prevent compaction, ensuring that plants enjoy plenty of air around their roots. There are environmental advantages, too. Most composted plant material begins as recycled waste from lumber and food-processing industries; in addition, it may include composted leaves collected from the yard.

Nurserymen like using bark-based mediums because of their excellent drainage and low cost. Many plants like them because they break down slowly and mimic soil conditions in crevices between tree branches — the native niche of many bromeliads and orchids. Naturally, specialty potting mixes for these plants include abundant composted bark. In regular potting soil, a very dark black color often indicates the presence of composted plant material.

SAND. Compared to other types of soil particles, grains of sand are quite large, so water flows quickly through soils that include plentiful sand. Coarse sand has long been used to create potting soils that drain quickly. The trade-off is that sand cannot retain moisture well, so a very sandy mix will dry out fast. This is a plus for cacti and other plants that prefer moisture in brief gulps, so sand is often added to soils blended for cacti and succulents. Palms and other plants originating along seashores, such as screw pine (*Pandanus*), also respond well when grown in a sandy mixture. Indeed, whenever you suspect that a plant is suffering from poor drainage or needs drier root conditions, amending the soil with sand is a good first step. A half-and-half mixture of peat moss and sand also makes a fine medium for rooting stem cuttings. For all uses, be sure to use sand that has been washed to remove salt and other impurities, such as sand packaged for use in aquariums. Sand used in children's sandboxes also may be used, though it's a good idea to give it a quick rinse in a bucket of fresh water before mixing it into potting soil for your plants.

PERLITE. In place of heavy sand, many potting soil manufacturers improve the drainage of their mixes by adding perlite — the small, white puffs that resemble broken pieces of popcorn. Perlite is made from a naturally occurring volcanic rock that pops when it is quickly heated to 1600°F. The popping process riddles each perlite piece with thousands of tiny air spaces, which makes it possible for perlite to take up and release water very quickly. Perlite is chemically inert, with a neutral pH (7), so it has no chemical influence on soil beyond regulating water and oxygen. When adequate nutrition is provided, plants can grow in 100 percent perlite, and it makes a great medium for rooting cuttings. Many potting soils include perlite, and those created for cacti and succulents often contain an extra helping. Small bags of perlite are widely available at garden centers. Many houseplant growers keep some on hand for rooting cuttings or lightening up soil that seems too heavy for certain plants.

VERMICULITE. Like perlite, vermiculite is made from naturally occurring mineral deposits that are mined, crushed, and then heated to the popping point. Vermiculite shares perlite's water-handling talents, so it helps hold soil moisture while improving drainage. Vermiculite mixes very easily with peat moss, and this mixture is the basis for most seed-starting mixes. Always dampen these mixes — or pure vermiculite — when handling it, because some vermiculite contains small amounts of asbestos-like particles, which should not be inhaled. These particles, if present, are not likely to become airborne unless they are quite dry. Using moist vermiculite to root cuttings and start seeds, and mixing it into potting soil to lighten its texture, pose no health risks.

MINERALS. As a finishing touch, most potting soils include a dusting of various minerals, such as lime, gypsum, or rock phosphate. Lime (ground limestone) raises the pH of mixes that are too acidic and provides plants with slow-release calcium. Gypsum and rock phosphate also serve as very slow-release fertilizers, so they are a welcome addition to many potting soils. As a casual houseplant keeper, the only mineral amendment you might want to keep around is a little lime, especially if you have heavily fluoridated water or mix your own peat-based potting mixes. A pinch of extra lime in a pot helps keep the pH high, which in turn helps some plants cope with the uptake problems associated with chemically tainted water. Never add lime to soil used for plants that like acidic soil conditions, such as azaleas, gardenias, and most ferns. In rare instances, however, a batch of potting soil may be so acidic that plants have trouble taking up nutrients. If plants fail to grow well after they have been repotted and do not respond to an increase in fertilizer, you can try giving them a drench with lime water, made from mixing a teaspoon of powdered lime into a quart of water.

Sooty Mold

Insects that feed by sucking plant sap, such as aphids and scale, excrete a sticky substance called *honeydew,* which in turn serves as an ideal home for dark-colored sooty mold. Sooty mold is often mistaken for fungus, but there is a major difference in that sooty mold does not invade leaf tissues. It can be removed using a soft cloth dipped in soapy water, and once leaves are clean they usually appear perfectly healthy. Sooty mold can occur on either side of a plant's leaves, or on both sides. When a plant shows patches of sooty mold, be sure to check for the presence of the pest that created the honeydew and take appropriate

- Look for products labeled as potting soil or potting mix, with houseplants mentioned somewhere on the label. You can pot up container-grown outdoor plants with the same potting mix you use for houseplants. Do not use products labeled as garden soil or topsoil, which are too heavy for houseplants. Exceptions to this rule are noted in the plant profiles, because a few long-lived houseplants benefit from having clean, bagged garden soil added to their growing medium.

- A few potting mixes contain insecticides that are taken up by plants. These can be an answered prayer if your palm is plagued with scale, but they should not be used to pot up plants with edible parts, such as calamondin orange or rosemary.

- If you are not sure how much potting mix you need, check the label. Many products have charts on the package to help you compute how much is needed to fill containers of various sizes. When in doubt, buy a little more rather than less.

- Store leftover potting soil tightly sealed in a cool, dry place. Use packing tape or clothespins to secure the top if the bag does not have a zipper-type closure.

- If you grow orchids, bromeliads, or other plants that need special potting soil, mail-order the potting medium you need if you cannot find it locally. See Resources on page 337 for a starter list of specialty soil suppliers.

measures to bring it under control. In some situations, the sucking insect that began the problem cycle is gone by the time sooty mold develops on plant leaves.

Staking and Training

See also Pruning (page 308), Repotting (page 309)
Just as newly planted trees often need stakes to hold them straight until their roots are able to function as firm anchors, so it is with houseplants. A stake can be used as a temporary prop for a plant that insists on falling over, or it can be a permanent fixture in the pot of a vining plant. You can also stake and train a plant to alter its shape. Topiary, for example, trains plants to assume the shape of their "stake," which is usually a wire form filled with moss. Some plants can be trained to grow into tree forms, called *standards*, which are comprised of a lean, upright main stem topped by a mass of foliage. Training guidelines for topiary and standards are discussed below.

Routine pruning and grooming may be all your plants need to keep them looking handsome, so you may never venture into involved plant training projects. But do go to the trouble of training naturally floppy plants, such as abutilon, and vines that are willing to grow on pillars — the best way to obtain a plant with a strong vertical posture. Vertical plants take up small footprints and offer tremendous versatility in interiorscapes, where they combine beautifully with other plant forms.

Simple staking. Plants that flop over may be stressed by too much or too little light, or they may emerge from the repotting process without sufficient roots to hold them upright. In either case, their postures can be improved by tethering them to a stake for a few weeks. Any type of stake will do, from a slender stick or piece of bamboo to a length of stiff, heavy-gauge wire. A single stake should suffice if only a little support is needed. Loosely secure the plant to the stake using soft string, twist ties, or a large paper clip bent out into an S shape that can be looped around the stake and the plant. Tight bindings can girdle stems, so it is better to use multiple loose attachments as opposed to a single tight one. (See at A.)

Plants with several floppy stems are better held up with a cage made from several slender stakes slipped inside the edges of the pot, which can be netted together with string, twine, or pliable wire. However, plants that require this level of support for more than a few weeks after repotting probably need a permanent support, or they may have grown so top-heavy that they are more in need of propagation than support. It is also possible that they might look better if allowed to cascade out of a hanging basket. (See at B.)

Twining plants such as jasmine will twist around their support, which can be as simple as a tripod of bamboo stakes secured together at the top with jute or wire. Or, make a hoop with heavy-gauge wire, with each end of the wire pushed down into the pot, or use green, pliable saplings less than .5 in/1.25 cm inch in diameter to create a twig trellis for twining vines. (See at C.)

A

A simple stake to which a plant is loosely tied will quickly improve its posture. Whenever possible, install a stake as part of the repotting process.

B

After repotting a floppy plant, you can make a temporary support cage by tying together stakes pushed inside the edges of the pot.

Semi-climbers such as pothos, climbing philo-dendron, ivy, and tree ivy *(Fatshedera)* slowly anchor themselves in place with strong aerial roots when provided with a support material that retains moisture, because the plants respond to the moisture by more vigorously producing aerial roots. Moisture-retentive osmunda posts or moss-filled wire posts are widely available at craft and florist shops. (See at D.)

The stakes, trellis, or post will become a per-manent part of a vining plant, so try to begin training at a young age. Install the post slightly off center in the pot, and attach the plant to it with pieces of wire or florist tape. Plants more than 12 in/30 cm tall may need to be attached at sev-eral points. Aerial roots are most likely to emerge from nodes, so these are the best places to create close contact between the plant stem and the post. You can further encourage aerial roots to grow by misting the attachment points with water every few days.

After the initial attachment of the main stem is complete, new lateral stems may emerge. You can shorten these by pruning back the tips, or you can secure them to the post. Lateral stems that pop out high on the plant can cause it to be top-heavy. To keep the plant from falling over, top it back or trim the lateral stems off entirely. As a general rule, vining and climbing plants should be pruned and trained into a pyramidal shape, which ensures that all parts of the plant receive abun-dant light.

Twining vines need little help to scramble up a stake, or to wind around a moss-filled topiary form.

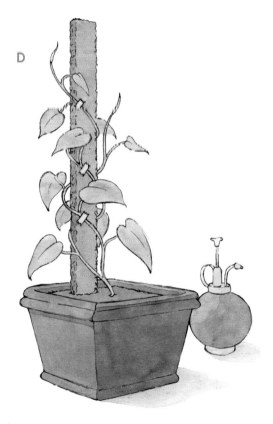

Plants that attach themselves to a post with aerial roots often need encouragement. Tape or wire them in place, and provide moisture to help the roots attach themselves to the post.

LEARNING THE JAPANESE ART OF BONSAI adds a huge dimension to growing houseplants. Beautiful bonsai results from growing selected foliage and flowering plants in broad containers in which stones, moss, or other materials are used to make the base of the plant almost as attractive as the stems and leaves. Stems often are sculpted and trimmed to help them reflect natural forces of wind and weather. Bonsai can be practiced with cold-hardy woody plants or houseplants. Regardless of the botanical subjects used, it can become a lifelong passion. Dozens of excellent books are available to get you started with bonsai, or you can seek out experienced bonsai growers through a club such as the American Bonsai Society, which has numerous local chapters (see Resources on page 339).

Topiary training. The art of training plants to grow into the shape of a special form, called *topiary,* can be practiced with several houseplants, including creeping fig, small-leafed varieties of English ivy, and varieties of rosemary that develop long, pliable stems. Craft and floral shops sell special topiary forms, which may be shaped like animals, cones, or wreaths. The forms are made from wire mesh stuffed with sphagnum moss; you can also make one yourself if you want to create a uniquely shaped topiary.

Before beginning a topiary project, soak the form in water for 30 minutes to make sure it is completely hydrated. Start topiary training during routine repotting, or buy new plants especially for the project. Large topiary forms or wreaths usually are sculpted from two or more plants situated at opposite sides of the form.

Once the plants and the form are settled into the container, attach primary stems to the form using fine wire. Prune off stems that show little promise for your training plan, but do not weaken the plants by trimming them too aggressively. Set the container in a hospitable spot and allow it to grow for a few weeks. Spritz the form with water every day or so to keep it lightly moist.

Every 4 to 8 weeks, work your topiary by removing old training wires that are no longer needed, installing new ones, and trimming off errant, untrainable stems. Use bright light to help energize growth spurts following each training session. Beginners often enjoy great success with topiary, but as with all creative arts, practice and patience lead to more pleasing results.

Training a vining plant onto a topiary form is not difficult, though it is important to trim the plant often, and to provide growing conditions that encourage rapid growth.

Year 1: The first phase of creating a standard form is to train the plant to grow very tall and straight, which usually requires the help of a stake.

Year 2: When the plant's trunk is strong enough to provide good support, prune the top of the plant to the shape you want.

Standards.

A few houseplants, such as rosemary, can be trained to grow as standards. The process requires 2 years or more, and commercial growers use varieties with growth habits that make them especially responsive to this type of training.

Year 1. Training begins by encouraging the plant to grow stiffly upright. With the plant's main stem secured to a stake, pinch off any lateral branches that attempt to grow from the lowest third of the plant.

Year 2. Remove any remaining lateral stems, and tip back stems at the top of the plant to a few inches long.

As the remaining stems fill out, the standard form is finally attained. However, even the best standard forms are usually not sustainable for more than one or two seasons. Eventually, the topknot becomes too heavy for the main stem, or it thins out as buds held in reserve in latent nodes are used up. Enjoy it while you can.

Terrariums

See also Humidity (page 266)

Where space is limited (for example, in an office cubicle or a small apartment), you can enjoy the companionship of plants with no risk of mess by growing them in a terrarium. Nestled into a goldfish bowl or little aquarium tank, a comely collection of plants will thrive with very little care. Terrariums that have an opening through which air can circulate need small amounts of water added from time to time, while those that are completely closed often can go months without watering. And because the conditions within terrariums are naturally moist, they make it possible to grow filigreed ferns and other dainty plants that require very high humidity levels.

About terrariums. In 1842, Dr. N. B. Ward of London published a book on what he called *The Growth of Plants in Closely Glazed Cases.* Today we know these as terrariums. Rather than botanical curiosities (which coincided with the invention of flat plates of glass), terrariums are most practical for growing small plants that require humid conditions in otherwise dry indoor environments. And because they require scant watering and feeding, terrariums are ideal for forgetful gardeners. The fluorescent lights in windowless offices usually provide enough light to satisfy high-humidity terrarium plants, which are often native to the damp conditions of the jungle floor.

A terrarium can be a completely enclosed glass jar or box, such as a fish tank, or you can use a fishbowl or large brandy snifter with its top left open. Open terrariums seldom have problems with disease since air circulates around the plants' foliage, but they need to be watered more often than enclosed terrariums. This is easily done by spritzing plants with water from a small spray bottle. If an open terrarium must be left unattended for a long period of time, covering the opening with glass or plastic will prevent loss of moisture.

Very small plants, which are often quite inexpensive, make fine members of a terrarium community. You can buy plants at floral shops or garden centers, or order unusual species from online or mail-order nurseries. Depending on the size and shape of the container, you may want three, five, or several more plants. Before planting them

in your terrarium, experiment with arranging them on a tabletop. Terrariums are usually viewed from one side, so it's best to place the tallest plants to the rear, with smaller plants in front of them. Include one variegated plant, but let various shades of green provide most of the color in your terrarium. The differing leaf textures of the species you choose will provide plenty of visual interest. As you plan placement, make sure that the leaves of plants do not actually touch the glass, which can cause them to stay wet for long periods, leading to problems with disease. Use a small pair of scissors to snip off any leaves that are less than perfect.

Like an enclosed miniature jungle, terrariums showcase small plants that thrive under very humid conditions.

Planting a terrarium. Most of the discount stores sell all the materials you need for your terrarium. In addition to a container, purchase a package of clean pebbles and another of charcoal, which you will find among aquarium supplies. In the garden department, buy a small bag of sphagnum peat moss and a fresh, unopened package of potting soil. Starting with clean, packaged materials is the best way to avoid introducing fungi that can cause diseases in the artificial world you are creating.

1. Wash the container with clean, soapy water and dry it thoroughly. Place a .5 in/1.25 cm layer of pebbles in the bottom of the container, followed by .5 in/1.25 cm of aquarium charcoal. Soak the sphagnum moss in a bowl of water for a few minutes. Squeeze out the excess water and then carefully place the sphagnum moss over the charcoal. The moss will work like a filter, keeping the soil from seeping down into the pebbles.

2. Use a ladle or small cup to place about 2 in/5 cm of moist potting soil over the moss. Try not to get soil on the sides of the container.

3. Set your plants in place, then use a fork, chopstick, or long kitchen tongs to nudge them into their permanent positions.

4. Use a wine cork stuck onto the end of an ice pick or the back of a spoon to tamp the surface of the soil, thus ensuring that all roots are firmly in contact with soil. For a touch of whimsy, add a few small stones or perhaps a figurine of a frog or snail if you wish.

5. Use a spray bottle or mister to rinse off any soil that has stuck to plant leaves and to lightly dampen the potting soil. Cover the terrarium for a day, then mist or spritz the plants again. The second spraying should provide ample water for an enclosed terrarium, but open containers may need a little more water. Watch the plants for signs that they need more water, but err on the side of dryness. Especially in an enclosed terrarium, it is very difficult to get rid of too much water.

Every 2 to 3 weeks, check your terrarium to see if it needs water, which is easily supplied by spritzing plants with a spray of water. Two or three times a year, add a small amount of all-purpose

ALL TERRARIUMS are not humidity chambers. You can also use a terrarium to grow a miniature garden made up of tiny succulents and cacti — a good way to enjoy prickly plants with no risk that people or pets will be hurt by spines. Arid terrariums should be left open to allow air circulation, which is also practical in the high-light situations these plants prefer. Glass enclosures kept in bright light quickly overheat if they are not left open.

houseplant food to the water, mixing it at half the rate recommended on the package. Groom plants periodically by snipping off failing leaves with a small pair of cuticle scissors. Allowing withered foliage to remain in the terrarium can lead to problems with disease.

Beyond overwatering, the only other problem you might have in a terrarium is overheating. Never place a terrarium in direct sun or near appliances that give off heat. If the terrarium's light comes from a window, rotate it weekly so that all plants get a chance to respond to directional light. Should some of the plants in your terrarium grow too large, you can either cut them back or take them out, pot them up, and install small replacements in the terrarium. Changing the scene is part of the fun of working with a terrarium. Sometimes switching out one plant is all that is needed to bring new life to a composition that has visually gone stale.

Top-Dressing

When plants grow so large that repotting is impossible, or they have a cascading growth habit that will be ruined by handling, you can *top-dress* the soil instead of repotting the plant. It is usually more practical to top-dress than to repot large, woody plants such as Norfolk pine or weeping fig, and you may also opt to top-dress tall, columnar cacti and big palms. To top-dress, allow the soil surface to dry, then use a table fork to loosen the top inch of potting medium. Remove it with a tablespoon. You may be able to dig a little deeper just inside the rim unless you have encountered a

tight ball of roots. Use the fork to make shallow perforations in the soil and roots below where you have excavated, then refill the container with fresh, high-quality potting soil. Plants that are not repotted should usually be top dressed once a year, preferably in spring.

When top-dressing, loosen the surface soil with a fork, and then remove it with a spoon. Be sure to perforate the excavated surface before replacing the top layer with fresh potting soil.

Watering

See also Drainage (page 259), Fertilizer (page 261), Humidity (page 266)

Though all houseplants need water, they are all a little different in this respect. Species vary in how much water they must take up and push to their leaves, and whether they prefer steady or fluctuating moisture levels around their roots. Containers and soils introduce more variables, but the most important factor is the air. It seems reasonable to expect that actively growing houseplants that are enjoying the warm temperatures of summertime would need more water than plants resting their way through winter, but this is not necessarily true. Indoor air in winter is often so dry that some plants need as much water in January as they do in June.

The bottom line is that every plant is an individual where watering is concerned. Getting to know the drinking preferences of each of your plants and satisfying them with your watering practices is one of the fundamental satisfactions of growing indoor plants. See the individual plant profiles in Parts 1 and 2 to learn about each of your plant's watering needs.

Rhythms of watering.
The lingo used to describe routine watering practices includes these phrases: "lightly moist," "moderately moist," and "allow to dry out between waterings." These are general tendencies, open to interpretation by different plants.

LIGHTLY MOIST. This first moisture level means that the plant benefits from soil that is never truly wet yet never completely dry. To achieve this result, you simply provide water frequently and take care to distribute it evenly in the container. Many plants that come from forests — both tropical and temperate — like to be kept lightly moist at all times.

MODERATELY MOIST. Plants that need moderate moisture often are fast growers with high light requirements. They include most of the indoor plants that produce beautiful flowers and a few robust foliage plants as well. Although somewhat demanding, these plants provide color and drama, and they often go into an annual recovery period of slow growth or dormancy when they need little or no water. The challenge is to provide ample moisture without getting carried away, because even plants that need abundant water can develop root rot or other problems if they are watered too much.

ALLOW TO DRY OUT BETWEEN WATERINGS. Many plants with succulent leaves or stems love to exercise their talent for hoarding moisture when water becomes available the same way they might if they were living in a climate where rains were few and far between. These are the plants that benefit from brief periods of dryness, and they often like their wet intervals to be short lived too. But all succulents are not alike in this respect, so it's best to pay attention to your plants' responses to watering and fine-tune your practices to please them. Aloe, for example, seems to thrive on moisture extremes, while holiday cactus likes consistent moisture in summer and drier conditions in fall and winter.

Gauging soil moisture.
The most common way to check the moisture level in plant containers is to wiggle your finger into the soil, up to the first knuckle, and decide if the soil feels moist about an inch below the surface. Even professionals use this method, along with other low-tech tricks such as tipping the pot to see if it feels heavy or light. But the finger method has its limitations. You can't tell how much moisture is present deep in the container, and you know nothing about the most difficult area to water, the center of the plant's root mass. To find out how much water is present in those areas, you can use a

probe or meter (which are not always reliable) or assess the container's weight.

There is always some guesswork involved in plant watering, but the finger method combined with regular weight checks should get you started in the right direction. Of course, the most important thing is to pay attention to your plants. Either underwatering or overwatering can cause a plant to droop, as can incomplete watering, in which only part of the root mass receives moisture. To prevent this problem, learn to water your plants from both the top and the bottom.

Top and bottom watering. The best way to water most plants is from the top, by slowly pouring water from a bottle or watering can around the plant's crown until water drips out through the drainage holes in the bottom of the container. There is always a possibility that water applied this way will run over the top of the soil, down the insides of the pot, and then out the drainage holes in the bottom. When this happens, the plant's roots may remain much too dry. To avoid this difficulty, poke holes in the soil and root mass using an ice pick or a wooden skewer to create spaces through which water can flow and then percolate into surrounding soil. You should also make plans to repot the plant, since this problem is often a symptom that more root space and a fresh supply of potting soil are needed.

Another potential problem with top watering are water spots that form on plant leaves, which is a common issue with African violets, gloxinias, and other plants that have downy leaf surfaces. When any of these top-watering complications are present, water plants from the bottom. To do this, pour water into a tray or saucer, set the plant in it, and allow the plant to drink its fill for up to

Water will percolate more easily to a rootbound plant's interior roots if you make small holes in the soil with a skewer or ice pick.

Although time consuming, bottom watering plants is often the best way to be certain that the lowest half of the root ball receives adequate moisture.

PALMS, DRACAENAS, TI PLANT (*Cordyline*), peacock plant (*Calathea*), and several other house-plants are sensitive to fluoride, which is often added to public water supplies. The most common symptom of fluoride sensitivity is browning leaf tips, which can also be caused by fluctuating soil moisture or erratic fertilization. Where fluoride is suspected as a problem, it can help to place pinches of lime on the surface of the pots every few months. This helps raise the pH of the soil, which makes the fluoride more soluble in water. Flushing pots from time to time (see page 263, under Fertilizer) is also quite helpful. The ultimate solution is to use distilled water or rainwater to water plants that are sensitive to fluoride.

30 minutes before emptying out any excess water. The biggest risk with bottom watering is water-logging of roots, which is seldom a problem in small containers but may be if the pot is very large and made of plastic or another material that holds water well. Never leave a pot sitting in standing water for more than 30 minutes.

Most plants flourish when they are watered both ways — most often from the top, but occasionally from the bottom. Top watering is easy and practical, and leaf spotting can be minimized by watering in the morning and not soaking the leaves. Occasionally, do go to the trouble of bottom watering your plants. Bottom watering every month or so is an excellent way to avoid the formation of dry pockets in the container, a common problem with plants that are infrequently repotted.

Best water for plants. One of the facts of modern life is that we often don't know what's in our water. And some of the things we do know about, such as chlorine, are abhorred by plants. Confined to pots, indoor plants have no way to escape tainted water, so it's crucial to give them water that's at least as good as the water you like to drink. If you filter your drinking water, filter the water you give your plants too. If you suspect that your tap water contains too much chlorine for plants, allow the water to sit out overnight, which gives chlorine and other chemicals time to escape as gas. If you make a habit of refilling the

containers you use to water your plants each time you finish watering chores, gases will slowly escape and the water will be ready to use by the time your plants need watering again.

Some people like to collect rainwater for their plants, an ancient ritual worth repeating whenever it's convenient. Or you can use melted snow, which often contains traces of beneficial micronutrients.

Most plants prefer "soft" water to "hard" water. Soft water contains very low amounts of calcium and magnesium salts, while hard water, which often flows through deposits of mineral-rich rock, contains high amounts of these elements. Many people who have very hard water utilize water softeners, which remove these mineral salts through filtration, magnetization, or a combination of processes. Water softened in these ways still contains high levels of salt, which leads to problems when it is used to water plants. In place of softened water, use water that is naturally soft, such as rainwater or bottled distilled water for your houseplants.

Regardless of its source, make sure water is at room temperature when you give it to your plants. Giving cold water to tropical plants chills their roots, which can cause them to rot.

Rehydrating parched plants. If a plant dries out so severely that it collapses, promptly place it in a pail or sink of lukewarm water. It may be so dry that it floats! Use a large spoon or cup to ladle water into the top of the container, and then allow the plant to soak for about 30 minutes. Remove the plant and place it on a rack (such as a dish rack) until all excess water drains away and the base of the container no longer drips. Wait until the next day to decide if any leaves need to be trimmed off. Most plants recover well from drying out for short periods of time. However, repeated trauma can cause stems and leaves to die.

This is also a good procedure to try with plants that seem to stay dry even though you water them regularly. Sometimes the middle of a container dries out so much that water applied to the surface runs down the inside of the pot and out through the drainage holes before the roots have a chance to drink their fill. Rehydration can help, but you should also make plans to repot the plant.

Rescuing waterlogged plants. When plant roots sit in excess water too long, they start to rot. As the roots deteriorate, they cannot take up water, so the plant wilts. What seems like the thing to do — providing more water — can actually make things worse! If the container feels heavy yet the plant droops, you probably have a

Five Tips for Better Watering

- **COMPANIONABLE CONTAINERS.** Position plants with similar watering needs together whenever you can. You will be less likely to skip over plants that need frequent watering, and the mess that sometimes results from giving plants a thorough soaking can be limited to one area of your house.

- **OVERHEAD IRRIGATION.** To water plants in hard-to-reach hanging planters, use a bulb-type turkey baster or a special watering bottle with an extra-long neck, which you can usually find at a garden center. If you're bothered by drips on floors or furniture, use string, hooks, and an aluminum roasting pan to create a drain tray to hang under the planter for a little while after watering. Or buy some inexpensive shower caps to temporarily enclose the bottoms of freshly watered hanging baskets.

- **HELPFUL HEADSPACE.** When potting up indoor plants, always leave at least ¾-inch of space between the top edge of the container and the top of the soil. This space works like a reservoir when you're watering, giving water a place to sit until it can soak in. It also helps prevent spills of soil or water.

- **HIDE A WATER SUPPLY.** If you have only one or two plants in a room that's far from your kitchen (or wherever you keep your watering can or bottle), hide a bottle of water behind the pots so it will always be there, ready to offer a few sips.

- **CLEAN OUT DRAINAGE TRAYS.** Many plants benefit from sitting on a bed of damp pebbles, which increases humidity while catching excess water that drains from the pots. As this water evaporates, salts are often left behind on the pebbles. This becomes a problem when plants take up water from the trays, which may be heavily laced with salts. To avoid problems, empty and thoroughly rinse drainage trays, and the pebbles within them, about once a month.

Rescue a waterlogged plant by slipping it out of its pot and laying the root ball on a layer of newspapers to dry overnight.

waterlogging crisis. To save the plant, place several thicknesses of newspaper in a pan or basin, lay the pot on its side, and slide out the root ball. Allow the root ball to dry on the newspapers overnight. Use clean sharp scissors to trim off any dark-colored or slimy roots before repotting the plant in a clean container with fresh potting soil. Adding small stones or pieces of a broken clay flowerpot — or even broken china — to the bottom of containers helps prevent this problem.

Indeed, overwatering is the leading cause of houseplant death. When you're getting to know a new plant, it is better to err on the dry side than to drown its roots with too much water. In addition, be careful in the autumn. The reason? New growth slows as days become shorter, so plants need less water. And when plants are moved indoors after spending the summer outside, the absence of wind, combined with radically reduced light levels, further limits their need for water. Indoor humidity levels are often moderate in fall, too. When indoor humidity levels drop as the winter heating season begins, you can carefully increase watering until plants appear content.

Wind

Just as plant leaves make physical changes to adapt to increasing or decreasing levels of light, stems alter their structure to better cope with movement, which typically comes from wind. As long as plants are kept indoors, they encounter very little moving air. Their stems do not need to be tough, and so they often are comprised of cells arranged in straight patterns. In comparison, plants that are exposed to moving air respond by arranging their stem cells in more twisted patterns, which makes them less prone to bruising and breakage.

The transition from tender stems to tougher, wind-resistant stems takes time, so you should acclimate plants to wind that are being moved outdoors the same way you acclimate them to increasing light. Frequently these two goals can be accomplished together. Begin by placing plants in a shady spot that is protected from strong wind and sun, and gradually move them to a more open environment, over a period of 1 to 2 weeks.

Even properly acclimated houseplants may suffer wind damage when exposed to high winds outdoors. When very blustery weather is predicted, move houseplants to a protected spot, such as against the outer walls of your house, or simply bring them indoors until calm weather returns. In addition to twisting or breaking stems and leaves, wind can easily topple plants, which can lead to devastating damage.

You also can condition your plants indoors by running a gentle fan, which will cause enough air movement to trigger a response from the plants' stems. In winter, you can keep your plants physically fit by talking to them as you water and groom them. The gentle puffs of air from your breath causes slight air movement, too.

Beautiful form, flawless texture, and a well-chosen container combine to make a mounding philodendron glow with satisfaction.

If you're not sure about the meaning of a word, the following short definitions should help. More thorough explanations are included in the text and illustrations in other parts of this book, so check the index if you need more information on a word or concept.

ACIDIC. Soil with a pH below 6.5, as is typical of soils comprised of peat moss or tree by-products, such as bark. Acidity can be reduced by adding lime, a mineral powder made from ground limestone.

ADVENTITIOUS ROOT. A root that emerges from above the soil line, often in unusual places such as leaves or nodes. Plants that develop adventitious roots are easy to propagate from stem cuttings.

AERIAL ROOT. A root that emerges from a plant's stem above the soil line. An aerial root may eventually reach down into the soil or attach itself to a support post.

ALKALINE. Soil with a pH above 7.0, which naturally occurs in low rainfall areas and some other places where abundant weathered limestone is present. Alkaline soil can be made more acidic by adding sulphur, which is produced from ground sulphuric rock.

ANNUAL. A plant that grows from seed, to flower, and then to seed again within one year.

ANTHER. The male reproductive part of a flower that bears the blossom's pollen supply. The stalklike structure that supports the anther is called the stamen.

AREOLE. A plant structure unique to cacti from which spines or hairs emerge. Areoles are often round, raised bumps, but in some species they are difficult to see.

AUXINS. Plant hormones that stimulate plant cell growth, particularly the growth of new roots. Auxins are usually sold as rooting powder, but nurseries also use liquid forms for some plants.

BONSAI. Training method in which plants are maintained at a small size and often set in miniature landscapes that dramatize primal forces of nature such as wind, gravity, and the passage of time.

BRACT. A specialized leaf that frames a plant's true flower. Bracts may be very leaflike, as in poinsettia, or they may resemble blossoms, as in bromeliads. Bracts are usually more long-lived than a plant's flowers, which are typically fleshy and fragile.

BULB. A type of storage root that includes cells that are poised to grow into leaves and flowers. Most bulbs are comprised of layered scales, like an onion's. Leaves and flowering stems emerge from the center of the top of a true bulb.

CACHEPOT. A container, usually decorative, in which a slightly smaller container can be placed.

CALLUS. A cut plant part that dries to form a solid surface that prevents the loss of plant sap while sealing out water, fungi, and bacteria.

CHLOROPLASTS. Special cells within plant leaves that take in light and transform it into energy.

CHLOROSIS. Yellowing of leaves, due to the failure of chloroplasts, which may be caused by nutritional problems, environmental stress, or old age.

CORM. A type of underground storage root, found at the base of a stem. Most corms are dense and somewhat woody compared to bulbs, rhizomes, or tubers.

CRAWLER. The juvenile, most mobile form of scale insects.

CROWN. A cluster of stems, closely attached to each other just below or above the soil's surface, that emerges from the roots together as a visible tuft or clump.

CULTIVAR. A distinct variety of a plant that is propagated vegetatively to preserve its unique or desirable characteristics.

DEADHEADING. The removal of aged or dead flowers, which often encourages a plant to produce additional blossoms.

DECIDUOUS. A plant that sheds its leaves and then grows new ones, usually after a period of dormancy.

DISH GARDEN. A single container planted with several different plants.

DOMINANT BUD. The bud at the tip of a stem, where most new growth occurs. Removing the dominant buds often causes latent buds, located farther down the stem, to begin growing.

DORMANT. A natural part of a plant's life cycle when it grows very little, often without benefit of leaves or stems, as do many bulbs, corms, and tubers.

DOUBLE FLOWERS. Flowers with roughly twice the number of petals present in the single-flowered version of that plant. Double flowers usually have two layers of petals.

EPIPHYTE. A plant that lives on another plant, as do some bromeliads, cacti, and orchids that live on tree branches in tropical forests. Epiphytes are not true parasites because they do not take nutrients from the plant on which they live.

EPSOM SALTS. Used in very small amounts, this drugstore staple can provide magnesium for selected houseplants.

EVERGREEN. A plant that retains its leaves year-round, even when grown outdoors.

FAMILY. A large group of plants that have botanical similarities, which are further divided into genera.

FOOT-CANDLE. The amount of light cast by a candle 1 foot away. Low-light indoor plants need 100–300 foot-candles of light. Those that need medium light need 300–600 foot-candles, while high-light plants need a minimum of 700–1,200 foot-candles.

FROND. A type of leaf comprised of finely divided sections, which are characteristic of ferns and some palms.

FUNGUS. A primitive, plantlike organism that lacks chlorophyll and is usually a parasite, drawing nutrients from a host plant or animal.

GENUS. A group of similar plants within a plant family. The first word in a botanical name is the plant's genus.

GLOCHID. A hooked spine present on some cacti.

GRAFT. The union where the rooted portion of one plant grows together with the stem or leaf of a different plant. Some cacti, trees, and shrubs are grafted plants.

HONEYDEW. The sticky liquid excreted by insect pests that suck juices from houseplants.

HYBRID. A novel plant developed by crossing different parent plants when they flower, usually by transferring pollen of one parent to the ovary of another. When the seeds mature, the generation grown from those seeds is the hybrid. In houseplants, once a hybrid is created, it is usually propagated vegetatively rather than by seed. Complex hybrids often involve hybrid parents created by crossing different species. These often include an × in the variety name.

HYDROPONICS. The practice of growing plants in nutrient-enriched water that is continuously circulated around the plants' roots.

HYGROMETER. An instrument that measures the amount of water vapor present in the air.

ISOLATE. To separate new or pest-ridden plants from other plants by a distance of at least 10 feet.

KEIKIS. Small plantlets that develop on the flower stem, close to the parent plant, of certain orchids, including some Phalaenopsis and Dendrobium orchids.

LATENT BUDS. Growing tips, often not visible, that plants possess along their stems, usually at leaf nodes. When the dominant bud, or tip bud, is removed, latent buds begin to grow.

LATERAL. A branch or stem that emerges sideways from another stem. Pinching off a stem tip often leads to the development of lateral branches.

LATEX. A milky sap present in some plants, which often tastes bitter and becomes sticky as it dries.

LEAFLET. A small leaf that is part of a larger arrangement comprising a compound leaf, as is seen in schefflera.

LEGGY. Term used to describe overly tall or elongated plants. The condition often results when plants are not pruned or are deprived of sufficient light.

MICRONUTRIENTS. Nutrients that are needed by plants in very small amounts, such as calcium, iron, magnesium, and copper. Fresh potting soil contains micronutrients, as do some fertilizers. Micronutrient sprays made from seaweed or synthetic substances can be applied to plants to provide micronutrients.

MONOPODIAL. Term used to describe orchids that grow upright from a crown, or foot, as do lady's slippers *(Paphiolpedilum)* and most moth orchids *(Phalaenopsis)*.

NODE. The place where leaves attach to stems. When cuttings are set to root, new roots usually emerge from the nodes.

OEDEMA. A condition caused by low light and overwatering in which leaves and stems rupture, evidenced by weeping of water droplets from leaves, or the appearance of raised bumps or ridges on leaves or stems.

OFFSET. A small plant that grows from a new crown while still attached to the parent plant. Offsets receive moisture and nutrients from the parent plant until they develop their own set of roots.

ORCHID MIX. A mixture of coarsely chopped fir bark, redwood bark, and small amounts of peat moss, perlite, or vermiculite, or a similar mix, created especially for orchids.

OSMUNDA POST. A moisture-retentive plant support made from the roots of osmunda ferns.

OVARY. The female part of a flower, often hidden from view at the base of the petals, where seeds form.

PEAT MOSS. Dark brown, acidic, organic matter harvested from peat bogs, which absorbs water well and hosts few plant diseases. Peat moss may be whole and stringy (sphagnum peat) or milled into a coarse powder.

PENDANT. Growth habit in which flowers or plantlets are produced on stem ends, like jewels at the end of a chain.

PERENNIAL. A plant that regrows for 2 years or more after dying back and becoming dormant (or semi-dormant) for several weeks, or sometimes months.

PERLITE. Popcorn-like pieces of chemically inert volcanic rock that are infused with tiny openings as a result of being exposed to high heat. Perlite lightens a potting soil's texture and improves its ability to hold water and air.

PETIOLE. The thickened leaf vein, resembling a stalk, that attaches a leaf to the stem. Plants such as African violets, begonias, and peperomias have long, fleshy petioles.

PHOTOPERIOD. Time period, usually measured in hours, that light is available to a plant. Many plants bloom in response to changes in the photoperiod.

PHOTOSYNTHESIS. The process plants use to create growth by taking in light energy and combining it with energy from moisture and nutrients.

PHOTOTROPISM. The tendency of plants to stretch or turn toward the best source of available light.

PINCH. Removing new growth from stem tips, usually by pinching it off with one's fingers. Stem tips also can be trimmed using scissors or pruning shears.

PISTIL. The female part of a flower, which supports the stigma, the organ that receives male pollen.

PLANTLET. A small plant that may grow from a stem, root, or leaf and will grow into a new plant if it is given a suitable environment for developing roots.

PLUG. A term used by plant growers to describe little wedges or thimbles of soil containing very young plantlets that have been raised from seed or tissue culture.

POT-BOUND. Word used to describe plants in which roots have become so dense within the container that no new root growth can occur.

PSEUDOBULB. A swollen stem common in several types of orchids that is used by the plant to store moisture and nutrients.

RHIZOME. A type of storage root that develops from a modified stem, usually with an elongated shape, and often featuring several nodes that can grow into new stems or roots.

ROOTING POWDER. Natural or synthetic plant hormones (auxins) that help stimulate the growth of roots in stem cuttings.

ROSETTE. A cluster of leaves of similar size that bunch together, often in a circular pattern.

RUNNER. A long stem or stolon (surface root) that develops roots and leaf buds to form new plants.

SEEDLING. A young plant grown from a germinated seed.

SPATHE. A fleshy bract that is joined to a flower spike, as is seen in anthuriums and spathiphyllums.

SPECIES. A distinctive form of a plant within a genus. The second word in a botanical name is the species name. If there is a third word, it is called the subspecies.

SPHAGNUM MOSS. Stringy, unmilled peat moss.

SPORE. A small reproductive structure produced by ferns and fungi, which germinates and grows but does not have stored nutrition or specialized cells typical of seeds.

STAMEN. The male flower part that supports the pollen bearing anther.

STANDARD. A lean, upright plant form comprised of a main stem topped by a mass of foliage, sometimes called tree-form. Standards are pruned and trained plants that may also include grafts.

STIGMA. A female flower part, usually located at the outer end of the pistil, that accepts male pollen.

STOLON. A modified stem that spreads out from the parent plant and has buds capable of growing into new plants.

STOMATA. Pores in plant leaves that "breathe" by exchanging gases.

STYLE. The female flower part that attaches the stigma to the ovary.

SYMPODIAL. Term used to describe the growth habit of some orchids, which develop shallow creeping rhizomes. The tip of the rhizome sends out a green shoot that eventually flowers. Cattleya, Dendrobium, and Oncidium orchids are usually sympodial.

SYSTEMIC PESTICIDES. Pesticides that are taken up by the plant and spread through its sap and tissues, which are then taken up by insects as they feed. Most (but not all) systemic pesticides should not be used indoors.

TISSUE CULTURE. A vegetative propagation method in which new plants are grown from a few cells taken from a parent plant. Tissue-cultured plants are sometimes called clones.

TOP-DRESS. To replace the topmost layer of soil in a large container with fresh potting soil. Or, to spread fertilizer, compost, or other substance over the top of the soil above a plant's roots.

TOPIARY. Method of training plants to assume the shape of their support, which is usually a wire form filled with moss.

TRADEMARKED PLANT. A plant with a unique parentage for which a patent has been obtained. Trademarked or patented plants cannot be propagated for sale without permission of the patent holder.

TUBER. A specialized underground root that stores nutrients and features buds that can grow into new stems and roots.

VARIEGATED. Foliage in which some of the natural green color has been replaced by other colors, such as white, cream, or red.

VARIETY. A distinctive form of a species, which can be a hybrid or simply a form that has unique or remarkable characteristics. In a botanical name, the variety name follows the Latin name, is usually within single quotation marks, and is not italicized.

VERMICULITE. Mica-like material made from naturally occurring mineral deposits that lighten the texture of potting soil and improve its ability to hold water and air.

Plants and Supplies

When you cannot find plants locally, the following companies stand ready to provide unusual varieties, as well as special potting mixes, fertilizers, and pest-control products.

Alanna's Greenhouses
Box 1342
Grand Forks, BC
Canada V0H 1H0
250-442-2552
or
P.O. Box 2
Danville, WA 99121
www.alannas.com
Achimenes and other gesneriads, geraniums, and numerous tropical vines

Bob Smoley's Gardenworld
3720 SW 183rd Terrace
Dunnellon, FL 34432
362-465-8254
www.bobsmoleys.com
Huge selection of cacti and succulents

Brent and Becky's Bulbs
7900 Daffodil Lane
Gloucester, VA 23061
804-693-3966
www.brentandbeckysbulbs.com
Extensive catalog notes varieties that are best for forcing into bloom indoors

Evans Orchid Lab
160 W. Coconut Avenue
Englewood, FL 34223
941-474-5982
www.evansorchidlab.com
Rare orchids shipped in small flasks for the orchid enthusiast

Excelsa Gardens
12839 25th St. N
Loxahatchee, FL 33470
800-649-5348
www.excelsagardens.com
Bromeliads, crotons, philodendrons, and many other rare tropical plants

Glasshouse Works
P.O. Box 97
Stewart, OH 45778
740-662-2142
www.glasshouseworks.com
Incredible selection of plants for indoor culture

Hidden Valley Hibiscus
2411 E. Valley Parkway
PMB 281
Escondido, CA 92027
760-749-6410
www.hiddenvalleyhibiscus.com
Common and uncommon hibiscus, including the newest hybrids

Hobbs Farm and Greenery
979 Barnestown Road
Hope, ME 04847
207-763-4000
www.hobbsfarm.com
Extensive selection of English ivies, geraniums, and numerous other houseplants

Kartuz Greenhouses
1408 Sunset Drive
P.O. Box 790
Vista, CA 92085
760-941-3613
www.kartuz.com
Begonias, gesneriads, and numerous other flowering houseplants

Langeveld Bulbs
725 Vassar Avenue
P.O. Box 2105
Lakewood, NJ 08701
732-367-2000
www.langeveld.com
Every bulb imaginable, for forcing or garden planting

Lauray of Salisbury
432 Undermountain Road
Salisbury, CT 06068
860-435-2263
www.lauray.com
Begonias, gesneriads, orchids, cacti, and succulents

Logee's Greenhouses
141 North Street
Danielson, CT 06239
888-330-8038
www.logees.com
Comprehensive selection of superior cultivars of over 700 houseplants

Lyndon Lyon Greenhouses
P.O. Box 249
Dolgeville, NY 13329
315-429-8291
www.lyndonlyon.com
African violets, orchids, and a fine selection of terrarium plants

Planet Natural
1612 Gold Avenue
Bozeman, MT 59715
800-289-6656
www.planetnatural.com
Beneficial mites for spider mite control

Stokes Tropicals
4806 E. Old Spanish Trail
Jeanerette, LA 70544
800-624-9706
www.stokestropicals.com
Bromeliads, ferns, and over 500 more tropical plants

The Violet Barn (Rob's Violets)
P.O. Box 9
Naples, NY 14512
585-374-8592
www.robsviolet.com
African violets, orchids, and an array of small plants for terrariums and dish gardens

Organizations of Interest to Houseplant Enthusiasts

Below are more than a dozen national organizations whose members share expertise about, and often plant material of, their favorite houseplants. Many have local chapters, which are listed at the websites of the national associations.

African Violet Society of America
2375 North Street
Beaumont, TX 77702
www.avsa.org

American Bonsai Society
P.O. Box 351604
Toledo, OH 34635
www.absbonsai.org

American Fern Society
c/o Missouri Botanical Garden
P.O. Box 299
St. Louis, MO 63166
www.amerfernsoc.org

American Gloxinia and Gesneriad Society
118 Byron Road
Lawrence, MA 01841
www.aggs.org

American Orchid Society
16700 AOS Lane
Delray Beach, FL 33446
www.orchidweb.com

American Primrose Society
P.O. Box 210913
Auke Bay, AK 99821
www.americanprimrosesoc.org

American Rose Society
P.O. Box 30000
Shreveport, LA 71130
www.ars.org

Bromeliad Society International
1608 Cardenas Drive NE
Albuquerque, NM 87110
www.bsi.org

Cactus and Succulent Society of America
P.O. Box 2615
Pahrump, NV 89041
www.cssainc.org

International Aroid Society
P.O. Box 43-1853
South Miami, FL 33143
www.aroid.org

International Geranium Society
P.O. Box 92734
Pasadena, CA 91109
www.geocities.com/rainforest/2822

International Palm Society
P.O. Box 1897
Lawrence, KS 66044
www.palms.org

The Cyclamen Society
Little Pilgrims
2 Pilgrims Way East
Otford, Sevenoaks
Kent TN14 5QN
United Kingdom

Botanical/Common Name Cross Reference

BOTANICAL NAME	COMMON NAME
Abutilon hybridum	flowering maple
Achimenes hybrids	cupid's bow, hot water plant, magic flower, orchid pansy
Adiantum capillus-veneris	maidenhair fern
Aechmea fasciata	urn plant, silver vase plant
Agave species	agave, American aloe, century plant
Aglaonema commutatum	Chinese evergreen
Aloe barbadensis, *A. vera*	aloe, burn plant
Aloe variegata	partridge-breasted aloe, tiger aloe
Ananas comosus 'Variegatus'	ivory pineapple, variegated pineapple
Anthurium hybrids	flamingo flower
Aphelandra squarrosa	zebra plant, saffron spike
Aporocactus flagelliformis	rat's tail cactus
Araucaria heterophylla	Norfolk Island pine
Asparagus densiflorus	asparagus fern
Aspidistra capitosa	jade ribbons aspidistra
Aspidistra eliator	aspidistra, cast iron plant
Asplenium nidus	bird's nest fern
Beaucarnea recurvata	ponytail palm
Begonia boweri	tiger begonia
Begonia masoniana	iron cross begonia
Begonia rex	rex begonia, painted leaf begonia, fancy-leafed begonia
Begonia × *corallina*	angel wing begonia
Begonia × *hiemalis*	winter-blooming begonia, Reiger hybrid begonia
Billbergia nutans	queen's tears, friendship plant
Caladium hybrids	caladium angel wings
Calathea rufibarba	lance-leaf calathea
Calathea	peacock plant, zebra plant
Capsicum frutescens	Christmas pepper
Cattleya hybrids	corsage orchid
Cereus peruviana	Peruvian apple cactus, column cactus, Peruvian torch
Chamaedorea species	parlor palms
Chamaerops humilis	European fan palm, Mediterranean fan palm
Chinodoxa luciliae	glory of the snow
Chlorophytum comosum	spider plant, airplane plant
Chrysalidocarpus lutescens	areca palm, feather palm
Cissus Antarctica	kangaroo vine
Cissus discolor	begonia vine
Cissus rhombifolia	grape ivy
Citrus × *citrofortunella mitis*	calamondin orange, miniature orange
Clivia miniata	clivia, Kafir lily
Codiaeum variegatum pictum	croton, Joseph's coat

BOTANICAL NAME	COMMON NAME
Columnea gloriosa	goldfish plant
Cordyline terminalis	ti plant, Hawaiian ti, good luck tree
Crassula arborescens, C. cotyledon	money plant, silver dollar plant
Crassula ovata	jade plant
Cryptanthus acaulis	earth star, starfish plant
Cyclamen persicum hybrids	cyclamen, Persian violet
Cyrtomium falcatum	holly fern, Japanese holly fern
Davallia canariensis	deer's foot fern
Davallia fejeensis	rabbit's foot fern
Davallia trichomanoides	squirrel's foot fern
Dendranthema morifolium	chrysanthemum
Dendrobium hybrids	dedrobium, spray orchid
Dieffenbachia	dumb cane
Dizygotheca elegantissima	false aralia, finger plant
Dracaena	corn plant, rainbow plant
Echeveria species	hen and chicks
Echinopsis hybrids	sea urchin cactus
Epipremnum aureum	pothos, devil's ivy
Euphorbia milii hybrids	crown of thorns, Siamese lucky plant, silverthorn, Christ's thorn
Euphorbia pulcherrima	poinsettia
Exacum affine	Persian violet, German violet, Arabian violet, tiddly winks
Fatshedera lizei	tree ivy, fat headed lizzy, aralia ivy, botanical wonder
Faucaria tigrina, F. felina	tiger's jaws
Ficus benjamina	weeping fig, weeping Chinese banyan
Ficus elastica	rubber plant, India rubber tree
Ficus lyrata	fiddle-leaf fig, banjo fig
Ficus pumila	creeping fig
Fittonia verschaffeltii	nerve plant, silver net leaf
Freesia corymbosa	freesia
Gardenia jasminoides	gardenia
Guzmania lingulata	scarlet star
Gymnocalycium mihanovichii 'Red Cap'	red top cactus, ruby ball
Gynura aurantiaca	velvet plant, purple passion
Gynura sarmentosa	trailing velvet plant
Hatiora gaertneri	Easter cactus
Haworthia species	haworthia
Hedera canariensis	Algerian ivy
Hedera helix	English ivy
Hibiscus rosa-sinensis	hibiscus, Hawaiian rose
Hippeastrum hortorum	amaryllis

BOTANICAL NAME	COMMON NAME
Howea belmoreana	sentry palm
Howea forsteriana	kentia palm
Hyacinthus orientalis	hyacinth
Hypoestes phyllostachya	polka dot plant, freckle face, measles plant
Iris reticulata	dwarf iris
Jasminum polyanthum	jasmine, Chinese jasmine, winter-blooming jasmine
Jasminum sambac	Arabian jasmine
Kalanchoe blossfeldiana	kalanchoe, flaming Cathy, flaming Katy
Kalanchoe diagremontiana	mother of thousands, devil's backbone
Kalanchoe tomentosa	panda plant, pussy ears
Lilium longiflorum	Easter lily
Lithops species	living stones, split rocks
Mammillaria bocasana	snowball cactus
Mammillaria elongata	golden star cactus, lady fingers cactus
Mammillaria species	powder puff cactus
Maranta leuconeura	prayer plant
Monstera deliciosa	Swiss cheese plant, split-leaf philodendron
Muscari armeniacum	muscari, grape hyacinth
Narcissus species and hybrids	daffodil, paperwhite narcissus
Neoregelia carolinae 'Tricolor'	blushing bromeliad, cartwheel plant
Nephrolepis exaltata	Boston fern, sword fern
Oncidium hybrids	dancing ladies orchid
Oxalis regnellii	oxalis, shamrock plant
Pandanus veitchii	screw pine, veitch screw pine
Paphiopedilum hybrids	lady's slipper orchid
Parodia leninghausii	yellow tower cactus
Parodia mammulosa	tom thumb cactus
Parodia scopa	silver ball cactus
Parodia species	ball cactus
Pelargonium graveolens	rose geranium
Pelargonium odoratissimum	apple geranium
Pelargonium species	geranium, scented geranium
Pelargonium × *domesticum*	regal geranium, Martha Washington geranium
Pelargonium × *fragrans*	nutmeg geranium
Pelargonium × *hortorum*	zonal geranium, fancy-leafed geranium
Peperomia argyreia	watermelon peperomia
Peperomia caperata	peperomia, waffle peperomia
Peperomia obtusifolia	baby rubber plant
Phalaenopsis hybrids	moth orchids
Philodendron bipinnatifidum	lacy-tree philodendron, anchor philodendron
Philodendron erubescens	blushing philodendron, climbing philodendron

BOTANICAL NAME	COMMON NAME
Philodendron hybrids	bird's nest philodendron, mounding philodendron
Philodendron scandens oxycardium	heartleaf philodendron
Phoenix canariensis	Canary Island date palm
Phoenix roebelinii	pygmy date palm
Pilea cadierei	aluminum plant, watermelon pilea
Platycerium bifurcatum	staghorn fern
Polypodium aureum	polypody fern, hare's foot fern
Primula polyantha	English primrose
Primula malacoides	fairy primrose
Primula obconica	German primrose
Pteris cretica	brake fern
Pteris ensiformis	ribbon fern, Victoria fern
Pteris species	table fern
Puschkinia scilloides	striped squill
Rebutia species	red crown, cluster cactus
Rhaphis excelsa	lady palm
Rhododendron hybrids	azalea, florists azalea
Rosa chinensis hybrids	rose, miniature rose, micro-rose
Rosmarinus officinalis	rosemary
Saintpaulia hybrids	African violet
Sanseveria trifasciata	mother-in-law's tongue, snake plant
Saxifraga stolonifera	strawberry begonia, roving sailor, mother of thousands
Schefflera actinophylla	umbrella tree
Schefflera arboricola	dwarf schefflera
Schlumbergera hybrids	Christmas cactus, Thanksgiving cactus, holiday cactus
Scilla species	scilla
Sedum morganianum	donkey tail, burro's tail
Senecio rowleyanus	string of pearls, bead plant
Senecio × *hybridus*	cineraria
Sinningia speciosa	gloxinia
Solanum pseudocapsicum	Jerusalem cherry, Christmas cherry
Spathiphyllum species	peace lily
Streptocarpus × *hybridus*	streptocarpus, cape primrose
Syngonium podophyllum	arrowhead plant, nepthytis, goosefoot plant
Tillandsia species	pink quill, air plant, sky plant
Tolmiea menziesii	piggy-back plant, youth-on-age, thousand mothers
Tradescantia albiflora	wandering jew, inch plant, wandering sailor
Tulipa species and hybrids	tulip
Vriesea splendens	flaming sword, painted feather, zebra bromeliad
Zantedeschia hybrids	calla lily
Zebrina pendula	wandering Jew, inch plant, wandering sailor

COMMON NAME	BOTANICAL NAME
African violet	*Saintpaulia* hybrids
Agave	*Agave* species
Air plant	*Tillandsia* species
Airplane plant	*Chlorophytum comosum*
Algerian ivy	*Hedera canariensis*
Aloe	*Aloe barbadensis*, *A. vera*
Aluminum plant	*Pilea cadierei*
Amaryllis	*Hippeastrum hortorum*
American aloe	*Agave* species
Anchor philodendron	*Philodendron bipinnatifidum*
Angel wing begonia	*Begonia* × *corallina*
Angel wings	*Caladium* hybrids
Apple geranium	*Pelargonium odoratissimum*
Arabian jasmine	*Jasminum sambac*
Arabian violet	*Exacum affine*
Aralia ivy	*Fatshedera lizei*
Areca palm	*Chrysalidocarpus lutescens*
Arrowhead plant	*Syngonium podophyllum*
Arum lily	*Zantedeschia* hybrids
Asparagus fern	*Asparagus densiflorus*
Azalea	*Rhododendron* hybrids
Baby rubber plant	*Peperomia obtusifolia*
Ball cactus	*Parodia* species
Banjo fig	*Ficus lyrata*
Barroom plant	*Aspidistra eliator*
Bead plant	*Senecio rowleyanus*
Begonia vine	*Cissus discolor*
Bird's nest fern	*Asplenium nidus*
Bird's nest philodendron	*Philodendron* hybrids
Blushing bromeliad	*Neoregelia carolinae* 'Tricolor'
Blushing philodendron	*Philodendron erubescens*
Boston fern	*Nephrolepis exaltata*
Botanical wonder	*Fatshedera lizei*
Brake fern	*Pteris cretica*
Burn plant	*Aloe barbadensis*, *A. vera*
Burro's tail	*Sedum morganianum*
Caladium	*Caladium* hybrids
Calamondin orange	*Citrus* × *citrofortunella mitis*
Calathea, lance-leaf	*Calathea rufibarba*
Calla lily	*Zantedeschia* hybrids
Canary Island date palm	*Phoenix canariensis*

COMMON NAME	BOTANICAL NAME
Cape primrose	*Streptocarpus × hybridus*
Cartwheel plant	*Neoregelia carolinae* 'Tricolor'
Cast iron plant	*Aspidistra eliator*
Century plant	*Agave* species
Chinese evergreen	*Aglaonema commutatum*
Chinese jasmine	*Jasminum polyanthum*
Christ's thorn	*Euphorbia milii* hybrids
Christmas cactus	*Schlumbergera* hybrids
Christmas cherry	*Solanum pseudocapsicum*
Christmas pepper	*Capsicum frutescens*
Chrysanthemum	*Dendranthema morifolium*
Cineraria	*Senecio × hybridus*
Climbing philodendron	*Philodendron erubescens*
Cluster cactus	*Rebutia* species
Column cactus	*Cereus peruviana*
Corn plant	*Dracaena*
Corsage orchid	*Cattleya* hybrids
Creeping fig	*Ficus pumila*
Croton	*Codiaeum variegatum pictum*
Crown of thorns	*Euphorbia milii* hybrids
Cupid's bow	*Achimenes* hybrids
Cyclamen	*Cyclamen persicum* hybrids
Daffodil	*Narcissus* species and hybrids
Dancing ladies orchid	*Oncidium* hybrids
Deer's foot fern	*Davallia canariensis*
Dendrobium	*Dendrobium* hybrids
Devil's backbone	*Kalanchoe diagremontiana*
Devil's ivy	*Epipremnum aureum*
Donkey tail	*Sedum morganianum*
Dumb cane	*Dieffenbachia*
Dutch hyacinth	*Hyacinthus orientalis*
Dwarf iris	*Iris reticulata*
Earth star	*Cryptanthus acaulis*
Easter cactus	*Hatiora gaertneri*
Easter lily	*Lilium longiflorum*
English ivy	*Hedera helix*
English primrose	*Primula polyantha*
European fan palm	*Chamaerops humilis*
Fairy primrose	*Primula malacoides*
False aralia	*Dizygotheca elegantissima*
Fancy-leafed begonia	*Begonia rex*

COMMON NAME	BOTANICAL NAME
Fancy-leafed geranium	*Pelargonium × hortorum*
Fat-headed lizzy	*Fatshedera lizei*
Feather palm	*Chrysalidocarpus lutescens*
Fiddle-leaf fig	*Ficus lyrata*
Finger plant	*Dizygotheca elegantissima*
Flaming Cathy	*Kalanchoe blossfeldiana*
Flaming Katy	*Kalanchoe blossfeldiana*
Flaming sword	*Vriesea splendens*
Flamingo flower	*Anthurium* hybrids
Florists azalea	*Rhododendron* hybrids
Flowering maple	*Abutilon hybridum*
Freckle face	*Hypoestes phyllostachya*
Freesia	*Freesia corymbosa*
Friendship plant	*Billbergia nutans*
Gardenia	*Gardenia jasminoides*
German primrose	*Primula obconica*
German violet	*Exacum affine*
Glory of the snow	*Chinodoxa luciliae*
Gloxinia	*Sinningia speciosa*
Golden star cactus	*Mammillaria elongata*
Goldfish plant	*Columnea gloriosa*
Good luck tree	*Cordyline terminalis*
Goosefoot plant	*Syngonium podophyllum*
Grape hyacinth	*Muscari armeniacum*
Grape ivy	*Cissus rhombifolia*
Hare's foot fern	*Polypodium aureum*
Hawaiian rose	*Hibiscus rosa-sinensis*
Hawaiian ti	*Cordyline terminalis*
Haworthia	*Haworthia* species
Heartleaf philodendron	*Philodendron scandens oxycardium*
Hen and chicks	*Echeveria* species
Hibiscus	*Hibiscus rosa-sinensis*
Holiday cactus	*Schlumbergera* hybrids
Holly fern	*Cyrtomium falcatum*
Hot water plant	*Achimenes* hybrids
Hyacinth	*Hyacinthus orientalis*
Inch plant	*Zebrina pendula, Tradescantia albiflora*
India rubber tree	*Ficus elastica*
Iron cross begonia	*Begonia masoniana*
Ivory pineapple	*Ananas comosus* 'Variegatus'
Jade plant	*Crassula ovata*

COMMON NAME	BOTANICAL NAME
Japanese holly fern	*Cyrtomium falcatum*
Jasmine	*Jasminum polyanthum*
Jerusalem cherry	*Solanum pseudocapsicum*
Joseph's coat	*Codiaeum variegatum pictum*
Kafir lily	*Clivia miniata*
Kalanchoe	*Kalanchoe blossfeldiana*
Kangaroo vine	*Cissus antarctica*
Kentia palm	*Howea forsteriana*
Lacy-tree philodendron	*Philodendron bipinnatifidum*
Lady fingers cactus	*Mammillaria elongata*
Lady palm	*Rhaphis excelsa*
Lady's slipper orchid	*Paphiopedilum* hybrids
Living stones	*Lithops* species
Magic flower	*Achimenes* hybrids
Maidenhair fern	*Adiantum capillus-veneris*
Martha Washington geranium	*Pelargonium × domesticum*
Measles plant	*Hypoestes phyllostachya*
Mediterranean fan palm	*Chamaerops humilis*
Micro-rose	*Rosa chinensis* hybrids
Ming Thing cactus	*Cereus peruviana monstrosus*
Money plant	*Crassula arborescens, C. cotyledon*
Moth orchid	*Phalaenopsis* hybrids
Mother of thousands	*Kalanchoe diagremontiana* or *Saxifraga stolonifera*
Mother-in-law's tongue	*Sanseveria trifasciata*
Mounding philodendron	*Philodendron* hybrids
Muscari	*Muscari armeniacum*
Nephytis	*Syngonium podophyllum*
Nerve plant	*Fittonia verschaffeltii*
Norfolk Island pine	*Araucaria heterophylla*
Nutmeg geranium	*Pelargonium × fragrans*
Orange, miniature	*Citrus × citrofortunella mitis*
Orchid pansy	*Achimenes* hybrids
Orchid	*Cattleya, Dendrobium, Oncidium, Paphiopedilum, Phalaenopsis*
Oxalis	*Oxalis regnellii*
Painted feather	*Vriesea splendens*
Painted leaf begonia	*Begonia rex*
Panda plant	*Kalanchoe tomentosa*
Paperwhite narcissus	*Narcissus jonquilla*
Parlor palms	*Chamaedorea* species
Partridge-breasted aloe	*Aloe variegata*

COMMON NAME	BOTANICAL NAME
Peace lily	*Spathiphyllum* species
Peacock plant	*Calathea*
Peperomia	*Peperomia caperata*
Perisan violet	*Cyclamen persicum* hybrids
Persian violet	*Exacum affine*
Peruvian apple cactus	*Cereus peruviana*
Peruvian torch	*Cereus peruviana*
Piggy-back plant	*Tolmiea menziesii*
Pineapple, variegated	*Ananas comosus* 'Variegatus'
Pink quill	*Tillandsia cyanea*
Poinsettia	*Euphorbia pulcherrima*
Polka dot plant	*Hypoestes phyllostachya*
Polypody fern	*Polypodium aureum*
Ponytail palm	*Beaucarnea recurvata*
Pothos	*Epipremnum aureum*
Powder puff cactus	*Mammillaria* species
Prayer plant	*Maranta leuconeura*
Purple passion	*Gynura aurantiaca*
Pussy ears	*Kalanchoe tomentosa*
Pygmy date palm	*Phoenix roebelinii*
Queen's tears	*Billbergia nutans*
Rabbit's foot fern	*Davallia fejeensis*
Rainbow plant	*Dracaena marginata*
Rat's tail cactus	*Aporocactus flagelliformis*
Red crown	*Rebutia* species
Red top cactus	*Gymnocalycium mihanovichii* 'Red Cap'
Regal geranium	*Pelargonium* × *domesticum*
Reiger hybrid begonia	*Begonia* × *hiemalis*
Rex begonia	*Begonia rex*
Ribbon fern	*Pteris ensiformis*
Rose geranium	*Pelargonium graveolens*
Rose, miniature	*Rosa chinensis* hybrids
Rosemary	*Rosmarinus officinalis*
Roving sailor	*Saxifraga stolonifera*
Rubber plant	*Ficus elastica*
Ruby ball	*Gymnocalycium mihanovichii* 'Red Cap'
Saffron spike	*Aphelandra squarrosa*
Scarlet star	*Guzmania lingulata*
Scented geranium	*Pelargonium* species
Schefflera, dwarf	*Schefflera arboricola*
Scilla	*Scilla* species

COMMON NAME	BOTANICAL NAME
Screw pine	*Pandanus veitchii*
Sea urchin cactus	*Echinopsis* hybrids
Sentry palm	*Howea belmoreana*
Shamrock plant	*Oxalis regnellii*
Siamese lucky plant	*Euphorbia milii* hybrids
Silver dollar plant	*Crassula arborescens, C. cotyledon*
Silver net leaf	*Fittonia verschaffeltii*
Silver vase plant	*Aechmea fasciata*
Silverthorn	*Euphorbia milii* hybrids
Sky plant	*Tillandsia* species
Snake plant	*Sanseveria trifasciata*
Snowball cactus	*Mammillaria bocasana*
Spider plant	*Chlorophytum comosum*
Split rocks	*Lithops* species
Split-leaf philodendron	*Monstera deliciosa*
Spray orchid	*Dedrobium* hybrids
Squirrel's foot fern	*Davallia trichomanoides*
Staghorn fern	*Platycerium bifurcatum*
Starfish plant	*Cryptanthus acaulis*
Strawberry begonia	*Saxifraga stolonifera*
Streptocarpus	*Streptocarpus × hybridus*
String of pearls	*Senecio rowleyanus*
Striped squill	*Puschkinia scilloides*
Swiss cheese plant	*Monstera deliciosa*
Sword fern	*Nephrolepis exaltata*
Table fern	*Pteris* species
Thanksgiving cactus	*Schlumbergera* hybrids
Thousand mothers	*Tolmiea menziesii*
Ti plant	*Cordyline terminalis*
Tiddly-winks	*Exacum affine*
Tiger aloe	*Aloe variegata*
Tiger begonia	*Begonia boweri*
Tiger's jaws	*Faucaria tigrina, F. felina*
Tree ivy	*Fatshedera lizei*
Tulip	*Tulipa* species and hybrids
Umbrella tree	*Schefflera actinophylla*
Urn plant	*Aechmea fasciata*
Velvet plant	*Gynura aurantiaca*
Velvet plant, trailing	*Gynura sarmentosa*
Victoria fern	*Pteris ensiformis*
Vietch screw pine	*Pandanus veitchii*

COMMON NAME	BOTANICAL NAME
Wandering jew	*Zebrina pendula, Tradescantia albiflora*
Wandering sailor	*Zebrina pendula, Tradescantia albiflora*
Watermelon peperomia	*Peperomia argyreia*
Watermelon pilea	*Pilea cadierei*
Weeping Chinese banyan	*Ficus benjamina*
Weeping fig	*Ficus benjamina*
Winter-blooming begonia	*Begonia* × *hiemalis*
Winter-blooming jasmine	*Jasminum polyanthum*
Youth-on-age	*Tolmiea menziesii*
Zebra bromeliad	*Vriesea splendens*
Zebra plant	*Aphelandra squarrosa* or *Calathea*
Zonal geranium	*Pelargonium* × *hortorum*

Index

Page numbers in **bold** indicate tables; those in *italic* indicate illustrations.

floral wrappings, *260*

Florida hybrids, 220

florist's azalea *(Rhododendron)*, 134–35

florists cyclamen *(Cyclamen persicum)*, 92–93

flowering maple *(Abutilon hybridum)*, *2*, 2–3, *3*

flowers

    forcing bulbs, 32–37

    forms and parts, *296–97*

    inducing blooming, 289, 309

    See also plant name; plant type

fluorescent light, *288, 289,* 290, 322

fluoride, 328

foam packing peanuts, 259, *259*

foot-candle, 290

forcing bulbs, 32–37

freckle face. *See Hypoestes phyllostachya*

Freesia (freesia), **32,** *40*

    corymbosa (freesia), xv, **39,** 44, *44*

friendship plant *(Billbergia nutans)*, 25

fungal diseases, 254–55, *255*

fungicides, 255

fungus, 265

fungus gnats, 270–71, *271*

G

Gardenia jasminoides (gardenia), xv, *102*, 102–3, *103*

    'Radicans', 102

    'Veitchii' (everblooming), 102

    'White Gem', 102

geraniums. *See Pelargonium*

German violet *(Exacum affine)*, 100–101

glochid, 54

gloxinia *(Sinningia speciosa)*, *146*, 146–47, *147*, 327

Gnatrol *(Bacillus thuringiensis)*, 271

golden cane palm *(Chrysalidocarpus lutescens)*, 222

goldern star *(Mammillaria)*, **65,** 72

goldfish plant. *See Columnea gloriosa*

good luck tree. *See Cordyline terminalis*

goosefoot plant *(Syngonium podophyllum)*, 240–41

grafting cacti, 61

grape hyacinth. *See Muscari*

grape ivy. *See Cissus rhombifolia*

grooming plants, 265, *265*

grouping, plant, 282

Guzmania lingulata (scarlet star), xv, xvi, *16*, 17, **22,** 27, *27*

    'Luna', 27

Gymnocalycium mihanovichii 'Red Cap' (red top cactus, ruby ball cactus), xiv, **65,** 70, *70*

Gynura (velvet plant, purple passion), xiv, 250

    aurantiaca, 204–5

    sarmentosa, *204*, 204–5, *205*

gypsum, 316

H

hanging plants, 251

hare's foot fern. *See Polypodium aureum*

Hatiora gaertneri (Easter cactus), xv, xvi, *59*, **65,** 71, *71*

Hawaiian rose. *See Hibiscus rosa-sinensis*

Hawaiian ti. *See Cordyline terminalis*

Haworthia species and hybrids (haworthia), xvi, 54, **76,** 82, *82*

healing power of plants, ix–x

heartleaf philodendron. *See Philodendron*

Hedera, 279, 319

    canariensis (Algerian ivy)

        'Floire de Marengo', 206

    helix (English ivy), xvii, *206*, 206–7, *207*, 282, **298**

        'Duck Foot', 206

        'Golden Ingot', 206

hen and chicks. *See Echeveria*

Hibiscus rosa-sinensis (hibiscus, Hawaiian rose), xv, *110*, 110–11, *111*

    'Dragon's Breath', 110

    'The Path', 110

high-intensity discharge (HID) lights, 291

Hippeastrum hortorum (amaryllis), xv, xvi, **32,** 37, *38*, **39,** *45*, *45*

    'Appleblossom', 45

    'Baby Star', 45

    'Scarlet Baby', 45

history of houseplants, viii–ix

hitchhikers (insect pests), 270, 291

holiday cactus *(Schlumbergera)*, 75

holly fern *(Cyrtomium falcatum)*, **189,** 191, *191*

lei orchid. *See Dendrobium*

light, 284–91

    artificial, 289–91

    effects of, 284–86

    measuring, 290

    natural, *280,* 286–87

    photoperiod (light time), 289

    seasonal changes, 287, *287,* 289

    See also plant name; plant type

Lilium (Easter lily), **32**

    longiflorum (Easter lily), xv, *36,* **39,** 47, *47*

lime, 316

Lithops species (living stones, split rocks), xiv, xvi, *64,* 65, **76,** 84, *84*

    aucampiae, 84

    marmorata, 84

"little" spring-flowering bulbs, 35, **36**

living stones. *See Lithops*

Livistonia chinensis (Chinese fan palm), 221

Lobivia, 69

longevity. *See plant name; plant type*

M

magnesium, 18, 262, 328

maidenhairs *(Adiatum),* 184, 185

Mammillaria species, xiv

    bocasana (powder puff, snowball cactus), *57,* **65,** 72, *72*

    elongata (golden star, lady fingers), **65,** 72

Maranta leuconeura (prayer plant), xvii, *210,* 210–11, *211,* 279

    containers for, 254

    'Erythoroneura', 210

    'Fascinator', 210

    'Kerchoveana', 210

    'Massangeana', 210

Martha Washington geranium. *See Pelargonium* × *domesticum*

mealybugs, 272–73, *273*

measles plant. *See Hypoestes phyllostachya*

Mediterranean fan palm *(Chamaerops humilis),* 221

micronutrient fertilizers, 262

micro-rose *(Rosa chinensis),* 136–37

milk, for leaf shine, 249

minerals, soil, 316

miniature orange *(Citrus* × *citrofortunella mitis), 88,* 88–89, *89*

miniature rose *(Rosa chinensis), 136,* 136–37, *137*

misting, 267

Monstera deliciosa (monstera, Swiss cheese plant, split-leaf philodendron), xvii, *212,* 212–13, *213,* **298**

mother-in-law's tongue. *See Sanseveria trifasciata*

mother of thousands. *See Saxifraga stolonifera*

moth orchids. *See Phalaenopsis*

mounding philodendron. *See Philodendron*

moving plants, *291,* 291–93

Muscari (grape hyacinth), *31, 32,* **32**

    armeniacum (muscari, grape hyacinth), xv, **39,** 48, *48*

        'Christmas Pearl', 48

        'Valerie Finnis', 48

N

Narcissus (daffodil, paperwhite narcissus), xv, 32, **32,** *34,* **39,** *40,* 49

    'February Gold', 49

    'Grand Soleil d'Or', 49

    'Jenny', 49

    jonquilla, 49

neem (azadirachtin), 278–79

Neoregelia carolinae 'Tricolor' (blushing bromeliad, cartwheel plant), xvii, *15,* **22,** 28, *28*

    'Compacta', 28

    'Martin', 28

Neos *(Neoregelia carolinae),* 28

Nephrolepis exaltata (Boston fern, sword fern), xvi, 185, 186, **189,** 193, *193, 285*

    'Bostoniensis', 193

    'Compacta', 193

    'Fluffy Ruffles', 193

nepthytis *(Syngonium podophyllum),* 240–41

nerve plant *(Fittonia verschaffelti), 202,* 202–3, *203,* 279

nitrogen, 261

nodes. *See* propagation

Nolina recurvata, 162

water, *(cont'd)*

  recommended amounts, 326–27, 329–30

  rehydrating, 328–29

  in terrariums, 324–25

  tips on applying, 329

  top and bottom watering, *327*, *327–28*

  See also plant name; plant type

waterlogged plants, rescuing, 329–30

watermelon pilea. *See Pilea cadierei*

weeping Chinese banyan. *See Ficus benjamina*

weeping fig. *See Ficus benjamina*

weeping of water droplets, 256

whiteflies, 277, *277*

wind, 330

winter-blooming begonia. *See Begonia × hiemalis*

winter-blooming jasmine. *See Jasminum polyanthum*

workplace plants, 258, 284

  See also terrariums

wrappings, floral, *260*

Y

yellow butterfly palm *(Chrysalidocarpus lutescens)*, 222

youth-on-age *(Tolmiea menziesii)*, 242–43

Z

Zantedeschia (calla lily, arum lily), xv, xvi, **32, 39,** 52, *52*

  rehmanii, 52

zebra bromeliad *(Vriesea splendens),* 30

zebra plant. *See Calathea*

zebra plant *(Aphelandra squarrosa),* 6, *6–7, 7*

Zebrina pendula (wandering Jew, inch plant, wandering sailor), xv, xvii, *244, 244–45, 245*

  'Quicksilver', 244

zonal geranium. *See Pelargonium × hortorum*

Acknowledgments

My words may comprise the heart of this book, but its soul was created by people with remarkable creative vision. From the beginning, my gifted editor, Gwen Steege, generously shared her knowledge of houseplants — and even lent me her favorite books — to make sure readers missed no chance to learn more about their green companions. Working with little more than lists and dull manuscript pages, photographer Rosemary Kautzky joined the team. Day after day, undeterred by attacks from prickles and spines, she lugged plants into her home, rearranging furniture and draperies and hoping for fair weather so she could show you the plants as they appear in natural daylight, in a real home. Finally, creative director Kent Lew and art director Cynthia McFarland focused their expert eyes on the pages and gently worked the elements until they achieved a perfect balance. Sincere thanks are also due to Judy Becker and George Wulster for their help with bulbs, and to Lisa Broberg Quintana for her guidance with orchids. To these and the many other people who provided the small puffs of air that helped breathe life into this book, I am deeply grateful.

Other Storey Titles You Will Enjoy

Garden Stone, by Barbara Pleasant
Practical information and more than 250 inspiring photographs explain how to use stone and plants together to create contrasting textures and colors in the garden. 240 pages. Paperback. ISBN 1-58017-544-9.

The Gardener's Guide to Plant Diseases, by Barbara Pleasant
Here are antidotes for the 50 most common plant diseases, with information on what they look like, where they occur, what they will do to the plant, and how to control them organically. 192 pages. Paperback. ISBN 0-88266-274-0.

The Gardener's Weed Book, by Barbara Pleasant
This easy-to-use reference guide covers the pros and cons of the presence of weeds, recommends proven organic methods for controlling unwanted weeks, and presents an illustrated encyclopedia of dozens of the most common weeds. 208 pages. Paperback. ISBN 0-88266-921-4.

The Gardener's Bug Book, by Barbara Pleasant
Working with nature to reduce the presence of garden pests, Pleasant shows how to produce bountiful, environmentally safe, and chemical-free gardens. 160 pages. Paperback. ISBN 0-88266-609-6.

Window Boxes, by James Cramer and Dean Johnson
150 full-color photographs, step-by-step instructions, and useful plant-care tips accompany 10 projects and quick design ideas for year-round window boxes. The authors combine container gardening with flower arranging to create visual treasures for every season. 176 pages. Paperback. ISBN 1-58017-518-X.

The City Gardener's Handbook, by Linda Yang
Here is an invaluable resource for any gardener facing the challenge of growing plants where space is limited, whether in the dooryard of a suburban townhouse or on a mid-city rooftop. 336 pages. Paperback. ISBN 1-58017-449-3.

The Perennial Gardener's Design Primer,
by Stephanie Cohen and Nancy J. Ondra
Learn how to create stunning perennial gardens using basic design principles for putting plants together in pleasing and practical ways. 320 pages. Paperback. ISBN 1-58017-543-0.

These books and other Storey books are available wherever books are sold,
or directly from Storey Publishing, 210 MASS MoCA Way, North Adams, MA 01247,
or by calling 1-800-441-5700. www.storey.com